Critical Essays on
GEOFFREY CHAUCER

CRITICAL ESSAYS
ON
BRITISH LITERATURE

Zack Bowen, General Editor

University of Miami

Critical Essays on

GEOFFREY CHAUCER

edited by

THOMAS C. STILLINGER

G. K. Hall & Co.
An Imprint of Simon & Schuster Macmillan
New York

Prentice Hall International
London   Mexico City   New Delhi   Singapore   Sydney   Toronto

Copyright © 1998 by G. K. Hall

G. K. Hall & Co.
An Imprint of Simon & Schuster Macmillan
1633 Broadway
New York, NY 10019

Library of Congress Cataloging-in-Publication Data

Critical essays on Geoffrey Chaucer / edited by Thomas C. Stillinger.
    p. cm. — (Critical essays on British literature)
  Includes bibliographical references and index.
  ISBN 0-7838-0024-X (alk. paper)
    1. Chaucer, Geoffrey, d. 1400—Criticism and interpretation.
2. Chaucer, Geoffrey, d. 1400. Canterbury tales.   3. Chaucer,
Geoffrey, d. 1400. Troilus and Criseyde.   4. Christian pilgrims and
literature.   6. Tales, Medieval—History and criticism.
7. Civilization, Medieval, in literature.   8. Trojan War—Literature
and the war.   9. Storytelling in literature.   I. Stillinger, Thomas
C. II. Series.
PR1924.C77   1998
821'.1—dc21   98–21545
                                                        CIP

This paper meets the requirements of ANSI/NISO Z3948-1992 (Permanence
of Paper).

10 9 8 7 6 5 4 3 2 1

Printed in the United States of America

Contents

◆

General Editor's Note

◆

The Critical Essays on British Literature series provides a variety of approaches to both classical and contemporary writers of Britain and Ireland. The formats of the volumes in the series vary with the thematic designs of individual editors and with the amount and nature of existing reviews and criticism, augmented, where appropriate, by original essays by recognized authorities. It is hoped that each volume will be unique in developing a new overall perspective on its particular subject.

Thomas Stillinger's introduction encapsulates the dialogical polemics of Chaucer debate during the early decades following World War II, and their evolution into a plethora of more specific historical and critical approaches in the last 20 years. The neatly divided critical positions were personified by D. W. Robertson's exegetical insistence on matters of Christian doctrine in interpretation of the texts, as opposed to E. T. Donaldson's New Critical interpretation of Chaucer's work as less a product of Christian medieval culture than a contemporary text dealing with the portrayal of timeless characters and situations applicable to the lives and imaginations of modern readers.

In Stillinger's summary the previous commitment to a single view of Chaucer's work has given way to a plethora of theoretical and historical approaches to Chaucer's individual works, much of the scholarship retaining some of the characteristics of the earlier critics, but adding new dimensions to both history and imaginative reading.

The selected essays were all written in the last 20 years and include such critical approaches as reader-response theory, deconstruction, gender and queer theory, among others, together addressing as wide a range of Chaucer's works as the space allows. Two essays, by Elizabeth Fowler and Winthrop Wetherbee, were written especially for this volume.

ZACK BOWEN
University of Miami

Publisher's Note

◆

Producing a volume that contains both newly commissioned and reprinted material presents the publisher with the challenge of balancing the desire to achieve stylistic consistency with the need to preserve the integrity of works first published elsewhere. In the Critical Essays series, essays commissioned especially for a particular volume are edited to be consistent with G. K. Hall's house style; reprinted essays appear in the style in which they were first published, with only typographical errors corrected. Consequently, shifts in style from one essay to another are the result of our efforts to be faithful to each text as it was originally published.

Introduction

Thomas C. Stillinger

Thow most a fewe of olde stories heere.
—Cassandra, in *Troilus and Criseyde* 5.1459

In 1987, Lee Patterson wrote that Chaucer criticism was still obsessed, as it had been for several decades, by the debate over the "Exegetical method" espoused by D. W. Robertson and others.[1]

> . . . Exegetics remains, apparently against all odds, the great unfinished business of Medieval Studies. The point is not simply that the Exegetical method continues to be practiced but that it continues to arouse passions. Unable to absorb Exegetics and move on, Chaucer studies instead circles back almost compulsively to an apparently irrepressible scandal, a recursiveness that itself bespeaks a scandalous limitation to its own critical creativity.[2]

One rereads this statement in 1998 with a sense of recognition and surprise: recognition because Patterson so neatly characterized a long-standing syndrome, and surprise because, a mere decade later, his claim would be hard to defend. Well into the 1980s, Chaucer criticism—for all the brilliant scholarship and criticism that was produced—was shaped by a single, somewhat repetitive debate. Now, though Exegetical and what we might call counter-Exegetical work continues to be done, the debate somehow seems over. Chaucer criticism has begun to move outward and forward.

This volume gathers together some of the very best Chaucer criticism written in the last two decades. The restriction to recent work is unusual for this series, and there are two reasons for it. The first is merely practical: good anthologies of criticism already exist that give a sampling of Chaucer criticism throughout this century. With the help of these anthologies and the bibliographic assistance provided by the *Riverside Chaucer* and by various guides and companions, it is not hard to trace the fortunes of criticism from Kittredge on.[3] The second reason is more substantial: I believe that Chaucer criticism

1

has recently arrived at a new stage, and that these 11 essays and chapters provide a complex picture of the state of the art.

To explain what kind of corner has been turned, it is necessary to revisit the debate that preoccupied Chaucer criticism for several decades. The debate is not staged, or even discussed in any detail, in any of the following essays: they engage long Chaucerian traditions in responsible, imaginative ways, but their relative indifference to the Exegetical Question is, as I have suggested, one of the signs that they belong to a new moment. So I shall attempt a brief overview here. Again, it is possible to find more detailed accounts elsewhere;[4] this will be a rather schematic sketch. My tutelary figure is the character quoted in the opening epigraph: Cassandra, who, asked to interpret Troilus's dream, responds by summarizing the entire history of Thebes in eight stanzas. As it happens, the relationship between interpretation and history is at the heart of the debate.

For centuries now, it has been possible to think about Chaucer in two quite different ways. He is an ancient writer, his texts silent monuments of a lost world; and, at the same time, he is a living poetic voice. The same could be said for any number of dead poets, of course, but the split is especially pressing in Chaucer's case because of historical events in the two centuries immediately following his death in 1400: an interrelated set of transformations—including the Reformation, the Great Vowel Shift, and the Renaissance's invention of "the Renaissance" and "the Middle Ages"—created a chasm in British cultural history, stranding Chaucer in a mysterious and intriguing past. In 1546, Peter Ashton wrote that "Chaucers wordes" are "by reason of antiquitie . . . almost out of vse";[5] in the 1580s, Sir Philip Sidney, as distant from Chaucer as we are from Jane Austen, could marvel that "in that misty time [he] could see so clearly."[6] Sidney and Spenser and Shakespeare (and Austen) still seem connected to us by a continuous tradition; Chaucer stands on the other side of a divide.

Yet something in Chaucer's poetry speaks to postmedieval readers with astonishing power. The paradox that Sidney describes—marvelously clear vision in a misty time—occurs with many variations in appreciations of Chaucer. If the Middle Ages are by definition strange and distant, then it is necessary to separate Chaucer from his time, even if his time clings persistently to him. Dryden, in 1700, echoes Peter Ashton in associating Chaucer's antiquity with his *words:* Chaucer labored under the disadvantage of "want of words in the beginning of our language," and, with regard to meter, "he lived in the infancy of our poetry, and . . . nothing is brought to perfection at the first."[7] On the other hand, says Dryden, "I see . . . all the Pilgrims in the *Canterbury Tales,* their humours, their features, and their very dress, as distinctly as if I had supped with them at the Tabard in Southwark."[8] Somehow, according to Dryden, Chaucer's outmoded means convey an unmediated reality.

Of course Dryden's distinction between words (medieval) and persons (present) cannot be maintained for long. Words must be cousin to the deed

(General Prologue 742), and words have other cousins as well: gestures, customs, opinions, expectations, social appearances, even persons. Separating the medieval from the timeless in Chaucer is precisely as difficult as separating the words from the poems. On the one hand, everything in Chaucer's texts points to a cultural universe we can reconstruct only with difficulty. Teachers of Chaucer learn to expect a stream of questions from readers new to the Middle Ages: What did a reeve do? How were women supposed to act? Would the Knight have seemed longwinded?—all asked as if the teacher will be able to rattle off an answer or at least look it up (possible for the first question, tricky for the others). Students justifiably feel hesitant to interpret a poet who so manifestly addresses a world they know so little of; professors presumably know something more about Chaucer's world, but perhaps not enough. Yet, on the other hand, of all medieval English poets, Chaucer is the one who can most easily be *read* rather than deciphered. This is partly due to historical circumstance: though the language changed enormously after 1400, Chaucer's own London dialect happened to be the direct ancestor of Modern English, so with a little practice moderns can say and hear his words. And it is partly due to Chaucer's clear seeing, however we describe it.

These two views of Chaucer—medieval monument and living voice— have been available, perhaps inevitable, ever since Chaucer's time was designated "the Middle Ages" and marked off as irretrievably past. As the example of Dryden shows, individual readers can take both views at once. In the early part of this century, that is what critics and scholars did, negotiating between antiquarian learning and engaged interpretation, between philology and appreciation. In the middle of this century, however, the two contrasting views were separated into two full-blown critical positions, represented diversely by diverse critics but associated especially with two figures, D. W. Robertson and E. T. Donaldson.

Donaldson is conveniently labeled a New Critic. In his essays and in the interpretive notes to his edition, *Chaucer's Poetry: An Anthology for the Modern Reader* (1958), he reads closely and elegantly; he finds ironies, paradoxes, complexities in Chaucer's texts; he celebrates the power of poetry to express truths beyond the grasp of nonliterary discourse;[9] and he treats Chaucer's texts as, more or less, autonomous creations, arising from a historical situation but in no way answerable to history. The goal is not to recover a lost, medieval Chaucer, but rather to read the poetry Chaucer left:[10] an extraordinary *listener,* Donaldson hears the undertones, the ambiguities, the deliberate silences in these complex verbal performances. The text isn't merely a framing of pre-textual realities; instead, Chaucer builds in layers of interpretation and characterization, and these layers, rather than the objects at the center, are what matter most. Donaldson's most famous critical contribution is surely his rich interpretation of Chaucerian narrators: in the General Prologue to the *Canterbury Tales,* we see the Prioress through the eyes of "Chaucer the Pilgrim," and the interplay between these two figures, implied in the selection of details in the Prioress's portrait, is finally more interesting than either figure alone. If the Canterbury pilgrims, so vividly present to Dryden, seem veiled in ironies and afterthoughts for Donaldson, what is always vivid and present is the poem itself. Donaldson's Chaucer speaks as clearly to "the modern reader" as he ever did to his contemporaries.

Donaldson did not polemicize about his method, and he did not need to: as a New Critic in the 1950s and 1960s, he was very much in tune with his time. Chaucer studies found a brilliant polemicist, and a radical challenge to its notions of common sense, in D. W. Robertson.

Robertson practiced, and preached, what he called "historical criticism." His 1950 essay of that name and his monumental *Preface to Chaucer* (1962) set forth his interpretive principles with admirable clarity. These principles might be summarized thus: First, culture is historical and determines both meaning and "style" (a crucial term for Robertson), so that what can be said and thought, in art and literature and daily life, changes over time. Medieval culture is fundamentally different from modern (Romantic and post-Romantic) culture; to understand the productions of medieval culture one must abandon one's own assumptions and think, instead, historically. *Within* the Middle Ages, however, there is surprisingly little change or variation. Medieval culture is all of a piece, homogeneous across regions, across social milieus, and across a millenium. The homogeneity of medieval culture makes it possible to explain texts by invoking other texts (or, strikingly, works of visual art) of very different periods or genres. Medieval people valued order, hierarchy, clarity, and orthodoxy. At the center of their Christian orthodoxy was the doctrine of charity. Augustine said in *On Christian Doctrine* that the Bible teaches nothing but charity and that any passage that does not seem to recommend charity should be read allegorically so that it does; the Middle Ages followed this interpretive rule at all times, applying it not only to the Bible but to all writing and all art. As Robertson says, "Medieval Christian poetry, and by Christian poetry I mean all serious poetry written by Christian authors, even that usually called 'secular,' is always allegorical when the message of charity or some corollary of it is not evident on the surface."[11] Finally—and here I quote the first "scholarly premise" listed in the introduction to Robertson's 1980 collection, *Essays in Medieval Culture*—"the cultural products of any age, or for that matter its general history, can be understood only in terms that would have been comprehensible at the time."[12] That is, it is not enough to know that medieval people would have read a certain poem in a certain way; such knowledge imposes upon the modern critic a responsibility to read that poem as it was originally read.

It will be clear that Robertson's principles, as I have skeletally summarized them, are a mixed lot: they include empirical claims, methodological recommendations, and theoretical positions. It would be possible to adopt some of these principles and leave others behind, in any number of ways. For example, one could agree with Robertson about how medieval people interpreted their poems, without agreeing that this is the only way they can be interpreted; or one could agree that biblical commentary and religious art and secular literature belong to the same cultural world, and that they can usefully gloss one another, without agreeing that they all say the same things at all times. Robertson and his fellow "Exegetical critics," however, had little patience with such compromises. The total interconnectedness that Robertson saw within the Middle Ages inhered in his critical principles as well. The word *exegetical* nicely captures Robertson's fusion of different elements: *exegesis* refers to the body of medieval commentary on the Bible (a major research tool), the medieval *practice* of biblical commentary (an important element in medieval intellectual life), the medieval approach to literary interpretation in general (an important part of the medieval "style"), and, finally, the interpretative method that *any* reader of medieval literature should follow. Again, it would be possible to value medieval commentaries as sources of information without taking them as models for one's own work, but the term *exegetical,* in its simplicity, militates against such choosiness: the method is all of a piece, a package that has to be accepted or rejected in its entirety.

It was difficult, then, to assimilate Robertson's work into the mainstream of Chaucer criticism, to treat it as one productive way of reading among others. But it *was* productive, and found followers, so it occasioned what amounted to a long-running debate. I have cast Donaldson as the anti-Exegetical opposition, because he has often been cast that way, and because he did explicitly write against Exegetical criticism.[13] But the debate was *about* Robertson: Donaldson did not argue for his own critical suppositions with anything like the polemical vigor Robertson did, and the attack on Exegetics was usually conducted in the name of common sense and moderation. Still, now that New Criticism no longer seems like mere common sense in the way it once did, it is possible to see a curious symmetry between Donaldson and Robertson: on the one hand a critic who, deploying enormous learning and philological expertise, reads Chaucer as in effect a contemporary; on the other hand a critic who, armed with a great interpretive imagination, insists that Chaucer belongs to the past, that the past is another world, and that nothing we know about our world can help us read Chaucer. For several decades the choice between these two opposing views of Chaucer aroused, as Patterson says, "passions." The debate was carried out in explicit polemics, in footnotes, in careers. In practice most critics learned from both Robertson and Donaldson and found their own compromises, but this was a hard position to theorize; the space of theory was given over to the great debate.

And now, I have suggested, the debate seems to have subsided. It did not end with one decisive blow; there were knockout punches all along, according to one side or the other ("If all of Chaucer's tales promote charity, why does he retract the ones that 'sownen into synne'?"). Rather, I think the issues have been reframed so that the Exegetical Question finally seems like a historical matter rather than a pressing concern. Several related developments have, in my view, brought this about: First, metacritical work like the Patterson essay from which I have quoted—and perhaps that essay in particular. (Sometimes the best way out of an impasse is to *describe* it as an impasse.) Second, the discipline-wide boom in "theory," which created such a proliferation of theoretical positions that Robertsonianism eventually did come to seem one (extreme) stand among many. And, third, the development of new kinds of historicism within Chaucer studies.

Historicism has returned, in the last decade,[14] but with a difference—or with many differences. To describe the Middle Ages as a thousand years of uniformity is to overlook some details, as anti-Robertsonians observed long ago; rather than belaboring the anti-Robertsonian point, however, historicist criticism has been exploring the details. In fact a good many things *happened* in the Middle Ages, not only chronicle events but also slow and subtle and crucial changes—in society, in economic conditions, in subjectivity, in the conventions of authorship, in gender, in the very notion of history. Exploring the differences *within* the Middle Ages, historicism also finds differences within itself: there are many histories, because there are many topics for history and many ways of framing historical questions.

Most of the articles in this volume could be described as historicist, but they read Chaucer in many different lights: in the light of folk traditions (Lindahl), the construction of subjectivity (Leicester), medieval political thought (Fowler), and class antagonism (Patterson), to name only four. The other disciplinary development I have mentioned, the engagement with "theory," is also in evidence here: readers will find in these essays, for example, traces and sometimes more than traces of reader-response criticism (Carton), deconstruction (Leicester and Scanlon), feminism (Dinshaw and Hansen), queer theory (Kruger). The distinction between historicist and theoretical work is not nearly as neat as it might seem, however; feminism, for example, includes the history of women and the history of patriarchy. It would be possible to describe *all* of these essays as representing different versions of "cultural studies," if that term implies a historically inflected, self-conscious, theoretically sophisticated investigation of cultural productions. But I have no wish to erase the differences between these essays, because the differences are in many ways the most important things about the group.

Needless to say there are still debates among Chaucer critics. For example, one of the essays in this collection is the subject of an indignant explanatory note in the *Riverside Chaucer*.[15] There are disagreements within the collection, too. The essays by Dinshaw and Hansen are both feminist, but they are feminist in different ways; the two important books from which the essays are drawn, published in 1989 and 1992, represent two complementary and partially contradictory feminist approaches to Chaucer. The three essays on *Troilus and Criseyde* highlight different aspects of the poem and configure its main characters in different ways. Readers will have no difficulty finding many such differences of emphasis, of method, of terminology, of interpretation. But there is no longer any single issue to polarize Chaucer criticism, the way Donaldson v. Robertson once did.

The situation in Chaucer criticism now is reminiscent of a moment near the beginning of the General Prologue to the *Canterbury Tales*. As all readers of the poem know, the long opening sentence establishes a cosmic framework: the hierarchy of the natural spheres is matched by the grammatical hierarchy created by the sentence's heavily subordinated construction. An inventory of nouns produces a list in which there seems to be only one item in every category: two months, but then one wind-god, one zodiac sign, one sun, one flower, one animal species, one island, one shrine, one saint. Of course, as readers also recognize, there is at least the potential for a conflict in this orderly scheme, a conflict focused on the human heart: do people go on pilgrimages because, like the birds, they are pricked by nature in their "corage," or do they go because they want to thank Saint Thomas for their recovery from sickness? The phrase "Thanne longen folk" can be glossed by what precedes it or what follows; the desiring human subject is situated in a cosmic framework that may actually be two frameworks, natural and spiritual. So the opening sentence of the *Canterbury Tales* could be said to open up a debate about the very largest of issues.

It is the *next* moment that seems to me evocative of Chaucer criticism today: the moment when the vertical, idealized, highly structured scheme of the first sentence gives way to the horizontal circumstantiality of a particular pilgrimage. Instead of one (or two) of everything, we have a hard-to-allegorize number of pilgrims, 29; instead of the resonant "Engelond" and "Caunterbury," we have the seemingly accidental "Southwerk" and "the Tabard." The writing opens up:

> The chambers and the stables weren wyde,
> And wel we weren esed atte beste.
>   (28–29)

After the opening sentence, there *is* "ease" in this simple, paratactic phrasing. The two lines make a sentence but not a couplet—unlike the emphatic *rime riche* that seals off the opening sentence, these lines rhyme outwardly, connecting with what comes before and after. Even the wideness of the accommodations suggests the horizontal extension, the accumulation of accidental observations, that is to follow in the General Prologue and in the *Tales* as a whole.

In Chaucer criticism the great debate generated by Exegetical criticism, truly a cosmic dispute over the most fundamental aspects of reading Chaucer, has passed by. What is left is not a void but a rich, circumstantial world, or perhaps more accurately a *set* of worlds. Chaucer criticism as a whole is no longer positioned around the stark bipolar Question: critics can explore bodies of evidence and theoretical problems and see where they lead.[16] If a single new issue emerges to galvanize Chaucer criticism as the Exegetical debate once did—and I have no wish to speed such an emergence—it will arise out of the extraordinarily productive, extraordinarily *attentive* work that is now being done. Perhaps there is something anticlimactic about the debate simply subsiding, but the future of Chaucer criticism is better for it.

Yet, as in the General Prologue, it seems important to admit that the current opening-out has been energized and crucially shaped by the extreme visions that preceded it. In the General Prologue, the debate between body and soul implied in the opening sentence is played out in myriad ways in the persons and performances of the particular pilgrims. In Chaucer criticism, the large methodological and ideological problems raised by Robertson's work keep returning, now as generative puzzles rather than stumbling blocks. Criticism has largely rejected Robertson's simplicities—his picture of a monolithic Middle Ages, his insistence that modern readers should read as medieval readers did—but Robertson's complexities have returned in new, sophisticated forms in the work of historically and even theoretically minded critics. When he affirmed the determining role of culture, and culture's historicity, and the necessity of interrogating one's own culturally determined assumptions, Robertson helped invent a specifically medieval cultural studies.

In selecting these essays I have been guided by several principles of my own. First, of course, I chose from among the best work I knew. Second, I aimed for at least partial "coverage" of the texts most likely to be encountered by students in their first Chaucer courses, though of course I wish more were covered.[17] My chief criterion, though, was to value work that introduces readers to *worlds*. Each of the essays opens a new way into Chaucer's texts and into the traditions of Chaucer scholarship.[18] For that matter, most of the essays come from a complete Chaucer book,[19] and if readers are led from these essays to those books, they will receive a magnificent (though of course still selective) education in Chaucer and in medieval culture. Finally, each essay reveals realms of inquiry and bodies of evidence and ways of thinking: each essay finds new contexts for Chaucer's texts, from the remarkable folk celebrations described by Lindahl to the intertextual weave of classical and Italian poetry explored by Wetherbee. For this reason I have been reluctant to abridge—so reluctant that I have not done it at all. It would have been possible, in a few cases, to make these essays flow more easily for readers new to medieval literature, to highlight the passages that offer Chaucerian interpretations and summarize the supporting material. But that would be to miss the point. Patterson's detailed account of class relations and Kruger's discussion of a *New Yorker* story and Scanlon's careful argument with Paul de Man—these are not detours but essential steps in a self-conscious critical effort to read Chaucer's texts in the Middle Ages *and* to read them now. We all, Chaucer included, inhabit several worlds.

Notes

I thank Disa Gambera for her help with this introduction and with the collection.

1. In this introduction I begin by discussing an entire debate and subsequently sketch out the debate's opposing positions; "Exegetical criticism" will be defined later in the discussion.

2. Lee Patterson, *Negotiating the Past: The Historical Understanding of Medieval Literature* (Madison: University of Wisconsin Press, 1987), 5.

3. A very brief selection, beginning with critical anthologies: C. David Benson, ed., *Critical Essays on Chaucer's* Troilus and Criseyde *and His Major Early Poems* (Toronto: University of Toronto Press, 1991); Malcolm Andrew, *Critical Essays on Chaucer's* Canterbury Tales (Toronto: University of Toronto Press, 1991); Harold Bloom, ed., *Geoffrey Chaucer* (New York: Chelsea House, 1985); the older standard Richard J. Schoeck and Jerome Taylor, eds., *Chaucer Criticism: An Anthology*, 2 vols. (Notre Dame, Ind.: University of Notre Dame Press, 1960); see also the historical anthologies edited by J. A. Burrow and by Derek Brewer, cited in notes 5 and 6. Guides and companions: the Oxford Guides to Chaucer, consisting of A. J. Minnis, ed., with V. J. Scattergood and J. J. Smith, *The Shorter Poems* (Oxford: Oxford University Press, 1995), B. A. Windeatt, *Troilus and Criseyde* (Oxford: Clarendon Press, 1992), and Helen Cooper, *The Canterbury Tales,* 2d ed. (Oxford: Oxford University Press, 1996); Piero Boitani and Jill Mann, *The Cambridge Chaucer Companion* (Cambridge: Cambridge University Press, 1986). For bibliographic help: Larry D. Benson, ed., *The Riverside Chaucer,* 3d. ed. (Boston: Houghton Mifflin, 1987); Mark Allen and John H. Fisher, *The Essential Chaucer: An Annotated Bibliography of Major Modern Studies* (Boston: G. K. Hall, 1987); and two multivolume series, the Chaucer Bibliographies from the University of Toronto Press and the Variorum Chaucer from the University of Oklahoma Press.

4. See especially the essay I have already quoted from, Patterson's "Historical Criticism and the Development of Chaucer Studies," in *Negotiating the Past.*

5. Peter Ashton, quoted in Derek Brewer, ed., *Chaucer: The Critical Heritage* (London: Routledge & Kegan Paul, 1978), 1:102.

6. From Sidney's *Apology for Poetry,* cited in J. A. Burrow, ed., *Geoffrey Chaucer: A Critical Anthology* (Harmondsworth, England: Penguin, 1969), 51.

7. Dryden, from the preface to the *Fables,* in Burrow, 69 and 64. Joseph Addison concurs: "But age has rusted what the poet writ, / Worn out his language, and obscur'd his wit" (from *Account of the Greatest English Poets,* 1694, in Burrow, 60).

8. Dryden, from the preface to the *Fables,* in Burrow, 61.

9. In a statement that could have been written by Cleanth Brooks, Donaldson writes: "The fact is that we do not read poetry with the intellect alone, and that when poetry makes two contradictory statements they do not cancel each other out. Both remain as part of the essential poetic truth, which is not the same thing at all as logic" (*Chaucer's Poetry: An Anthology for the Modern Reader,* 2d ed. [Glenview, Ill.: Scott, Foresman, 1975], 1134).

10. In the title of Donaldson's edition, the word *poetry* is more tendentious than it may seem. Of course it has literal application: the edition doesn't include Chaucer's prose. But it also evokes the New Critical sense of poetry as the paradigm for all literature: the bibliography of New Criticism is full of titles like "*Macbeth* as Poem" and "*The Golden Bowl* as Poem."

11. D. W. Robertson, "Historical Criticism," in *Essays in Medieval Culture* (Princeton: Princeton University Press, 1980), 10.

12. D. W. Robertson, *Essays in Medieval Culture,* xi.

13. See E. T. Donaldson, "Patristic Exegesis in the Criticism of Medieval Literature: The Opposition," *Critical Approaches to Medieval Literature,* ed. Dorothy Bethurum (New York: Columbia University Press, 1960), 134–53.

14.   For a critique of recent historicist developments in medieval literary criticism, see Gayle Margherita, *The Romance of Origins: Language and Sexual Difference in Middle English Literature* (Philadelphia: University of Pennsylvania Press, 1994).

15.   See my editorial note to Evan Carton's "Complicity and Responsibility in Pandarus' Bed and Chaucer's Art," his essay reprinted in this volume.

16.   I have been repressing the impulse to hedge my schematizing remarks with moderating concessions, but I will here offer one that must stand for many: Of course great scholarship and criticism was produced in the decades and centuries before 1979 (the date of the earliest essay here), and of course Robertsonian work continues to be written, sometimes by avowed anti-Robertsonians. No bell has rung announcing a change of consensus. Yet something has, I believe, palpably changed.

17.   In particular, I regret the lack of work on the Prioress's Tale and the Franklin's Tale. And the principle of coverage is itself in some ways regrettable: I would have been glad to include brilliant work on the Manciple's Tale, the Squire's Tale, and the dream-visions.

18.   It may be worth mentioning that, although each of the essays focuses on one particular text, the General Prologue or a Tale or *Troilus,* almost all of them extend their discussion to include other Chaucerian texts; the index should be consulted.

19.   The essays by Lindahl, Leicester, Dinshaw, Hansen, and Aers are literally chapters from books. In two cases, those of Patterson and Scanlon, I chose an earlier article that was later transformed into a book chapter, because the article seemed to serve as a freestanding introduction better than the book chapter did. Wetherbee's article is a special case: in an important new piece written especially for this volume, he revisits (or, as he modestly says, "reworks") the issues raised by his *Chaucer and the Poets,* in my view the single best study of *Troilus and Criseyde.*

Chaucer and the Shape of Performance

CARL LINDAHL

The road as stage, the pilgrim players: both aspects of Chaucer's setting incorporate the folkloric structures of fourteenth-century thought and society. Yet the *Canterbury Tales* presents far more than the general conditions for generating stories: it gives us a game, described in some detail, with well-delineated rules, clearly executed roles, distinct and consistent patterns of interaction. Is this game Chaucer's invention? If not, from what source did he derive it? Does the game itself—*as a game*—have a shaping role in the poem? Critical interpretations of the structure of the *Tales* range from the exasperatingly vague to the excruciatingly specific.

At one extreme are the allegorical readings that address the poem as if it were a riddle, the least obvious solutions often found the most intriguing. For seventy years various critics have claimed that the pilgrimage was contoured as a foil for theological doctrine, that the characters and their stories symbolized, for example, the Seven Deadly Sins.[1] Later, the shapes of Gothic architecture were invoked as blueprints for the deep symbolic structure of the poem.[2] As these imaginative reconstructions multiply, Chaucer's own concrete and explicit setting—a company of pilgrims engaged in a festive storytelling contest—becomes lost in a crowd of icons and symbols.

At the opposite pole are literal interpretations that view the poem as a chronicle, much as fundamentalists read the Bible. Frederick Furnivall, for example, counted miles and days to reassure us that, yes, it was indeed possible that the Cook would have had enough time during the eight-and-a-half-mile ride between Ospringe and Harbledown to drink himself into the stupor that caused him to fall from his horse.[3]

My approach is more abstract than that of the literalists, but more firmly rooted in social reality than the answers most recently in favor. *Chaucer shaped his poem to simulate the structure of the medieval festival, fitting the patterns of action within the frame and links to a model of oral group performance thoroughly familiar to his contemporaries.* The audience's knowledge of such oral shapes influenced their response to the poem, which—whether or not it was read aloud—became a model oral entertainment in their eyes.

From *Earnest Games: Folkloric Patterns in the Canterbury Tales.* © 1987 Carl Lindahl. Reprinted by permission of Indiana University Press.

It is puzzling that, of the innumerable critical works devoted to the *Canterbury Tales,* there is not one which closely examines its possible structural relationship to the patterns that governed the presentation of oral arts in medieval festival.[4] Critics have closely examined the debt of Renaissance artists to festive forms. Citing many of the rituals I will discuss, C. L. Barber has demonstrated their influence on Shakespeare's comedies, and Mikhail Bakhtin has presented an imaginative assessment of their importance to Rabelais.[5] Why not a similar study of Chaucer? Perhaps because festival form is not merely conspicuous in the *Canterbury Tales,* but inseparable from the work itself. Barber and Bakhtin demonstrate how Renaissance authors *preempt folk forms and reshape them into literature.* I contend that Chaucer *reshapes literature into festival,* crafting a frozen representation of a lively play form never before (or since) rendered in writing, a world fully consonant in its rules and interactions with celebrations witnessed and enacted by the poet's contemporaries. Shakespeare's comedies may be festive, they may incorporate festive structures, but in their larger form they adhere to the conventions of Renaissance drama. Rabelais' prose may be festive, but (according to Bakhtin) it is not based principally on festival, nor is it imitative of festival in its overall structure: Rabelais used festive modes to shatter, rather than refashion, preexisting molds of all kinds, oral and literary. Chaucer's narrator, on the contrary, claims to be reporting act-by-act the progress of a game. I contend that Chaucer the Pilgrim and Chaucer the poet stand here in formal accord. Whether or not there was ever a pilgrimage-*cum*-storytelling-contest that proceeded exactly in the manner of the *Canterbury Tales,* there were many contemporary celebrations that shared the poem's pattern.

If, in creating his poem, Chaucer has also *re-created* a consummately medieval festival, the tale he tells must have specific artistic and social dimensions, and these two factors must hold each other in constant balance. Festive art, the antithesis of closet art, must appeal broadly. There are no Emily Dickinsons among the practitioners of oral poetry: the concerns of the audience must surface in the artist's plan. Therefore, festive art not only entertains, but also gives voice to the concerns of an entire group, providing a mixture of social critique and compensation fantasy.[6] Accordingly, to demonstrate that Chaucer has re-created the medieval festival, I must first show that he has chosen festive actions appropriate to the social status of his performers. I will examine the players and moves of historically documented games, and derive their most broadly representative social and artistic patterns. The evidence presented here comes principally from nine festivals well-known to Chaucer and his contemporaries; it is likely that Chaucer witnessed or participated in specific enactments of most of them. I will identify the nine most common shaping features of these games, then describe each rule in some detail, and show how Chaucer incorporated each into his poem.

All nine festivals were mounted by groups similar in social background to some or all of the Canterbury pilgrims. The performances took two basic forms, determined by the status of the players. Such *noble and bourgeois* entertainments as the *Cour Amoureuse,* the love debates, the London Pui, and the courtly Mayings were large and elaborate contests in which poets strove for the favorable judgment of a mock prince. A close look at one reveals the form common to all four:

> The *Cour Amoureuse* was monumental both in size and formality. Over six hundred members are listed on one of its registers, about seven hundred on another, all ranked according to a rigid system. Membership was exclusively male, though ladies were present at the meetings and played an important role in the proceedings. On St. Valentine's Day, following a series of masses, the group assembled under the direction of the Prince of Love, an accomplished minstrel. Then ensued a competition among *gentil* poets, whose work had earlier been screened for entry by the twenty-four ministers of the *Cour.* The subject matter was love, and the entrants' goal was to please the ladies who were called upon to judge. The winning poet was awarded a crown and chaplet made of gold.

There is evidence to connect Chaucer to the *Cour,* the Pui, and the courtly Mayings.[7] Though all such links are speculative, the *Canterbury Tales* shows he knew their general rules. Among his fictional players, the Knight, Squire, Monk, Prioress, and Franklin would share a familiarity with these elite games.

The *Mixed-Class* entertainments—the Feast of Fools, Boy Bishop ceremonies, Riding of St. George, mystery plays, Christmas guisings and Lord of Misrule performances—were massive events in which commoners took on the roles of their masters, ruling as kings-for-a-day over the entire play society. The *Festum Stultorum* is broadly representative:

> The Feast of Fools was mounted by members of the lower clergy in open mockery of their ecclesiastical superiors. The deacons and choirboys chose from their ranks a "Bishop" to perform his role in the most absurd manner possible. The festivities began with a church service marking his investiture. Within the church, he delivered bawdy sermons and read a parody mass, which often contained the ludicrous "Prose of the Ass," performed in Latin as the congregation called out a derisive response in the vernacular. Outside the church, celebrations continued, assuming even wilder forms whose indecencies "would shame a kitchen or tavern," and involving the participation of the entire community. The outside revels also featured oral performances, most often "verses scurrilous and unchaste."[8]

Such feasts took place throughout England and embraced the entire range of its citizenry, but the principal performers and primary beneficiaries were members of the lower classes, people whose positions in life corresponded with those of the Reeve, Miller, Manciple, and Summoner. Thus, medieval performance, like Chaucer's pilgrimage, engaged two distinct classes of players: *gentils* and churls. The accompanying chart describes the two performance types, which differed according to this broad social division.

Festive Structures in Medieval Life and Literature

Traits	Gentil Celebrations (Nobles and Bourgeois)				Mixed-Class Celebrations	
	Cour Amoureuse (Feb. 14)	London Pui	May Day (Floure and Leafe)	Love Debates	Mystery Plays (York, N-Town, Beverley)	Feast of Fools
1. Autocratic ruler	Prince d'Amour	Prince du Pui	Queen of Love	Queen of Love	—	Pope (Bishop, Archbishop) of Fools
2. Amateurs as major performers	noble and *gentil* poets	*gentils* perform their songs	noble and *gentil* poets	noble and *gentil* poets	lead roles *sometimes* professional; others amateur	occasional pay for leader; other roles amateur
3. Measures to enforce participation	noncompetitors buy supper for all	dues waived for competitors	?	?	fines for nonparticipants	townsmen force participation of clergy
4. Rigid formality	quasilegal written charter	quasilegal written charter	patroness and retinue have specific tasks*	debates duplicate legal procedures	very formal written charters	choosing of Pope and retinue; special masses, sermons
5. Processionality	?	horseback procession to Prince's home	procession to the fields	?	massive procession preceding plays	parade through street after mass
6. Mingling of sacred and profane	religious observances precede *Cour*	gild dedicated to holy works, maintaining altar	?	?	pious plays, *interludi* sacred and profane mingle in performance	masses and revels mingle
7. Wider festive context	masses, supper, games	holy feast and supper for poor precede competition	tourneys, jousts, dances	dances, other amusements	masses, parades, revelry	Christmas celebrations
8. Competitive elements	*individuals* compete for crown	*individuals* compete for crown	*teams and individuals* compete	*individual* competition and judgment	*group* rivalry among tradesmen	social *factions*: laity vs. clergy, intrachurch fights
9. Hierarchical structure	17 ranks *duplicate* social order	*duplicates* social order	queen and court *duplicate* social order	queen and court *duplicate* social order	participants' place in parade and plays assigned to gilds *duplicate* social order	lowly Pope and retinue *invert* social order

? Indicates insufficient evidence for the presence of a given trait

— Indicates that the trait is not present

* Indicates the hypothetical reconstruction of the Floure and Leafe ceremony, according to Bédier, Kittredge, and Pearsall

Mixed-Class Celebrations (continued)			Festive Fictions			Traits
Boy Bishop	*Lord of Misrule and Mummings*	*Riding of St. George*	*Canterbury Tales*	*Decameron*	*Sercambi's Novella*	
Boy Bishop	Captain of mummers; Lord of Misrule	St. George	Host (Herry Bailly)	rotating dictatorship	Leader (Aluizi)	1. Autocratic ruler
occasional pay for leader; other roles amateur	amateur players	amateur players	amateur players	all tellers perform as amateurs	teller not paid	2. Amateurs as major performers
forced participation of clergy	fines for nonparticipation	gild members must attend or pay fine	noncompetitors must pay bill for all players	—	—	3. Measures to enforce participation
choosing of Bishop, retinue; masses, sermons	specially delegated roles, regimented performances	elaborate procession with delegated roles	Host dictates rigid rules to company	each dictator chooses theme	Leader appoints storyteller, entertainers	4. Rigid formality
parade through street after mass	guisers ride and march in procession	all participants join in procession	pilgrimage	—	pilgrimage	5. Processionality
masses and revels mingle	masses and revels mingle	religious gild funds masses	pilgrimage and profane tales	—	pilgrimage and profane tales	6. Mingling of sacred and profane
Christmas celebrations	Christmas celebrations	masses and feasting on St. George's Day	pious frame indicates sacred procession	—	—	7. Wider festive context
social *factions*: laity vs. clergy, intrachurch fights	social *factions*: lower classes mock superiors	?	*individual and factional* competition (trade vs. trade, class vs. class)	—	—	8. Competitive elements
lowly Bishop and retinue *invert* social order	lowly king (abbot) and court *invert* social order	lowly servants play St. George and retinue, *invert* social order	Host attempts to *duplicate* social order as *gentils* defer to him; churls attempt to *invert* social order	—	Leader appoints treasurer, stewards; no evidence of class status of appointees	9. Hierarchical structure

In the first seven of their nine shaping traits, the *gentil* and churl festivals resembled each other closely. First, both featured an *autocratic ruler,* a Master of the Revels, who governed absolutely within the festive frame. This leader was a temporary despot whose preemptive powers made him a formidable, if playful, counterpart of the real king. The merchant membership of the London Pui chose a prince to serve as uncontested judge of their song competitions. He was endowed with royal stature by the contesting poets, who addressed their *envois* to him and strove for his approval.[9] The Floure and Leafe rivalry was probably ruled in similar fashion. One of Deschamps' *ballades* exalts John of Gaunt's daughter, Philippa: to the poet, the leader of the floures is not merely a duchess, but the very "Queen of Love, who surpasses all in wisdom and honor."[10]

Among the *gentil* celebrations, only the *Cour Amoureuse* recognized multiple leaders. The Prince assumed the autocrat's position, but he was a minstrel, more a decoration than a ruler. The real power was vested in an oligarchy of ministers who controlled the festivities and a company of noble ladies who judged the entries. Yet it is important to note that the *fiction* of rule by one mock prince was preserved even at the *Cour,* as revealed in a surviving poem addressed to the Prince:

> Noble, so powerful prince,
> valiant Pierre d'Auteville,
> holding, as sovereign, in your hand
> the Court of Love. . . .[11]

A like penchant for dictatorship is apparent in mixed-class entertainments. In his play role, the Boy Bishop enjoyed great authority—and an audience with the real-life King of England. The Pope of Fools also ruled supreme in his mock domain: he was empowered to raise funds for mounting dramas which he directed.[12]

Chaucer's Herry Bailly is an autocrat of the same playful stamp. From the beginning of the ride, the Host claims control over the artistic and behavioral destinies of the pilgrims: he sets the rules and determines who tells the tales. The Host's relatively low social status among the pilgrims has its medieval parallels—as when the minstrel Hauteville reigned as Prince of Love over real-life lords at the *Cour.* As Master of the Revels, the Host shares a pedigree with the mummers' captain, the May Day king, and a host of anonymous autocrats who have governed folk performance as far back in time as it can be traced.

Second, in medieval celebrations the featured performers were *amateurs who comprised both the cast and the audience.* The festive play world gave the stage to those who would not normally mount it. Sometimes, as at the Pui and the *Cour,* accomplished minstrels attended the rites, and occasionally they held positions of esteem. Nevertheless, professionals did not figure in the central performances. At the *Cour* and in the love debates the nobles contended for honor; at the Pui the wealthy *gentils* competed. Men who customarily paid others to entertain them here entertained their peers. The knight Boucicaut, who had servants read to him on Sunday afternoons, was among the composers of the *Cent Ballades,* and he presented these pieces as questions of love at the Papal Palace in Avignon.[13] The late Middle Ages marked the birth of one kind of renaissance man—the *gentil* who also served as occasional artist.

Mixed-class feasts were also primarily amateur affairs: only a handful of players were compensated. The Paston family of Norwich retained a servant, William Woode, "to pleye Seynt Jorge" in the Riding, but Woode also worked day-to-day as a Warden in the Paston household.[14] By and large, the roles of audience and participant were even less distinct for the lower classes than for the *gentils.* As Bakhtin has stated, festival "does not know footlights, in the sense that it does not acknowledge any distinction between actors and spectators."[15] From time to time—as during the Prose of the Ass, when the Pope of Fools read his profane sermon to all assembled in the church—one performer set himself apart from the crowd. But the pattern of the churls' celebration allowed for a looser period of entertainment during which the entire group performed variously and severally, or in unison: after the sermons of the Boy Bishop and the *Rex Stultorum,* the crowd carried its rough artistry into the streets.

Chaucer himself was one of the Middle Ages' accomplished amateur artists, of the same status as the merchants who performed at the Pui and the untitled *gentils* who submitted poems to the *Cour.* It is not surprising, then, that the composer of the *Canterbury Tales* describes a festive amateur performance. In keeping with the festive rules, Chaucer's audience and cast (with the exception of Herry Bailly, the Master of the Revels himself) are one and the same. E. K. Chambers once suggested that the Canterbury pilgrims tell tales only because there are no professional entertainers in the company.[16] But Chambers has misread the purpose of this traveling game: it is simply festival decorum that the entertained must also entertain.

Third, the autocrat's powers were most pronounced in his *strictures to ensure the players' participation.* The edict of Chaucer's Host—"And whoso wole my juggement withseye / Shal paye al that we spenden by the weye" (1.805–6)— finds a perfect echo in the bylaws of the *Cour Amoureuse:* any minister who failed to submit songs was required to host a dinner for his fellows.[17] Both the *Canterbury Tales* and the medieval celebration offer systems of rewards and punishments designed to cajol every member of the audience into the spotlight. For the lower classes, urging often turned into coercion. In Beverley even the gildsmen who did not act in the mystery plays were called upon to attend, wearing uniforms. Fines and dues were also levied by the King of Fools and Lord of Misrule: their subjects were required to play—and to pay for their fun.

Fourth, medieval games were marked by a *rigid formality* that would seem forbiddingly constrained in modern play contexts. In the twentieth century, only the driest of "festivities" (college commencements, for example) are structured as severely as were the most playful pastimes of Chaucer's England. The Canterbury game is no exception. In addition to setting an enormous fine for failure to join in his game, Herry Bailly passes down general rules for participation, specifies a prize and the means of funding it, appoints certain storytellers, and reserves the right to stop a teller in the middle of a tale (1.788–809, 828–41). He works out a system of protocol for the pilgrims to follow. At the journey's outset, though many outrank him in real life, they sheepishly—"by oon assent" (1.817)—acknowledge his privilege to "seye his voirdit as hym leste" (1.787). As the journey progresses, the Host maintains his rigid authoritarianism. Though from time to time he is challenged, even overridden, the pilgrims' defiance is directed not at the festive rules themselves, but at Herry Bailly's failure to apply those rules correctly (a point to which I will return).

Gentil celebrations were often governed by written statutes. The charter of the *Cour* orders ministers to register and seal the verses submitted for competition. The subjects of the poems, even the exact words of the refrains, were dictated to the entrants. If the *Cour*'s codes can be taken as representative, punishments for noncompliance were severe. Anyone guilty of composing

> . . . ditties, complaints, rondeaux, virelais, ballades, lays [or similar pieces], rhymed or in prose, to the dishonor, diminution, or blame of a certain woman or women in general . . . will have his coat of arms erased. His shield will be painted the color of ashes, as if he were an infamous man, an enemy of honor, and dead to the world.[18]

This ruling raises questions concerning Chaucer's punishment as described in the *Legend of Good Women* (F 431–41): to atone for having created a faithless Criseyde, he must write poems in praise of virtuous ladies. Though many have read this sentence simply as a product of the poet's imagination, the *Cour* would have punished the author of the *Troilus;* the Pui, with its like set of prohibitions, would also have censured him.[19]

A similar sense of protocol attended mixed-class revels. Surviving "missals" attest that the parody mass celebrated during the *Festi Stultorum* was as elaborate as the regulation mass itself: the text requires, for example, that during the performance of this sometimes rather orthodox service, the celebrant bray three times at specific moments, and that the congregation respond by braying, providing comedy on cue.

Fifth, the *Canterbury Tales* and fourteenth-century festivals share a sense of *processionality* which conjoins the act of entertainment with the parade. In the *Tales,* the procession provides the major motivation for the game: stories are told to soften an otherwise hard and joyless road. Tales and songs made the journey more pleasant for the traveler. Yet it was an intrinsic aspect of medieval performance that, even without a goal to move toward, travel was inseparable from entertainment. Medieval performances—particularly those involving the entire community—were seldom stationary affairs.

Of the nine games examined here, not one can be said for certain not to have included a procession. Among the *gentil* celebrations the Floure and Leafe was introduced by a morning procession into the fields, and the London Pui included a horseback progress to the home of the newly chosen Prince. The Feast of Fools and the Boy Bishop ceremonies ended with cavalcades in which the mock potentate was carried through the city. And the Corpus Christi pageant often included two processions: one, the more pious ecclesiastical march, in which the town's governmental and trade officials went with church officers through the streets; the other, the plays themselves, in which it seems the procession traveled to the performers, as the audience visited dozens of fixed stages.[20] Both processions were so highly valued that at York (1426) it was ruled that they be held on separate days, so that one parade would not engulf the other.[21]

Like the mixed-class festivals, medieval pilgrimage oscillated between the poles of utmost formality and utter chaos. Shorter processions tended to be formal. Local pilgrimages in fourteenth-century France, for example, featured groups of riders followed by pilgrims afoot, all proceeding in rank, *cierges* in hand, toward a nearby shrine.[22] On the longer processions it was likely that at some point the ranks would break into an ungoverned flow, often a near riot, which was as much a part of the festivities as were the measured marches. Similarly, the investitures of the Boy Bishop and Pope of Fools were marked by processions down the church aisles during which hierarchical decorum was observed. Afterward, however, the crowd became riotous and moved formlessly through the streets. Orderly and disorderly parades would alternate.

The length of the Canterbury pilgrimage dictates that it follow the long form just described. Chaucer does occasionally indicate that some order is being imposed on the ranks. We know, for example, that the Miller plays the bagpipe for the company and that his music leads them out of Southwark. Here is a partial image of procession, one that is reinforced to some extent by the observation that the Reeve rides always at the end of the group. At St. Thomas's watering hole, however, the Host breaks up this parade, gathers the group in a flock (1.824), and initiates a less orderly progress, which loosens as the journey wears on and reaches a peak of disorder when the Cook becomes drunk and falls off his horse, just before the last secular tale is told.

Sixth, in all the medieval celebrations, *sacred and profane elements intermingle* in an easy and complementary fashion. Even the most secular (the Court of Love, presenting erotic themes in governmental guises) and the most anticlerical (the Feast of Fools, observed in patent mockery of the Church) entertainments openly embraced the most conventional aspects of piety. Masses and sincere prayer marked these otherwise unholy rites.[23] Similarly, the overtly religious events possessed a second, secular, impious side. After the Boy

Bishop's mass, prayers were supplanted by obscene songs as celebrants filed from the church.

Chaucer's poem opens with a melding of sacred and profane—invoking in one breath spring breezes, mating birds, and the holy blissful martyr, Thomas of Canterbury. The subsequent tales freely interweave piety and play. This combination is characteristic not only of the nine games examined here, not only of the *Canterbury Tales,* but also of medieval pilgrimage in general, where piety was penetrated with nearly every gradation of play—from simple levity to open blasphemy, from gambling to sex acts in sacred places.

Seventh, even the most elaborate medieval games were simply parts of greater celebrations, fragments embedded in a *wider festive context.* Each feast was a mere motif in a complex ritual design, and each must be seen within its frame to be fully understood. In general, the framing event was a foil to offset the celebration: the more austere events were temporally flanked by revelry, the more playful events by austerity and order. The wildest celebrations were set in the midst of the holiest seasons. The Feast of Fools, the Feast of Boys, and the reign of the Lord of Misrule were fixtures on the church calendar, small and relatively uncharacteristic segments of the long, devotion-filled chain of Christmas holidays. The Riding of St. George occurred at the end of the Lenten season, on the day (April 23) dedicated to the patron saint of England—in the very time of year that Chaucer's pilgrims begin their ride.

The *Canterbury Tales,* like its real-life medieval analogs, is a celebration within a celebration, a profane event embedded in a sacred procession. Beginning with a seasonal allusion, the poem places the pilgrimage at the onset of spring, in the neighborhood of Holy Week and St. George's Day, a time when both spiritual faith and secular life are revitalized by the return of warmth and greenery. The pilgrims' play and their holy destination are both appropriate to the season. The allusion to St. Thomas which opens the poem and the sermon on sin which ends it are as true to the nature of medieval play as are the raucous tales which fall between these sacred markets. Like those contemporary games which were framed by pious activities, Chaucer's poem emphasizes the impious side of things, thus providing a contrast to the larger, more serious celebration the pilgrims are keeping. Herry Bailly's first address to his guests, as they end their supper the night before the ride, describes the dual nature of the journey they will soon undertake:

> Ye goon to Caunterbury—God yow speede,
> The blisful martir quite yow youre meede!
> And wel I woot, as ye goon by the weye,
> Ye shapen yow to talen and to pleve. . . .
> (1.769–72)

The Host, like the great majority of his co-celebrants, sees no ambiguity in this juxtaposition. As Canterbury is reserved for praying, the road there favors playing. And as the journey lengthens, the Host does all in his power to maintain a mood of levity: he calls repeatedly for merry tales and condemns excessive religiosity wherever he finds it. The pilgrims generally affirm that the playful make the best prayers.

The seven traits examined thus far apply equally to the games of the *gentils* and those of the churls, but the remaining two break down according to class lines. Until now, I have stressed how Chaucer created a middle world mediating the extremes of society and behavior. His cast excludes most gradations of nobility and peasantry, his pilgrims generally foreswear pious and impious excesses. Yet, as some of the gild records have suggested, this newly formed middle-class community, no yet officially recognized in Chaucer's time, was marked by internal tension. The more *gentil* members sought the power and privilege traditionally accorded the nobles, and the churls sometimes claimed the few concessions the older order had granted the peasants. In the *Canterbury Tales* both groups exploit the play roles of the venerable three-estate system. The *gentils* imitate the behavior appropriate to noble games; the churls adopt performance patterns characteristic of the peasants.

Eighth, medieval games were marked by strong *competitive elements*. There was a marked tendency among the *gentil* celebrants to compete for a prize: often a crown of gold or of leaves, as at the *Cour* and the Pui. There was an acknowledged winner and a prescribed means by which he was chosen. Entrants played hard, and not always fairly, for this prize: the Pui's statutes dictated punishments for prejudicial action on the part of the judge, and the bylaws of the *Cour* went to great lengths to ensure that entries were honestly submitted.[24]

The churls, however, competed as a rule not individually, but by factions. Individual competitions sometimes occurred, but these generally *preceded* the feast. The Boy Bishop and Pope of Fools were chosen from among many candidates well before the celebration; the festivities began with the winner's investiture. Within the feast the real contest was one of class and occupational rivalry. Such fights were often the unsanctioned side effects of play. Nevertheless—as Le Roy Ladurie has shown—they constituted perhaps the most important aspects of the performance, as far as the lower classes were concerned.[25]

At the *Festi Stultorum* and the Feast of Boys, the competition was often between the laity and the permanent clergy. At Rheims in 1390, the vicars and choirboys dressed themselves in bourgeois fashion; in reprisal, offended laymen mounted plays satirizing the clergy. At Auxerre, a similar rivalry was institutionalized, as laymen and lower clergy competed in the singing of "doggerel songs." The winning faction often subjected the losers to intense mockery.[26] Occupational rivalry surfaced continually on Corpus Christi Day. Members of each gild tried to outdo all others, both within the dramatic framework and outside it. Trade competition often surged into violence. At York in 1419 the Carpenters and Cordwainers attacked the Skinners, using axes to hew apart the torches carried by the latter to light the Corpus Christi procession. Later, there was a four-year wrangle between York's Cordwainers and Weavers. The issue was precedence in the procession: the Cordwainers, who felt slighted by protocol, refused to bear torches. The quarrel led to the arrest of many tradesmen and was submitted to civic arbitration before it was resolved.[27]

In the *Canterbury Tales,* the Host—a man of no small social standing, who wants to be a respectable "play" lord to his betters—favors the *gentil* approach. He sets up a prize and announces rules favoring individual competition. And the *gentils* respond, with characteristic grace. The Knight temporarily renounces the privilege of his rank and signals his submission to the rules. Like real-life entrants in *gentil* contests, he is interested in the prize. His remarks reveal a competitive bent, but affirm his intent to compete in *gentil*-manly fashion:

> I wol nat letten eek noon of this route;
> Lat every felawe telle his tale aboute,
> And lat se now who shal the soper wynne. . . .
>   (1.889–91)

Other *gentils* begin their tales humbly, lamenting their lack of artistic skills, a rhetorical ploy also found in extant poems from the *Cour* and the love debates.[28]

True to *their* rules, however, the churls bolt: they tell their stories not for the free lunch but for blood. The Miller, Reeve, Cook, Manciple, Friar, and Summoner appear on stage not merely as artists, but as verbal duelists, using their tales as vehicles for thinly-veiled blows against occupational and class rivals, in a manner reminiscent of the mixed-class celebrations. In general, the fights between pilgrims of roughly equal status are the most overt and intense. Furthermore, the intensity of their competitions is generally proportionate to the intensity of the rivalry between the trades represented by the duelists. Thus, when the Miller faces off with the Reeve, it is not merely personal animosity, but a long-standing trade conflict between the estate of reeves and the estate of millers which lies at the root of their fight. Similar occupational rivalries lie behind the slurs traded by Summoner and Friar, and Cook and Manciple. Their quarrels evoke the fights held on Corpus Christi, when intertrade conflict was an essential, if unofficial, motivating force for the players.

Ninth, the churls' readiness to fight is rooted in the fact that all the games were marked by *elaborate hierarchical structure.* In these festivities, the "craving for symmetry" which Johan Huizinga finds everywhere in medieval culture is clearly evident.[29] The *Cour* was divided into seventeen orders, from *grands conservateurs* to "gardeners," each play role yielding powers commensurate with its title. The *Cour* duplicated the actual machinery of government and society—the entire upper and middle portions of French society were mirrored in play. The Prince of the Pui, the patroness of the Floure and Leafe, and the Boy Bishop were all given play roles corresponding exactly to the functions of the leaders for whom they were named.[30]

Such duplication pervades the entire social range of performance. In the mumming performed before Richard II, the masked procession represented the most powerful elements of upper-class society and marched in ranks which followed the dictates of protocol. First came the knightly estates: squires, riding two by two, preceded knights riding in similar fashion, heralding the Emperor; then followed the clerical procession, with a Pope and a retinue of twenty-four Cardinals. In the processions preceding the mystery plays the entire town marched in uniform, with the lowly Porters in the lead, followed by other groups in exact ascending order of municipal importance. At Beverley the most powerful gilds also acted the most important plays, with the Gild Merchant, which controlled the town, significantly assigned to mount the *Last Judgment*.[31] Deference to rank entered even into the wage scales of the paid performers. At the Coventry Corpus Christi plays, the player of God was the most highly paid actor, followed by the players of Souls, Common Men, the Worm of Conscience, and Judas. The same connection between social and metaphysical hierarchies is seen in the plays assigned the gilds: "play" life imitated day-to-day life as closely as possible. At York, the shipwrights, fishers, and mariners staged the *Noah* play; the goldsmiths the *Magi;* the bakers *The Last Supper.*

One important factor, however, divides the *gentils'* play hierarchy from that of the churls. While the elite games *duplicated* the social order, placing players in roles correspondent to their real-life status, the churls *inverted,* even *subverted,* that order. The Pope of Fools was chosen from the lowest ranks of the inferior clergy, the Boy Bishop from the choirboys, St. George from among the servants—and their retinues as well from among other lowly groups.

Although mixed-class feasts mocked the highborn, the mockery itself presented a hierarchical conception of society. This fact cannot be overstressed; interpreters of medieval festival often fail to note the importance of hierarchy even for the churls. In an otherwise impeccable depiction of carnival, Bakhtin declares:

> The suspension of all hierarchical precedence during carnival time was of particular significance. Rank was especially evident during *official* feasts . . . [which produced in effect] a consecration of inequality. On the contrary all were considered equal during carnival.[32]

In emphasizing freedom, Bakhtin distorts the nature of the game. *Relative* license was indeed extended to the lower classes during carnival, but absolute, ungoverned freedom was not. The freedom of festival, like that of yoga, is based upon constraint. Mixed-class celebrations featured the same formal aspects that governed *gentil* pastimes: both had their autocrats and enforced participation. Even as, during the Feast of Innocents, choirboys marched down the aisles proclaiming the fall of the mighty (to the strains of *Deposuit potentes*), a new Bishop—a boy bishop, granted rank and privilege over his fellows—came forward to assume the mitre and reinforce the paradigm of hierarchy. Festive churls did not destroy hierarchy; rather, they rearranged its content, from the bottom up—much as when the Pope of Fools wore his holy breeches on his head.

Such inversions were not only desirable but necessary for the lower classes. Festival presented their only opportunity for sanctioned social ascent. It was a time when a miller *could* "quite" a knight, as Chaucer's Miller does. The subservience of the churls at all other times made them not only relish, but demand, exalted treatment on holidays. And the lowly were generally granted greater power at festival than at any other time. This power extended from the license to act like clowns and louts to the more directed animosity of imitating and ridiculing their social superiors, and to requesting and receiving clear concessions from the upper classes. Such obligatory charity marked the Boy Bishop ceremonies: the chosen boys were not only granted the pleasure of ruling for a day, but were also given money, lavish meals, and the permission to skip classes the following day, as the rest of the community resumed its ordinary work. And at the Feast of Fools, the Bishop who surrendered his role to the play Bishop was required to host a sumptuous feast for the mobs that mocked him. Clearly, these were real as well as "play" rewards.

Furthermore—and this is perhaps the most important point—the churl denied such holiday offerings would feel no inhibitions about seizing them outright. At wedding feasts in northern France, the hosts customarily offered wine to the crowds, whether or not the watchers had been invited to the wedding. In 1427 at Magnieux, a group of peasants, when refused this wine, started a riot; another such scene in 1381 ended with a death. A record dated 1375 from Chalon-sur-Marne records the tradition (*acoustumé et de longtemps*) that newly married nobles must give their servants wedding gifts; in 1391 a servant denied his due killed the bridegroom.[33] Similar violence, most often taking the form of riots, and occasionally leading to murder, is found in various fourteenth-century accounts of the *Festi Stultorum*. Defiance of uncharitable *gentils* also occurred on pilgrimage. In 1431 four hostelries near the shrine of Our Lady of Walsingham were burned to the ground. The explanation advanced for the arson was that pilgrims were enraged by the high cost of lodging.[34]

The Canterbury pilgrims follow the performance paradigms appropriate to their respective estates. Chaucer the Pilgrim, like Chaucer the poet, is a *gentil* who introduces the players in customary fashion: his list of *dramatis personae* reads in nearly exact descending order, just as do the two surviving membership lists of the *Cour Amoureuse*. When the festival begins, Herry Bailly reinforces that order, setting up his game strictly along *gentil* lines. He manipulates the straws in his hand so that the Knight—the most exalted pilgrim—may tell the first tale. Attempting to use this planned accident to create an elite hierarchy, the Host invites the Monk to tell the second tale. In seeming irony, but true to the nature of medieval performance, it is the highborn pilgrims who bow before the less-than-worshipful Herry Bailly. The Knight, Man of Law, Squire, and their peers "wol nat rebelle" against his pleasure (5.5), but proclaim his requests their obligations (2.41).

The churls, however, have another game plan. True to his pedigree, the Miller defies the Host's attempt to keep him in check. As Herry Bailly asks the Monk to tell a tale to follow the Knight's, Robyn steps in and says he has a noble tale himself. The Host, trying to maintain gentility's control, says that some man better than the Miller should speak next (1.3130). This proves too much for the Miller—he must endure servitude at all other times, but not on holiday. The Host's condescension only strengthens the Miller's resolve: if refused his holiday rights, he will simply seize them.[35]

As the celebration continues, the two factions continually evince their predictable behavior. The Squire, Merchant, Franklin, Man of Law, and Prioress all speak only when spoken to, using the most deferential language in addressing their often indelicate leader. But the churls seldom acknowledge the man's existence. Like the Miller, the Reeve, Cook, and Summoner all break into the session without so much as speaking to the Host, let alone asking his permission.[36] The Summoner, Pardoner, and Friar interrupt other pilgrims, defying the Host and assuming his leadership functions. From the Miller's Tale to the Manciple's, the churls mount a revolt against the Host, rendering the *Tales,* in effect, a double celebration: an abortive *gentil* entertainment and a churls' brawl, both at once.

Over this mixed event the Host rules precariously, in both modes. He is the exalted Prince of the Pui, sometimes delicate (as in his address to the Prioress, 7.445–51), sometimes speaking "lordly as a kyng" (1.3900). But as the festivities wear on, he assumes more and more the ludicrous aspects of the Pope of Fools. His gaucheness, malapropisms, and anticlerical jokes partake of the slapstick of the *Festi Stultorum*. Herry Bailly's mock panegyric to the Physician is set in a comic style common to surviving texts from mixed-class festivals. Just as the Host praises the most ignoble tools of the doctor's trade—

> I pray to God so save thy gentil cors,
> And eek thyne urynals and thy jurdones,
> Thyn ypocras, and eek thy galiones,
> And every boyste ful of thy letuarie;
> God blesse hem, and oure lady Seinte Marie!
> (6.304–8)

—the office of the Feast of Fools magnifies the most asinine qualities of the ass:

> Behold the son
> Yoked below his massive ears!
> Extraordinary ass!
> Lord of Asses!
> That strong jaw . . .
> Pulverizes the fodder . . .
> He consumes barley grains
> Together with their ears;
> Wheat from chaff
> He separates on the threshing-room floor![37]

In both texts, the more extravagant the rhetoric, the sillier its object is made to seem. Herry Bailly expends similar mock praise on such *gentil* clerics as the Monk (7.1924–64). But he is less subtle in deriding churchmen of lower rank (the Parson and Pardoner, for example), and he is openly abusive to his secular inferiors (Miller, Cook, Reeve).

But in the end, the Host's balancing act fails. To salute one's betters while slandering inferiors is not festival decorum. Because Herry Bailly never relinquishes his real-life social position, he cannot control the churls. When he insults the Miller (1.3130, 3134–35) and the Cook (1.4344–55), both in terms of their class status, he is asking for trouble. And when, in a passage worthy of the Prose of the Ass, he proposes to enshrine the Pardoner's testicles in a hog's turd (6.947–55), he very nearly forfeits his role. His speech is a quintessential festive inversion, momentarily substituting the Pardoner's sexual "relics" for St. Thomas's shrine, and invoking the comic principles present at the Feast of Fools when dung rather than incense was burned in church censers to convert the sacred to the utterly profane. But the Host himself is not the appropriate person to mock the Pardoner. Unlike the Bishop of Fools, he is not a lowborn man assuming temporary control over his equals. Instead he has been pulling rank, assuming he can have the best of both worlds: the authority of the *gentils* and the churls' tongue. It is necessary here that the Knight step in to reimpose order. This *gentil,* who has acted in a manner consistent with his class, merits the respect he demands in telling Host and Pardoner to kiss and make up. He displays the deference wise nobles extended to churls on holiday and reasserts the festive equality of the two men. After this, the Host never regains his former stature. The Knight, breaking his promise not to interrupt any man's tale, shuts up the Monk; even the lowly Manciple prevails over Herry Bailly, convincing him not to make the Cook perform (9.25–68).

Just as the General Prologue proclaims the end of the three-estate society, the dissolution of the Host's rule prefigures the death of the medieval festival, which is deeply rooted in the estates system. At the poem's beginning, Chaucer the narrator attempts to offer an idealized picture of medieval society, but adds much information revealing that medieval ideals are no longer being observed. In the General Prologue class distinctions are blurred: the riders are seldom what they would have themselves seem. The humble attire of the Knight clashes with the pretentious dress of the Miller and Gildsmen. The older estates model is not adequate to describe the society of these fourteenth-century pilgrims, who take advantage of newfound wealth and social freedoms to dress and act in ways that reflect their aspirations rather than their origins.

Similarly, the medieval festive forms which Chaucer uses to shape the *Canterbury Tales* are absolutely dependent on the estate system. Medieval festival flows from the premise that *gentils* and churls can and should be distinguished. If bourgeois Herry Bailly can pretend to be a noble, but cannot defer to his inferiors at Holiday, a festival can become a riot. Just as violence resulted when mass celebrations were repressed, the *Canterbury Tales* tends toward dissolution as the Host is overridden and the pilgrimage wears toward its end.[38]

No surviving work of medieval literature could have given Chaucer the festive outline of his poem.[39] No contemporary social theory could have supplied the structure or details of the internal divisions in his pilgrim community. But the records of medieval festivals mark the same rules, roles, and tensions that surface in the *Canterbury Tales*. Chaucer drew upon the traditional play forms he had witnessed all his life and crafted them into a lifelike shape of performance.

Notes

A much more detailed version of this argument appears in Carl Lindahl, "The Festive Form of the *Canterbury Tales*," *ELH* 52 (1985): 531–74. I thank Johns Hopkins University Press for allowing me to use material from that article. [Ed. note: This note was originally endnote 1 in "Chaucer and the Shape of Performance"; all subsequent notes have been renumbered.]

1. See, for example, Frederick Tupper, "Chaucer and the Seven Deadly Sins," *PMLA* 29 (1914): 93–128.
2. Robert M. Jordan, *Chaucer and the Shape of Creation: The Aesthetic Possibilities of Inorganic Structure* (Cambridge, MA: Harvard University Press, 1967).
3. Frederick J. Furnivall, "A Temporary Preface to the Six-Text Edition of Chaucer's *Canterbury Tales*," Part I, [Publications of the Chaucer Society], 2nd series 2, no. 3 (London, 1868), pp. 25–26, 35.
4. In discussing the interaction of Miller and Host in the Prologue to the Miller's Tale, Alfred David treats some of the festive precepts to be examined here; see his *Strumpet Muse* [Bloomington: Indiana University Press, 1976], pp. 92–95. My argument owes much to it, as well as to Mr. David's comments and suggestions.
5. C. L. Barber, *Shakespeare's Festive Comedy: A Study of Dramatic Form and Its Relation to Social Custom* (Princeton: Princeton University Press, 1959); Mikhail Bakhtin, *Rabelais and His World*, trans. Hélène Iswolsky (Cambridge, MA: M.I.T. Press, 1968).
6. In addition to Bakhtin, see Natalie Z. Davis, *Society and Culture in Early Modern France* (Stanford: Stanford University Press, 1975), pp. 97–123, 152–87; Emmanuel Le Roy Ladurie, *Carnival in Romans*, trans. Mary Feeney (New York: Braziller, 1979).

7. Among Chaucer's contemporaries and acquaintances connected with these events are Othon de Graunson, John Gower, and Sir John Clanvowe, whose poems on Valentine's Day are similar to Chaucer's; Jack B. Oruch, "St. Valentine, Chaucer, and Spring in February," *Speculum* 56 (1981): 557. Eustace Deschamps's name is found on one of the membership lists of the *Cour Amoureuse;* he also wrote a floure and leafe ballade in honor of Philippa, daughter of Chaucer's patron, John of Gaunt. Chaucer's possible links with the Pui are sketched by John Fisher in *John Gower: Moral Philosopher and Friend of Chaucer* (New York: New York University Press, 1964), pp. 77–83; his connection with the Floure and Leafe is most thoroughly examined by Kittredge, "Chaucer and Some of His Friends," *Modern Philology* 1 (1903–4): 1–18. Although Chaucer died the year the French *Cour Amoureuse* was instituted, he may have participated in an English version of the celebration; indeed, Oruch believes that Chaucer's "Parliament of Fowls" represents the beginning of the Valentine's ritual. Lydgate and Charles d'Orleans also mention lovers' lotteries on Valentine's Day (Oruch, pp. 534–65).

8. EKC [*The Mediaeval Stage,* ed. E. K. Chambers (London: Oxford University Press, 1975)] 1:274–335 discusses the feast of fools; the quotations in this description are found on pp. 292 and 294.

9. Thomas H. Riley, *Munimenta Gildhallae Londoniensis,* 2 vols., Rerum Britannicarum Medii Aevi Scriptores, no. 12 (London, 1860), vol. 2, pt. 2, pp. 216–20, 589–90; Fisher, *John Gower,* p. 78. Similar powers were granted the Lord of Misrule; see EKC 1:411–12.

10. *Oeuvres complètes de Eustache Deschamps,* ed. Marquis de Queux de Saint-Hi-laire, SATF [Société des Anciens Textes Français] (1884), vol. 4, ballade no. 765 (my translation).

11. Arthur Piaget, "La Cour Amoureuse: Dite de Charles VI," *Romania* 20 (1891): 452 (my trans.); the poet, Amé Malingre, was a "squire" of the *Cour Amoureuse.*

12. EKC 1:391; the Boy Bishop was also fully invested, as real-life bishops were.

13. *Les Cent Ballades: Poème du XIVe siècle,* ed. Gaston Raynaud, SATF (1905), pp. xvi–lxviii.

14. EKC 1:177, 223.

15. Bakhtin, p. 7.

16. EKC 1:56.

17. Piaget, "Cour Amoureuse," p. 451; R. Howard Bloch, *Medieval French Literature and Law* (Berkeley: University of California Press, 1977), p. 153.

18. Piaget, "Un Manuscript de la Cour Amoureuse de Charles VI," *Romania* 31 (1903): 602 (my trans.).

19. Richard F. Green, "The *Familia Regis* and the *Familia Cupidinis,*" in *English Court Culture,* ed. V. J. Scattergood and J. W. Sherborne (New York: St. Martin's, 1983). Green sees the poetic allusions to punishment as generally fictional in nature.

20. The opinion that the plays moved to the spectators, rather than vice versa, does not have universal support. Anna J. Mill gives a brief summary of the debate in "The Miracle and Mystery Plays," part 12 of *A Manual of the Writings in Middle English,* general ed. Albert B. Hartung, vol. 5 (New Haven: Connecticut Academy of Arts and Sciences, 1975), pp. 1317–18.

21. *Records of Early English Drama: York,* ed. Alexandra F. Johnston and Margaret Rogerson, 2 vols. (Toronto: University of Toronto Press, 1979), 2:22–44.

22. Many examples of the formal nature of local pilgrimages in fourteenth-century France are found in RV [*Le Folklore de la Guerre de Cent Ans, d'après les lettres de rémission du Trésor des Chartres,* ed. Roger Vaultier (Paris: Guénégaud, 1965)], pp. 125–74.

23. Piaget, "Un Manuscrit," p. 601; EKC 1:286. A measure of piety is shown even in the burlesque "Prose of the Ass"; the Beauvais "missal" of this service (c. 1160) directs the congregation to bray, but also has them sing the pious *Vincit* and pray for their ecclesiastical and political leaders.

24. Piaget, "Un Manuscrit," pp. 599–601; Riley, *Munimenta* 2, pt. 2, pp. 216–20, 589–90.

25. Le Roy Ladurie's *Carnival in Romans* details inter-class conflicts in a sixteenth-century Mardi Gras; for medieval parallels, see EKC 1:305–315; RV, pp. 54–57.

26. EKC 1:305, 315.

27. Johnston and Rogerson 1:32–33 (for the Skinners' offenses), 158–59, 162–63, 166–74 (for the Cordwainers'); cf. EKC 2:331–32.

28. Richard F. Green presents the courtly model for such refined obsequiousness, provides a few examples, and presents some explanations for its pervasiveness in *Poets and Prince-pleasers,* [Toronto: University of Toronto Press, 1981], pp. 112, 131–82, 204.

29. *The Waning of the Middle Ages,* trans. F. Hopman (New York: St. Martins, 1949), p. 72.

30. Thus the titles "Queen" of the "Floures," "Prince du Pui"—and "Bishop," *Archepiscopus,* and *Dominus* for the Boy Bishop.

31. The wage scales and gilds assigned the various roles and plays are recorded in EKC 2:117–18, 131, 139, 341; for the order of the torchbearers at York (1415), see Johnston and Rogerson, p. 24.

32. Bakhtin, p. 10; emphasis mine.

33. RV, pp. 22–25.

34. H. M. Gillett, *Shrines of Our Lady in England and Wales* (London: Samuel Walker, 1957), p. 308.

35. Alfred David (*Strumpet Muse,* pp. 92–95) has analyzed the Miller's behavior in terms of "holiday rights."

36. *Canterbury Tales* 1.3860–64, 3909 (Reeve); 1.4325–28 (Cook; Roger does indeed speak to the Host later in the poem [1.4365ff.], but only after the Host has slandered him); 3.1665–68 (Summoner).

37. EKC 2.279–82; my trans.

38. David shows how the depicted action (*Strumpet Muse,* pp. 220–21) and even the literary style (pp. 215–31) of the *Tales* breaks down in the poem's final sections; the increasing diffuseness of the action is in a way quite realistic, reflecting the logical consequences of the Host's violations of festive decorum. The breakdown of style offers an interesting artistic parallel.

39. As the chart indicates, Boccaccio's *Decameron* and Sercambi's *Novella* are literary creations of Chaucer's time which observe, to some extent, the rules of folk festivals. But these works reproduce only parts of the festive pattern that Chaucer renders in full; see Lindahl, "Festive Form," pp. 558, 566.

The Disenchanted Self

H. MARSHALL LEICESTER JR.

I was wondering myself if I know where I am going. So I would answer you by saying, first, that I am trying, precisely, to put myself at a point so that I do not know any longer where I am going.

> Jacques Derrida, "Structure, Sign, and Play in the Discourse of the Human Sciences"

I am nat wont in no mirour to prie,
But swynke soore and lerne multiplie.

> *The Canon's Yeoman's Prologue* (VIII, 668–69)

As an institution, the author is dead: his civil status, his biographical person have disappeared; dispossessed, they no longer exercise over his work the formidable paternity whose account literary history, teaching, and public opinion had the responsibility of establishing and renewing; but in the text, in a way, I *desire* the author: I need his figure (which is neither his representation nor his projection), as he needs mine.

> Roland Barthes, *The Pleasure of the Text*

What seem to me to be the two best treatments of the *General Prologue*, E. Talbot Donaldson's "Chaucer the Pilgrim" and Jill Mann's *Chaucer and Medieval Estates Satire,* between them outline the general structure of Chaucerian practice in the *Canterbury Tales,* the telling of tales as the interaction between a subject and an institution. Donaldson, of course, concentrated on the subject side of the interaction in his influential characterization of the naive narrator of the *General Prologue* and the links, who so often misses the point of the complex phenomena he describes in order that Chaucer the satirist or the poet or the man can make sure that *we* see how complex they are. Donaldson was the first to call attention to the issue of voicing in the

From *The Disenchanted Self: Representing the Subject in the Canterbury Tales.* © 1990 the Regents of the University of California. Reprinted by permission of the Regents of the University of California and the University of California Press.

prologue and the first to apply to the poem the dramatic method that had previously been used only on the tales.

By contrast, Mann firmly established for the first time the genre of the *General Prologue* by demonstrating that the poem is an estates satire, one of a class of medieval treatments of the orders, or estates, of society. These works generally list the various members of society according to the traditional scheme of the estates and comment on their abuses—themselves stereotyped. Though she notes that Chaucer shows a freedom typical of him in the selection of the particular estates he presents, Mann proves that he "does cover the elements of social anatomisation made familiar by estates literature" as a means "to suggest society as a whole by way of [a] representative company of individuals" (*Medieval Estates Satire,* 4, 5). The traditional classification provides Chaucer with a conceptual framework shared with his audience (what I have been calling an institution) for organizing his observations of individuals in society, an underlying structure of common assumptions about what society is and the way it is put together. I shall briefly consider each of these approaches in turn before trying to combine their best features for a fuller reading of the poem.

CHAUCER THE PILGRIM

Donaldson's formulations of Chaucer the pilgrim are made with an awareness of the complexity of the actual performance situation, which he images as social: the author (Chaucer the man), reading aloud to a court audience, projects a fictional caricature of himself (Chaucer the pilgrim), which both masks and emphasizes the complex ironic sensibility Donaldson calls Chaucer the poet. When he asserts "the probability—or rather the certainty—that [the three Chaucers] bore a close resemblance to one another, and that indeed, they frequently got together in the same body" ("Chaucer the Pilgrim," I), Donaldson is close to an image of the poet as subject, a site from which multiple selves, roles, and so on emerge simultaneously and undecidably. Such oxymoronical characterizations of the poet's "elusion of clarity"[1] as "that double vision that is his ironical essence" ("Chaucer the Pilgrim," II) reflect similar intimations of the absence, in the last analysis, of a determinate Chaucer.

Nonetheless, Donaldson in concerned in "Chaucer the Pilgrim" and elsewhere to construct a self for the fictional pilgrim, a distinct, finished personality whose attitudes toward all the other pilgrims he describes in the *General Prologue* can be made fully consistent with a set of root tendencies or traits in him: snobbishness, overreadiness to please, Babbittry, and the like. In "Chaucer the Pilgrim," at least, these traits again appear to be grounded in social typification. Donaldson is aware of the estates tradition as a general background of the poem, which he refers to in passing as "the ancient stock satirical characters" that "it was left to Chaucer to turn . . . into real people assembled for a pilgrimage" (9). For him, however, these classifications are of interest not as what lies behind the depiction of the *pilgrims* (as they are for Mann) but as a source of the attitudes of the *speaker,* whose membership in the third estate is loosely held to account for his personality, "a bourgeois exposed to the splendors of high society, whose values, such as they are, he eagerly accepts" (4). Though there is much to be said for this turn toward the historical and institutional situation of the poet (which he normally brackets out of his readings, often for good reasons),[2] Donaldson himself does not follow it out far, nor does he fully textualize the poet's self-representation. The idea of Chaucer the pilgrim requires that in any given passage we first decide what Chaucer the pilgrim means by what he says and then what Chaucer the poet means by what the pilgrim means, and this division of the speaker leaves a certain residual uncertainty about the distinction between the voice of the text and a presence behind and beyond it who somehow guarantees the meaning we find there. Some of Donaldson's characterizations of Chaucer the poet take on a distinctly metaphysical cast:

> Undoubtedly Chaucer the man would, like his fictional representative, have found [the Prioress] charming and looked on her with affection. To have got on so well in so changeable a world Chaucer must have got on well with the people in it, and it is doubtful that one may get on with people merely by pretending to like them: one's heart has to be in it. But the third entity, Chaucer the poet, operates in a realm which is above and subsumes those in which Chaucer the man and Chaucer the pilgrim have their being. In this realm prioresses may be simultaneously evaluated as marvellously amiable ladies and as prioresses. (II)

A moment's reflection establishes that this third realm can only be the text; that is where Donaldson reads the simultaneous double evaluation. The text is here being hypostatized, in the New Critical fashion that locates Donaldson's own historical situation, as an "entity" that hovers in a paradoxical nonplace that is both in the text and outside it, somewhere between the two institutional sites called the work and the author.[3]

But even at the level Donaldson is working at, the representation of the self, I do not see the need to reify these tensions in the text into separate personalities of the same speaker, and I think this way of talking about the narrator of the *General Prologue* has proved misleading because it has promoted not just the detextualization but the oversimplification of the speaker as well. It has encouraged us not only to treat him as if we knew who he was apart from his utterances and could predict his responses but to treat him as more of a simpleton than the evidence warrants. The general personality traits of Chaucer the pilgrim have themselves become reified in the Chaucer criticism of the last thirty years, and this frozen concept of the character has fostered a carelessness in reading that Donaldson himself rarely committed. I suspect that the success of this reified partial object, despite a few attempts to put him back together,[4] has been due in large part to a natural desire on the part of critics to evade the feelings of contingency and responsibility that haunt the act of interpretation and the indeterminacy of the text.[5] The notion of Chaucer the pilgrim at least offers an *homme moyen sensuel* with whom we can feel we know where we are and whose apparent mistakes can serve as the stalking horses of our more accurate—though no less assured—moral judgments, which we authorize through the equally assured poet who must have "meant" us to see them. Chaucer the pilgrim thus becomes another version of the more general phenomenon of the self-betraying speaker already encountered in the criticism of the Wife's and Pardoner's tales. But I think that it is just this sense of knowing where we are and with whom we are dealing that the *General Prologue,* like those tales, deliberately and calculatedly denies us.

Consider, for instance, the following passage from the Monk's portrait, a notorious locus—and one fastened on by Donaldson—for the naiveté of the narrator:

> He yaf nat of that text a pulled hen,
> That seith that hunters ben nat hooly men,
> Ne that a monk, whan he is recchelees,
> Is likned til a fissh that is waterlees—
> This is to seyn, a monk out of his cloystre.
> But thilke text heeld he nat worth an oystre;
> And I seyde his opinion was good.
> What sholde he studie and make hymselven wood,
> Upon a book in cloystre alwey to poure,
> Or swynken with his handes, and laboure,
> As Austyn bit? How shal the world be served?
> Lat Austyn have his swynk to hym reserved!
> Therfore he was a prikasour aright.
>
> (I, 177–89)

If we think of these lines as the performance of a speaker who is blind to their "real" significance, as apparent praise of the Monk that actually dispraises him, we immediately run into the following difficulties. First, the Monk's own bluff manner is present in these lines. I agree with most commentators that he is being half-quoted and that we hear his style, for example, in a phrase like "nat worth an oystre."[6] This semicitation already introduces a measure of uncertainty as to who is speaking, or at least a question about the extent to which the narrator really does agree with what he cites. Second, the standards of the Monk's calling, against which, if we will, he may be measured, are also present. The social and moral worlds indeed display their tension here, but *who brought these issues up?* Who is responsible for the slightly suspended enjambment that turns the deadly precision of "As Austyn bit?" into a small firecracker? For the wicked specificity with which, at the beginning of the portrait, the Monk's bridle is said to jingle "as dooth the *chapel belle*" (171, emphasis added)? Who goes to such pains to explain the precise application of the proverb about the fish, "This is to seyn, . . ."? Who if not the speaker? The Monk? Given the quasi-citational character of the passage, it is possible to see not only the narrator but also the Monk himself as a man who is aware of the discrepancy between the impression he makes and the ideals of his estate and whose no-nonsense utterances are attempts to face it directly, if not quite squarely. Who is talking here? Third, even if we confine this sort of awareness to the narrator, these observations do not permit us to say that he is only making a moral judgment or only poking fun at the Monk. Donaldson and Mann are surely right to point to the way the portrait registers the positive claims made by the pilgrim's vitality and "manliness."[7] The speaker's amused enjoyment of the Monk's forthrightness is too patent to let us see him as just a moralist. Fourth, the way the speaker's voice evokes complex possibilities of attitude is neatly caught by "And I seyde his opinion was good." The past tense reminds us that the *General Prologue* is a retrospective account of a meeting that took place at some unspecified time in the past, "in that seson on a day" (19). The virtual now of the prologue is situated not only after the first night at the Tabard but after the whole of the rest of the pilgrimage as well, including the telling of all the tales. It thus opens up a gap between the past of meeting and the now of telling that has room for any amount of reconsideration and revision of first impressions. "And I seyde his opinion was good": that is what he said when he and the Monk had their conversation, but is he saying the same thing now in this portrait? Did he really mean it at the time? Does he now? In what sense?

The point of this exercise is not merely to show that the speaker's attitude is complex and sophisticated but also to stress how obliquely expressed it is, all in ironic juxtapositions whose precise heft is hard to weigh, in part because we have no clear markers for tone as we might if we heard the prologue spoken. What we have, in fact, is a speaker who is not giving too much of himself away and who is not telling us, any more than he told the Monk, his whole mind in plain terms. The tensions among social, moral, and existential worlds are embodied in a single voice here, and they are embodied *as tensions,* not as a resolution or a synthesis. We cannot tell exactly what the speaker thinks of the Monk *or* of conventional morality, and it is not fully clear that he can tell either. One of the things that turning the speaker into Chaucer the pilgrim may deny him is his own ambivalence about the complexity of his own responses to the pilgrims. I will have more to say about this point later, but we can tell here that we are dealing with a speaker who withholds himself from us, with the textual traces of a presence that asserts its simultaneous absence. The speaker, even as a performer, a self, is present as uncomprehended and not to be seized all at once in his totality. He *displays his difference* (or, textually, his *différance*) from his externalizations, his speaking, in the act of externalizing himself.

Thus even at the level of self-presentation, before the issue of subjectivity is broached, the reification involved in making the speaker of the *General Prologue* into Chaucer the pilgrim seems unsatisfactory. At this level textuality manifests itself as the sort of humanist richness Donaldson locates only in Chaucer the poet as a quasi-*hors-texte* but which is in fact operating as the unspoken of the narrator's textual utterances to generate a kind of *effet du réel*. In literature (as in life, come to think of it), the "reality effect" of characters is a function of their mystery, the extent to which we are made to feel that there is more going on in regard to them than we know or can predict. Criseyde is a well-known and well-analyzed example elsewhere in Chaucer's poetry of this effect,[8] and the general narrator of the *Canterbury Tales* is another. His lack of definition may in fact explain why he can be taken for Chaucer the pilgrim. Because his "identity" is a function of what he leaves unspoken—that is, because it is derived from implication, irony, innuendo, and the potentialities of meaning and intention that occur in the gaps between observations drawn from radically different realms of discourse[9]—there is room for the temptation to reduce his uncomfortable indeterminacy by forcing the gaps shut and spelling out the connections. But suppressing the indeterminacy in this way involves reducing complex meanings to simpler ones that may not be "meant" (may not function in the discourse of the text) in the first place. One infers Chaucer the pilgrim by displacing the things the speaker does not say (since, after all, he does not *say* them but only suggests them) and by insisting that he "means" his statements in only the plainest, most literal sense. Such an interpretation does not fail to recognize that the displaced complexities are there; it simply relocates them in "the poem" or "Chaucer the poet," thus *choosing* to constitute from the manifold of the text a social (or moral, or intellectual) dope, a speaker who is unaware of the import of his own language, which is being fed to and through him by a "higher" entity.

"Chaucer the pilgrim" thus does function as a hedge against textuality and the play of semiosis: the construct both contains them and sets them free under controlled conditions. The pilgrim himself is the representative of determinate, communicative meaning, which is both preserved and criticized in him. At the same time textual, disseminated, ironic signification is displaced to the poet, who functions as a place where such literary effects can be acknowledged yet still treated as meant or authorized. But my first objection to this procedure is that once again it denies the speaker—who in this case seems clearly to be the maker as well—his agency in the production of the performance. It is not that there is no such thing as Chaucer the pilgrim, first of all in the sense that the text does represent a human agent who undertakes the project of describing a set of events that he represents as having actually happened to him. These events are in some important sense fictional, and that makes their protagonist some kind of a fiction as well. Nor would I want to deny that there is an issue in the poem about whether or not the speaker is always in complete command of the project. The trouble is that the notion of Chaucer the pilgrim as it has been used displaces what is complex or problematic about this activity to the author or the work, even before we bring our Foucaultian guns to bear on those notions. It has thus made it too easy to miss the ways in which the poem is itself a representation of the speaker's active encounter with the difficulties of judging and classifying others and the extent to which the question of his control of the description (including the play of semiosis) is an issue first and foremost for him. My problem with Chaucer the pilgrim, even before the question of the subject enters into the matter, is that he has not yet been sufficiently recognized as a self.

ESTATES SATIRE

One of the most valuable features of *Chaucer and Medieval Estates Satire* is the attention Mann pays to Chaucer's unique treatment of the estates form itself. The *General Prologue* is not, she argues, merely an example of estates satire but also an alteration and revision of estates techniques that produces a different, we might say a more "modern," image of society. As she shows, Chaucer consistently displaces or complicates the relatively straightforward moral judgments of traditional estates literature in favor of the more ambiguous details of the immediate social impression his pilgrims make. Whereas we are never in doubt about what we are to think of the monks, friars, or townsmen in other estates satires, we are almost always unsure of exactly how good or bad their counterparts in the *General Prologue* are. This uncertainty produces what Mann describes as the effect of an estates satire from which the purpose of moral classification has been removed and at least suggests a view of society as constituted more by the behavior and performances of individuals and groups than by an a priori scheme. Chaucer "ironically substitut[es] for the traditional moral view of social structure a vision of a world where morality becomes as specialized to the individual as his work-life" (*Medieval Estates Satire,* xi).[10]

Though I agree, Mann's way of formulating and presenting her case seems to me to go at once too far and not far enough: too far in that she applies her unquestionably valid insights too broadly and generally to all the portraits and the prologue as a whole; and not far enough in that in practice she, like Donaldson, neglects the ways the poem actively challenges not only the traditional assumptions of moral classification in general but also those of estates satire in particular. Both of these difficulties stem from a neglect of the poem's voicing and especially the temporal inflections of voice that are registered in, and as, its *sequence*. Thus in the first instance Mann's discussions of individual portraits take them out of sequence and relocate them in new groupings according to the various methods of characterization she analyzes in separate chapters: in chapter 4, the omission of the victim (the Man of Law, the Doctor, the Merchant, the Five Guildsmen); in chapter 7, portraits organized around scientific classifications (the Pardoner, the Franklin, the Miller, the Reeve); and so on. As a result, in her treatment all the portraits make essentially the same point about the displacement from moral classification to social impression without registering differences of emphasis and degree. Mann frequently makes observations that cry out for further explanation. She notes, for instance, that one of Chaucer's techniques of complication involves the application of attractive images to characters who are also critically presented—the Friar's eyes twinkling like stars, for example. She goes on to note that sometimes "the imagery works *with* the moral comments. . . . The animal imagery in the portraits of the Miller, Pardoner, and Summoner persuades us that we are dealing with crude or unpleasant personalities" (*Medieval Estates Satire,* 193–94). What she does not notice is that all three of these pilgrims are closely bunched together in the cluster of five rogues that ends the portrait gallery in the prologue. That is, there is a conjunction of moral and social unpleasantness at this point in the poem, a locally consistent use of imagery to create negative moral comment at a structurally significant juncture in a way that works against the more global tendency in the poem to render such judgments problematic.

Similarly, Mann notes the undoing of determinate signification, "Chaucer's constant exploitation of the different semantic values of words," in the poem:

> The adjective "worthy" is used as the keyword of the Knight's portrait, where it has a profound and serious significance, indicating not only the Knight's social status, but also the ethical qualities appropriate to it. In the Friar's portrait, the word is ironically used to indicate the Friar's lack of these ethical qualities—but it can also be read non-ironically as a reference to social status.[11] . . . The reference to social status seems to be the only one in the portrait of the Merchant, who "was a worthy man with alle" (283). By the time we reach the Franklin's portrait, the word is used with a vague heartiness which seems to indicate little beside the narrator's approval: "Was nowher swich a worthy vavasour" (360). (*Medieval Estates Satire,* 195–96)

As this passage shows, Mann is not unaware of the sequential character of the process, and she sees that it has something to do with the narrator, whom she earlier calls "a representative for the rest of society in its relation to each estate" (*Medieval Estates Satire,* 194). The fact of sequence has no real significance for her argument, however, as it might if it were correlated with the parallel sequence through the estates—from Knight to Friar to Merchant and Franklin—that the poem also displays. That is, "worthy" becomes *progressively* less informative and more indeterminate as the narrator moves *through* the traditional estates classifications; the undoing of determinate meaning is connected to the categories of social classification and their progression in the text.

One thing that keeps these features of the text from pulling their weight in Mann's reading is her generally distant and unfocused treatment of the speaker: her inattention to sequence is an effect of her relative disinterest in the poem as a performance. Though she is aware of the Donaldsonian tradition and pays it lip service at points, she is more interested in the poem as a record of the poet's original use of estates conventions. As she sees it, this transaction takes place as it were behind the scenes of the poem. She is willing to accord the poet as maker a considerable range of independent authorial activity, including the deliberate deployment of intertextualities with both the *Decameron* and Langland,[12] but she sees the poem itself as the trace or product, rather than the depiction, of authorship. *Auctoritas* itself is not a problematic notion for her except at the level of large-scale historical process, the gradual drift of medieval society toward modernity that she seems to feel the poem registers. For Mann, the poet *uses* the institution of estates classification richly and often critically, and she has brought that institution into the center of the poem in a way Donaldson does not. What is missing from her reading that Donaldson supplies is an attention to how the text *represents* the act of description and classification itself in the person of its narrator.

In what follows I will combine the Donaldsonian emphasis on voice-oriented reading with Mann's institutional perspective to explore how the text itself represents and revises—at once uses and questions—both. I will begin by sketching a prospective reading of the *General Prologue* that follows the sequence of the performance the poem depicts—the unfolding deployment of available conventions of social and moral classification by a speaker who attempts to use them to organize the practical task of making sense of his experience. Such a prospective reading is appropriate as a way of acknowledging the *specificity* of the prologue, its representation of a particular intentional agent, or self, under concrete institutional and social conditions of performance. I will end by considering the prologue as a disenchanted text that retrospectively identifies its own agency and its own textuality as central facts about itself, thereby undoing its own prospective ambitions to objectivity, completeness, and closure and opening itself to indefinite rereadings. This redefinition of the text necessarily entails a reevaluation of the "self" it has generated as only an effect of its prospective (or prologal) character, and this revision provides a model, I will suggest, for the representation of subjectivity in the *Canterbury Tales.*

THE PROLOGUE AS PERFORMANCE:
NOTES TOWARD A PROSPECTIVE READING

But nathelees, whil I have tyme and space,
Er that I ferther in this tale pace,
Me thynketh it acordaunt to resoun
To telle yow al the condicioun
Of ech of hem, so as it semed me.

(35–39)

The *General Prologue* presents itself prospectively as the record of an experience, but not the experience of meeting the pilgrims on the way to Canterbury. Rather, as Donald Howard has shown, the poem purports to represent
the experience of the speaker in putting together the memory of that meeting, which took place at some time in the past, so as to give it to us reordered
"acordaunt to resoun."[13] This is the task he undertakes *now,* in the present of
narrating, "whil I have tyme and space / Er that I ferther in this tale pace,"
after the pilgrimage itself has been completed. The experience is of course a
fiction, the textual representation of a virtual "I" addressing a virtual audience "To telle yow al the condicioun / Of ech of hem." As I have suggested,
the fiction is one of *performance,* the logocentric illusion, as we say nowadays,
of a performer who unfolds his meaning to us as he speaks, but it is no less
consistently presented for all of that. The poem keeps us aware of this fictional or virtual now of audience address from its beginning to its end, when
"now is tyme to yow for to telle / . . . al the remenaunt of oure pilgrimage"
(720, 724). The rational ordering of the pilgrims is thus a *project* the narrator
proposes at the outset of the prologue, one we watch him enact as the poem
unfolds.

If the ordering of the pilgrims is a project of the narrator's, it does not initially seem difficult or challenging to him or to us. Like the famous opening
sentence, with its effortless progression from the impersonal cosmic eros of seasonal change through vegetable growth and animal (or at least avian) sexuality
to the *amor spiritualis* that drove Saint Thomas, the presentation of the pilgrims in the first half of the *General Prologue* is a richly embroidered and elegantly varied expression of "what everybody knows" about the shape of society.[14] The progression of portraits from the Knight through the Wife of Bath
is consistently, though complexly, structured on the time-honored model of
the three estates. The tally of the pilgrims begins with a preeminent representative of the estate of *milites* and pauses for a moment to list the Knight's hierarchically ordered entourage—his son the Squire and his servant the Yeoman—before passing on to the second group, the three members of the
regular clergy. As Mann notes (*Medieval Estates Satire,* 6), it would be more correct in conventional estates terms to place the clerical figures first, and this fact
suggests that the estates organization is modified by hierarchical considerations of another sort: the Knight is in some sense the highest-ranking pilgrim.

This displacement does not, however, affect the overall organization in estates terms. With the clerical figures too there is room for flexibility and play—the Prioress's entourage is also listed briefly at the end of her portrait. But here, as with the treatment of the Five Guildsmen as a single unit, the choice to stress the portrait as more basic than the individual person by brushing past the Second Nun and the Nun's Priest(s) points to the importance of estates classification over individuality as such. In any case, the basic structural outline is clear: three religious presented in order of official rank, a prioress, a monk as monastery official ("kepere of the celle"), and an ordinary friar. This grouping is followed by the inevitably more miscellaneous list of the pilgrims of the third estate, which by the late Middle Ages had become a kind of catchall for those who were not knights or clergy and which is itself variously carved up by other estates satires.[15] The first part of the poem, viewed from a certain distance, displays a complex articulation of interrelated hierarchical schemata within a basic triadic structure continued through the Wife of Bath's portrait, at least in the sense that the portrait groupings continue to be divisible by three. The triad of the Franklin, the Five Guildsmen, and the Cook, for instance, outlines a modern, citified, bureaucratic, and competitive parallel—a knight of the shire, burgesses who aspire to rank,[16] and a proletarian craftsman in the temporary hire of his betters—to the more traditional and naturalized sociomoral hierarchy of the first triad, the Knight, the Squire, and the Yeoman, who are bound together by ties of blood and homage.

If there are problems with the order I have sketched so far—and there are—they are not allowed to emerge in the unfolding of the poem for some time. Like the opening sentence, the order of the pilgrims in the first half of the prologue, which is rooted in conventional and collective norms, reflects "what everybody knows" about the exfoliation of natural and spiritual energies in springtime and the relation of these energies to the shape of society and its estates. This is perhaps one reason why the portraits in this part of the poem exhibit the relatively relaxed tone and the lack of overt moralization that Mann notes. These descriptions draw easily on the shared framework of assumptions in whose name our representative, the narrator, speaks. That the kind of loving the Squire currently practices is more closely allied to the energies of the animal soul than to the rational love of *ecclesia* and *respublica* his father embodies need not be spelled out. It is carried in the implications of the image that links him to the sleeplessly amorous birds of the first eighteen lines—"He sleep namoore than dooth a nyghtyngale" (98)[17]—birds that are themselves balanced between the immanent "gravitational" love that moves the sun and the other stars through the round of the seasons and the focused and rational divine love that calls to and through the saint. Similarly, our common expectation that any literary friar will be a bad one makes it unnecessary for the narrator to condemn the pilgrim Friar explicitly. One reason the Friar's portrait is the longest in the prologue is the extreme popularity and ubiquity of antifraternal satire in the fourteenth century: there is a rich fund of conventional material to draw on, and the poet-narrator can count on this tacitly shared background to enforce his ironies.[18]

As Mann's discussion of "worthy" may suggest, however, the precise placing of these pilgrims does create some difficulties, and, as I want to insist, these difficulties are experienced by the speaker, and experienced progressively. An overview of the pilgrims of the third estate reveals an increasing strain between what the poet's common culture tells him he ought to be able to say about people ("what everybody knows") and what his actual experience of trying to describe them provides. It is preeminently in this section of the poem that technical and scientific jargon and the language of craft, for example, become conspicuous, with the effects Mann notes: the felt absence of more widely applicable and less specialized role definitions, and a sense of the disjunction between the moral and professional spheres that emphasizes the fundamentally amoral character of professional expertise; think of the Shipman's navigational skill, which appears to make him a more efficient pirate, or the learning of the Doctor, whose tag, "He was a verray, parfit praktisour" (422), calls attention to the difference between his *skills* and the Knight's *virtues* (72). Details of dress and appearance become less informative. The end of the Man of Law's portrait, with its abrupt dismissal "Of his array telle I no lenger tale" (330), stresses how little we can learn about him from his off-duty dress, especially compared to the amount of symbolic information about character carried by the estates uniform of the Knight with his armor-stained "gypon"; likewise the portrait of the Friar with his double-worsted semicope. The same indefiniteness characterizes such things as the Cook's "mormal," the name of the Shipman's barge, the *Maudelayne* (what would that mean if it meant?), and most of the details of the Wife of Bath's portrait: her deafness, her complicated love life, and her big hat. The Wife's portrait is the culmination in the poem of the progressive tendency of particular qualities of individuals to shift their area of reference from the exemplary to the idiosyncratic. The often-noted excellence of each pilgrim becomes rooted more and more in the existential being and activity of the individual and less and less in his or her representative character as the symbol of a larger group. The individual's place in a hierarchy becomes less important than his or her performances; consider again the difference between a "verray, parfit gentil knyght" and a "verray, parfit praktisour." These are persons whose stories we would have to tell to understand them—or who would have to tell their stories.

This need for more information is overtly recognized in the Wife of Bath's portrait, the only place in the portraits that refers beyond them to the tale-telling to come:

> Housbondes at chirche dore she hadde fyve,
> Withouten oother compaignye in youthe—
> But thereof nedeth nat to speke as nowthe.
>
> (460–62)

"What everybody knows" is not enough to account for the Wife either morally or socially, and the promise of more to come points to the narrator's awareness that she will have to do it herself later. As I have suggested, following Hoffman, the hierarchy of the opening lines of the prologue, in terms of which the pilgrims are organized and against which, broadly speaking, they are measured, is fundamentally a hierarchy of loves. It ought therefore to be possible "acordaunt to resoun" to place the Wife's loves in relation to that order. But that is just what the speaker does not do. The details of the Wife's portrait are as vibrant as the woman we sense behind them, but their vividness only stresses their lack of coherence in traditional terms. Prospectively neither we nor the speaker can arrange them in a hierarchy of significance with respect to the hierarchies of nature, society, and the divine order. It is clear that the question interests the speaker since he allows it to take over the latter part of the portrait. The list of the Wife's pilgrimages (463–66), a record of travel that competes with the Knight's, is made an excuse to remind us, with an elbow in the ribs, that "She koude muchel of wandrynge by the weye" (467)—unlike, no doubt, that proper father and head of an extended family unit. Her gap teeth and "hipes large" keep the issue before us, and the portrait ends "Of remedies of love she knew per chaunce, / For she koude of that art the olde daunce" (475–76). This continued fascination does not, however, allow the speaker to rest secure in a neutral, "objective" presentation of the Wife's love life and its place in the scheme of things, as his mildly chauvinist tone reveals. The Wife certainly raises the questions that gender and sexuality put to the standard, patriarchal hierarchies, questions of the relations between sensual love, "felaweshipe," marriage, *amor dei,* and *remedia amoris,* but these relations, as she will remind us in her prologue and tale, are matters of controversy, and the description of her here does not begin to resolve them.

It seems to me to be no accident that the portrait of the highly idealized and morally transparent Parson occurs at just this point, forming the strongest possible contrast to the ambiguities of the Wife of Bath. Even more significant, however, is the fact that now the organizing principle of the poem changes. After the closely linked Parson-Plowman grouping, the final five pilgrims are bunched together and announced in advance as completing the tally: "Ther was also a REVE, and a MILLERE, / A SOMNOUR, and a PARDONER also, / A MAUNCIPLE, and myself—ther were namo" (542–44). As opposed to the complex complementarity and hierarchy of the ordering of the portraits in the first half, we are here presented with rather simple oppositions: two against five, bad against good. If the initial organization of the poem is indeed that of the three estates, we obviously do well to ask why the Parson's portrait is not included with the second, clerical, triad and why it interrupts the account of the third estate (to which all the remaining pilgrims in the list belong) instead. In the sort of sequential or prospective reading I am urging here, the question does not arise until we reach the Parson's portrait, but it certainly does arise then. The effect is to make the initial three-estates ordering, *in retrospect,* look much more selective and ad hoc than it did at first, much more the product of tacit choices and decisions on the part of the narrator who now alters and abandons it.

The two most striking features of the final sequence of seven portraits from the Parson through the Pardoner are, first, a drive to ultimate moral clarification that I will call *apocalyptic,* in the etymological sense of the word as an unveiling, a stripping away of surface complexity to reveal the fundamental truth beneath it,[19] and second, the conspicuous emergence of the narrator as the source of this drive. The effect of the insertion of the Parson-Plowman dyad is to provide a golden "ensample" against which not only the remaining pilgrims but also the previous ones—the Parson's portrait contains a number of "snybbing" critical references to previous portraits such as those of the Monk and Friar—are measured and found wanting.[20] Besides the animal imagery cited by Mann (*Medieval Estates Satire,* 194–95), which is itself susceptible of typological and physiognomical interpretation *in malo,* as Curry, Robertson, and others have shown, there are other patterns that cut across the last portraits and produce the effect of a uniformly wicked and worsening world. The Miller, whose badness is qualified by the energy of his animal spirits, carries a sword and buckler. The more sinister-sounding Reeve, who does not just defraud a few village yokels but undermines a whole manor from lord to laborers, carries a "*rusty* blade" (618, emphasis added), and the Summoner's failure to sustain and defend ecclesiastical order is pinned down by the allegory of his armory: "A bokeleer hadde he maad hym of a cake" (668). Read across the portraits and, once more, against the image of hierarchy and vigilant order embodied in the first triad, where the Yeoman keeps the Knight's weapons "harneised wel" (114) for use at need, the symbolic progression of weapons here implies that as evil becomes more spiritual and intense, its outward signs become clearer and more concrete emblems of the inner state, and that such progressive evils are increasingly revealed as demonic parodies of the good. The Summoner and the Pardoner in particular have the *privatio boni* theory of evil written all over them.

At the same time the narrator moves forward out of the relatively anonymous "felaweshipe" of "what everybody knows" into a position of isolated prominence as he takes a God's-eye view more akin perhaps to the Parson's. He says "I" more often; he addresses us more overtly, breaking off description to do so; he warns and exhorts and judges: "Wel I woot he lyed right in dede" (659). The effect is well represented by the Manciple's portrait, which is, notoriously, not about the Manciple but about the lawyers he works for. As the speaker moves toward the end of the portrait, he idealizes them more and more, stressing the power for social good bound up in them who are "able for to helpen al a shire" (584) and then managing to suggest that it is somehow the Manciple's fault that they do not help: "And yet this Manciple sette hir aller cappe" (586). Because the speaker so conspicuously wrenches us away from the Manciple, he calls attention to himself and his own social concerns. For this reason, among others, all this apocalyptic processing registers, I think, as a failure of vision on the narrator's part. In sequence and in context it looks like a reaction to the complexities and uncertainties of classification and judgment generated by the enterprise of the first half of the *General Prologue,* a retreat to simpler and more rigorous standards of moral classification that, because its psychological motives emerge so clearly, also looks like name-calling, a product less of objective appraisal of the pilgrims in question than of the speaker's own wishes and fears about the evils of society.

The pattern of this psychology is fairly precisely that of what I have called "masculine" disenchantment since it is focused on the ways human agents like the Manciple and the Summoner manipulate and subvert what should be a transcendent and stable order, and is marked by nostalgia for what it knows has been lost. The Summoner is an actively disenchanted cynic, whose perversion of what ought to be the justice of God is accompanied by an articulate conviction that it is only the justice of men as corrupt as himself: " 'Purs is the ercedekenes helle,' seyde he" (658). If the speaker protests this blatant assertion, he seems nonetheless to agree that it is all too often true, as the Pardoner's portrait affirms even more strongly:

> But with thise relikes, whan that he fond
> A povre person dwellynge upon lond,
> Upon a day he gat hym moore moneye
> Than that the person gat in monthes tweye;
> And thus, with feyned flaterye and japes,
> He made the person and the peple his apes.
> (701–6)

Like the pilgrims in their tales, the narrator of the *General Prologue* does not simply use categories to make neutral descriptions but also has attitudes toward the descriptions he makes and the things he describes. The pervasive symbolic processing of the end of the portrait gallery shows that there is more at stake for him here than the features and foibles of individuals. By the end of the prologue the pilgrims are being made aggressively to stand for estates as images of the state of society. Once again it seems no accident, in retrospect, that the tale of the pilgrims ends with the Pardoner, the darkest example and the most trenchant spokesman of an attitude the speaker here comes close to sharing.

This reading of the narrator's psychology is the more convincing, at least to me, because of the character of the passage that immediately follows the portraits. An address that begins confidently with a straightforward statement of what has been achieved, "Now have I toold you soothly, in a clause" (715), becomes more and more tentative and apologetic as it proceeds and more and more nervous about the *effect* not only of what remains to say but also of what has already been said:

> But first I pray yow, of youre curteisye,
> That ye n'arette it nat my vileynye,
> Thogh that I pleynly speke in this mateere,
> To telle yow hir wordes and hir cheere,
> Ne thogh I speke hir wordes proprely.
> For this ye knowen al so wel as I:
> Whoso shal telle a tale after a man,
> He moot reherce as ny as evere he kan
> Everich a word, if it be in his charge,
> Al speke he never so rudeliche and large,
> Or ellis he moot telle his tale untrewe,
> Or feyne thyng, or fynde wordes newe.
> He may nat spare, althogh he were his brother;
> He moot as wel seye o word as another.
> Crist spak hymself ful brode in hooly writ,
> And wel ye woot no vileynye is it.
> Eek Plato seith, whoso kan hym rede,
> The wordes moote be cosyn to the dede.
>
> (725–42)

The passage is dogged by the speaker's repetitions of the attempt to deny responsibility for the descriptions of the pilgrims he is about to give and haunted by his sense that the denials are not convincing because he is too clearly responsible for the descriptions he has already given. He ends oddly, after a discussion of the tales that are to come, where we might have expected him to begin, with an apology for having failed to order the pilgrims correctly, and this peculiarity suggests what is really on his mind: "Also I prey yow to foryeve it me, / Al have I nat set folk in hir degree / Heere in this tale, as that they sholde stonde" (743–45).[21] In strong contrast to the atmosphere of shared understandings and common agreements he projected at the beginning of the prologue, the speaker here appears nervously isolated, as if surrounded by an audience of Millers, Manciples, Reeves, Summoners, and Pardoners, whose accusation of "vileynye" he might have some cause to anticipate.

What seems to *happen* in the performance represented in the *General Prologue* is that two rather different procedures of classifying the pilgrims, which I have called hierarchical and apocalyptic and which seem to correspond in emphasis to the classificatory and the moralizing impulses respectively in estates satire, are adopted and then discarded by the speaker. In the final movement of the poem he turns to the pilgrims themselves, in part as a way of getting himself off the hook. The movement of the prologue is within two versions of "resoun," understood, as it can be in Middle English, as a translation of Latin *ratio*.[22] The distinction I have in mind is between, on the one hand, underlying cause, the reasons in things that are patterned on the *rationes seminales* in the mind of God, the basic rational structure of reality; and, on the other hand, account, argument, and especially opinion, as with the Merchant: "His resons he spak ful solempnely, / Sownynge alwey th'encrees of his wynnyng" (274–75). The poem goes from an account "acordaunt to resoun," which seems to want to claim the first definition, to the moment when the Knight begins his tale, "As was resoun, / By foreward and by composicioun" (847–48)—that is, according to an explicitly man-made, ad hoc, and open-ended *ratio* or plan, the tale-telling project, which will require the activity not of the narrator but of the pilgrims themselves in telling their tales and of the reader in putting together and evaluating the various performances. This movement is paralleled by a shift in the meaning of the word "tale" from "Er that I ferther in this tale pace" at the beginning of the prologue to the force the word takes on contextually in the apology just quoted. In the first instance the primary meaning would seem to be "tally," "reckoning," in the sense of a completed list or account, which is also one of the primary meanings of *ratio*. By the time the end of the portrait gallery is reached, however, the developed sense of the speaker's contribution to the way the list has unfolded lets the meanings "Canterbury tale"—that is, traveler's tale, whopper—and more generally "fiction," "story," such as the pilgrims will tell, speak out. These transformations of "tale" and "resoun" have in common the disenchanted view in the more technical sense that they enforce of the enterprise of the poem and its speaker.

I began by suggesting that the *General Prologue* actively challenges the traditional assumptions of estates satire. An analysis of the prologue's detailed representation of the practice of classifying establishes that the poem is in fact not an estates satire but a critique of an estates satire in the mode of deconstruction. That is, its narrator's gradual and eventually conspicuous questioning of his own procedures operates as a miming of traditional classifications so as to bring out gradually the tensions and contradictions that underlie and constitute them. As the representation of an unfolding experience, the poem is also a representation of the coming into something like discursive consciousness of the problematic character of what begins as the relatively unreflective practical activity of classifying people, and it presents that coming into consciousness as an awakening to disenchantment. The speaker of the poem eventually encounters his own agency, the inescapable likelihood that he has made use of estates conventions to *create rather than discover* the order of society, so that the *General Prologue* turns out to be, like the tales that follow, much more a representation of the voice generated by a certain kind of activity in the moment-by-moment, line-by-line process of describing than an objective narration. The stalking horse of this enterprise is indeed the performing narrator, a self-conscious version of Chaucer the pilgrim, who appears to find himself enmeshed in the tensions and bedeviled by the impasses that lead to what I take to be a central theme of the prologue, the question of what it means to judge and classify one's fellows. If the speaker feels and fears that he may have falsified the pilgrims in describing them, the corollary is that the poem is indeed a performance in exactly the way that the tales are. It is the self-presentation of a speaker, far more the Poet's portrait than an account of the other characters, who must now be expected to present themselves in their tales. What for the represented speaker is an experience of disenchantment is for the textualizing poet the representation of practical disenchantment.

It is one thing to have such an experience but quite another to write it down, in particular to make *a written representation of a failed performance.* If the aim is to give a satisfactory account of the pilgrims, one might start over on a different plan or, having learned one's lesson, discard the prologue. But to read the poem prospectively as a fictional performance—a reading it initially encourages—is finally to be made aware of the inadequacies of that mode of reading, and this awareness I take to be one of the aims of the representation. From this point of view, what the poem is criticizing, in estates satire and elsewhere, is the notion that once having heard what you say, I know what you mean and who you are. This is the assumption that seems to underlie the speaker's project to classify a group of pilgrims whose own performances he has already heard before we have gotten to them. It is the logocentric supposition that would make of the prologue a version of Derrida's characterization of Hegel's preface to *The Phenomenology of Mind:* something written last and put first, something meant, in an odd way, to do away with the need for the work itself.[23] What replaces this notion, what moves into the gap created by the undoing of definitive classification and interpretation, is the notion of reading and rereading, or to put it another way, the replacement of the poem as performance by the poem as text. The *General Prologue* ends, in a typically deconstructive move, with an act of *différance,* a deferring of the meaning of the pilgrims and the pilgrimage as something different from what the poem as performance achieved. The deferral is what makes the difference, and makes difference possible, because it frees up the prologue to be reread as a piece of writing in all sorts of new conjunctions with the tales. And of course it frees up the speaker too, who is not really, or at least not only, the somewhat more ambitious version of Chaucer the pilgrim that my performance analysis has been making him out to be, a matter to which I will now turn.

VOICE AND TEXT, PILGRIMS AND POET

A definitive version of the retrospective rereading that the prospective "failure" of the *General Prologue* opens up is in principle impossible and in practice impracticable—this book is only one version of a part of it. Nonetheless, a sketch of its implications will bring my own reading here to a close. I begin by observing that a prospective reading of the prologue, and the kind of reading of the poem as a whole that it encourages, is both overly traditional—perhaps even "establishment"—and overdominated by institutional perspectives at the expense of those of individuals. One index is the way the prospective unfolding of the prologue tries to control textuality by enforcing the importance of certain details in the portraits at the expense of others. The placing of the last five portraits over against the Parson-Plowman dyad and the stress given to patterns of imagery that run across portraits, like the weaponry pattern analyzed above, make such things as the Reeve's rusty blade, his top "dokked lyk a preest biforn" (590), or his governance of "His lordes sheep" (597) to his own advantage stand out as emblems of an estate and its responsibilities misused to the detriment of society. In doing so, they make other details, like the Reeve's actual trade of carpenter or his "wonyng . . . ful faire upon an heeth; / With grene trees yshadwed" (606–7), recede in importance or take on an anomalous feel, as in Mann's analysis of the Friar's twinkling eyes. Such details come into their own in a retrospective rereading, where the perspective of the tale can play back on the prologue to open up new lines of interpretation. The Reeve's assessment of the dignity owed his trade, as it combines with the generalized paranoia the portrait sketches and the tale confirms, motivates his attack on the Miller, for example, and the Friar's eyes twinkling "As doon the sterres in the frosty nyght" (268) are given point by the cold, distant, calculated way the Friar in his tale tries to watch and control his own performance before others, a kind of role-playing that brings out the element of technique and false heartiness in "rage he koude [that is, knew how], as it were right a whelp" (257).[24]

In a more general way, the institutional overdetermination of the prologue as performance and the repression of textual indeterminacy that rereading reveals are present in the portraits that go with the tales analyzed in this book. Prospectively the Knight's portrait is tied to an idealized image not only of the man but also of his estate and the place it occupies in a larger image of social hierarchy. The portrait has to do duty for so much in the way of symbolic support of estates hierarchies and the like that it makes less than it might of questions about the historical state of the institution of chivalry. The concreteness of the details of the description—all those named battles, for instance—has led disenchanted readers like Terry Jones to give them a weight of historical reference that many other critics have felt the portrait itself does not use or pushes to one side. Though I have yet to see a convincing argument that the portrait is ironic about the Knight, the more we know about the places he has been, the less confidence the institution of knighthood he seems so ideally to uphold inspires. This impression is in line with my reading of the prologue as a text that gradually reveals its own disenchantment. By its end the poem has become—or shown itself as—an analysis of the social and ideological commitments that are entailed in estates satire itself, in particular analysis of the form's "establishment" commitments to tradition, authority, and hierarchy such as might lead us—or the narrator— to try to make a "good" knight into an image of the health of knighthood. The tensions that make such commitments problematic are only present in the portrait as suppressed or latent textual possibilities that are not directly used in the prologue. Where they turn up, of course, is in the tale, as *problems about his estate that the Knight himself must engage,* and I have argued at length for the disenchanted realism of his portrayal of the temple of Mars as it bears on Theseus's chivalry, a portrayal that matches anything Froissart—or Jones—has to say about Peter of Cyprus at Atalia ("Satalye") or the siege of Alexandria. Thus it is probably accurate to think of the fundamental institutional grounding of character in the *Canterbury Tales* as the estate, and that this grounding holds for the pilgrims themselves as well as for the poet and the reader. Estates classification looks like a set of fundamentals about character in the sense of a foundation or a place to start, which is to say that such classifications represent not the *essences* of the pilgrims but *pre-texts,* ways of naming that they have to draw on, what they are confronted with about themselves socially, and what they have to enact, sustain, alter, and above all *negotiate* in their lives and their tales.

A rereading of this sort thus returns to both the prologue and the tales the historical and social, as well as personal, specificity of that negotiation, which the relatively abstract and idealizing thrust of the prospective reading initially denies them. To come back to the Knight's portrait after reading the tale is to see more readily how its details might support a reading of the Knight that is less idealized in the sense of less faded, unreal, and outmoded or late medieval than the criticism, or indeed the prospective thrust of the prologue itself, often allows.[25] For instance, the prospective encouragement the portrait unquestionably gives to a reading of "Ful worthy was he in his lordes werre" (47) as a shorthand representation of the Knight's crusading defense of God's Christendom in his numerous campaigns (as if he were himself a Peter of Cyprus) recedes in the light of the tale because of the tale's consistent and principled refusal of a providential interpretation of history. Despite the perennial temptation, reenunciated by A. J. Minnis, in *Chaucer and Pagan Antiquity,* to read the Knight's (and Chaucer's) awareness of historical difference as finally loaded in favor of modern Christianity over pagan antiquity, it will be clear by now that I see the tale and the Knight as deeply protohumanist in the credit they extend to the ancient world, a credit that is no doubt critical but far more in the emulative mode of the Renaissance than in some "medieval" theological one. Our own historical hindsight can locate the tale's undoing of such pieties precisely in historically conditioned disenchantment: the Knight's approval of olden times can be read as an index of his disenchanted failure to be convinced by a style of providential reading of historical process in relation to the kind of history making he knows best that had become increasingly ideologized and conspicuously political since at least the time of the investiture controversy. It is a style whose continuing use by the propagandists of two rival popes and a Holy Roman Emperor in the Knight's own time cannot have made it *more* convincing. The Knight thus joins Boccaccio and Chaucer as a progenitor of a project to restore and renew the epic that has, like a certain version of knighthood, a future; and if the English were not as quick as the Italians to make effective political and ideological use of this humanism, the fact that Chaucer thought a knight an appropriate voice for it suggests that he understood the social valence of the kind of change it represented.

From this retrospective angle the Pardoner too escapes the twin misrepresentations as contemptible body and apocalyptic symbol of social decay that the prologue's prospect foists on him. Out of place like the Parson in the estates structure of the prologue, the Pardoner is an "ecclesiaste" whose relation to both orders and degree is genuinely problematic and felt as such in the poet's voicing. But to read this problematic quality back to the prologue portrait from the Pardoner's assault in his tale on the church he represents is to see how these moments of strain in the classification project of the poem register more than the confusions of an inept performing speaker, as if such difficulties only beset comic unreliable narrators. What are from one point of view psychological tensions are from another registrations of a culture that is genuinely in tension with itself about its own structure and the adequacy of its own principles of classification—orders and estates—to its developing historical actuality. The Pardoner is an extension and complication of a relatively familiar type in the period, a radical-conservative social critic of the abuses of the church, the commodification of the sacramental system, and the secularization of the clergy, all of which are part of his own subjectivity since he is a site of them all. As such, he joins a chorus of disenchanted voices, from spiritual Franciscans to Lollards to satirical poets, chroniclers, and the Sultan of Turkey,[26] who condemn the debasement of what ought to be a divine institution by human manipulation and urge a revolutionary return to primitive gospel standards. From a longer perspective he participates as well in the Reformation project, carried on by Luther, Calvin, and Kierkegaard, of reconceiving Christian subjectivity on neo-Donatist, individualistic, and psychological grounds whose radical conservatism might be summed up in the phrase *neo-Augustinian*—which is no doubt why modern exegetical neo-Augustinianism is so helpful in reading him.

In the case of the Wife of Bath there is a similar moment of social tension evident in the transition from her portrait to that of the Parson, reflected in the "feminine" questioning of various economic, social, and gender boundaries and categories that she and her description embody and in the "masculine" retrenchment of authority, orthodoxy, and male dominance that comes with the Parson. If the wider sociocultural sources and repercussions of this central moment are harder to evoke in the mode of glancing allusion I have adopted with the Knight and the Pardoner, I suspect that is due less to the

absolute modernity of feminist gender theory than to the fact that the historical work needed to ground an understanding of the social and economic
meaning of gender difference in the period, which needs to be directed by
that theory as well as inform it, is only beginning to get done—and that I
have only begun to read it. Certainly it is clear enough that the Wife's own
prologue and tale are, among other things, an engagement with precisely the
kind of authority the Parson is made to carry in the *General Prologue,* and it
seems likely that read retrospectively, her portrait announces, and her prologue and tale carry out, her participation in a late medieval gynesis, or contribution to the discourse on woman, that such figures as Margery Kempe,
Juliana of Norwich, and Christine de Pisan also have something to do with
and that we are just beginning to learn to read.[27] For my purposes here, however, I want to use the issues the Wife raises about gender to return to the
question of the subject, impersonation, and "Chaucer."

The three pilgrims whose tales occupy most of this book are situated at
the beginning, middle, and end of the portrait gallery in the *General Prologue*
(though I did not select them for that reason). They thus outline the sequence
of the poem in a way that is particularly telling with respect to the themes of
desire, gender, and the paternal law. The poem begins in an atmosphere of
official hierarchy, plenitude, and male power ("vertu," from Latin *virtus,*
"maleness," derived from *vir,* "man") that are specifically associated in the
opening lines with phallic assertion. Those lines give, one might say, a very
gendered representation of what April does to March to get the world moving
in spring:

> Whan that Aprill with his shoures soote
> The droghte of March hath perced to the roote,
> And bathed every veyne in swich licour
> Of which vertu engendred is the flour . . .
> (1–4)[28]

Consistent with this opening, the first portrait, the Knight's, supplies the
image of a powerful patriarch, worthy and vir-tuous. He is a victorious
fighter, a defender of the church, and the legitimate father of a squire who
will succeed legitimately to the paternal estate—the very person to justify the
speaker's tacit faith in the links between authority, determinate transmissible
meaning, and male gender dominance. By the time those assumptions have
been put in question by the anomalies of the third estate and the breakdown
of hierarchy associated with them, it seems more than fortuitously appropriate that the boundaries of the third estate, and of the project to order the performance hierarchically, should be marked by a woman, and a markedly competitive, combative, and threatening one at that. And just as it seems no
accident that the Parson's portrait, which is a strident reaffirmation of male
authority as well as ideal Christian order, follows the Wife's and initiates the

last phase of the portraits, it seems even less of one that the gallery ends in an atmosphere of divine order undermined by human abuses, of active disenchantment, and with the Pardoner, the one pilgrim who is lacking the phallus, the embodiment of the not-masculine, castrated: "I trowe he were a geldyng or a mare" (691). His song "Com hider, love, to me!" (672) may even remind us, in context, that the opening paragraph itself ends not in stable order and fulfillment but in desire and lack: "The hooly blisful martir for to seke, / That hem hath holpen whan that they were seeke" (17–18).

What a rereading of the prologue in terms of these gender themes reveals is the emergence of another kind of plot and a different sort of psychological structure for the poem. As I have been arguing, the disenchanted perspective on its own unfolding that characterizes the end of the prologue stresses retrospectively the extent to which the poem is the representation not of the objective reality of others but of the undeclared (and perhaps unconscious) motives that lie behind a particular attempt to classify them. The particular inflection of this general pattern that a focus on gender produces is the way the speaker associates gender and its vicissitudes (if that is the right word for the Pardoner's portrait) with order or the lack of it. But precisely because this way of reading brings the speaker out from behind the concealment of "objective" description, it also reveals the extent to which these portraits are carriers of the speaker's projections. They are aspects of his own attitudes toward his undertaking, markers of his own "masculine" rage for order and its vicissitudes, apparently unconscious roles that he plays. They are also, of course, clues to his own instability of gender and his own proper (improper) subjectivity.

The reading of the *General Prologue* I have been calling prospective is also masculine in the terms developed in this book. That reading traces a *project* of the speaker's to generate a decisive account of the pilgrims that will establish them as stable sources or origins of the tales they tell and which therefore encourages the kind of bad, old-fashioned, dominated-by-the-frame reading I have been continually fighting from the beginning of my own project here. It is important to see that a version of the speaker's project is fundamental to the poem and the poet—that it is what they begin with in one sense, and equally, given the prologue's claim to come after the pilgrimage, what they end with in another. The desire of this project is to find, establish, or make *selves* for the pilgrims that their tales will embody without alteration, and reflexively that desire makes the project a version of *the poet's desire to be and to have a self of his own.* The prologue and the links—the entire frame that punctuates the *Canterbury Tales,* as Lacan might say—testifies to its maker's desire to establish and inhabit stable structures of gender and genre, to record and preserve the social status quo and its workings, to delineate and maintain clear boundaries between the self and others, and to be a transmitter of the phallus, an authority, and what his culture calls a man. The poem *represents* this desire, and represents it as the poet's from beginning to end. It is particularly important to recognize this about the poem because the recognition supports the fundamental validity of the dramatic method in reading it. No textually responsible reading of the poem, including a deconstructive one, can ignore or factor out the pilgrim tellers, the issue of agency, and the problem of voice. These are things that must be read *through* rather than around. If the *Canterbury Tales* is, as I have maintained, one of the major explorations and analyses of subjectivity and its implications—of the escape of the self from itself—in the Western tradition, it founds that exploration and analysis in an understanding of the human fact of the self as that impossible thing, that insatiable desire, that ceaselessly escapes and returns.

Thus if we desire the author, as Barthes suggests, there is evidence in the poem that Chaucer did too. But that desire is of course only part of the story. There is further evidence that "Chaucer," the voice of that text, desires the other as well, and *that* desire speaks in the most characteristic act of the *Canterbury Tales,* impersonation. "Thereof nedeth nat to speke as nowthe" (462) in the Wife's portrait in effect allies the feminine with supplementarity, with what is *left out* of the "masculine" prospect, what has to come "after." The edge of masculine locker-room innuendo that dominates the portrait combines with this admission/promise of more to come to suggest just how inadequate a "masculine" (indeed a male) perspective is for understanding the Wife and the virtual necessity of finding a way to let her own point of view speak out even if it means dressing in drag to do it. Moments like this, or like the apology at the end of the portrait gallery, call attention to the fact that the *General Prologue* does not do justice to the pilgrims and therefore, by the same token and for the same reasons, does not do justice to the poet-speaker and his understanding of his world. From this point of view it can be said that the voice of the textual working we call "Chaucer" shares the Derridian desire to escape knowledge and certainty, to reach a point of not knowing any longer where he is going because of the constraints such "knowledge" imposes. Out of the dramatized insufficiency of traditional social, moral, and gender classifications, and the dramatized insufficiency of the kind of self that goes with them to deal with the complexity of individuals and their relations, the poet turns to the pilgrims, and turns to them as texts.

After all, one of the first things that is obvious about the voice-of-the-text of the *Canterbury Tales,* the agency or self we are led to construct for it, is that "he" is an impersonator in the conventional sense: he puts fictional others between himself and us. Each of the tales is, we know, Chaucer impersonating a pilgrim, the narrator speaking in the voice of the Knight or the Reeve or the Second Nun. They are his creatures; he gives them his life. One of the motives of this enterprise—certainly one of its effects—is to slow us down, to keep us from grasping the central consciousness, the author's self, too quickly and easily by directing our attention to the variety and complexity of the roles he plays and the voices he assumes. Though he is—he must be—each of the pilgrims and all of them, he seems to insist that we can only discover him by discovering who the Knight is, the Parson, the Pardoner, the Wife of Bath. But this self-protective motive is again only half the story. We might as easily say that the poet takes his own life from the pilgrims he impersonates, and the amount of time and effort spent on making the pilgrims independent, the sheer labor of consistent, unbroken impersonation to which the poem testifies, suggests that this perspective is at least as compelling for Chaucer as for us. The enterprise of the poem involves the continual attempt, continually repeated, to see from another's point of view, to stretch and extend the self by learning—and practicing—to speak in the voices of others.

This perspective seems not only opposed to the "masculine" reading of the prologue and the tales but also allied to the kind of impulses I have been calling feminine. It is associated with a fluidity of identity and identification: the desire and ability to appreciate and enact a variety of positions, including gender positions. It is allied with the desire and ability to see the "feminine" in men and the "masculine" in women and imagine how subjects who occupy those bodies within those social constructions might feel, act, desire, and "go on" practically in the circumstances. It seems allied as well with a preference for individuals over society, with private life as opposed to public life, and with the escape from self and the phallus called *jouissance*. It indeed has something to do with bisexuality, and it allows us to locate that feature of all the pilgrims/texts analyzed here in their putative maker as well. In fact Chaucerian impersonation itself has this consistently double or bisexual quality. It oscillates continually and simultaneously between, on the one hand, the desire and practice of dominating others and turning them into versions and extensions of the self that I have analyzed in the Pardoner and, on the other hand, the desire and practice of exploring new roles, possibilities, and personalities that I have examined in the Wife of Bath. Though one mode is dominant in those two pilgrims, each is constantly engaged in both modes, and how should the poet who makes, and is made by, them both escape the same fate and the same desire?

As the foregoing list may suggest, however, the pair "masculine"/"feminine" begins to take on an allegorical reach at this point that is both a genuine and important fact about the symbolic ramifications of gender and a difficult opposition to work with in finishing up here. I have been playing with a number of (to me) dauntingly complex oppositions, most centrally perhaps "masculine"/"feminine" and self/subject. Like Chaucer, I do not think I can control all their relations in my text (to say nothing of elsewhere), and I want now to veer again to the latter pair, remarking only that though the two sets of terms are intimately related, they are neither reducible to one another nor even always consistently parallel.

I have argued that the end of the *General Prologue* enacts a shift from the poem as performance to the poem as text. In doing so, it focuses attention on the speaker as performer in the act—prospectively—of giving way to what I have called the voice of the text. It thus identifies itself—retrospectively—as another instance of what the tales also are (and were first), a representation of the agency of an individual subject in its dealings with language, if language is considered as the most general instance of an institutional construct. That last formulation might do as a definition of the key term I have not defined in this book, *voice*. If so, however, the definition will have to be glossed so as to encompass the dynamics of self and subject, the undecidable play between the coalescence of the subject site into a shapely, self-mastering humanist agent, and the undoing of that position into the place of a fluid, multifarious polyvocality. Voice ought to be a term for that process, a way of referring to the tug toward undoing the self and letting loose the dance of the signifiers, and the complementary drive to contain the plurivocal unruliness of what goes on where subjectivity happens. This is the dynamic Chaucer's poem represents between "masculine" and "feminine," speaker and pilgrims, prologue and tales, self and subject. It is the dynamic as well of reading in general—the movement between the "decoding" of meaning and the pleasure of the text—and of the kind of reading this particular text represents and invites.

The version of the opposition that seems most apposite for understanding voice, however, remains that between performance and text. This is so first of all because of the fairly obvious ways *performance* as a notion evokes location, the willed agency of the performer and the dominance of "his" voice in what is performed, the humanist self, embodiment, and the like, whereas *text,* as now understood, suggests dissemination, the deconstruction of the self in favor of larger, structural forms of agency, the ironing out of relations of dominance and recession among voices, loss of location or disembodiment, and so on. To make voice the swing term of this opposition, more or less in the way *estate* is the hinge between personal and social in the poem, is to make it the field within which those doings and undoings go on, that is, to make it the site of its own other and, as I have maintained, the central concern, along with estate, of the *Canterbury Tales.* Second, the appropriateness of thinking of voice as the site of the play between performance and text is enhanced if we recall again that the *Canterbury Tales* proposes and presents itself patently, right on the surface, as the textual representation of oral performance, that is, as something that represents the location of language in the agency of individuals but does so in a form that is also bound to undo that location and agency and put them in question.

Such a definition, or collocation of definitions, of voice allows us to respond to the rhythms of performing and textualizing, the doing and undoing of voice in the poem, as part of its larger structure and of what it represents—allows us to attend to them not simply as what the poem evinces or enacts because all uses of language do but also as a large part of what the poem is about. This response in turn helps draw attention to what I have been focusing on throughout this reading: those moments in the poem when its performing subjects encounter their own living-out of the condition I have tried to describe. These are the moments, and they come in every tale, when the subject represents and experiences itself as unselfed, textualized, and escaping itself at the same time that it continues to produce performance effects from its location in body and book. As one of the readers of an earlier version of this book, Paul Strohm, remarked, "I still believe that some uncertainty in the attribution of narrative perspective is a property of Chaucer's texts, and that at least some multiplication of narrative voices and perspectives loose within individual tales is inevitable." Exactly. This is a very Chaucerian predicament, one that is represented over and over in his poetry as the situation that poetry both represents and confronts, struggles with and exploits, and it is, not surprisingly, a predicament of his readers as well. The end of the *General Prologue* multiplies a performing self into a textual subjectivity, and the crucial feature of that subjectivity is impersonation. To appear as a disenchanted self in one sense—as one who is aware of the human construction of society and self—is to appear as a disenchanted self in another: as a self-constructing activity that continues into the rest of the poem *in the form* of an impersonation, a practice of voicing, that is always its own undoing and therefore demands continual rereading. The advent of the poem as text identifies the speaker of the *General Prologue,* like the pilgrim tellers of the tales, as simply one of the poet's many self-representations, a multiplicity he is no mere (though no less) in control of than any of those other tellers or than any other human subject. That textualization sets the terms of both his writing and our reading and serves notice that we—all of us—will have to read his "real nature" differently, and keep reading.

Notes

[Ed. note: This essay is the conclusion ("Conclusion: The Disenchanted Self") to Leicester's 1990 book, *The Disenchanted Self: Representing the Subject in the Canterbury Tales;* occasionally, toward the end of the essay, Leicester refers to arguments made earlier in his book. In the notes, I have silently added bibliographic information (drawn from Leicester's own bibliography).]

1.   The phrase is taken from Donaldson, "Chaucer and the Elusion of Clarity," in T. E. Dorsch, ed., *Essays and Studies 1972 in Honor of Beatrice White* (New York: Humanities Press, 1972), 23–44.

2.   See the quotation [earlier in Leicester's book] from Donaldson, *Chaucer's Poetry:* "In my criticism I have been reluctant to invoke historical data from outside the poem to explain what is in it. . . . I have therefore eschewed the historical approach used both by the great Chaucerians of the earlier part of this century and by those scholars who have recently been reading Chaucer primarily as an exponent of medieval Christianity. The fact that the difference between what these two historical approaches have attained is absolute—if Chaucer means what the older Chaucerians thought he meant he cannot possibly mean what these newer Chaucerians think he means—has encouraged me to rely on the poems as the principal source of their meaning" (E. T. Donaldson, *Chaucer's Poetry: An Anthology for the Modern Reader,* 2d ed. [Glenview, Ill.: Scott, Foresman, 1975], vi).

3.   See Michel Foucault, "What Is an Author?" trans. Josué V. Harari, in Josué V. Harari, ed., *Textual Strategies: Perspectives in Post-Structuralist Criticism* (Ithaca, N.Y.: Cornell University Press, 1979), 141–60.

4.   Most notable is the valuable and neglected article by John M. Major, "The Personality of Chaucer the Pilgrim" (*PMLA* 75 [1960]: 160–62), but see also Donald Howard, who makes the parsimonious Aristotelian move of putting the ideal form back into the matter in "Chaucer the Man" (*PMLA* 80 [1965]: 337–43).

5.   See Donaldson's brilliant and humane critique of stemma editing on similar grounds in "The Psychology of Editors of Middle English Texts," in *Speaking of Chaucer* (Durham, N.C.: Labyrinth Press, 1983), 102–18.

6.   See, e.g., Charles A. Owen, Jr., "Development of the Art of Portraiture in Chaucer's *General Prologue*," *Leeds Studies in English* 14 (1983): 125–27.

7.   See Donaldson, "Chaucer the Pilgrim" (in *Speaking of Chaucer,* 1–12), 5, and Jill Mann, *Chaucer and Medieval Estates Satire: The Literature of Social Classes and the General Prologue to the* Canterbury Tales (Cambridge: Cambridge University Press, 1973), 17–37, esp. 20. See also Larry Sklute, "Catalogue Form and Catalogue Style in the General Prologue of the *Canterbury Tales*" (*Studia Neophilologica* 52 [1980]: 35–46), 43.

8.   See Arthur Mizener, "Character and Action in the Case of Criseyde" (*PMLA* 54 [1939]: 65–81), and Robert P. apRoberts, "The Central Episode in Chaucer's *Troilus*" (*PMLA* 77 [1962]: 373–85).

9.   This observation suggests that a paratactic style is conducive to producing the kind of effect I am describing because the information (syntax) that would *specify* the connection between statements is left out. See Erich Auerbach, *Mimesis: The Representation of Reality in Western Literature,* trans. Willard Trask (Garden City, N.Y.: Doubleday, Anchor, 1953), 83–107. Parataxis is one of the main descriptive techniques of the *General Prologue,* particularly noticeable in the three central portraits of the Shipman, the Physician, and the Wife of Bath but widely employed throughout. Further, the structure of the prologue is itself paratactic (composed of juxtaposed, relatively independent portraits), and so is the poem as a whole (composed of juxtaposed tales).

10.   See also the last chapter of *Medieval Estates Satire,* "Conclusions," 187–202.

11.   See Mann's discussion of the Friar's portrait, *Medieval Estates Satire,* 53.

12.   This is an interesting and suggestive feature of Mann's treatment of the poem, which appears to have gone unremarked, perhaps because she simply assumes the poet's knowledge of these works that an older generation of Chaucerians was inclined to deny. Her evidence is generally convincing because it is firmly textual and detailed. See *Medieval Estates Satire,* 46–47, 198, 208–12.

13.   Donald R. Howard, *The Idea of the* Canterbury Tales (Berkeley and Los Angeles: University of California Press, 1976), 134–58.

14.   See the fine discussion of the organization of the poem in Arthur W. Hoffman, "Chaucer's Prologue to Pilgrimage: The Two Voices" (*ELH* 21 [1954]: 1–16).

15.   See Mann, *Medieval Estates Satire,* Appendix A, 203–6.

16.   Sylvia L. Thrupp, in *The Merchant Class of Medieval London (1300–1500)* (Chicago: University of Chicago Press, 1948), has demonstrated how typical was the desire, in men of the Five Guildsmen's class, to crown a career in the city by buying land, moving to the country, and becoming gentry. These pilgrims thus "belong" with the Franklin in part because they are trying to become him.

17.   See Hoffman, "Chaucer's Prologue to Pilgrimage."

18.   See Muriel Bowden, *A Commentary on the General Prologue to the* Canterbury Tales, 2d ed. (New York: Macmillan, 1967), 119–45, and my discussion of the Monk's portrait above.

19.   And more or less in the sense that Morton W. Bloomfield uses it with respect to Langland in *Piers Plowman as a Fourteenth Century Apocalypse* (New Brunswick, N.J.: Rutgers University Press, 1961).

20.   For example, "He was a shepherde and noght a mercenarie" (514) or "He was to synful men nat despitous, / Ne of his speche daungerous ne digne, / . . . But it were any persone obstinat, / What so he were, of heigh or lough estat" (516–17, 521–22). See also Donaldson, "Adventures with the Adversative Conjunction in the General Prologue to the *Canterbury Tales;* or, What's Before the But?" in Michael Benskin and M. L. Samuels, eds., *So Meny People Longages and Tonges: Philological Essays in Scots and Medieval English Presented to Angus McIntosh* (Edinburgh: Benskin and Samuels, 1981), 355–60, esp. 356.

21.   Laura Kendrick notices the changing tone of this apology in *Chaucerian Play: Comedy and Control in the* Canterbury Tales (Berkeley and Los Angeles: University of California Press, 1988), 144–45.

22.   See the excellent account of the word and its medieval uses in Richard McKeon, *Selections from the Medieval Philosophers* (New York: Scribners, 1930), 2:488–90.

23.   See "Outwork, prefacing," in *Dissemination,* trans. Barbara Johnson (Chicago: University of Chicago Press, 1981), 2–59. The supplementarity of prefacing is presented by Derrida pretty much as something Hegel encounters (or is oblivious of), outside his project, unwillingly, as an effect of a blindness. In this sense Chaucer's prologue is unlike one view of *The Phenomenology of Mind* because the poem is patently *not* finished and does not, therefore, form a completed system and because the prologue itself points conspicuously to the inadequacy of its prefacing. Hence it becomes, as I say in the text, an analysis of the impulse to such completion rather than an instance of it. What if these things were true of "Hegel" as well? Though de Man raised this question with respect to Derrida's reading of Rousseau in *Blindness and Insight,* and Harry Berger, Jr., has raised it about the reading of Plato in "Plato's Pharmacy," it has never to my knowledge been followed up.

24.   See Leicester, "'No Vileyn's Word': Social Context and Performance in Chaucer's *Friar's Tale"* (*Chaucer Review* 17 [1982]: 24–25) and the discussion of the Physician's portrait earlier in Leicester's *Disenchanted Self,* 11–12.

25.   See, for example, Howard, *Idea of the Canterbury Tales,* 94–97.

26.   See Leicester, *The Disenchanted Self,* 223 n. 2.

27.   For gynesis, "the putting into discourse of 'woman' as [a] *process* . . . neither a person nor a thing, but a horizon, that toward which the process is tending" (25), see Alice Jardine, *Gynesis: Configurations of Woman and Modernity* (Ithaca, N.Y.: Cornell University Press, 1985). For bibliography on the developing study of this field in the Middle Ages, the reader might start with E. Jane Burns and Roberta L. Krueger, eds., *Courtly Ideology and Woman's Place in Medieval French Literature* (special issue, *Romance Notes* 35, no. 3 [1985]), and their "Selective Bibliography of Criticism: Women in Medieval French Literature," 375–90; Mary Erler and Maryanne Kowaleski, eds., *Women and Power in the Middle Ages* (Athens: University of Georgia Press, 1988); Mary Beth Rose, ed., *Women in the Middle Ages and the Renaissance: Literary and Historical Perspectives* (Syracuse: Syracuse University Press, 1986); and *Medieval Feminist Newsletter.*

28.   See Joel Fineman, "The Structure of Allegorical Desire," in Stephen Greenblatt, ed., *Allegory and Representation: Selected Papers from the English Institute,* n.s., no. 5 (Baltimore: Johns Hopkins University Press, 1981), 26–60.

The Afterlife of the Civil Dead: Conquest in the Knight's Tale

ELIZABETH FOWLER

THE INTERRUPTED TRIUMPH

In many manuscripts of the *Canterbury Tales,* the Knight's Tale begins with an epigraph:

> Heere bigynneth the Knyghtes Tale.
> *Iamque domos patrias, Scithice post aspera gentis*
> *Prelia, laurigero, &c.*

The editors of the *Riverside Chaucer* translate the Latin as "And now (Theseus, drawing nigh his) native land in laurelled car after fierce battling with the Scithian folk, etc."[1] These lines describe a triumph, a popular cultural form in the late Middle Ages and a civic ceremony that is still alive in the modern world—I might cite for example the parade of the New York Yankees down Manhattan's Avenue of the Heroes after they won the 1996 World Series. The triumph is a genre that ranges especially freely across media: sports, music, painting, theology, architecture, drama, lyric poetry. The Tale's epigraph sets the stage by introducing the triumph as the first event of Chaucer's story and by announcing that the story has been told by other authors: notably Statius (in the *Thebaid*), whom the epigraph quotes, and Boccaccio (in *Il Teseida delle nozze d'Emelia*). The *Riverside* expands the "&c.," continuing Statius's account of how Theseus's triumphal entry "is heralded by glad applause and the heaven-flung shout of the populace and the merry trump of warfare ended" (p. 828). Chaucer tells the story differently: when the epigraph breaks off, we catch a glimpse of the kind of revision he will accomplish in the course of the Tale. The Knight's Tale takes up the topic of the aftermath of conquest and invites more ambivalent responses to the triumph than those Statius attributes to the Athenians.

Theseus's triumphal entry into Athens, his own dukedom, occurs in celebration of the most recent victory in what the Knight tells us is a record-

This essay was written specifically for this volume and is published here for the first time by permission of the author.

breaking series of conquests of "Ful many a riche contree" (864). According to old stories, the Knight says, Theseus is "swich a conquerour / That gretter was ther noon under the sonne" (862–63). The Knight's Tale proves to be, as I shall argue throughout this essay, a consideration of conquest and its claims to dominion.[2] How good can a government be, Chaucer asks, if it is established by force? As the topic of the Knight's Tale, conquest has two aspects, the political and the sexual. When the Tale begins, Theseus is coming home from victory in the wars between the sexes, a victory over the "regne of Femenye" itself, located in those days, Chaucer tells us, in a land called Scithia. Together with "muchel glorie and greet solempnytee" (870), Theseus's trophies include the captured queen of the Amazons, Ypolita, and her young sister Emelye. By winning the war, Theseus takes both political and sexual dominion over others, both memorialized in his *raptus* of the Amazon queen. As a figure of conquest, Theseus is set moving in a plot that is framed by two marriages: Ypolita's at its beginning and Emelye's at its end. Thus conquest, expressed in the topos of the *raptus*, is contrasted to marriage, an institution founded entirely on consent. The triumph and the *raptus* trumpet the claims of conquest, but the "weddynge" unsettles those claims with its implicit recourse to the criterion of consent.

Conquest is by definition supremely indifferent to consent; according to legal theorists then and now, consent is invalidated by force or coercion. If we wonder what Ypolita thinks of her marriage, knowing what she said under the pressure of Theseus's sword would hardly satisfy us. Perhaps this is why Chaucer never tells us what she thinks; why, in the first Tale of a long poem otherwise so obsessed with what women say, desire, and do, he so radically restrains and qualifies the representation of women. Not only are we perpetually cut off from what Ypolita thinks, feels, or speaks in this account of her conquest, but our attention is sharply and immediately drawn to this omission by the narrator himself. Lines 875–92 constitute a famous example of the rhetorical figure *occupatio*,[3] in which the Knight elaborately tells us what he will not tell us: about the war against "the regne of Femenye" and what happened to Ypolita in the course of it. The occupatio is a characteristic feature of the narrator's voice throughout the Tale and plays an important role in helping us define what it is we are hearing and seeing. The Knight's Tale does not tell Ypolita's story; neither does it strictly confine itself to the story of Theseus, because we are so often invited to wonder about conquest from points of view outside that of the duke—especially women's and prisoners' points of view. Chaucer ingeniously suggests perspectives critical of those represented in the Tale by means of the narrator's rhetorical devices, his very fussiness about the business of telling the story.

Theseus's opening triumph is interrupted twice: first, within the fictional time of the narration, by the Knight's occupatio about the Scithian women and, second, within the fictional time of the triumph, by a crowd of Athenian women who have been waiting for him in the temple "of the goddesse Clemence" (928) outside the city gates. In both interruptions Chaucer opens a window onto ways of responding to the triumph that differ from the joy and exultation appropriate to triumphal forms. "What folk been ye, that at myn homcomynge / Perturben so my feste with criynge?" asks Theseus (905–6). The Athenian widows exhibit extreme grief, the opposite passion to that invited by Theseus's victory celebrations. The rift in the social fabric caused by war and slaughter is the source of their liminal status, which is characterized by means of age, gender, emotion, class, architecture, and geography. Their grief issues in the rhetorical form of the complaint (915–51), and their interruption of the triumph proves definitive: it launches the plot of the Knight's Tale and opens up the story to a kind of suspense only resolved by the final, long marriage scene that closes the Tale. For Theseus does not complete his *raptus* and triumphal entry of Athens: rather than enjoying his spoils, he leaves his trophy-wife at the gates of the city-state and marches off to Thebes on another pillaging mission.

The appeal that cultural rituals make to the passions (triumphs appeal to joy) and the need that the passions have for cultural rituals (grief needs funerals) together become a structuring principle of the Tale.[4] Like the occupatio that alerts us to the possibility of differing emotional reactions to Theseus's conquest, rhetorical forms throughout the Knight's Tale provide a lens through which the reader can see conflicts between human passions and the ceremonies of social life. The contrast between the triumph and the lament enacts a breach in decorum that provokes Theseus to the ritual of war. Theseus's pity, an apparent index of his character's suitability for rule, is quickly converted to avenging anger.[5] These passions result in the funeral the widows wanted (described in the occupatio of lines 991–1000), but also in the gruesome ransacking and pillaging of Thebes. Only when Thebes is leveled does Theseus complete his triumph:

> And whan this worthy duc hath thus ydon,
> He took his hoost, and hoom he rit anon
> With laurer crowned as a conquerour;
> And ther he lyveth in joye and in honour
> Terme of his lyf; what nedeth wordes mo?
> (1025–29)

Yet this is no closed couplet; as the poem continues, "mo" is rhymed with "wo" and Theseus's joy is paired with the imprisonment of Palamon and Arcite:

> And in a tour, in angwissh and in wo,
> This Palamon and his felawe Arcite
> For everemoore; ther may no gold hem quite.
> (1030–32)

The verb "lyveth" serves equally for Theseus's joy and the knights' woe: for all the existential despair and appeals to fortune and fate that abound in the Tale, these experiences of triumph and abjection are not arbitrary—they are causally related.[6] Theseus's triumph and joy depend on Palamon and Arcite's defeat and woe—these cultural forms and passions are not produced by a god or by nature; they are all produced by conquest, a particular political act and structure.

THESEUS AND THE CHARACTER OF POLITICAL THOUGHT

As he frequently does throughout the *Canterbury Tales,* in the Knight's Tale Chaucer associates ideas with certain characters, aspects of astrology, heraldry, genres, rhetorical topoi, rituals, grammatical constructions, lexical clusters, and even colors. All of the Tale's highly organized iconographical system repays attention, but here I would like to concentrate on the connection between ideas and characters. Chaucer's choice of a crusader as storyteller in itself helps to raise the topic of conquest: the narrator of the Tale is a knight who, as we know from the General Prologue, has been fighting in religious wars across Europe and the Middle East. The crusades were the most important impetus for the legal and ethical thinking about conquest before fifteenth-century European forays into the New World.

Then there is the prominent figure of Theseus himself, the great conqueror. When he chooses to tell part of Theseus's story, Chaucer makes him a figure out of political philosophy. His Theseus exemplifies a category in Aristotle's *Politics* as it is explicated by the fourteenth-century political thinker, Marsiglio of Padua:

> There is and was a fifth method of kingly monarchy, whereby the ruler is made lord *(dominus)* over everything in the community, disposing of things and persons according to his own will, just as the head of a family disposes at will of everything in his own household.[7]

Theseus's acts also fit a category of tyranny included in the Parson's Tale:

> And forther over, understoond wel that thise conquerours or tirauntz maken ful ofte thralles of hem that been born of as roial blood as been they that hem conqueren. (Parson's Tale, 764)

Both such tyranny and Marsiglio's "fifth" kind of absolute monarchy are inimical to the English political settlement, which John Fortescue will soon praise as a mixed or limited monarchy, *dominium politicum et regale.* His fifteenth-century formulation of the English version of the mixed constitution plays upon an ideal that is well accepted by Chaucer's time, one given strong impetus by the interpretations of Aristotelian constitutional theory established by Thomas Aquinas. The ideal of the mixed constitution is expressed in late medieval English government by the elevation of parliament's role in circumscribing the autonomy of the monarch. In a passage that strictly curtails interpretation of the Roman maxim *quod principi placuit,* the authoritative medieval treatise on English law known as "Bracton" places much stronger constraints upon the English king than those Richard II wished to recognize:

> For the king, since he is the minister and vicar of God on earth, can do nothing save what he can do *de jure,* despite the statement that the will of the prince has the force of law *{quod principi placet legis habet vigorem},* because there follows at the end of the *lex* the words "since by the *lex regia,* which was made with respect to his sovereignty"; nor is that anything rashly put forward of his own will, but what has been rightly decided with the counsel of his magnates, deliberation and consultation having been had thereon, the king giving it *auctoritas.* . . . For he is called *rex* not from reigning but from ruling well, since he is a king as long as he rules well but a tyrant when he oppresses by violent domination the people entrusted to his care.[8]

Richard II tested the limits of this institutional settlement severely throughout the height of Chaucer's career and was deposed in 1399 by a magnate he had dispossessed.

In the Knight's Theseus we have not a bad holder of a limited monarchy, as Richard is often described, but something like its mirror-opposite: a benevolent wielder of an absolute imperial dominion.[9] This is the kind of idealized representation that Richard's ideological campaigns attempted to create. Theseus's dominion over Scithia and Thebes is absolute, but the internal constitution of Athens is represented as uncertainly mixed. Though he seems to take freestanding military action against Thebes, Theseus does consult the Athenian "conseil and the baronage" (3096) on the question of Emelye's marriage (perhaps because it is the plan of the Athenian parliament for complete control of Thebes [2970]). Throughout, Theseus is shown to be a master of political as well as military persuasion. But as pleasing as it might have been to Richard II, Theseus's model of the imperial polity appears in a story that suggests the enormity of its costs and offers a rather bleak view of (even aristocratic) life under such political arrangements.

Surprisingly, perhaps, the Knight's Tale does not idealize violence; it presents violence as another in a series of social rituals imbued with aesthetic ambitions, but not as heroic, spiritually transcendent, or beautiful. In fact the Knight goes to some lengths to depict the horror of war. Theseus's defeat of Creon in "pleyn bataille" is an action that takes only three lines and is then followed by a lengthy evocation of the rather unheroic destruction of Thebes:

> But shortly for to speken of this thyng,
> With Creon, which that was of Thebes kyng,
> He faught, and slough hym manly as a knyght
> In pleyn bataille, and putte the folk to flyght;
> And by assaut he wan the citee after,
> And rente adoun bothe wall and sparre and rafter
>
> (985–90)

> Whan that this worthy duc, this Theseus,
> Hath Creon slayn and wonne Thebes thus,
> Stille in that feeld he took al nyght his reste,
> And dide with al the contree as hym leste.
> To ransake in the taas of bodyes dede,
> Hem for to strepe of harneys and of wede,
> The pilours diden bisynesse and cure
> After the bataille and disconfiture.
>
> (1001–9)

Ransacking the heaps of corpses for equipment and clothing, the Athenians seem more like scavenging vultures than like noble heroes. The god of war, the patron of Arcite, and the object of Theseus's primary devotions, Mars himself is unstintingly "grym as he were wood" (2042). He is associated with felony, anger, theft, dread, betrayal, arson, murder, open war, strife, suicide, murder, outrage, mass slaughter, tyranny, and an extraordinary list of other calamities personified in the course of the vivid ecphrasis that describes the ornamentation of the temple (1995–2040). They are all presided over by the figure of Conquest in a scene I shall return to at the end of this essay. The effect of such depictions is to invite us to experience fear, of course, but it is also to disassociate fighting from the realm of cultural achievements and to discredit it by assimilating it to disease, misery, and the willful destruction of civility. In short, the effect of Theseus's actions on social bonds is more destructive than generative. Theseus sacralizes violence by instituting it as a ritual; he then instructs his people to praise him when he draws limits to what he has instigated.

Much criticism of the Knight's Tale has focused on Theseus and whether he is understood to be idealized or satirized, whether he is a philosopher, a virtuous pagan, a mercenary, or a tyrant.[10] Many critics have justified Theseus's role in terms of his aspirations to civilize the brutal disorder of life; but this is to take a view that must ignore Theseus's role as the source of much of the brutal disorder of life.[11] Theseus and his "chivalrie" ([865], a pun that invites us to question whether his cavalry is chivalrous) tear down two civilizations within the first 200 lines of the poem. By this I do not mean simply that Theseus is motivated by self-interest, but that our understanding of the benefits of order must be considered through a reading of a story in which Theseus's benevolent attempts at order appear to do little more than keep violence from being directed at him. At several points in the story the Theban knights consider mounting a full-scale attack on Theseus's rule, but with luck and high rhetoric he manages to arrange that they fight each other rather than him. The view of Theseus as a paragon cannot account for the Theseus who appears in Chaucer's shorter poems: *The House of Fame* (405–26), *The Legend of Good Women* (VI, VIII), and *Anelida and Arcite.* With the exception of the *Anelida,* which, like the Knight's Tale, begins with his triumph over Ypolita, in these poems Theseus is excoriated as traitorous, pitiless, and false.

Critics who are, on the other hand, disturbed by the absolutist aspects of Theseus's behavior encounter the problem of explaining why Chaucer makes him seem so nice. Jill Mann defends the importance of Chaucer's attribution of pity to Theseus within the sphere of sexual relations and the emotions, an interpretation that must be extended further, I think, into the realm of politics if it is to account for the political ambitions of the Tale.[12] There is nothing wrong with benevolence, but benevolence is insufficient for good rule: the grounds of dominion must be sound and the shape of the polity just in order for good government to build human society. The project of my reading of the Knight's Tale is to focus upon Theseus's role as the plot's embodiment of a *dominus* who holds his power by conquest. The task that Chaucer sets the reader is, I think, not to decide whether Theseus's character is good or bad, a dilemma perceived as central by much of the criticism of the Knight's Tale to date, but rather it is to question whether conquest can be compatible with good governance, whether it can be detached from absolutism, and whether, as a justification for rule, it can make a good showing against the competing argument, that the proper establishment of dominion lies not through conquest, but through consent. An ethical evaluation of Theseus must be complemented by a political one.

CIVIL DEATH AND OTHER FORMS OF SOCIAL LIFE

Ethics comes from the Greek word for character, *ethos:* looking for the social meanings embedded in Chaucer's representations of characters is a good way to investigate the political and social setting of his ethical inquiry. Attributes that we may read as psychological, personal, and individual also have important roles to play in the social space between characters. That space is given a curious, shifting shape and emotional charge in the Tale as the plot takes up the issue of governance. Chaucer chooses to think about conquest in a surprising setting: the story of particularly intense affective bonds among a small group of characters. These bonds are turbulent and vulnerable, fraught with passions that are seeking social forms in which to be satisfied. Such forms of social life might include an action such as an assault or a kiss; a ceremonial ritual such as a funeral, a triumph, or a tournament; a bond such as sworn brotherhood or marriage; a status such as Athenian citizen, ruler of Thebes, or courtier. Civic and religious ceremonies and rituals motivate the narrator's recourse to formal rhetorical figures and fill up an enormous proportion of the lines of the Tale.

With the help of figures of speech and their textual traditions, rituals and ceremonies are like molds that the passions can be poured into. These molds help to solidify the passions, giving them social shape and meaning, and memorializing them publicly. Emotions have meaning insofar as they find such forms; thus there is a sense in which the passions can be understood as the interface between the forms of social life and the feeling suffered by individual bodies. The passions are the glue that (whether securely or insecurely) attaches individual human bodies to the institutional forms of social life. They can do this work when they are interpreted in a way that allows them to be glue: that is, when they are understood through language, ideologically. This is the process that interests Chaucer in the Knight's Tale and throughout the *Canterbury Tales*. He loves to think about the tricky connections between the passions suffered by individual bodies and the forms of social life in a polity—and in a world in which polities conflict.

The empire built upon the grounds of Theseus's conquest is not society in general, but a particular kind of society. Its justification by conquest has a number of consequences, and the story drives them home by taking, as its main focus throughout, characters who have suffered civil death. Palamon, Arcite, and Emelye are all trophies and prisoners of war. In the physiological state of the cousins when they are first discovered, "Nat fully quyke, ne fully dede" (1015), we find an accurate description of the civil death that these characters endure as prisoners under Theseus's rule. *Civil death* is a legal term describing the status of a person who has been stripped of all civil rights and capacities. Palamon and Arcite are recognized as privileged members of the Theban social body by the Athenian heralds, who are practiced in reading the signs of elite status "by hir cote-armures and by hir gere" (1016). The knights are "torn" out of the "taas," the heap of dead Theban bodies that suggests the demolished polity of Thebes, to become Theseus's prisoners, for whom he will take no ransom. The duke refuses to recognize, as medieval practices of ransom did, the priority of aristocracy over war's geographical antagonisms. Chaucer himself was captured and ransomed in war, so he must have considered this detail keenly.[13] Theseus causes Palamon and Arcite to suffer a more complete civil death than Chaucer's audience might expect their capture alone to cause.

Stripped of their status by conquest, the knights respond in a peculiar and interesting way. The sole social bond that might be possible for them to sustain, the bond between them, they quickly abjure. Though it has multiple bases—kinship, citizenship, class, sworn brotherhood, knightly obligation—they are each willing, even eager, to sacrifice their mutual bond in order to dedicate themselves to a new explanation of their abjection. Palamon's woe at his imprisonment turns almost immediately (in the plot—in the story, years have passed) to the woe of love-longing. Unable to tell his cousin's "A!" from previous cries, Arcite counsels him to patience by instigating a series of explanations and objects to blame for their imprisonment. First, Arcite blames Fortune, Saturn, and their horoscopes. Palamon denies these causes and claims he is hurt by beauty:

> This prison caused me nat for to crye,
> But I was hurt right now thurghout myn ye
> Into myn herte, that wol my bane be.
> The fairnesse of that lady that I see
> Yond in the gardyn romen to and fro
> Is cause of al my criyng and my wo.
> I noot wher she be womman or goddesse,
> But Venus is it soothly, as I gesse.
>
> (1095–1102)

He prays to Venus that she will deliver them from tyranny. Notably, it is the word "tirannye" that brings Arcite to the window, where he suffers the same sight and fate. Emelye's beauty "sleeth" him; if he cannot have her grace, he says "I nam but deed" (1118, 1122). In this sequence, blame for the misery of conquest, civil death, and imprisonment is transferred by the knights away from Theseus to the gods, then onto their imaginative (indeed wholly visual) relation to Emelye. The theme of murder has permeated the poem's language since the account of Thebes's destruction and the knights' civil death; now it permeates their discussion of love. Chaucer's diction allows us to trace murder's transfer from politics to love. We see that here the passions remain intact in their content and structure despite their changing objects, and that they seek an ideologically intelligible and effective social form.

The slide between objects seems to serve at least two purposes: first, it allows the cousins to regain a kind of paradoxical nobility in abjection because it is noble to declare oneself subject to the feminine beloved's tyranny according to the ideological conventions of courtly love, whereas it is ignoble to be subject to Theseus's conquest, and it is hopeless to be subject to fortune or the stars. There is no future in admitting their "disconfiture" and loss at Theseus's hands, so a second purpose for the transfer is that it gives them a goal: the quest for what they call Emelye's pity and grace. Palamon and Arcite's declarations of mortal love soon transform into anger at each other. This is the cost of attributing their abjection to Emelye, which disallows anger toward her and so cannot accommodate their primary emotional reaction to Theseus. In the course of their debate in prison, their double reaction to conquest—woe and anger—is divided and redirected toward two objects: Emelye and each other. Conquest succeeds in bringing them to civil death and then further stripping them of their sense of solidarity and binding identification with each other. Denying his obligations to Palamon, Arcite says:

> Wostow nat wel the olde clerkes sawe,
> That "who shal yeve a lovere any lawe?"
> Love is a gretter lawe, by my pan,
> Than may be yeve to any erthely man;
> And therfore positif lawe and swich decree
> Is broken al day for love in ech degree.
>
> (1164–68)

Tracing their rage back to its origins in conquest, we can see that it is con-quest rather than love alone that destroys the bond of "felawshipe" between Palamon and Arcite. As the Knight cries in an impassioned apostrophe while the knights prepare to kill each other in the grove:

> O Cupide, out of alle charitee!
> O regne, that wolt no felawe have with thee!
> Ful sooth is seyd that love ne lordshipe
> Wol noght, his thankes, have no felaweshipe.
> Wel fynden that Arcite and Palamoun.
>
> (1622–26)

The kind of tyrannical love and lordship generated by conquest are equally intolerant of the horizontal social bonds that securely bind the good society. "Felaweshipe" is an important word for Chaucer: like Aristotle's earlier *philia* and Edmund Spenser's later "friendship," Chaucer's "felaweshipe" is a general word that covers all kinds of voluntary social bonds—from the marital to the political.[14] Whether it is expressed in sexual or political arrangements, dominion by conquest dissolves such voluntary social bonds.

With the encouragement of Theseus's frequent pronouncements, the knights' abject state seems to them to represent the general condition of human life that many critics have taken it to represent. In fact, their status is particular and political in its origins: they are the captives of conquest, liter-ally "caytyves" as the wretched queens also call themselves (924). Soon the original cause of their abject condition is nearly forgotten and the knights come to experience everything in terms of the paradox of paradise and prison, now imaginatively inverted by the presence of Emelye. As Arcite puts it: "In prison? Certes nay, but in paradys!" (1237). *Prima pars* closes with their dilemma expressed in a conventional narrative device of medieval romance, the *demande d'amour,* to show how thoroughly their political condition has become a sexual condition:

> Yow loveres axe I now this questioun:
> Who hath the worse, Arcite or Palamoun?
> That oon may seen his lady day by day,
> But in prison he moot dwelle alway;

> That oother wher hym list may ride or go,
> But seen his lady shal he nevere mo.
> (1347–52)

The most intense conflict between social bonds takes place in *pars secunda*. Arcite's condition is entirely changed by his mania and melancholy:

> And shortly, turned was al up so doun
> Bothe habit and eek disposicioun
> Of hym, this woful lovere daun Arcite.
> (1377–79)

Abjection make him unrecognizable as a social being; he offers himself as a "povre laborer" (1409) to Theseus's court, thus beginning a transformation out of civil death that will be completed, as we shall see, only in his funeral pyre. In the grove, both knights are again brought to the brink of death before Theseus causes them to be reborn into civil life as part of his body politic.

Once Palamon and Arcite accept total abjection by engaging in mortal combat in the grove, they are able to accept Theseus's lordship, completely reversing their original relation to him. It seems to come as a kind of relief to them to reimagine as noble what they once would have seen as treason; in their vows of loyalty to Theseus, they are able to embrace a social structure that redresses their original loss and civil death. In its arc, the Knight's story tracks the cousins and Emelye through the transformation of their rebellious, captive selves to the oath-taking, loyal subjects of imperial rule. How does this conversion take place? It is accomplished through astute political management of the relation between the passions and cultural rituals. Can conquest produce social forms that genuinely serve and satisfy human passions? In order to pacify the passions of its subjects, Theseus's government must attempt to convert dominion that has been established by conquest into a dominion that will be held by consent. The horrors of war must give way to such voluntary and productive social bonds as marriage. Theseus controls the passions of the civil dead by harnessing them to his social order—by memorializing their rage in his own honor, making a ceremony of it in his theater of war, and making Emelye the trophy.[15]

THE POLITICS OF DEATH

The threats to Theseus's social order caused by the rebellious pain of the civil dead, without whom there would be no one to rule after conquest, have been redirected in their object and converted into pageantry and civic ritual through the course of the Tale. It is important to see how the funeral and the wedding are cultural rituals that preserve the social body of Athens in Theseus's interest. As we shall see, the extinguishing of consent that is accomplished by conquest provides final closure to the Knight's Tale in *pars quarta*. The distinguishing rhetoric of *pars quarta* is imperative. Theseus appears "Arrayed right as he were a god in trone" (2529) and causes his herald to declare the rules of the trial by battle. Built so that no sight line is impeded, the very architecture of the lists participates in the process of judgment.[16] The knights are ordered to do their *devoir* (2598, as jurors are still ordered to do). When Palamon is taken, Theseus pronounces his judgment:

> He cryde, "Hoo! namoore, for it is doon!
> I wol be trewe juge, and no partie.
> Arcite of Thebes shal have Emelie,
> That by his fortune hath hire faire ywonne."
>
> (2656–59)

More imperatives and edicts follow. Once Arcite is injured, Theseus is anxious to calm the knights and contain the violence of the ritual. He issues another judgment:

> For which anon duc Theseus leet crye,
> To stynten alle rancour and envye,
> The gree as wel of o syde as of oother,
> And eyther syde ylik as ootheres brother;
> And yaf hem yiftes after hir degree,
> And fully heeld a feeste dayes three,
> And conveyed the kynges worthily
> Out of his toun a journee largely.
> And hoom wente every man the righte way.
> Ther was namoore but "Fare wel, have good day!"
>
> (2731–40)

The banality of this last line is to the point: the ritual of the tournament is designed both to incite and exhaust political anger, and it is effective only if it does both. At Arcite's death, Theseus makes another formal judgment and then commands the funeral rites. Finally, his long speech closes the Knight's Tale with a special set of commands that usurp the consent of Emelye, Palamon, and all of Thebes in a single speech act that will occupy our attention in the last section of this essay. The imperative mode and the speech acts it generates—rulings, judgments, edicts, declarations, commands—focus our attention on Theseus's style of governing the funeral and wedding of *pars quarta*.[17]

The opening interruption of Theseus's triumph is echoed at the close of the tournament: Arcite's fall takes place in the middle of his own triumph, during his victory lap, and he too is prevented from enjoying a trophy-wife. The accident instigates a series of four images of the dying Arcite's body that are crucial to the rest of the Tale and fill a large portion of *pars quarta*. Here it is worth paying attention to the different uses of space made by the story and the plot: in the story, Arcite has but one body that is injured, treated, abandoned by its soul, dressed, and burned; in the plot, in contrast, there is a series of bodies, many Arcites bearing vividly different descriptions. Good analogues to Chaucer's series of Arcites can be found in other media: we might compare his technique to simultaneous narration in medieval painting and illustration or, in funerary sculpture, to the *transi* tomb, which enclosed the remains of the person invisibly but employed two effigies of the dead, one below (the *transi* figure) and one above the body's remains.[18]

Language too can convey multiple images of a single body in order to present a program of ideas about its social meanings. In this sense, fiction better represents social space than does the world itself. A text in English reads left to right and top to bottom, in a linear thread that can multiply the image of a single character into many images, but in doing so creates each new image on a new part of the page. In the Knight's Tale, there are far more images of Arcite's body than of the ostensible romance object of visual desire, the body of Emelye.[19] Our first encounter with the series of Arcites comes with the apparition of the injured body in place of the noble heraldic victor. Rather than using an extended epic simile, the Knight rather simply compares Arcite to a coal or a crow because of the black blood that has run into his face (2692). This stunned, punctured, crying body is cut out of the social shell of heraldic armor that it is no longer capable of animating. The interior disorder of his body suddenly cannot be accommodated within the "harneys" of his role in the tournament, the role of the champion knight.

The second body of the series appears at line 2743, after Theseus has calmed the competing legions with soothing rhetoric, feasting, and gifts. The other knights are returned to their places in the social and political fabric of the world without further disruption or damage. Not Arcite, of course—his body seems at this point to take upon itself all the paradoxical violence and fragile vulnerability of the flesh: its subjection to illness, injury, the passions, chance, and death. The gruesome description of his suffering reduces and deflates Arcite's emotional distress to his physiology. As readers have often noticed, the metaphors of the love complaint are literalized in his physical distress:

> Swelleth the brest of Arcite, and the soore
> Encreesseth at his herte moore and moore.
> (2742–43)

His deathbed complaint itself makes Emelye the source of his injuries:

> Allas, the wo! Allas, the peynes stronge,
> That I for yow have suffred, and so longe!
> Allas, the deeth! Allas, myn Emelye!
> Allas, departynge of oure compaignye!
> Allas, myn hertes queene! Allas, my wyf,
> Myn hertes lady, endere of my lyf!
>
> (2771–76)

The theme of murder, which had originated in the knight's near death in Thebes and civil death in Athens and had then been transferred to his suffering in love, finds simultaneous fulfillment and bathos in Arcite's accidental bodily death.

In the course of the long description, the paradox of heat and cold, a trope drawn from courtly love lyrics, is used rather baldly to suggest the way death strips Arcite of the social meanings he helped construct for himself. At the point of death, Arcite becomes a third body:

> For from his feet up to his brest was come
> The coold of deeth, that hadde hym overcome,
> And yet mooreover, for in his armes two
> The vital strengthe is lost and al ago.
>
> (2799–2802)

> His spirit chaunged hous and wente ther,
> As I cam nevere, I kan nat tellen wher.
> Therfore I stynte; I nam no divinistre;
> Of soules fynde I nat in this registre,
> Ne me ne list thilke opinions to telle
> Of hem, though that they writen wher they dwelle.
> Arcite is coold, ther Mars his soule gye!
>
> (2809–15)

His medically abandoned, theologically abandoned, socially exhausted dead body is quite forlorn, but in this blank third state becomes free to acquire a new role, becoming a kind of effigy upon which social meanings can be reinscribed. The paradox of temperature provides Theseus with a symbolic location for the funeral rites:

> Duc Theseus, with al his bisy cure,
> Caste now wher that the sepulture
> Of goode Arcite may best ymaked be,
> And eek moost honurable in his degree.
> And at the laste he took conclusioun
> That ther as first Arcite and Palamoun
> Hadden for love the bataille hem bitwene,
> That in that selve grove, swoote and grene,

> Ther as he hadde his amorouse desires,
> His compleynte, and for love his hoote fires,
> He wolde make a fyr in which the office
> Funeral he myghte al accomplice.
>
> (2853–64)

The "office funeral" is carefully designed to redress the loss of Arcite and the injury that his life and death seem to pose to the social body of Athens.

As it cooled and lost its social meaning, the gruesome second body represented a threatening violence and vulnerability that are now redressed by the vital fire and the careful, luxurious presentation of the fourth image in the series of Arcites, the perfected corpse. It appears at line 2873, in the midst of Theseus's preparations:

> And after this, Theseus hath ysent
> After a beere, and it al overspradde
> With clooth of gold, the richeste that he hadde.
> And of the same suyte he cladde Arcite;
> Upon his hondes hadde he gloves white,
> Eek on his heed a coroune of laurer grene,
> And in his hond a swerd ful bright and kene.
>
> (2870–76)

Here, Arcite is memorialized not as a Theban "caytyf," but as a conqueror in a laurel crown. The bathos of the ignoble fall that interrupted his triumph is reversed by the elevation of his arms upon three great white steeds (2889–98). The threats Arcite represented to Theseus as an angry prisoner, as a banished lover, as a disguised retainer, and as a rehabilitated champion of conquest are all symbolically cured in the ceremony. Theseus mourns grandly and publicly assigns Arcite arms and honors as a nobleman, a place in the Athenian body politic. In fact, the hierarchical structure of Athens is carefully represented as intact in the funeral procession. There is much smoothing over of conflict throughout the ceremony and even the fantasy of a retrospective marriage: Emelye is given the role of grieving widow, though for all we know she has never spoken a word to Arcite.

Like the *transi* tomb, the poem provides an ideational program that relates the various bodies of Arcite to one another. An idealized, immutable Athenian body politic is reasserted by the funeral and symbolized by the triumphal fourth body of Arcite that wears the crown and sword. The gruesome second body of Arcite seems to have absorbed everything rebellious, as if resistance to Theseus's rule had been nothing but a bodily disease that could be cauterized by the funeral pyre. The political rift that had been exacerbated by the conquest of Thebes by Athens and represented by the civil deaths of the Theban knights is now erased. The triumphal Arcite is the full subject of Duke Theseus, dead but completely assimilated into the social order of

Athens. The opening funeral conducted by the widows of *prima pars* recognizes above all the political antagonism between Athens and Thebes; among possible social divisions, this closing funeral recognizes only class: it forgets or refuses to memorialize Arcite's conquered, "caytyf" status.

After the procession, the narrative takes a turn. The descriptions of the funeral preparations have to this point been represented as a series of Theseus's commands, but after the procession the narrative shifts into the passive voice and removes itself a degree from Theseus's point of view. The elaborately ornamental, anastrophic occupatio that stretches its syntax across nearly 50 lines (2919–66) includes a description of the chaos caused by the minor gods, birds, and beasts who are "Disherited of hire habitacioun" (2926) by the destruction of the standing wood of the grove. The epic catalog of trees cites a conventional figure for political civilization, and its felling is correspondingly disturbing. As a whole, the occupatio suggests the social costs of Arcite's death and Theseus's ceremony. Among other points of view he demurs to express, the Knight will not tell us what Emelye "spak, ne what was hir desir" during the funeral service (2944). As so often in the Tale, elaborate rhetorical figures show Theseus's brilliant ideological control of passions and persons through public ritual. The occupatio opens up the possibility of responding in ways very different from those his ceremonies prescribe.

THE POLITICS OF MARRIAGE

The cultural work of the ceremonies of the Knight's Tale is not complete with the gorgeous funeral. Though the battle and the funeral reassert social hierarchies by honoring knightly ideals and denying Arcite's political abjection, they do not solve the problem of the future relation of Athens to its "caytyves" and conquered lands. Theseus's plans for Thebes are publicly announced at the moment when the polity's mourning for Arcite ceases:

> By processe and by lengthe of certeyn yeres,
> Al stynted is the moornynge and the teres
> Of Grekes, by oon general assent.
> Thanne semed me ther was a parlement
> At Atthenes, upon certein pointz and caas;
> Among the whiche pointz yspoken was,
> To have with certein contrees alliaunce,
> And have fully of Thebans obeisaunce.
> For which this noble Theseus anon
> Leet senden after gentil Palamon . . .
> (2967–76)

The rhymed opposition of "alliaunce" and "obeisaunce" leaves nothing to the imagination about the contrast between the civil status of Thebans and Athenians. The Greeks resolve to consolidate their dominion over Thebes, and the means of this consolidation is to be the marriage of Palamon and Emelye. Both characters seem to have been reduced to tractable rubble by the horrors of the ritual battle and its aftermath. Theseus's brilliant long speech attempts further to shape the Theban and the Scithian "caytyfs" to "obeisaunce" and thus to assimilate Thebes into his dominion through a marriage—precisely the way he first managed to assimilate Scithia. The high watermark of the imperatives of *pars quarta,* Theseus's speech commands the marriage with considerable persuasive force. Its main object, however, is to model the political world as imperial and to integrate a rehabilitated Thebes and Palamon into that idealized, centralized polity.

Theseus opens with a depiction of the world's creator as a conqueror who captured the four elements with a "faire cheyne of love" and imprisoned them "In certeyn boundes, that they may nat flee" (2988, 2993). The language of capture and imprisonment carefully echoes the events of *prima pars,* suggesting to the reader that Theseus's metaphysics may have a particular political purpose. The "Firste Moevere" turns out to be very like Theseus, a "Prince" and "kyng" against whom it is foolish to rebel or complain (versions of the disdainful word "grucchen" reappear throughout the speech):

> And whoso gruccheth ought, he dooth folye,
> And rebel is to hym that al may gye.
> (3045–46)

The deaths of polities are also apparently inevitable, biologically to be expected: Chaucer has Theseus contentiously add human cities to a list, drawn from Boccaccio, of the life spans of natural features of the landscape—an oak, a stone, a river:

> The brode ryver somtyme wexeth dreye;
> The grete tounes se we wane and wende.
> Thanne may ye se that al this thyng hath ende.
> (3024–26)

The speech treats the damage caused by conquest as if it were as natural as the ordinary course of death and to be regretted only briefly. The image of the towns recalls the death of Thebes, as well as an earlier image in the temple of Mars:

> The tiraunt, with the pray by force yraft;
> The toun destroyed, ther was no thyng laft.
> (2015–16)

The death of towns in the Tale has never been as natural as Theseus presents it, nor as self-determined as his grammar suggests: the image opens up another crack in the smooth surface of his logic. Throughout the speech, there is a self-interested assertion that a stable governor supervises all such destruction. His talk against rebellion is focused on the passions rather than on armed resistance, and on the loss of Arcite rather than on the loss of Thebes. That allows his rhetoric to move easily between its politically quietist metaphysics to his directives to Palamon and Emelye.

The contrast between corruption and perfection that structured Arcite's funeral is repeated in two new contexts: in Theseus's reassurances that nature is perfect despite its cycles of mutability and then in his exhortation to marry:

> What may I conclude of this longe serye,
> But after wo I rede us to be merye
> And thanken Juppiter of al his grace?
> And er that we departen from this place
> I rede that we make of sorwes two
> O parfit joye, lastynge everemo.
>
> (3067–72)

To marry, in this logic, is to choose joy rather than sorrow, the perfect rather than the "corrumpable" (3010), the eternal rather than the transient, life rather than death, wise Jupiter rather than foolish rebellion, the "faire cheyne of love" (2988) rather than the "foule prisoun of this lyf" (3061), the intact Athenian social body rather than the "taas" of Theban corpses. Theseus carefully lines up this long series of manufactured oppositions and asks that the audience accept some very loose reasoning by analogy. Like Arcite's funeral body, the marriage is presented as something that will repair the anger and the injury suffered by the social body during conquest. Theseus associates the known effects of conquest—bodily death, civil death, grief, and anger—with the processes of nature, and he offers marriage and obedience as their remedy. Logically, then, his account of the marriage reverses its actual purpose. It is designed to consolidate Athens's conquest of Thebes, yet he represents it as if it would repair the damage done by that conquest.

The logical contradiction of Theseus's speech is not buried—his series of oppositions attempts to harness our awareness of the contradiction and propel us, together with Palamon and Emelye, toward an acceptance of the marriage. Contradiction itself becomes a theme of the speech's appeal to the passions. Sorrow for Arcite's death becomes "contrarie . . . wilfulnesse" (3057), disobedience, and "grucchyng." Arcite has escaped from "this foule prisoun of this lyf," and the metaphor asks us to respond to the occasion of his death with the joy appropriate to his escape from Theseus's prison. Finally, Palamon and Emelye are reprimanded.

> Why grucchen heere his cosyn and his wyf
> Of his welfare, that loved hem so weel?
> Kan he hem thank? Nay, God woot, never a deel,
> That both his soule and eek hemself offende,
> And yet they mowe hir lustes nat amende.
>
> (3062–66)

Now their grief at Arcite's death is interpreted as an offense to him and his soul. They are urged to "amende" their "lustes," to reform their emotions along the pattern of Theseus's reasoning. That reasoning advises a fully contradictory experience of the passions: the substitution of merriment for woe and of joy for sorrow.

The rhetorical project seems to work, because no more complaints are heard from Palamon and Emelye; and, though it seems significant that, just as in Ypolita's case, we are never shown Palamon or Emelye voluntarily consenting to the marriage, they are reported to love each other blissfully from then on. The end of the Tale is surprising, for Theseus's forceful ideological reinterpretation of their experience of the passions glues them, apparently solidly, into a new social structure that they had resisted before: the Amazon Emelye resisted marriage and the Theban Palamon resisted Athenian governance.[20] However, Chaucer does not focus our attention upon their affective experience of these emotions or other aspects of their psychology: instead, he lavishes attention upon Theseus's rhetoric and shows how even within the voice of conquest at the height of its persuasive and ideological power, we have recourse to other political and ethical criteria of evaluation. Everything we have learned from the Knight's Tale so far helps us make sense of the closing act of Theseus's oration. The complex quadrangulation of human passions, rhetorical forms, ritual ceremonies, and social institutions is tightly, even starkly, represented in the last 30 lines of Theseus's great speech. In the opening triumph of *prima pars* we are asked to notice the gap between emotion and the ceremonies designed to commemorate the institutional form of conquest: the imperial polity is celebrated by Theseus's triumph over Scithia but interrupted by the grief suffered by the widows on the Theban front. The occupatio becomes an analytical rhetoric capable of opening a window into the ideological work of the triumph and suggesting to us the existence of suppressed emotional and political meanings. In the closing scene of the Knight's Tale, rhetoric again offers us rich analytic possibilities.

The meeting of the Athenian parliament returns the poetry to the fully imperative mode that has dominated *pars quarta*. Like the triumph, the speech acts here inaugurate a new institutional arrangement that consolidates Athenian dominion through a marriage. As ritual acts both are performed by Theseus unilaterally. The rhetorical form of marriage, however, evidences enormous strain. Rather than declarative marital vows performed by the two spouses, we have an imperative command uttered by Theseus. Rather than the expression of consent by the bride and groom that is considered legally central to the institution of marriage across so many cultures, Theseus proclaims that "this is my fulle assent, / With al th'avys heere of my parlement" (3075–76). The joining of the couple's hands that iconographically represents mutuality in genealogical charts and visual representations of many other kinds is produced here by Theseus's imperious directive to Emelye to "Lene me youre hond" and his equally dismissive treatment of Palamon's voluntary consent:

> I trowe ther nedeth litel sermonyng
> To make yow assente to this thyng.
> Com neer, and taak youre lady by the hond.
> (3091–93)

Like English customary law before it, canon law had, since the twelfth century decretals of popes Alexander III and Innocent III, required solely an exchange of mutual consent for the performance of legitimate marriage. Instead of what fourteenth-century Christians would recognize as a lawful, mutual contract between Emelye and Palamon, we are given Theseus's edict, which engulfs their wills in its expansive, sudden use of the royal first-person plural: "for this is oure accord" (3082). In a passive construction, the Knight declares:

> Bitwixen hem was maad anon the bond
> That highte matrimoigne or mariage,
> By al the conseil and the baronage.
> (3094–96)

Chaucer invites the reader to puzzle over this passage by observing the abruptness of Emelye's apparent emotional reversal. She seems to have forgotten the self we knew in the temple of Diana, where we were privy to her thoughts, prayers, and (especially) vows as never before or since. When we see how the rhetorical form of the marriage vow is strained by Theseus, it reveals the gap, familiar from so many of the earlier episodes, between social institutions and the passions they are designed to express, satisfy, and solidify. We see the workings of ideology as Theseus attempts to close that gap and to make Emelye's emotions accord with marriage, to make marriage accord with political conquest, and to make Thebes accord with Athens. We would not, I think, call such accord voluntary, nor would we call it concord. The best case that Chaucer makes for conquest, then, requires much silence. Even if we imagine it as a blissful silence, Chaucer never represents it as consent. The rhetorical form of the marital vow, which requires consent and specifies both its agents and its audience, clarifies the limits of conquest. Against that rhetorical form we can see conquest consolidating its dominion, but we can also see how a complete consolidation is impossible. To be effective, ideological pressure always seems to admit a residue that reminds us of the sources of human suffering; therefore such pressure always admits of its own political analysis. Decked out for burning, Arcite's body urges us to forget that Theseus annihilated Thebes. But the corpse is also an effigy of the repressed, a repository of memory.

The Knight's Tale is a story of the disturbances that the civil dead represent to the conqueror. The violence of conquest seems paradoxically, in its aftermath, to threaten the conquering social body itself. At the center of the Tale, presiding over the ecphrastic personifications that fill the temple of the god of war, sits the figure of Conquest in just such a vulnerable position:

> And al above, depeynted in a tour,
> Saugh I Conquest, sittynge in greet honour,
> With the sharpe swerd over his heed
> Hangynge by a soutil twynes threed.
> (2027–30)

The three temples architecturally organize the play of ideas in the Tale. Mars's prosecution of conquest, Venus's binding of humans into social affiliations, and Diana's critical and separatist feminist agency provide a network of motives that not only shape the plot, but direct the reader's ethical and political deliberation. When we judge conquest by the standards of war, it is conceded to be vulnerable to its own method and instrument, yet accorded all honor. When we judge it by the standards of Venus and Diana, however, we notice that it corrodes social bonds, tears down social structures, and forcibly extinguishes the capacity of the person for genuine consent—a capacity that is emblematized in the notion of female chastity. Though Theseus's original conquest of Scithia and *raptus* of the royal Amazon sisters is nearly forgotten by the end of the Tale, no amount of high rhetoric or good intentions can, according to Chaucer's account, turn this final political marriage into the expression of voluntary consent that characterizes the constitution of the good society. The tension between the triumph and the lament, between *raptus* and marriage, between the Athenian subjugation of Thebes and the Athenian parliamentary mixed constitution controls the thought experiment of the Knight's Tale. The best case for the conqueror never amounts to a defense: the pain of the civil dead haunts Theseus's triumphs and undermines the appeals of conquest for consent.

Notes

This essay is written in grateful memory of John Pope and Cleanth Brooks and has benefited from the counsel of Victor Luftig, Tom Stillinger, and my students at Yale University.

1.   All citations of Geoffrey Chaucer's works are to *The Riverside Chaucer*, ed. Larry D. Benson (Boston: Houghton Mifflin, 1987).

2.   For a treatment of the jurisprudence of dominion in the Knight's Tale, see my essay "Chaucer's Hard Cases," in *Medieval Crime and Social Control*, ed. Barbara Hanawalt and David Wallace (Minneapolis: University of Minnesota Press, 1998).

3.   This figure is also called *occultatio*, a term Richard A. Lanham and H. A. Kelly prefer. See Lanham, *A Handlist of Rhetorical Terms* (Berkeley: University of California Press, 1969).

4.   Medieval thinking about the passions is quite different from modern thinking about "the emotions." Because this essay attempts to trace the assignment of particular ideas and objects to what in Chaucer is a quite programmatic representation of affective states or drives (joy, grief, pity, anger, woe, fear, desire, etc.), I often use the word *passion* rather than *emotion*. The connections between the passions, ideology, rhetoric, and social institutions are at the heart of my inquiry.

5.   On pity as a heroic ideal, see Jill Mann, *Geoffrey Chaucer* (New York: Harvester Wheatsheaf, 1991), especially 171–76.

6.   Editors differ on how to treat line 1031. The alternative, "Dwellen this Palamon and eek Arcite," derives from the Hengwrt manuscript and is adopted by the editions of Robert A. Pratt and E. T. Donaldson.

7.   Marsiglio of Padua, *Defensor pacis*, trans. Alan Gewirth (Toronto: University of Toronto Press, 1980), 31; cf. Aristotle, *The Politics*, 1287a1–1288b1.

8.   Henry de Bracton, *De legibus et consuetudinibus angliae*, 4 vols., trans. Samuel E. Thorne (Cambridge: Harvard-Belknap, 1968–77), 2:305.

9.   The role of Theseus in political philosophy continues into the early modern period. In *Il Principe*, Machiavelli designates Theseus together with Moses, Cyrus, and Pomulus as men who founded new states by means of "virtù" rather than "fortuna." According to Niccolò Machiavelli, Fortune gave Theseus the occasion and the dispersed (*dispersi*) Athenians who then were, like Chaucer's Arcite and Palamon, material to be shaped to the form of his dominion (*The Prince: A Bilingual Edition*, trans. Mark Musa [New York: St. Martin's, 1964], 40–43). On the history of the figure of Theseus, see Patricia Eberle's forthcoming work.

10.   David Aers makes the case for Chaucer's criticism of Theseus's militarism and its "inquiry into problems of order in cultural and metaphysical dimensions, one which includes especial attention to the uses of metaphysical language by those in power, the transformations of metaphysics into an ideology of unreflexive secular domination" (*Chaucer, Langland, and the Creative Imagination* [London: Routledge & Kegan Paul, 1980], 195).

11.   For example, "Order, which characterizes the structure of the poem, is also the heart of its meaning," according to Charles Muscatine, *Chaucer and the French Tradition* (Berkeley: University of California Press, 1969), 181. Not so David Aers: "Although much of the misery the poet has displayed is based in specific human practices and choices encouraged by the culture over which Theseus presides, the duke never thinks of differentiating between 'that we may nat eschue' and what we *could* eschew with a change in outlook and practice" (*Chaucer, Langland, and the Creative Imagination*, 191).

12.   Jill Mann, *Geoffrey Chaucer*, 165–85. See Susan Crane's response in *Gender and Romance in Chaucer's* Canterbury Tales (Princeton: Princeton University Press, 1994), 21–23. On pity see also Aristotle, *Nichomachean Ethics*, 1105b20–30. For an introduction to the bibliography of the Knight's Tale, see the explanatory notes in *The Riverside Chaucer* by Vincent J. DiMarco (826–28), and see Monica McAlpine, ed., *Chaucer's "Knight's Tale": An Annotated Bibliography, 1900 to 1985* (Toronto: University of Toronto Press, 1991).

13.   See Derek Pearsall, *The Life of Geoffrey Chaucer: A Critical Biography* (Oxford and Cambridge: Blackwell, 1992), 40–41, and V. A. Kolve, *Chaucer and the Imagery of Narrative: The First Five* Canterbury Tales (Stanford: Stanford University Press, 1984), 99–101.

14.   See the chapters on friendship in Aristotle's *Nichomachean Ethics*, and see Spenser's *Faerie Queene*, bk. 5. Chaucer's Parson calls woman the "felawe" of man as he explains how a

good marriage is not hierarchical: "God made womman of the ryb of Adam, for womman sholde be felawe unto man" (Parson's Tale, 927). On "felaweshipe" as the form of the polity Chaucer most admires, see David Wallace, *Chaucerian Polity: Absolutist Lineages and Associational Forms in England and Italy* (Stanford: Stanford University Press, 1997), especially chaps. 2–3. Wallace contrasts the degradation of the fraternal bond between Palamon and Arcite with the "felaweshipe" developed in the General Prologue: see pp. 109–10.

15. The "macro-rhetorical," memorial features of the Knight's Tale are described by Mary Carruthers in "Seeing Things: Locational Memory in Chaucer's Knight's Tale" in *Art and Context in Late Medieval English Narrative: Essays in Honor of Robert Worth Frank, Jr.,* ed. Robert R. Edwards (Cambridge, England: D. S. Brewer, 1994), 93–106. She shows how places and buildings become storial locations for, among many other things, "primary emotion (woe, lust, anger, courage, awe)" (102). My essay attempts to extend her analysis by considering the cultural uses of the ceremonies that take place in those locations (the prison, garden, grove, etc.). As we have seen, an important role these rituals play is the ideological redefinition of the passions the characters experience. That redefinition repositions characters within the social structure that is represented in the Knight's Tale by the memorial architecture Carruthers describes. Similarly, the poem appeals to the passions and ethical judgment of the reader in ideological ways that I would describe, in Chaucer, as an invitation to deliberation. As Carruthers's work has consistently argued, memorial art draws our attention to the affective and ethical process it presents to the reader.

16. Susan Crane, *Gender and Romance,* 34–36.

17. A. S. G. Edwards has suggestively connected Chaucer's play with speech acts to the issues of medieval nominalist philosophy. See "Chaucer and the Poetics of Utterance," in *Poetics: Theory and Practice in Medieval English Literature* (Cambridge, England: D. S. Brewer, 1991), 57–67.

18. For important analogies between the Knight's Tale and the conventions of medieval visual composition, see V. A. Kolve, *Chaucer and the Imagery of Narrative,* especially 121–22. Chaucer's granddaughter Alice had a beautiful *transi* tomb built for herself that is well preserved at Ewelme, Oxfordshire. Both visible bodies are lying on their backs, the hands praying, the faces turned up. The upper effigy presents a clothed, serene, idealized young woman; the lower depicts an exposed, decaying, mortal corpse. On the connection between political theory and doubled representations of bodies in funerary art, see Nigel Llewellyn, *The Art of Death: Visual Culture in the English Death Ritual c. 1500–c. 1800* (London: Reaktion, 1991).

19. On Emelye's body, see Susan Crane, *Gender and Romance,* 79–84.

20. With respect to Emelye's plasticity, Carolyn Dinshaw writes that "women's desires must conform to the desires of men" in a society founded on the exchange of women (*Chaucer's Sexual Poetics* [Princeton: Princeton University Press, 1989], 107). This is a crucial reminder that gender is constitutive in the ideological redefinition of the passions that concerns us here. Chaucer elaborates the redefinition that the Theban knights experience; he gives just enough detail about Emelye to underline her difference, but not enough to clarify it. In other poetry (notably, the *Legend of Good Women,* the Wife of Bath's Tale, the Physician's Tale, *Troilus and Criseyde*), his focus is on the ideological components of the affective experience of women.

"No Man His Reson Herde":
Peasant Consciousness, Chaucer's Miller,
and the Structure of the *Canterbury Tales*

LEE PATTERSON

Aux yeux de l'historien, la rèvolte agraire apparâit aussi inséparable du régime seigneurial que, par exemple, de la grande enterprise capitaliste, la grève.

—Marc Bloch

In 1906 Robert Root described Chaucer's appeal in the following terms:

> We turn to Chaucer not primarily for moral guidance and spiritual sustenance, nor yet that our emotions may be deeply and powerfully moved; we turn to him rather for refreshment, that our eyes and ears may be opened anew to the varied interest and beauty of the world around us, that we may come again into healthy living contact with the smiling green earth and with the hearts of men, that we may shake off for a while "the burthen of the mystery of all this unintelligible world," and share in the kindly laughter of the gods, that we may breathe the pure, serene air of equanimity.[1]

This passage provides a remarkable synopsis of values that have always been at the center of Chaucer criticism: that the poet is a keen and genial observer of humankind who is himself emancipated from narrow self-interests, that because he is (as Root elsewhere put it) "in the world, but not of it," he is able to trace with forbearance what Blake called "the Physiognomies or Lineaments of Universal Human Life."[2] Hence some fifty years after Root's book, one of the greatest of the next generation of Chaucerians, E. Talbot Donaldson, described Chaucer as possessed of "a mind almost godlike in the breadth and humility of its ironic vision"; and in 1985 Derek Pearsall introduced his excellent book by insisting that the *Canterbury Tales* neither "press for [n]or permit a systematic kind of moral or ideological interpretation," while

From *South Atlantic Quarterly* 86 (1987): 457–95. © 1987 Duke University Press. Reprinted by permission of Duke University Press.

describing "the general moral purpose of the *Tales*" as being "always to give the advantage to a humane and generous understanding."[3]

But while this humanist tradition of criticism has, by and large, and with great success, established the terms by which Chaucer's poetry is interpreted, it has declined to subject its own central category—the poet's ideologically unconditioned, even transhistorical consciousness—to interpretation.[4] Yet surely Chaucer's uncanny ability to present himself as the historically undetermined poet of a correspondingly dehistoricized subjectivity is itself a historical event, just as we must similarly acknowledge that the unmasking of ideology is itself, inescapably, ideological (always understanding of course, that by ideology we mean not simply a crude false consciousness but rather an organized system of beliefs, meanings, and values by which people endow their world with significance and thereby make it accessible to practical activity). If an ideologically free space cannot exist, where then does Chaucer stand when he describes "the varied interest and beauty of the world"? And if we agree that Chaucer's subject is subjectivity itself—"the Physiognomies or Lineaments of Universal Human Life"—what interests of his own led him to this topic?

The current and virtually universally accepted interpretation of Chaucer's social position is that he stood between—and hence to some extent apart from—the two great cultural formations of his time, the court and the city. A bourgeois within the court, he was a royal official in the city—a complexity of allegiance that, it is argued, freed him from any narrowly partisan commitments. According to Paul Strohm, who has developed this argument in greatest detail, both within the court and the city, and in the transit between the two, Chaucer found himself negotiating a highly factionalized world that taught him that "the process of understanding [was] less a matter of ranking alternatives on some vertical scale of moral choice, than of adding alternatives on a horizontal and less judgmental plane in order to reveal the full range of possibilities inherent in a subject."[5] And Stephen Knight has translated this social mobility into economic terms, arguing that Chaucer stands between the natural economy of the feudal nobility and the exchange economy of his bourgeois origins.[6] To put a complex matter simply, Knight sees Chaucer as condemning the rampant cash nexus of the mercantile ethos while simultaneously insisting upon the rights of a newly emergent, market-generated subjectivity, a paradox that is finally resolved only by his escape into the orthodox piety of the Parson's Tale.

But there are serious historical problems with this kind of analysis, regardless of the terms in which it is articulated. For by accepting as the central division of Chaucer's social world an opposition between the city and the court, this understanding omits and effectively erases the rural world that was, recent historians have argued, the most socially combative and historically progressive element of late medieval English society. What makes this erasure possible is the widespread acceptance by literary critics of the idea that medieval society can be understood in terms of an opposition between the *Naturalwirtschaft* of a country that is economically inert, socially repressive, and culturally backward, and, on the other hand, an economically innovative, socially mobile, and culturally avant-garde town that is the locus of a progressive *Geldwirtschaft*. It is important to realize that what underwrites this account is the assumption that the town—and the open market that is its raison d'être—is the solvent of the feudal mode of production: urban freedom from the reciprocal dependencies of feudalism allows for the creation of a free-floating individual, capable of entering into contractual relations; labor is divided into the specializations necessary for the eventual triumph of industrialization; and an emergent civic humanism provides the foundations for the development of parliamentary democracy. What we have here, in other words, is the familiar and oddly inescapable Whig interpretation of history, with the heroic bourgeoisie, here instantiated in the form of the medieval merchant adventurer, as history's prime mover.[7] For as R. J. Holton has recently pointed out, this reading of the transition from feudalism to capitalism depends upon the classic Enlightenment notion that history proceeds

> in terms of the progressive realisation of a system of "natural liberty" achievable through free market relations. . . . The assumption is that given the removal of barriers economic freedom (or "capitalism") becomes established of itself. This position, as Talcott Parsons pointed out, implies that capitalism "needs no specific propelling force—if it consists merely in rational conduct why should it?" This he regards as the "orthodox Anglo-Saxon view of economic history."[8]

Indeed, even if one reads the changes brought about by the rise of a money economy negatively, the essential terms of the analysis do not change. Rather than arguing that individuals are now free to determine their own economic fates for themselves, with a consequent increase in innovative entrepreneurialism and technological development, we could instead, in a quasi-Marxist way, describe these changes in terms of the infection of personal relations with the cash nexus, the subjection of natural value to the relentless commodification of the market, and the process by which the worker, who under feudalism was either himself part of the means of production or, better yet, possessed them, becomes alienated from his own labor. But such a neo-Smithian Marxism, as it has been cogently termed, still sees the agency of economic and social transformation as the town-based market economy—and still stigmatizes the country as a regressive brake upon the productive forces.[9]

In fact, political interests quite apart, the idea that the dynamic of late medieval society can be understood in terms of the opposition between a feudal natural economy and a capitalist money economy has been for many years under attack by medieval historians. Over forty years ago, M. M. Postan

called the rise of the money economy "one of the residuary hypotheses of economic history: a *deus ex machina* to be called upon when no other explanation
is available"—cautionary words that have had too little impact upon literary
critics.[10] Similarly oversimple is the notion that the changes in late medieval
English society can be understood as a struggle between progressive urban
centers dominated by a mobile bourgeoisie and free citizenry and, ranged
against them, a hierarchical and static rural feudalism dominated by a conservative nobility and church. It is clear, for example, that the agrarian economy
was thoroughly monetized and exchange-oriented throughout the Middle
Ages, that peasant society had been for many centuries highly stratified and
differentiated, and that there existed since at least the twelfth century a vigorous, monetized, and even credit-based peasant land market, a market for
agricultural wage labor, and small-scale but essential rural industry and commodity production.[11] Similarly, both lay and ecclesiastical landlords were
engaged in sophisticated techniques of estate management and in the calcula-
tive pursuit of profit-maximization, many members of the seigneurial class
were deeply involved in the world of international trade, and even the quintessential noble activity of warfare was pervaded with the values of the cash
nexus. Finally, the notion that medieval cities were "non-feudal islands in a
feudal sea"—while pointing to an important truth—can too easily be exaggerated.[12] If in theory *Stadtluft machts frei,* in practice a city like London
tightly restricted access to citizenship, while civic life as a whole was dominated by a conservative merchant patriciate that imposed upon the city much
the same structure of dominance and subordination as was in force across the
feudal world as a whole.

It has been argued that what this revisionary history demonstrates is
that feudalism was really capitalism writ small, that the full-scale capitalist
development that took place from the sixteenth century forward was the realization of processes that were always present and that simply required technological developments and shifts in attitudes to bring about their triumph.[13] This is, of course, simply a variant on the Whig thesis that
capitalism represents the natural condition of economic man. Its only true
alternative is that offered by Marxist historians—Maurice Dobb, Rodney
Hilton, and Robert Brenner are the central figures—for whom the key component of *all* nonsocialist economies is the governing classes' exploitation of
the producers in order to extract surplus value.[14] These historians understand
feudalism not simply as an inefficient means by which the individual seeks to
fulfill his economic destiny but as a mode of production characterized by the
direct rather than indirect exploitation of labor by the ruling classes. Similarly,
markets—and the cities that developed around them—represent not an
alternative to the feudal mode of production but, given the need of the
exploiting class to extract surplus value in the form of money, an element necessary for the proper functioning of the feudal economy.[15] For Marx,
medieval merchant capital was never itself progressive or transformative but

remained parasitic upon the truly productive forces of society—forces that had always been and (until at least the eighteenth century) remained agricultural.[16] In sum, the prime mover in feudal society was thus not proto-capitalist trade but the growing surplus value that the landowning class was able to extract from the agrarian economy. Thus it is that contemporary medieval historians have discovered, to cite the title of Brenner's highly influential article, "The Agrarian Roots of European Capitalism"—a discovery that sees the agricultural sector as being the locus for Marx's "really revolutionizing path" of transition by which the producer becomes himself a capitalist.[17]

Understanding economic life in terms of class struggle, these historians have argued that what brought about the collapse of feudalism, and the transition to capitalism, was the growing ability of the late medieval peasant to withhold surplus value and turn it to his own economic interests. Thus they have followed Marx's lead in describing the period 1350 to 1450 as the golden age of the English peasant. As Hilton has pointed out. "Medieval peasants were quite capable, in economic terms, of providing for themselves without the intervention of any ruling class. In this they differed from ancient slaves, and from modern wage workers who have to work on the means of production in order to gain their living."[18] Since it always possessed (even if it did not yet own) the means of production, when the medieval peasantry developed sufficient strength to resist the grossest forms of seigneurial exaction it was able to retain the surplus value of the agrarian economy, which had up to this time been appropriated by the ruling classes. Hilton describes the results in the following terms:

> Between 1350 and 1450 . . . we find that relative land abundance was combined, for various reasons, with a relaxation of seigneurial domination and a notable lightening of the economic burden on the peasant economy. Peasant society, in spite of still existing within (in broad terms) a feudal framework, developed according to laws of motion internal to itself. The village community was dominated by the richer peasant families, who ran the manorial court in its jurisdictional, punitive and land-registration functions. The limits on rents and services were firmly fixed well below what the lords wanted.[19]

Hence, concludes Hilton, "it is possible that the century after the Black Death was the golden age of the middle rather than of the rich peasantry (the yeoman)."[20] But it is also the case that this rural economy is the seedbed for later capitalist development. As Dobb points out, and as Hilton and Brenner have shown in detail, "It is then from the petty mode of production (in the degree to which it secures independence of action, and social differentiation in turn develops within it) that capitalism is born."[21]

The effect of these arguments is to present a very different picture of late medieval English society from what we are used to seeing. Rather than the merchant class and the city functioning as the agents for change, they are to be understood as dependent upon an ever more profligate and financially insecure seigneurial class.[22] Conversely, however, the agricultural economy remains strong, but always at a local level: while the increased agricultural productivity of the postplague years does not, because of the decline in demand, lead to a substantial increase in money income, the small agricultural producers are able to keep more of their product and to expand their holdings, an expansion that takes place at the expense of both the large landholders and, on the other side, of their less successful peasant neighbors. It is thus the *rural* sector of the economy that is dynamic, and the solvent of feudal relations is neither merchant capital nor the trading activity it finances but a vigorous peasant economy, with the crucial element in the collapse of feudalism being peasant resistance to the seigneurial extraction of surplus profit. What we have, then, to conclude this discussion with a schematic description, is a feverish consumer boom in luxury goods masking irreparable structural weaknesses and set against a powerful, self-confident peasant economy—a self-confidence visible throughout the later medieval period and nowhere more dramatically than in the rising of 1381.

One clear effect of this account upon our understanding of Chaucer is that it should encourage us to dispense with the notion of the poet as ideologically free-floating. To begin with, the distinction between noble and bourgeois, feudal and urban, while real and visible, cannot be drawn as sharply as this kind of description requires. On the contrary, both sets of values, however different one from the other, are *together* part of the hegemonic ideology that dominates late medieval English society; and both are to be set against the largely inarticulate but nonetheless insistent pressure of rural commodity production and the political resistance it spawned. The crucial ideological distinction, in other words, is not between the seigneurial nobility and the urban merchant class but between both of these elements of the exploiting class, on the one hand, and on the other the increasingly independent and self-sufficient productive classes in the country.

The unity of the ruling classes, whether seigneurial or mercantile, is especially visible in the case of Chaucer himself. Far from being simply an ordinary London citizen, Chaucer was in fact the son of one of the members of the mercantile patriciate who controlled the city, a privileged position that is certainly reflected in his early entrance into the household of the Duchess of Ulster and in his successful career within the courts of Edward III, of John of Gaunt, and of Richard II. Moreover, as one of Richard's royal servants the poet did not, as is usually assumed, disclaim any interest or role in politics; on the contrary, he was very much the king's man in the crucial Parliament of 1386, suffered for his allegiance when the king's party failed, and was finally rewarded for his loyalty when the king regained power in 1389.[23] In other words, to see Chaucer as somehow caught between two worlds and therefore free of both is both to misunderstand the structure of late medieval English society and to underestimate the strength of the poet's political commitments, whether freely chosen or not. What this ultimately means, then, is that whatever signs of a turning away from the dominant ideology we recognize in the *Canterbury Tales*—and I believe there are a great many—should be understood not as a function of the instinctive pull of a natural origin (Chaucer returning to his bourgeois roots) but as a conscious and deliberate decision. Moreover, given the fact that the most powerful alternative to this dominance was embodied in a rebellious peasantry which we might expect Chaucer to have regarded with little natural sympathy, we can anticipate that any turn toward alternative values will be marked with a powerful ambivalence.

It is my argument that the *Canterbury Tales* stages Chaucer's rejection of the cultic values of the courtly world in explicitly political terms with the Miller's *quiting* of the Knight. But this embrace of peasant self-confidence is immediately registered as threatening, and the subsequent development of the *Tales* serves to contain this threat—a containment that is accomplished first by the Wife of Bath, with her privileging of a socially undetermined (and politically inert) subjectivity, and then in the complementary tales of the Friar and Summoner, in which peasant self-assertiveness is both dissipated into internecine squabbling among ecclesiastical agents and appropriated, at the end of the Summoner's Tale, by seigneurial authority. In the first eight of the *Canterbury Tales* the break from social orthodoxy is staged not once but twice. If the order of the best manuscript tradition is correct (and I believe that recent scholarship has shown that it is), then the first eight tales fall into the following pattern:[24]

I: Knight	II: Man of Law
Monk interrupted by	Parson interrupted by
Miller	Wife of Bath
Reeve	Friar
Cook [unfinished]	Summoner

With the choice of the Knight as the first tale-teller, the initial movement of the *Tales* begins by affirming the conservative social ideology of the three estates that has already governed, in however qualified a fashion, the articulation of the portraits in the General Prologue. Yet when Harry Bailly—true to his name—tries to enforce this repressive ideology by turning next to the Monk, the Miller interrupts, initiating a countermovement of *fabliaux* revelry that comes to a precipitous halt with the Cook's shameful anecdote. Then the process starts again, now with the Man of Law as the voice of orthodoxy, an orthodoxy with which Chaucer associates his earlier, now discarded poetic self by having this agent of the ruling classes be an admirer of the *Legend of Good Women*. After the Man of Law's Tale of the saintly and long-suffering daughter of the Emperor of Rome (derived from a chronicle written originally for one of the daughters of Edward I), Harry Bailly attempts to continue this comfortable line of development by turning to the apolitical Parson. Yet now the Wife of Bath interrupts, initiating a line of development that will continue without interruption until the definitive cancellation of the *Canterbury Tales* finally accomplished by the long-deferred Parson.

The important point for our purposes is to recognize that the agents of the break—the Miller and the Wife of Bath—are in both cases representatives not of the bourgeois mercantile world of the cash nexus, but rather of the aggressive rural economy that was threatening seigneurial/mercantile dominance. And the next question that arises is, why does the interruption succeed in the second case while it fails in the first? The answer to this question is, I believe, political: in the first case the challenge is class-determined and as a result too explicitly threatening, while in the second it is deflected into a traditional mode of ideological opposition—that is, into promoting the claims of a socially undetermined subjectivity that stands apart from *all* forms of class consciousness. In other words, Chaucer begins by posing his opposition to the dominant ideology in terms of class antagonism, but then retreats by setting up as his privileged category subjectivity per se, the free-floating individual whose needs and satisfactions stand outside any social structure— in short, the transhistorical being that criticism has traditionally taken Chaucer himself to be. And while we may see this move as politically timid, it is nonetheless crucial to Chaucer's subsequent dominance of our literary tradition. For it is as the great champion of the individual that Chaucer has displaced his more politically explicit rivals (like Gower and, especially, Langland—both of whom haunt the *Canterbury Tales* as rejected possibilities) and has established himself as the Father of English Poetry.

In choosing as his initial agent of disruption a miller, Chaucer is opening his poem to one of the major areas of discontent in medieval rural society. The millsoke—the toll paid by peasants who were required to have their grain ground at the seigneurial mill—was not only a significant source of income for the landlord but a bitterly resented imposition upon the rural producer and a central focus of peasant resistance to seigneurial authority. In the summarizing words of Marc Bloch,

> There were occasions when milling stones were seized by the lord's officials in the very houses of the owners and broken in pieces; there were insurrections on the part of housewives; there were lawsuits which grimly pursued their endless and fruitless course, leaving the tenants always the losers. The chronicles and monastic cartularies of the thirteenth and fourteenth centuries are full of the noise of these quarrels.[25]

That the disruptive energy with which Chaucer endows his Miller derives from this general condition seems clear, but the particular role that millers played in the struggle for peasant independence remains enigmatic. While there is evidence that suggests that millers were sometimes agents of seigneurial control, there are also indications that they were themselves part of the resistant village community, underlings who had their own grievances. So too, that millers stole is confirmed by both numerous documents and popular reputation, but were their victims primarily the peasants or the lord? Similarly, we do not really know how relatively prosperous millers were. There is some evidence to support the widespread opinion that "the miller was commonly one of the most considerable men in the village,"[26] and the sharp decline in mill rents in the postplague period suggests that millers were, like the other members of the peasant community, able to drive better bargains with mill-owners—a sign of growing strength that doubtless contributed to their unpopularity. Not coincidentally, millers were included in the various Statutes of Labourers whose fees the government sought to control. But other evidence suggests that, on the contrary, some millers suffered from both a degraded social status and economic disability. In sum, the evidence is contradictory—a contradiction that itself finds telling expression in the Miller's Tale.

But one thing we do know for certain is that millers were participants in the Peasants' Revolt of 1381. One John Fillol, for instance, a miller from Hanningfield, Essex, was hanged for his part in the revolt, and the records indicate that other millers played a prominent role.[27] Furthermore, if names are any indication of occupation, it is significant that a John Millere of London was charged with being one of those who stole wine from the Vintry, another John Meller of Ulford was hung and his goods confiscated, and the eloquent leader of the rebels at St. Albans was William Grindecobbe.[28] Moreover, when the rebels of Bury St. Edmonds beheaded John Cavendish, a king's justice who had enforced the Statute of Labourers with particular severity, the executioner was named Matthew Miller; given both the physical strength of millers and their reputation for violence, the name seems likely here to coincide with vocation.[29]

Most important, however, is the fact that the peasants themselves seem to have seen the figure of the miller as capable of embodying both their grievances and their desire for an almost apocalyptic reckoning. Two of John Ball's famous letters refer specifically to an allegorized miller:

> Johan the Mullere hath ygrownde smal, smal, smal;
> The Kyngis sone of heuene shalle pay for alle.
> Be war or ye be wo;
> Knoweth ʒour frend fro ʒoure foo,
> Haueth ynowe and seyth "Hoo":
> And do welle and bettre, and fleth synne,
> And seketh pees and holde therynne.

Jakke Mylner asketh help to turne hys mylne aright. He hath grounden smal smal; the kings sone of heven he schal pay for alle. Loke thy mylne go aright, with the foure sayles, and the post stande in stedfastnesse. With ryght and with myght, with skyl and with wylle, lat myght helpe ryght, and skyl go before wille and ryght before myght, than goth oure mylne aryght. And if myght go before ryght, and wylle before skylle, than is oure mylne mys adyght.[30]

No doubt there is a scriptural subtext to these threatening words (see, for example, Matt. 21:44, Luke 20:18), but they more immediately witness to the long history of peasant anger toward the seigneurial monopoly of the power of the mill—a power that the rebels of 1381 here seek to appropriate and turn to their own, retributive uses. Chaucer's Robin the Miller would have called such retribution *quiting,* and lest we think the analogy with John Ball's Jack the Miller is arbitrary, let us remember at the outset that Jack's message includes an ambiguous injunction—"Haueth y-now, and seith 'Hoo' "—that is also at the center of Robin's lesson:

> I have a wyf, pardee, as wel as thow;
> Yet nolde I, for the oxen in my plogh,
> *Take upon me more than ynogh.* . . .
> So he may fynde Goddes foyson there,
> Of the remenant nedeth nat enquere.[31]
>
> (3158–66)

Part of the peasant's claim to freedom, and what sets him apart from the extortionate lord who would bind him, is that he understands the natural fitness of things and knows when he has (and when he has had) enough.

There is thus a specifically political appropriateness to the fact that the Miller's Tale is a narrative staging of the vitality and resourcefulness of the natural world. In part, these values are embodied in Alisoun, whose vernal beauty serves to elicit the male desire that motivates the Tale. All three of the men attempt, with varying degrees of success, to constrain her to their needs: John holds "hire narwe in cage, / For she was wylde and yong, and he was old" (3224–25); to Absolon she is a prey to be caught—"if she hadde been a mous, / And he a cat, he wolde hire hente anon" (3346–47); and if Nicholas does manage to seize her, it is only for a moment: "she sproong as a colt dooth in the trave, / And with hir heed she wryed faste awey" (3282–83). Yet the Miller's Tale does not articulate a simple opposition between natural freedom and social constraint; on the contrary, it presents this opposition as itself mediated by a moderation that bespeaks a calm confidence in the just workings of natural law. The Tale everywhere displays an apparently flawless orderliness: not only does the random aimlessness of the plot reveal itself to be ordered by an exquisite logic, but the unthinking hedonism of the action leads to judgments of an impeccable exactness. The dandified Absolon suffers a scatological humiliation, the too-clever Nicholas—who "thoughte he wolde amenden al the jape" (3799)—becomes himself the butt of a jape executed by his intended victim, and the arrogantly know-nothing John is victimized by his violation of the natural law that "man sholde wedde his simylitude" (3228). Compared to the moral anarchy over which the Knight has (however unwittingly) presided, the Miller's Tale articulates a world of perfect moral sense. Although the Miller's ludic festivity bursts into the pilgrimage with rude insistence, it contains its own self-regulation: to attempt to control it is at once unavailing and unnecessary. The natural and the supernatural are in perfect harmony, the Tale tells us, and the "belle of laudes" (3655) that rings while the lovers are enjoying their sexual frolics harmonizes the "melodye" (3652) in Alisoun's and Nicholas's bed of love with the song of the friars in the chantry. The result is an unstinted hymn of praise: "what wol ye bet than weel?" (3370).

Criticism has traditionally read this claim as either an end in itself—an effect of the benign naturalism of the *fabliau*—or as an expression of the Miller's philosophical naiveté and spiritual culpability.[32] But in fact, I believe, the Miller's celebration of the natural—as a world of beauty, as a source of glad animal spirits, and (most important) as a principle of order—is best understood as a political statement that is consistent with the deeply political nature of the Tale as a whole.[33] Criticism has shown how the Tale launches a pointed attack upon the chivalric ideology so thoroughly, and critically, represented in the Knight's Tale. The heroic *Theseus artifex* is here represented by John the carpenter, his astrological credulity inciting him, to his cost, to pry into "Goddes pryvetee" (3454, 3558), just as Theseus's hubric oratories invoked planetary gods who then brought disasters down upon the world that worshipped them; and in its largest sense, the Tale teaches a lesson about the impossibility of constraining either people or events to the kind of overmastering will that characterizes chivalry. Similarly, Nicholas and Absolon travesty two forms of the chivalric love ethic that underwrites the Knight's Tale: Nicholas is the predatory seducer who deploys the forms of courtly wooing in order to gratify his appetites, Absolon the narcissistic, inefficient dandy who plays at lovemaking without understanding how to do it. And here too the critique is not only mocking, but includes as well a sharp sense of grievance: in directing their attentions to Alisoun, after all, Nicholas and Absolon seek to enact a characteristically seigneurial appropriation: "She was a prymerole, a piggesnye, / For any lord to leggen in his bedde, / Or yet for any good yeman to wedde" (3268–70).

Yet it is not only or even primarily the seigneurial class that is the target of the Miller's *quiting*. If the representations of Nicholas and Absolon serve to mock and subvert the Knight's chivalric culture, they are also vehicles for an attack upon an ecclesiastical establishment that is perceived as equally overbearing and exploitative; and given the fact, as Hilton has pointed out, that "the great ecclesiastical landlords [were] notorious for their bad relations with their tenants," the anticlericalism of the Tale, as of medieval peasant movements as a whole, is not to be wondered at.[34] To be sure, in the figure of the inefficient Absolon, a parish clerk who puts on snobbish airs, theatrically displays (in his role as Herod) a ferocity he clearly lacks in life, and laughably deforms the biblical text for seductive purposes, the Miller's critique is essentially mocking and contemptuous. But even here more than mockery is at issue. For by having Absolon use the Song of Songs as his text the Miller is calling attention to a tradition of interpretation in which the coercive manipulation inherent in the institution of biblical exegesis is particularly visible. As the frequency with which it was interpreted suggests (it was by far the most commonly interpreted book of the Bible throughout the Middle Ages), the Song of Songs was an especially provocative text to medieval exegetes, challenging them to rewrite a Hebrew love song into the dogmatic terms of church doctrine. And yet, implies the Miller, if their fascination bespeaks an awareness of the Song's destabilizing potential, it also witnesses to an unacknowledged pleasure in its seductive literality, a literality that Absolon here turns precisely to the purposes of seduction.[35] In other words, the Miller is arguing that Absolon's misuse of the Song of Songs is a characteristically clerical misappropriation: what exegetes typically do *to* the Song of Songs, Absolon here seeks to do to Alisoun *by means of* the Song of Songs.

If in the figure of Absolon clerical *dominium* is revealed as hypocritically self-regarding and yet comically ineffective, in the figure of Nicholas the ecclesiast is represented as a far more proficient manipulator. Here the instruments of manipulation are other forms of clerical culture—astrology, to be sure, but also, and most tellingly, the mystery plays to which allusion is made throughout the Tale. For it is Nicholas who stages the entire production, using as his primary text the Noah play.[36] It is the appropriateness of this choice that I wish to examine. In one sense, since the play focuses on the theme of *maistrye* in the relationship of Noah to his wife, the play has a natural affinity for "maister Nicholay" (3437, 3579)—who, as his unnecessarily elaborate plot shows, is seeking not just to seduce Alisoun but to demonstrate in particularly spectacular fashion his superiority over "men that swynke" (3491).[37] But it has as well, I believe, another, deeper relevance to the political dynamic that controls the Miller's Tale, the exploration of which will return us to the question of peasant consciousness and the nature of nature.

When Richard II revoked his charters of manumission and suppressed the rebellion, he told the peasants, "Rustics you were and rustics you are still; you will remain in bondage, not as before but incomparably harsher."[38] Behind these chilling words lies what Rodney Hilton calls "the caste interpretation of peasant status"—the idea that serfdom is a permanent condition of moral inferiority inherent in the peasant's very being rather than a social status capable of being both assumed and (at least in theory) left behind. The common medieval opinion that the grossly inequitable political order was a consequence of man's sinful nature, while implying a passive acquiescence in injustice, was not in a crudely direct way an instrument to enforce specific class interests: for Augustine, the distinction between Cain, the founder of the *civitas terrena* (in which we all live) and Abel, the precursor of Christ and thus founder of the *civitas Dei* (to which we all aspire), was less historical than moral and spiritual, an opposition fought out within the soul of each Christian.[39] But later writers gave the distinction a specific social instantiation: as one late medieval cleric misleadingly claimed, "Augustine said that the miserable calamity of bondage hath reasonably been brought into the world because of the demerits of the peoples, so that bondage is now fitly rooted among peasants and common folk."[40] And this distinction could then be scripturally authorized by identifying Abel as the father of all nobility, Cain—the *agricola* of Gen. 4:2—as the first *servus*.[41] The ultimate effect of this line of argument was not only to explain the peasant's subjection as a function of his sinfulness but to define the peasant as in effect belonging to another order of being, as a member of a different race, a nonhuman. Hence when Gower says, in book 5 of the *Vox clamantis,* that the peasantry "is a race without power of reason, like beasts," he is repeating a ubiquitous vilification—the peasant is an animal—in order to characterize the peasantry as a race of subhuman creatures whose fallen nature requires subjection.[42]

It was this definition of serfdom as an intrinsic and permanent condition of moral inferiority, and not simply as a social status that entailed certain economic disadvantages, that the 1381 rebels sought to efface. Froissart's well-known summary of the peasants' demands makes this abundantly clear:

> These unhappy people . . . said that they were kept in great servage, and in the beginning of the world, they said, there were no bondmen, wherefore they maintained that none ought to be bond without he did treason to his lord, as Lucifer did to God; but they said that they could have no such battle [*taille*] for they were neither angels nor spirits, but men formed to the similitude of their lords, saying why should they then be kept so under like beasts.[43]

As Hilton has said, the rebels "strove not merely for a reduction of rent but for human dignity."[44]

For all its comic tolerance, the Miller's Tale takes part in this struggle, and not least by subverting and mocking the very terms with which the reigning ideology sought to stigmatize and oppress peasants. For one thing, the Miller's witty, even elegant Tale—an achievement that even modern critics, who continue to wonder at the presence of so intelligent a Tale in the mouth of so obviously brutish a teller, have not been quite prepared to grant him—both proves that the peasant is not the inarticulate and brutal figure that hostile representations had depicted and establishes a countervailing set of values. In place of the Knight's paranoid insistence on the continual need for supervision and constraint, the Miller describes (as we have seen) a world that shatters all efforts at confinement but that nonetheless contains its own principle of equilibrium in a sense of natural fitness and decorum. In locating at the thematic center of his Tale a benign, virtually prelapsarian *lex naturalis,* the Miller is thus reversing the terms of antipeasant defamation. Far from being fallen and degraded, nature here serves as a beneficent and supportive principle; far from being in need of compensation by the *lex positiva* created by men, the *lex naturalis* is seen as providing an unerring standard. And what is striking is that the Miller's rehabilitation of nature as a principle of moral order is itself profoundly expressive of his class consciousness. For he promotes a view of the natural world that was—so far as we can tell from the fragmentary evidence—common to peasant movements throughout the late Middle Ages. That nature provides a self-evident norm of fairness, an originary and still authoritative principle of equality, is implicit in the famous couplet of 1381, "Whan Adam dalf, and Eve span / Wo was thanne a gentilman?"[45] And in their political program the rebels sought to return England to a similarly prelapsarian condition, in which both a people's monarchy and a people's church could subsist without any intervening hierarchy. Furthermore, both here and throughout the Middle Ages, one of the goals of peasant resistance was to achieve access to the bounty of the natural world—the woods, fish and game—that they felt was theirs by right of being natural creatures like their lords. In sum, stigmatized by their opponents as beings who expressed with special and culpable directness the fallenness of nature— "they so till the earth, they are so utterly earthly, that we may truly say of them: They shall lick the earth and eat it," as one particularly vicious prelate put it, while an English celebrant of peasant humility described them as "grobbyng aboute the erthe"[46]—peasants not only accepted this "natural" identity but redeemed it by insisting, like the Miller in his Tale, upon nature's essential goodness.[47]

Far from being the result of either misguided optimism or spiritual turpitude, then, the Miller's rehabilitation of nature is part of a political program that turns against the governing classes one of its own instruments of ideological control. The same thing can be said about his use of the Noah story. We have already seen how the distinction between Cain and Abel was used as an aristocratic *Gründungsage* to justify the subjection of the peasant. The story of Noah was upon occasion used for the same purpose. When human history was refounded after the flood, the original division of peoples established by Cain and Abel now became a threefold distinction to be drawn among Noah's three sons, Japhet, Ham, and Shem. Once again, a distinction that for patristic writers existed at the level of the spiritual and ecclesiastical life became defined in the later Middle Ages in terms of social opposition. The first writer to make this definition explicit was, it seems, Honorius of Autun in his *De imagine mundi* (1133):

At this time humankind was divided into three: into freemen, knights, and serfs [*servos*]. Freemen [are descended] from Shem, knights from Japhet, serfs from Ham.[48]

Ham's subjection was to be explained by the curse laid upon Ham's son Canaan by Noah when Ham mocked his drunken father's nakedness: "Cursed be Canaan, a servant of servants [*servus servorum*] shall he be unto his brethren" (Gen. 9:25). As exegetes had always insisted, Ham was of the race of Cain, and now this text identified that race with the *servi* who were so visible a part of medieval life. Needless to say, any argument that stigmatizes the vast majority of the population as damned beyond redemption—"curssed uppon þe grounde," as the York play put it—can hardly enter the mainstream of medieval political thought.[49] Yet there is evidence that, despite its exorbitance, this identification of the cursed Ham with rustics did achieve considerable currency. The popular *Cursor mundi,* first written in about 1300 and then rewritten into two other versions, appended to the usual geographical distribution of Noah's sons (Shem to Asia, Ham to Africa, and Japhet to Europe) Honorius's social analysis:

> Kny3t & þral and fre man
> Of þese þre briþeren bigan:
> Of Sem fre mon, of Iapheth kny3t,
> þral of Cam, waryed wi3te.[50]

More significant is the very popular *Liber de moribus hominum et officiis nobilium ac popularium super ludo scachorum,* written in the early fourteenth century by Jacobus de Cessolis and in the course of the century translated at least twice into French and then later four times into German and once (by Caxton) into English. For de Cessolis not only enforces the identification of peasants as members of the race of Cain, but he uses the story of Ham's mockery to introduce a discussion of the four kinds of drunkenness (like a lion, a lamb, a swine, and an ape), a vice that is then associated with the laborer and seen as a spur to social disturbance: wines (in Caxton's translation) "make the poure [man] riche as longe as the wyn is in his hed and shortly dronkenshyp is the begynnynge of alle euylles."[51]

But the text that is most interesting in terms of the Miller's Tale is the *Liber armorum,* a brief treatise on heraldry included in the early fifteenth-century *Boke of Seynt Albans,* a compilation that draws throughout upon much earlier materials.[52] For here the antipeasant myth of Ham is not only deployed in a way that makes its relevance to the Miller's Tale evident but that suggests that its late medieval currency was a response to the debate about the nature of serfdom that was at the center of the class struggle taking place in fourteenth-century England. The *Liber armorum* begins by demonstrating "how gentilmen shall be knowyn from vngentill men and how bondeage began first" specifically in order to counter peasant claims of natural equality:

> A bonde man or a churle wyll say, "All we be cummyn of Adam." So Lucifer with his cumpany may say, "All we be cummyn of heuyn."[53]

For Lucifer and his rebel angels were the first group to be placed in bondage, followed by Cain, who was damned by God and by Adam for his fratricide: "By that did Cayn become a chorle and all his ofspryng after hym" (cci[v]). Noah was descended from Abel's son Seth, and he in turn

> had .iii. sonnys begetyn by kynde; by the modre .ii. were named Cham and Sem and by the fadre the thirde was namyd Jafeth. Yit in theys .iii. sonnys gentilnes and vngentilnes was founde. In Cham vngentilnes was founde to his owne fadre, dooun to discuver his preuytes and laugh his fadre to scorne. Jafeth was the yongist and repreued his brodre. Than like a gentilman, take mynde of Cham: for his vngentilnes he was become a chorle and had the cursyng of God and his fadre Noe. And whan Noe awoke he sayde to Cham his sonne, "Knowyst nott thow how hit become of Cayn, Adam['s] soon, and of his churlish blode? All the worlde is drownde saue we .viii. And now of the to begynne vngentilnes and a cause to destroye vs all—vppon the hit shall be and so I pray to God that it shall fall. Now to the I gyuve my curse, wycked kaytife for euer, and I gyuve to the the north parte of the worlde to draw thyn habitacion, for ther shall it be where [are] sorow and care, colde and myschef. As a churle thow shalt haue . . . the thirde parte of the worlde, wich shall be calde Europe, that is to say the contre of churlys." (ci[v]–cii[r])

Nothing could more vividly illustrate the writer's sense of contemporary urgency than his (or her) willingness to override the traditional geographical endowments. Far from being exiled to distant Africa, the damned race of Ham is ubiquitously present in the here and now of late medieval Europe, a presence that requires the gentle reader to learn, for his own self-protection, the way "to deseuer Gentilnes from vngentilnes" (ci[r]).[54] Finally, lest we doubt the currency of this identification of the serf with Canaan and the children of Ham, we actually find a somewhat confused reference to it in that most orthodox of late-fourteenth-century texts, Chaucer's Parson's Tale: "This name of thraldom was nevere erst kowth til that Noe seyde that his sone Canaan sholde be thral to his bretheren for his synne" (X, 765).[55]

What the Miller's Tale does, then, is to turn the myth of Ham against the clerical culture from which it originally arose. For here the searcher into hidden "pryvetee," far from being a peasant, is instead the astrologer-cleric Nicholas, who uses his illicit knowledge to mock and scorn John the Carpenter, the father Noah of the play he is staging. Moreover, the characteristics that are ascribed to the biblical Ham by medieval clerical culture are here applied, with striking aptness, to Nicholas. Ham's name means, according to the commentators, *calidus,* and he embodies a spirit that is *impatiens, inquietus,* and *commotior.*[56] Moreover, he represents, according to Augustine's authoritative exegesis.

> those who boast the name of Christian and yet live scandalous lives. For it is certain that such people proclaim Christ's passion, symbolized by Noah's nakedness, in their professions, while they dishonour it by their evil actions. It was of such people that we read in Scripture, "You will recognize them by their fruits."[57]

Most centrally, Ham is the heretic who reveals that which ought to remain a mystery, the *corporis mysterium* enacted in the passion and reenacted in the Eucharist: he "makes manifest that which was for the prophets a secret," and with this illicit knowledge he "deceives the simple"—the sort of "lewed man," like John, "That noght but oonly his bileve kan."[58] As John succinctly says, with (as we know from his prologue) the Miller's approval, "Men sholde nat knowe of Goddes pryvetee" (3454–56). The relevance of these characteristics to the Miller's Nicholas is self-evident. In effect, Nicholas's play seeks to reaffirm the superiority of the cleric over the despised rustic—a superiority given mocking expression in a widespread clerical "prayer" that serves as virtually the blueprint for the Miller's Tale:

> O God, who brought forth a multitude of rustics and sowed great discord between them and us, grant, we beseech, that we may live off their labors and enjoy their wives.[59]

But what the Tale actually does is to outparody the parodists: in a way that strikingly prefigures the Wife of Bath's performance, the Miller turns the materials of clerical culture against its proprietors, revealing by his dazzling act of cultural criticism how defamatory are their misrepresentations.

Yet we must also recognize that the Miller's Tale, in its animosity toward John the Carpenter, contains as well an act of peasant self-criticism. In part, we have here an expression of the stresses and strains within the peasant community itself: John is a "riche gnof," and Robin represents himself in the Tale as a servant boy who can be packed off to London and (so John at least thinks) to death by drowning without a second thought. So that while others may have thought of millers as powerful and prosperous—hence the antimiller literature—the Miller thinks of himself otherwise, as a dependent and unregarded *famulus.* But the Miller's scorn for John has also a deeper political meaning. Despite being a successful village craftsman, John not only allows himself to be intimidated by his lodger but has, by marrying the youthful Alisoun, violated a natural law that he, of all people, ought to understand; and when the Miller says that John married Alisoun because "he knewe nat Catoun, for his wit was rude" (3227), he is mockingly invoking an *auctoritas* to support a truth that ought to be self-evident to the truly natural man.[60] As Langland put it, "kynde wit" is the companion of the commons and teaches "ech lif to knowe his owene."[61] Moreover, and more reprehensively, he has also betrayed his class interests by handing himself over to a smooth-talking clerical con man.

Thus it is John who is most severely punished at the end of the Miller's Tale: his wife is "swyved," his arm is broken, and his reputation as a man of probity is ruined. Yet even here, significantly enough, the Miller cannot finally withhold his sense that this punishment, however merited, is nonetheless enacted in the distasteful form of class victimization:

> The folk gan laughen at his fantasye;
> Into the roof they kiken and they cape,
> And turned *al his harm unto a jape.*
> For what so that this carpenter answerde,
> It was for noght; *no man his reson herde.*
> With othes grete he was so sworn adoun
> That *he was holde wood* in al the toun;
> For *every clerk anonright heeld with oother.*
> They seyde, *"The man is wood,* my leeve brother";
> And every wight gan laughen at this stryf.
>
> (3840–49)

Before beginning to rehearse the Miller's Tale, a nervous narrator had warned the "gentils" "nat [to] maken ernest of game" (3186); now at the end the Miller reverses the terms—and meaning—of the warning: when a group of clerks turn "al [a rustic's] harm unto a jape," more is at issue than simple comedy. The point is not just that the clerks band together against the rich artisan—an opposition that figures not just the traditional medieval antagonism between clerks and peasants but also, in an oblique but nonetheless historically corroborated fashion, the larger conflict between the classes that was the central social phenomenon of Chaucer's England. Rather, it is that the terms the Miller uses here to represent the carpenter's oppression bear a powerfully political valence and force us to attend to the class consciousness to which the Tale gives witness. The clerks do not here merely silence John's arguments—"no man his reson herde"—but deny him rationality itself. In twice insisting that the clerks considered John mad, the Miller is again invoking a terminology typical of medieval commentators (most of them, of course, clerics) on peasant behavior. And this madness is nowhere more visible than when the peasant seeks to promote his own interests. For the early-fourteenth-century chronicler of the Abbey of Vale Royal, the "bestial men of Rutland" who had recourse to the courts and the King in a vain effort to prove that they were not the Abbot's serfs were *rabicanes*—mad dogs.[62] And as we should perhaps expect, the chroniclers of the Peasants' Revolt consistently use the language of insanity to describe the rebels. For Walsingham, the Revolt as a whole is an expression of the *insania nativorum*—the madness of bondmen—and his account is saturated with terms like *dementes, irrationi-bile,* and *stulti* and invokes throughout the language of satanic possession: the rebels are *ganeones daemoniaci* (children of the devil), perhaps even *pejores dae-monibus* (worse than devils).[63] Gower also describes the Revolt as an expression of bestial madness: the rebels "were swine into which a cursed spirit had entered, just as Holy Writ tells of," and "just as the Devil was placed in command over the army of the lower world, so this scoundrel [Wat Tyler] was in charge of the wicked mob."[64] And even less vindictive observers invoke the language of madness and folly: a relatively disinterested macaronic poet calls the rebels "folus" and *stultes,* Knighton calls them *stultes* and refers to them as servants of the devil, Froissart compares them to devils from hell, and the monk of Westminster reinvokes *rabicanes.*[65]

"The man is *wood,*" say the clerks about John when he tries to tell "his reson"—a designation important enough that the Miller first invokes it in his own voice and then has the clerks repeat it. As we shall in a moment see in detail, the use of the language of folly and demonic possession to describe peasant resistance surfaces again in the *Canterbury Tales:* the lord in the Summoner's Tale begins by assuming that the churl Thomas is a "fool" (2292) or—a term that is applied twice and implied once—a "demonyak" (2240, 2292; and cf. 2221). The point is that these are not simply terms of casual abuse, but are derived from the language of moral censure with which the governing classes of medieval Europe, and particularly of fourteenth-century England, tried to stigmatize, and so to control, peasant protest. In having the unified mockery of the clerics pervert John's "resons" into the irrationality of madness, then, the Miller's Tale offers a bitter commentary upon not just the Peasants' Revolt but upon the official language that sought to censor peasant resistance at the level of discourse as effectively as the instruments of government suppressed it politically.

In searching for an ideological posture by means of which to distance himself from the cultic and increasingly caste-defined aristocratic culture of his time, Chaucer almost inevitably turned to the most vigorous oppositional force within his society—the rural world of peasant culture. In the General Prologue the Miller is represented in the conventional terms of peasant caricature: he is grossly ugly, with a flat nose, a huge mouth, and swinishly red hairs that protrude from a wart and match a beard also red "as any sowe or fox"—in sum, a threatening figure of peasant animality who uses his head not for rational thought (of which peasants are in any case incapable) but to enact invasive acts of violence: "Ther was no dore that he nolde . . . breke it at a rennyng with his heed" (I, 550–51).[66] And when he then invades the tale-telling game, he displays two of the most characteristic of peasant vices—drunkenness and a contempt for order. The essential terms of the Miller's representation are thus not moral and psychological but social and political, and the consciousness articulated by his Tale is derived from the politics of late-medieval English society.

It is a consciousness, moreover, to which Chaucer grants remarkable scope and force, allowing it both to counter the oppressive hegemonic culture of the aristocracy and to subvert the language of class hatred promoted by certain forms of clerical discourse. Yet as we should expect, this authority is immediately, and severely, circumscribed. For as soon as the claims of peasant class consciousness are put forward they are countered. The Reeve's Tale accomplishes this subversion in two ways. One is to reveal the disunity within the peasant class itself, not simply by the antagonism between the Reeve and the Miller but by the Reeve's own betrayal of class interests. He is himself both an agent of seigneurial control, and has social ambitions: he began life as a carpenter, is now a reeve, and his dress and diction reveal his clerical ambitions.[67] In short, he shows that the social identity asserted by the Miller is a fiction, that there is no class unity among the peasantry but only individuals. The second point is that Chaucer endorses this position by requiring us to read the Reeve's Tale as the expression of an individual psyche. By a whole variety of means, which criticism has well analyzed, the Reeve's Tale expresses a meaning that is not political or social but psychological and spiritual, thus undoing the reversal accomplished by the Miller. And this assertion of the primacy of the individual serves, of course, to depoliticize the Tale by moving it from the realm of history to that of psychology.

The stigmatizing of the Miller's interruption is then carried to its inevitable conclusion in the Cook's Tale. Although he means to recoup the disruptive energies of the Miller's Tale, the Cook unwittingly reveals them to be not enlivening but destructive, not a necessary alternative to the hegemonic ideology of the Knight's Tale but a riotous excess that threatens the social order as a whole. Hence his fragmentary Tale is itself about degeneration followed by ejection: it tells of the apprentice Perkyn Revelour whose ludic festivity declines into criminal riot and leads to his explusion from his master's house. The principle that governs the action of this Tale is phrased by the Cook as a proverb: "Wel bet is roten appul out of hoord / Than that it rotie al the remenaunt" (4406–7), a principle that is then revealed to be relevant as well to his own performance, which is terminated before it can defile the *Tales* as a whole. In locating this social menace in the figure of the Cook, Chaucer is stigmatizing not only the urban wage laborers (the very group who scandalously welcomed the rebellious peasants when they invaded London in 1381), but the craft guilds whose representatives are presented, within the fiction of the General Prologue, as the Cook's employers.[68] In other words, in making the Cook the voice of lower-class criminality, a criminality sponsored, however unwittingly, by the small, relatively powerless craft guilds, Chaucer places his poetry in the service of the dominant merchant patriciate from which he himself originally derived.

How, then, is the second effort at escaping from the tyrannical embrace of the dominant ideology accomplished in the next group of tales? Now the role of the establishment previously filled by the Knight is played by the Man of Law, a sociologically appropriate choice given the ease with which lawyers entered into the world of the aristocracy.[69] Moreover, the Man of Law is both a familiar companion of merchants (he learned the tale he is now about to tell, he informs us, from them) and a reader of Chaucerian poetry and specifically of the *Legend of Good Women,* a text he cites in his Prologue and that provides the paradigm for the Tale of the saintly and long-suffering Constance he then tells. The Man of Law represents, in short, that earlier Chaucerian self that is now to be rejected. If we think of Chaucer as a man with mercantile social origins, whose economic security depends upon fulfilling ministerial functions for the king, and who may even have himself received legal training, then we can see the way in which the Man of Law's Tale scrutinizes, and ironically inflects, the very social identity that led Chaucer to retreat from the experiment of Fragment A. Conversely, the Wife of Bath, who now fills the role previously played by the Miller, is one of those rural commodity producers—specifically, one of the independent weavers who were springing up all over England with the sudden growth of the English cloth industry—who were contributing so heavily to the threatening strength of the agrarian economy.[70] The scene is thus set for a replay of the Knight-Miller confrontation.

Yet this is not quite what we get. On the contrary, just as the Reeve's Tale drained away the political meaning of the Miller's Tale by an act of privatization, so the Wife of Bath's performance accomplishes a similar internalization of value. To be sure, the issue now is not spiritual salvation but psychological wholeness, and the topic is not social ambition but marriage. But the Wife of Bath's *social* challenge as an independent, postfeudal commodity producer is here set aside. Unlike the Miller, she insists upon the rights not of her class but rather of her selfhood. It is subjectivity per se that she promotes, a subjectivity that Chaucer (like many medieval writers) associates both here and throughout his work with women.[71] In other words, in substituting for the political threat posed by the Miller the Wife of Bath's insistence upon the priority of the individual self, Chaucer makes what we have come to recognize as the characteristic liberal move. What the Wife wants is not, despite her truculent tone, political or social change; on the contrary, the traditional order is capable of both generating her independent selfhood and of accommodating the marital happiness that would accomplish its fulfillment. To be sure, to acknowledge that the basic unit of social life is a socially undetermined selfhood has crucial political implications—beginning with the recognition of the equality of all people—that carry the possibility (but by no means the necessity) of social change. And to see that the bearers of this message are women is also a political statement. But the direction in which the politics of the individual moves is opposed to that dictated by the class consciousness of the Miller: after all, the socially undetermined selfhood privileged by individualism is by definition already common property. Thus the Wife avoids the kind of economic transformations entailed by the Miller's antagonistic social consciousness—transformations that were in fact overtaking late-medieval England but that were prevented from coming to fulfillment by the final destruction of the peasant economy in the sixteenth and seventeenth centuries.

The successful completion of the subversive process initiated by the Wife of Bath is possible, therefore, because her opposition is generated from a position that does *not* correspond to the most vigorous oppositional forces at work in Chaucer's historical world. On the contrary, her invocation of the rights of the subject derives its force from a dense and widespread web of precedents found in earlier medieval writing. For precisely the familiarity of her challenge, however brilliantly innovative the form in which it is articulated, makes it appealing and useful to Chaucer. Moreover, the final two movements of this staged, four-act drama of rebellion—the Friar's and the Summoner's Tales—are also constructed from highly traditional materials that while, again, brilliantly reaccented, nonetheless remain comfortably within the settled structures of medieval social ideology. Just how comfortably can be briefly indicated by a final glance at the key member of this pair, the Summoner's Tale. This Tale plays here, in the *Canterbury Tales'* second movement, the role that fell to the disgraced and excluded Cook's Tale in the first movement. Far from being chastened by the apparent failure of Fragment A, then, Chaucer seems defiantly to return here to the churlish world of mockery and retaliation that was forced into the pilgrimage by the Miller's interruption, the world of *quiting* that came to such a bad end in the Cook's Tale. The Summoner's Tale enacts *quiting* to an almost quintessential degree: not only does the Tale retaliate against the pompous Friar by deploying all of the traditional antifraternal arguments, but it even mocks fraternal propaganda by subjecting it to merciless ridicule. *Quiting* is thus definitively recuperated, and in order to enforce the parallelism with Fragment A, Chaucer chooses as his spokesman for this recuperation the one other diseased pilgrim among the group, the scabrous Summoner whose inflamed face seems an appropriate counterpart to the disgusting "mormel" or ulcer that adorns the Cook's leg.

Now our question becomes truly pressing: why does Chaucer complete this process with the Summoner while he apparently felt himself unwilling to go forward with the Cook? If the argument of this paper is correct, the answer lies in the realm of politics. And in terms of the conditions of fourteenth-century life, the Cook and the Summoner do indeed represent two very different worlds. The Cook derives from the threatening urban proletariat that stands as the economic and ideological counterpart to the emergent rural producers—a degraded urban version, in other words, of the Miller—while the Summoner, for all his gross immorality, is part of the apparatus of social control imposed upon medieval society by the church.[72] The Summoner, like the Reeve, is a bailiff, although in this case for the archdeaconal court that punished various spiritual and moral offenses, especially sexual ones. In other words, as his agent of successful subversion Chaucer has chosen not a genuinely rebellious figure but instead a representative of one of the most repressive forces in medieval society. This conservatism is also thematized in the Tale itself. As is appropriate for its place within the *Tales* as a whole, the Summoner's Tale is a recuperation of the churlish irreverence introduced into the *Tales* by the Miller, and it tells how a pompous representative of clerical learning is undone by the churlish wisdom of his intended victim. Yet the very traditional nature of the Summoner's attack—its deployment of the well-worn topoi of antifraternal satire—functions to remove the Tale from the specific context of late-fourteenth-century English history. As Penn Szittya rightly says about antifraternalism, "The poets, like the polemicists before them, are writing less about the friars than about an idea about the friars, less about men they have seen begging on the streets in London than about numberless and placeless figures who are the sons of Cain and allies of Antichrist, men whose final significance lies not in history but at its End."[73] Moreover, Thomas's churlish triumph is displaced from the peasant locale in which it is initially enacted to a seigneurial context: after receiving his insult from Thomas, the friar retreats to the manor house, where the insult is completed by the squire. For one thing, then, the lines of social opposition are here drawn not along class lines (as in the Miller's Tale) but instead according to the traditional division of lay versus clerical. And for another, Thomas's churlish wit is revealed to be in need of a supplementary interpretation that can be provided only within the context of aristocratic play.

It is quite true, of course, that the Tale leads us to think that his gift always contained within it the wonderfully deflating meaning that the squire makes explicit, that—to put it crudely—the seigneurial class lives off the humor of its agricultural workers as well as off their labor. This is part of the recuperation of churlishness that the second four Tales seek to accomplish. Yet live off it they do, and nothing in the Tale suggests that this is an arrangement that can or should be called into question. Far from there being any question of peasant independence or class antagonism, the Summoner's Tale presents us with a rural world united in its opposition to the fraternal orders—orders that had originally, of course, preached a dangerously radical social message but that are now represented as hopelessly, laughably corrupt.[74] The true forces of social change abroad in Chaucer's historical world are thus definitively disarmed, and we retreat into a world of aesthetic appreciation, in which peasant energy, however potentially threatening, is reduced to a playful manipulation of the images of the official culture that leaves the realities firmly in place.

Yet even here Chaucer does not wholly suppress the political. On the contrary, it returns at the end of the Summoner's Tale in a passage that both recalls (as I have already suggested) the end of the Miller's Tale and invokes, in an oblique but I think unmistakable fashion, the radical political program that informed late-medieval peasant belligerence. Presented with the churl's problem of how to divide a fart equally among a convent of thirteen friars, the seigneurial household is itself divided. The lady is instantly dismissive: "I seye a cherl hath doon a cherles deed" (2206). But the lord is intrigued, and when the terms of his puzzlement are located within the political context of rural discontent they take on a startling relevance:

> The lord sat stille as he were in a traunce,
> And in his herte he rolled up and doun,
> "How hadde this cherl ymaginacioun
> To shewe swich a probleme to the frere?
> Nevere erst er now herde I of swich mateere.
> *I trowe the devel putte it in his mynde.*
> In ars-metrike shal ther no man fynde,
> Biforn this day, of swich a question.
> Who sholde make a demonstracioun
> That *every man sholde have yliche his part*
> As o the soun or savour of a fart?
> *O nyce, proude cherle, I shrewe his face!*
> Lo, sires," quod the lord, "with harde grace!
> *Who evere herde of swich a thyng er now?*
> *To every man ylike? Tel me how.*
> *It is an inpossible, it may nat be.*
> Ey, *nyce cherl,* God lete him nevere thee!
> The rumblynge of a fart, and every soun,
> Nis but of eir reverberacioun,
> And evere it wasteth litel and litel awey.
> Ther is no man can deemen, by my fay,
> *If that it were departed equally.*
> What, lo, *my* cherl, lo, yet how shrewedly.
> Unto *my* confessour to-day he spak!
> I holde hum certeyn a *demonyak!*
> Now ete youre mete, and lat the cherl go pleye;
> *Lat hym go honge hymself a devel weye!*"
>
> (2216–42)

Taken aback by signs of mental power in a creature thought to lack the capacity, the lord is intrigued but finally retreats into typical defamations: the churl is either foolish ("nyce") or crazy ("a demonyak"). At issue, of course, is the burning peasant demand for equality: "To every man ylike? Tel me how. / It is an inpossible, it may nat be." Not only can a fart not be "departed equally," but neither can the goods of this world. Hence the lord closes with a curse on any who would think otherwise—"Lat hym go honge hymself a devel weye!"—and returns to his meat, itself one of those goods with which he is so abundantly supplied but which peasants like Thomas conspicuously lack. Chaucer here presents, then, a brief allegory of the seigneurial reaction to peasant demands, and then shows, in the squire's translation of Thomas's challenge back into the dehistoricizing language of antifraternal discourse, how those demands are displaced and finally appropriated to the traditional ideology of medieval society. And finally, of course, this is an allegory of Chaucer's own practice of articulating but ultimately silencing the voice of peasant protest.

Notes

[Ed. note: A later version of this essay appears as chapter 5 ("The *Miller's Tale* and the Politics of Laughter") of Patterson's *Chaucer and the Subject of History* (Madison: University of Wisconsin Press, 1991).]

1. Robert Kilburn Root, *The Poetry of Chaucer* (Boston, 1906), 44.
2. Root, *Poetry of Chaucer,* 32; William Blake, "Prospectus of the Engraving of Chaucer's Canterbury Pilgrims," in *Poetry and Prose of William Blake,* ed. Geoffrey Keynes (London, 1943), 637.
3. E. Talbot Donaldson, ed., *Chaucer's Poetry,* 2d ed. (1958; repr. New York, 1975), 1100; Derek Pearsall, *The Canterbury Tales* (London, 1985), xiv. I would like to dedicate this essay to the late Talbot Donaldson; although I suspect that he would disapprove of its argument, I am sure that he would support the attempt by one of his students to offer a revisionary reading.
4. The only real alternative that Chaucer criticism has provided to this tradition has been Exegetics, which I have discussed in this context in chapter 1 of *Negotiating the Past: The Historical Understanding of Medieval Literature* (Madison, 1987).
5. Paul Strohm, "Form and Social Statement in *Confessio Amantis* and *The Canterbury Tales,*" *Studies in the Age of Chaucer* 1 (1979): 33.
6. Stephen Knight, *Geoffrey Chaucer* (London, 1986).
7. Herbert F. Butterfield, *The Whig Interpretation of History* (London, 1931).
8. R. J. Holton, *The Transition from Feudalism to Capitalism* (New York, 1985), 35, 38–39. The citation by Parsons is from his *The Structure of Social Action,* 2 vols. (1937; repr. New York, 1968), 1: 157. For a recent account of the transition from the orthodox point of view, see Carlo M. Cipolla, *Before the Industrial Revolution: European Society and Economy, 1000–1700,* 2d ed. (1976; repr. New York, 1980), for whom "the urban movement of the eleventh to thirteenth centuries [was] the turning point of world history. . . . The urban revolution of the eleventh and twelfth centuries was the prelude to, and created the prerequisites for, the Industrial Revolution of the nineteenth century" (146–49).
9. Robert Brenner, "The Origins of Capitalist Development: A Critique of Neo-Smithian Marxism," *New Left Review* 104 (1977): 25–82.
10. M. M. Postan, "The Rise of a Money Economy," *Economic History Review* 14 (1944); reprinted in *Essays on Medieval Agricultural and General Problems of the Medieval Economy* (Cambridge, 1973), 28.
11. Rodney H. Hilton, *The English Peasantry in the Later Middle Ages* (Oxford, 1975), and Hilton, *Class Conflict and the Crisis of Feudalism* (London, 1985), a collection of many of his essays; see also P. D. A. Harvey, ed., *The Peasant Land Market in Medieval England* (Oxford, 1984).
12. Postan, *The Medieval Economy and Society* (Harmondsworth, 1975), 239.
13. This argument has been most vigorously advanced by Alan Macfarlane, *The Origins of English Individualism* (Oxford, 1978).

14.   For a discussion of the work of Dobb and Hilton, see Harvey J. Kaye, *The British Marxist Historians* (London, 1984).

15.   For a recent discussion, with extensive bibliography, see Holton, *Cities, Capitalism and Civilization* (London, 1986); see also Hilton, "Towns in Societies—Medieval England," *Urban History Yearbook* 9 (1982): 7–13, and Hilton, "Medieval Market Towns and Simple Commodity Production," *Past and Present* 109 (1985): 3–23.

16.   Marx's attack on merchant capital as not being what he calls in the first volume of *Capital* "the really revolutionizing path" of transformation can be found in chapters 20 and 47 of *Capital* III.

17.   Brenner's article appeared first in *Past and Present* 97 (1982): 16–113 and is now reprinted in T. H. Aston and C. H. E. Philpin, eds., *The Brenner Debate: Agrarian Class Structure and Economic Development in Pre-Industrial Europe* (Cambridge, 1985), 213–327.

18.   Hilton, *Bond Men Made Free* (1973: repr. London, 1977), 41.

19.   Hilton, "Reasons for Inequality Among Medieval Peasants," *Journal of Peasant Studies* 5 (1978): 271–83; reprinted in *Class Conflict and the Crisis of Feudalism,* 149.

20.   Ibid. Hilton's *The English Peasantry in the Later Middle Ages* provides a description of this golden age.

21.   Maurice Dobb, "A Reply," in Hilton, ed., *The Transition from Feudalism to Capitalism* (London, 1978), 59.

22.   For the classic discussion of "The Crisis of Seigneurial Fortunes," see Marc Bloch, *French Rural History: An Essay on its Basic Characteristics,* trans. Janet Sondheimer (Berkeley, 1970), 112–26. The growth of the luxury trade, and its impoverishing effect upon seigneurial fortunes, is stressed by Harry A. Miskimin, *The Economy of Early Renaissance Europe, 1300–1460* (Cambridge, 1975), 135–37, and passim.

23.   For this reading of Chaucer's role in the politics of the 1380s, disputed by some Chaucer scholars, see T. F. Tout, *Chapters in the Administrative History of Mediaeval England,* vol. 3 (Manchester, 1928), 417.

24.   An excellent discussion of this vexed issue, with persuasive arguments in favor of the authority of the Ellesmere order, is provided by Larry D. Benson, "The Order of *The Canterbury Tales,*" *Studies in the Age of Chaucer* 3 (1981): 77–120. In the discussion that follows, I have also accepted the disputed authenticity of the Man of Law's Epilogue and the argument that the interrupter of the Parson is indeed the Wife of Bath, whose Prologue and Tale then follow; for arguments supporting this view, see Donaldson, "The Ordering of the *Canterbury Tales,*" in *Medieval Literature and Folklore: Essays in Honor of Francis Lee Utley,* ed. Jerome Mandel and Bruce A. Rosenberg (New Brunswick, 1971), 193–204.

25.   Bloch, *Land and Work in Medieval Europe,* trans. J. E. Anderson (Berkeley, 1967), 157. For the extraordinary struggle over milling rights at St. Albans, see Rosamond Faith, "The 'Great Rumour' of 1377 and Peasant Ideology," in Rodney Hilton and T. H. Aston, eds., *The English Rising of 1381* (Cambridge, 1984), 66. For other examples of disputes over mill-soke, see Richard Bennett and John Elton, *The History of Corn Milling,* 4 vols. (London, 1898–1904), 3:202–70 and 4:40–53. Because of space restrictions, I have not been able to annotate the assertions made in the following paragraph about the place of the miller in the late-medieval economy—a topic that requires a full-scale investigation.

26.   George C. Homans, *English Villagers in the Thirteenth Century* (Cambridge, Mass., 1941), 285, who unfortunately offers no evidence.

27.   For John Fillol, see Christopher Dyer, "The Social and Economic Background to the Rural Revolt of 1381," in Hilton and Aston, *English Rising of 1381,* 38; for another anonymous miller, see Hilton and Aston, 16. In his account of the rebellion in *Vox clamantis,* John Gower also contemptuously testifies to the presence of millers among the rebels: "nor did the dog at the mill stay home" (*The Major Latin Works of John Gower,* trans. Eric W. Stockton [Seattle, 1962], 59).

28. On the two John Millers, see André Réville and Charles Petit-Dutaillis, *Le Soulève-ment des Travailleurs d'Angleterre en 1381* (Paris, 1898), 224 and 232; on William Grindecobbe, and his famous speech, see R. B. Dobson, ed., *The Peasants' Revolt of 1381* (London, 1970), 269–77.

29. Edgar Powell, *The Rising in East Anglia in 1381* (Cambridge, 1896), 13–14.

30. The verse letter is cited from Thomas Walsingham, *Historia anglicana,* ed. Henry Thomas Riley (London, 1864), 2:34; the second, from Knighton's *Chronicon,* is cited from Dobson, *Peasants' Revolt,* 381–82. These two texts have been recently put in relation to the Miller's Tale by Paul A. Olson, *The Canterbury Tales and the Good Society* (Princeton, 1986), 54–55, who sees the Miller as "cousin to the revolt's 'Jack the Miller' but seen through [Chaucer's] elite court eyes" (75).

31. All citations are from Benson, ed., *The Riverside Chaucer* (Boston, 1987).

32. For the first, see V. A. Kolve, *Chaucer and the Imagery of Narrative* (Stanford, 1985), 158–216; for the second, Morton Bloomfield, "The Miller's Tale–an un-Boethian Interpreta-tion," in Mandel and Rosenberg, *Medieval Literature and Folklore Studies,* 205–11.

33. Olson, *Canterbury Tales and the Good Society,* also sees the Miller as promoting the rebellious prelapsarianism of John Ball (75–80); where we disagree is over Chaucer's attitude, which for Olson remains that of the court. Another consistently political interpretation of the Tale is the excellent article by Robert P. Miller, "The *Miller's Tale* as a Complaint," *Chaucer Review* 5 (1970–71): 147–60, who also sees the Tale as providing a critique of the Miller's insurrectionist misunderstanding of the proper role of the three estates.

34. Hilton, *A Medieval Society: The West Midlands at the End of the Thirteenth Century* (London, 1966), 156. For the anticlericalism of peasant movements, see Hilton, *Bond Men,* 50–52, 101–3, 106–8, 124–25, 167–68, 198–206. According to Michel Mollat and Philippe Wolff, *Ongles bleus, Jacques et Ciompi: les révolutions populaires en Europe aux XIVᵉ et XVᵉ siècles* (Paris, 1970), "Evêques et abbés ont été des seigneurs particuliérement vigilants et combatifs, parce qu'ils s'estimaient comptables du patrimoine qu'ils avaient reçu et qu'ils devaient trans-mettre intact" (288).

35. This issue is present in the exegesis of the Song from its very inception: Origen prefaces his *Commentary* by warning "everyone who is not yet rid of the vexations of flesh and blood and has not ceased to feel the passion of his bodily nature, to refrain completely from reading this little book and the things that will be said about it" (*The Song of Songs: Commentary and Homilies,* trans. R. P. Lawson [Westminster, 1957], 23)—a threat from which Origen, as a castrate, was of course protected (which is perhaps why it is the effete Absolon who purveys the *Song* in the Miller's Tale). See also Augustine, *De doctrina christiana,* 2:6.

36. For an excellent discussion of the dramatic allusions in the Tale, see Sandra Pierson Prior, "Parodying Typology and the Mystery Plays in the Miller's Tale," *Journal of Medieval and Renaissance Studies* 16 (1986): 57–73. Refreshingly avoiding the spiritualizing readings of previ-ous critics, Prior argues that Chaucer is criticizing a general human propensity to "presume too much upon God's *pryvetee* and unique power" (73). But the plays are not socially neutral, and Prior is closer to the mark when she more specifically claims that "the outcome of Nicholas's play and game teaches us that clerks who rewrite salvation history may burn (here if not in hell)" (73)—but for their social rather than theological transgressions.

37. For the play of Noah as about *maistrye,* see Kolve, *The Play Called Corpus Christi* (Stanford, 1966), 146–51.

38. This is Walsingham's account, as translated in Dobson, *Peasants' Revolt,* 311. For the original, see Walsingham, *Historia anglicana,* 2:18.

39. Augustine, *City of God,* 19:15, trans. Henry Bettenson (Harmondsworth, 1972), 874–75.

40. Balthasar Reber, *Felix Hemmerlin voñ Zürich* (Zürich, 1846), cited by G. G. Coulton, *The Medieval Village* (Cambridge, 1925), 522.

41. Coulton, *Medieval Village,* 21, 247; and for the representation of Cain in the Towneley *Mactatio Abel* as a husbandman, see G. R. Owst, *Literature and Pulpit in Medieval England,* 2d ed. (Oxford, 1961), 491–92. It is this enrollment of the peasant in the damned race of Cain that accounts for his designation in antipeasant writings as a Jew (see Paul Lehmann, *Parodistische Texte* [Munich, 1923], where the peasant is described as being "ineptus et turpis ut Judeus" [21]), as a Christ-killer (see Francesco Novati, *Carmina Medii Aevi* [Florence, 1883], for a poem that asserts that "Christo fu da villan crucificò, / e stogom sempre in pioza, in vento e in neve, / perchè havom fato così gran peccò" [27, n. 1]), and as an *alter Judas* (Novati, 45).

42. Gower, *Vox clamantis* (trans. Stockton, 210); this is an identification that he later enforced by depicting the Peasants' Revolt as a rising of maddened animals. For examples of antipeasant writings that stress the animal nature of the peasant, see Novati, *Carmina Medii Aevi,* 32, n. 1, 34–38; as Matteo Vegio said in the early fifteenth century, a peasant's ox has a more human appearance than does the peasant himself (31, n. 1). See also the medieval proverb, "Rusticus asello similis est, hoc tibi dico" (Hans Walther, *Lateinische Sprichwörter und Sentenzen des Mittelalters und der Frühen Neuzeit,* ed. Paul Gerhard Schmidt [Göttingen, 1986], 9:511 [item 223]). The notion of the peasant as a creature capable not of love but only of animal lust is part of this identification of his fallen nature: as Andreas Capellanus famously said in his *De amore,* rustics "are impelled to acts of love in the natural way like a horse or a mule, just as nature's pressure directs them" (ed. and trans. P. G. Walsh [London, 1982], 223). See also the treatise on love included within *Li Hystore de Julius Cesar:* "Volentei d'amer ki en vilain se met estriner le fait ausi *comme une beste salvage,* ne il ne poet son corage aploiier a nule cortoisie ne a nule bonté, ains aime folement et sans coverture. Et che n'est mie amours, ains est ensi comme rage, quant vilains s'entremet d'amer" (ed. A. Långfors, *Romania* 56 [1930]: 367). Two well-known representations of the peasant as a subhuman, animal creature can be found in Chrétien de Troyes's *Le chevalier du lion* and in *Aucassin et Nicolette;* a particularly bestial visual image of a miller appears in the margins of the Luttrell Psalter, conveniently reproduced on the cover of the paperback edition of Postan's *Medieval Economy and Society.* Less prejudicial pictures that serve to link the peasant to the natural world can be seen in late medieval calendar illustrations, where the peasant serves as virtually a marker of the passage of the year. For examples, see Henrik Specht, *Poetry and the Iconograph of the Peasant: The Attitude to the Peasant in Late Medieval English Literature and in Contemporary Calendar Illustration* (Copenhagen, 1983).

43. Dobson, *Peasants' Revolt,* 370; the translation is by Lord Berners. For the original, see Kervyn de Lettenhove, ed., *Oeuvres de Froissart,* vol. 9 (Brussels, 1869), 387.

44. Hilton, "Peasant Movements in England Before 1381," *Journal of Peasant Studies* 1 (1974): 207–19; reprinted in *Class Conflict and the Crisis of Feudalism,* 138.

45. Walsingham, *Historia anglicana,* 2:32.

46. Roderigo, Bishop of Zamorra, *Speculum Vitae Humanae* (c. 1465), cited by Coulton, *Medieval Village,* 518; for the second citation, see Owst, *Literature and Pulpit in Medieval England,* 553.

47. The most explicit peasant assertion of the authority of the *lex naturalis* (which they identified with the *lex divina*) is to be found in the documents produced during the German Peasants' War of 1524–25; see Peter Blickle, *The Revolution of 1525: The German Peasants' War from a New Perspective,* trans. Thomas A. Brady and H. C. Erik Midelfort (Baltimore, 1981), 168, and Heiko A. Obermann, "The Gospel of Social Unrest," in Bob Scribner and Gerhard Benecke, eds., *The German Peasant War of 1525—New Viewpoints* (London, 1979), 39–51. Coulton is surely right when he says that the peasants' Twelve Articles "rest upon [an] appeal from oppressive human law and custom to natural law" (Coulton, *Medieval Village,* 546).

48. Honorius of Autun, *De imagine mundi:* "Huius tempore divisum est genus humanum in tria: in liberos, milites, servos. Liberi de Sem, milites de Japhet, servi de Cham" (J. P. Migne, ed., *Patrologia Latina* [PL] 172:166).

49. *Sacrificium Cayme and Abel,* in Richard Beadle, ed., *York Plays,* 1:86.

50.   Sarah M. Horrall, ed., *The Southern Version of Cursor Mundi,* col. 1 (Ottawa, 1978), 102–3, lines 2133–36.

51.   William Caxton, trans., *The Game and Playe of the Chesse,* 2d ed. (Westminster, 1481[?]), reprinted in facsimile by Vincent Figgins (London, 1855). For an edition of de Cessolis, see Ernest Rietz and Augustus Sjhoberg, eds., *De ludo scacchorum* (Lund, 1848–49).

52.   See E. F. Jacob, "The Book of St. Albans," *Bulletin of the John Rylands Library* 28 (1944): 99–118.

53.   *The Boke of Seynt Albans* (St. Albans, 1486), fol. ci^r; further folio numbers will be included in the text. I have supplied the punctuation.

54.   The essentially racist nature of the myth of Ham was made odiously explicit in early nineteenth-century America, where it functioned as a justification for slavery; see Thomas Virgil Peterson, *Ham and Japeth: The Mythic World of Whites in the Antebellum South* (Metuchan, 1978).

55.   This sentence is not found in the text that apparently served as Chaucer's source: Siegfried Wenzel, "The Source of Chaucer's Deadly Sins," *Traditio* 30 (1974): 368.

56.   See, e.g., Ambrose, *Liber de Noe et arca* (*PL* 14:435); Isidore, *Quaestiones in Veterum Testamentum: In Genesin,* 8:6 (*PL*83:235–36).

57.   Augustine, *City of God,* 16:2 (trans. Bettenson, 650–51). This interpretation is repeated throughout the Middle Ages, as by Isidore, *Quaestiones in Veterum Testamentum: In Genesin,* 8:6 (*PL* 83:235–36), and by Rhabanus Maurus, *Commentarius in Genesim,* 2:9 (*PL* 107:525–26). So too, the interpretation of Noah's drunken nakedness as representing Christ's passion is the standard exegesis.

58.   Rhabanus Maurus, *Commentarius in Genesim,* 2:9 (*PL* 107:525), and Remigius, *Commentarius in Genesim,* 9 (*PL* 131:78). Cassian defined Ham as a worker in secret arts: see David Williams, *Cain and Beowulf* (Toronto, 1982), 30–31, and Gower, *Confessio amantis,* 4:2396–2400, in *English Works,* ed. G. C. Macauley (London, 1901), 1:366.

59.   Lehmann, *Die Parodie im Mittelalter* (Munich, 1923): "Deus, qui multitudinem rusticorum congregasti et magnam discordiam inter eos et nos seminasti, da, quesumus, ut laboribus eorum fruamur et ab uxoribus eorum diligamur" (178; see also 117, and Lehmann, *Parodistische Texte,* 22).

60.   The same point has been made by E. M. W. Tillyard, *Poetry Direct and Oblique* (London, 1945), 88.

61.   George Kane and E. Talbot Donaldson, eds., *Piers Plowman: The B Text* (London, 1975), 121–22.

62.   A long extract from the *Ledger Book of Vale Royal Abbey* is translated by Coulton, *Medieval Village,* 132–35; for rabicanes, see 133.

63.   Walsingham, *Historia anglicana,* 1:457–60, 472, 2:13, 16; see Dobson, *Peasants' Revolt,* 169–74, 272–75, 307–10.

64.   Gower, *Vox clamantis* (trans. Stockton, 58, 65).

65.   For these terms, see Dobson, *Peasants' Revolt,* 144, 183, 189, 199, 278.

66.   For a discussion of the conventions governing the representation of peasants, see Alice M. Colby, *The Portrait in Twelfth-Century French Literature* (Geneva, 1965), 73–81.

67.   In theory the reeve was chosen by the tenants to represent them, and should therefore be distinguished from the bailiff, who was the lord's agent; but in practice the reeve often functioned as a bailiff: see H. S. Bennett, "The Reeve and the Manor in the Fourteenth Century," *English Historical Review* 41 (1926): 358–65.

68.   For the distinction between the powerful trade guilds or merchant companies, and the far weaker craft guilds, see Sylvia Thrupp, *Merchant Class of Medieval London* (Ann Arbor, 1948), 27–41.

69.   As Postan has said, with perhaps unconscious irony, "it is difficult to overestimate the continuous social advancement of lawyers and their ability to break into the upper ranks of society" (*Medieval Economy and Society,* 175).

70.   See Mary Carruthers, "The Wife of Bath and the Painting of Lions," *PMLA* 94 (1979): 209–22, and D. W. Robertson, Jr., " 'And for my land thus hastow mordred me?': Land Tenure, the Cloth Industry, and the Wife of Bath," *Chaucer Review* 14 (1979–80): 403–20.

71.   For a reading of the Wife's Prologue and Tale as a progressive discovery of the subject, its staging of questions of poetic authority and gender, and the many medieval precedents for this strategy, see my " 'For the Wyves love of Bathe' ": Feminine Rhetoric and Poetic Resolution in the *Roman de la rose* and the *Canterbury Tales*," *Speculum* 58 (1983): 656–95.

72.   See Thomas Hahn and Richard W. Kaeuper, "Text and Context: Chaucer's *Friar's Tale*," *SAC* 5 (1983): 67–101.

73.   Penn R. Szittya, *The Antifraternal Tradition in Medieval Literature* (Princeton, 1986), 230.

74.   That the fourteenth-century fraternal orders still had the capacity to participate in movements for social justice is suggested by objections earlier in the century to their participation in peasant protests against monastic landlords at Bury St. Edmunds, at Christ Church, Canterbury, and at Sandwich (see A. G. Little, *Studies in English Franciscan History* [Manchester, 1917], 98–99); similarly, complaints that they supported the rebels of 1381 (by Walsingham, for instance [*Historia anglicana* 2:13], and by the author of the *Fasciculus Zizaniorum,* ed. W. W. Shirley [London, 1858], 292–95) are probably antifraternal slanders, but they may just point to a shred of historical truth.

"Glose/Bele Chose":
The Wife of Bath and Her Glossators

Carolyn Dinshaw

The Man of Law has just concluded his tale of Constance, reuniting father and daughter in one big ideological embrace, and it has pleased that manliest of men, Harry Bailly. The Host's delight in this tale, expressed in the Epilogue of the *Man of Law's Tale,* comes as no surprise: as we've seen, the Man of Law's *vita* of Constance—like Chaucer's "Seintes Legende of Cupide" that the Man of Law mentions in his Introduction—has represented its heroine as a will-less blank and has thus controlled the threat that an independent female "corage" would pose to patriarchy. Such control of the "sleightes and subtilitees" of women (as he will put it later, in response to the *Merchant's Tale* [4:2421]) is immensely appealing to the henpecked Harry; impressed by the Man of Law's performance, he stands up in his stirrups and calls out: "Goode men, herkeneth everych on!" He then asks another one of "ye lerned men in lore," the Parson, to tell a tale. But the prospect of a suffocating sermon, especially after the *Man* of Law's tale, is too much for the Wife of Bath. Out of this company of "goode men" the voice of the woman bursts: "Nay, by my fader soule, that schal he nat! . . . He schal no gospel glosen here ne teche." Instead, "My joly body schal a tale telle," a tale having nothing to do with "philosophie, / Ne phislyas, ne termes queinte of lawe."[1] The Wife opposes her tale to the "lerned men's" lore: it is her "joly body" against their oppressive teaching and glossing.

The Wife—a clothier, dealer in *textus*—continues in her Prologue to oppose herself to glosses. "Men may devyne and *glosen,* up and doun" (3:26; my emphasis) about how many men one may have in marriage, but the Wife knows that God bade us to increase and multiply: "That gentil *text* kan *I* wel understonde." In this endlink to the *Man of Law's Tale* and beginning of the Wife of Bath's Prologue, woman is associated with the body and the text—as in the Pauline exegetical assimilation of literality and carnality to femininity I discussed in the Introduction—and is opposed to the gloss, written by men, learned, anti-pleasure, and anti-body.

From *Chaucer's Sexual Poetics.* © 1989 The Board of Regents of the University of Wisconsin System. Reprinted by permission of the University of Wisconsin Press.

Indeed, outfitted in her ostentatious garb—thick kerchiefs, fine stockings, new shoes, huge hat—and emphasizing that those "gaye scarlet gytes" are well used, the Wife of Bath herself is an embodiment of the letter of the text as Jerome has imaged it in his paradigm of proper reading: like the alien woman of Deuteronomy 21, she is a woman whose clothed appearance is centrally significant. But unlike that new bride, she retains her costume (which she intends, I argue, to be alluring, however overwhelming and repellent others might find it), revels in her seductive person and adornment: *her* hair isn't shaved, *her* nails aren't pared.[2] Unlike that silent bride—and unlike her virtually mute relations, the passive feminine bodies manipulated by the narrator of the *Legend of Good Women* and Constance in the *Man of Law's Tale*—the Wife speaks: whereas that alien captive is passed between men at war, her desire conforming to the desire of the men in possession of her, the Wife makes her autonomous desire the very motive and theme of her performance.[3] And if Jerome's paradigm—a forerunner of Lévi-Strauss's patriarchal paradigm, just as we have seen the *Man of Law's Tale* to be—runs on the assumption that all women are functionally interchangeable (an assumption on which Pandarus and Troilus operate as well), the Wife of Bath would seem to regard *men* as virtually interchangeable: "Yblessed be God that I have wedded fyve! / Welcome the sixte, whan that evere he shal," she declares (44–45), and elaborates:

> I ne loved nevere by no discrecioun,
> But evere folwede myn appetit,
> Al were he short, or long, or blak, or whit;
> I took no kep, so that he liked me,
> How poore he was, ne eek of what degree.
> (622–26)

The Wife of Bath, in fact, articulates, makes visible, exactly what that patriarchal hermeneutic necessarily excludes, necessarily keeps invisible. She represents what the ideology of that model—an ideology incarnated, as we've seen, by the Man of Law—can't say, can't acknowledge, or acknowledges only by devalorizing and stigmatizing as Other: she represents independent feminine will and desire, the literal body of the text that itself has signifying value and leads to the spirit without its necessarily being devalued or destroyed in the process.[4] The woman traded must be silent; the Wife talks. The woman's desire must be merely mimetic; the Wife chronicles her own busy "purveiance / Of mariage" (570–71). The gloss undertakes to speak (for) the text; the Wife maintains that the literal text—her body—can speak for itself. If the Man of Law must energetically suppress the feminine, the Wife vociferously speaks as that Other created and excluded by patriarchal ideology, and in this way she reveals the very workings of this ideology. Most penetratingly, as her *Tale* suggests in its narrative focus on a rapist, if the patriarchal economy of the trade of women proceeds without woman's necessary acquiescence, it is always potentially performing a rape. (The rape is, in fact, Chaucer's own innovation to the traditional stories that inform this tale, a deliberate alteration that argues for its significance in the whole of the Wife's performance.)[5]

We might say, then, that the Wife is everything the Man of Law can't say, everything Criseyde, everything Philomela might have said, given the chance. She makes audible precisely what patriarchal discourse would keep silent, reveals the exclusion and devalorization that patriarchal discourse performs. Speaking as the excluded Other, she explicitly and affirmatively assumes the place that patriarchal discourse accords the feminine. Far from being trapped within the "prison house" of antifeminist discourse, the Wife of Bath, I argue, "convert[s] a form of subordination into an affirmation," to adapt Luce Irigaray's words here; she *mimics* the operations of patriarchal discourse. As Irigaray has characterized it, such mimesis functions to reveal those operations, to begin to make a place for the feminine:

> There is, in an initial phase, perhaps only one "path," the one historically assigned to the feminine: that of *mimicry*. One must assume the feminine role deliberately. Which means already to convert a form of subordination into an affirmation, and thus to begin to thwart it. . . . To play with mimesis is thus, for a woman, to try to recover the place of her exploitation by discourse, without allowing herself to be simply reduced to it. It means to resubmit herself— inasmuch as she is on the side of the "perceptible," of "matter"—to "ideas," in particular to ideas about herself, that are elaborated in/by a masculine logic, but so as to make "visible," by an effect of playful repetition, what was supposed to remain invisible: the cover-up of a possible operation of the feminine in language.[6]

Irigaray's own project of mimesis is immense—it intends the thwarting of all patriarchal discourse—and I cannot engage here the complex context in which she develops the idea. Such a concept of mimesis is in itself, however, very powerful: it seems to me strikingly useful to the analysis of the Wife of Bath's performance, a performance that is at once enormously affirmative and adversative. But the Wife is also crucially unlike the woman Irigaray describes here; she "plays with mimesis," mimics patriarchal discourse ("Myn entente nys but for to pleye," she maintains [192]), not in order to "thwart" it altogether, to subvert it entirely, but to *reform* it, to keep it in place while making it accommodate feminine desire. What the Wife imagines in her Prologue and *Tale* is a way in which such patriarchal hermeneutics as imagined by Jerome, Macrobius, and Richard of Bury can be deployed to the satisfaction of everyone under patriarchy, according a place of active signification to both masculine and feminine: clerk and wife, gloss and text, spirit and letter, "matter" and "ideas" (Irigaray mentions the Aristotelian terms I've discussed in my Introduction). What would be necessary to the satisfying formulation of sexualized hermeneutics is, in fact, inherent in that Hieronymian image itself, an understanding of the feminine not as only the distracting veil but the fecund body, not as merely something to be turned away from, gotten rid of, passed through, but as something that is, in itself, at once a locus of pleasure *and* a locus of valuable signification. The Wife thus articulates the happy possibility of reforming the patriarchal and fundamentally misogynistic hermeneutic based on the economy of possession, of traffic in texts-as-women, to make it accommodate the feminine—woman's independent will and the signifying value of the letter.

The Wife of Bath, in fact, would seem to be Chaucer's favorite character, and the reasons for this become clearer and clearer. As Robert A. Pratt has put it in his analysis of Chaucer's evolving idea of the Wife, from her early characterization as teller of the *Shipman's Tale* to her fully fleshed-out form as we know it now,

> She appears to have interested Chaucer more, to have stimulated his imagination and creative power more fully and over a longer period, than any other of his characters.[7]

She pops up again and again: apparently irrepressible; she bursts out of even the confines of her "fictive universe," the *Canterbury Tales*—where she provokes the excited interjections of Pardoner and Friar and is deferred to as a certain kind of authority by both Clerk and Merchant—to be cited in Chaucer's own voice in "Lenvoy de Chaucer a Bukton."[8] The Wife is a source of delight for this male author precisely because through her he is able to reform and still to participate in patriarchal discourse; he recuperates the feminine *within* the solid structure of that discourse.

This is a male fantasy, of course. And when we consider that such desire for the reform—not the overturning—of patriarchy is represented as a woman's desire, it is even more apparent that this is a masculine dream. Granted that it is indeed such a fantasy, we might remark that it is not a bad one, after all; it is not exploitative of the feminine for purely masculine gratification. Through the Wife, Chaucer imagines the possibility of a masculine reading that is not antifeminist, that does acknowledge, in good faith, feminine desire; and further, he represents the struggle and violence to the feminine that accompany the articulation of this fantasy. Through the Wife, then, Chaucer recuperates the sexualized hermeneutic that he recognizes as both pervasive in the medieval literary imagination and manifestly flawed. He has shown its limits in *Troilus and Criseyde,* the *Legend of Good Women,* and the *Man of Law's Tale,* has shown the toll thereby taken on the feminine; he continues, in the Wife of Bath's Prologue and *Tale,* to register the toll taken on the feminine corpus in even the imagining of patriarchy's reform. The Wife expresses a dream of masculine reading that is not antifeminist and a feminine relation to the condition of being read that is not antimasculinist—but she does so after having been bruised and battered, permanently injured by that clerk Jankyn, in their concussive renovation of patriarchal discourse.

1

Crucial to the smooth passage of the alien woman between men at war, as we've seen time and again, is the exclusion of her independent desire. Criseyde is rejected by immasculated readers of her because she seems to them to be gratifying her own fickle desire; the women of the *Legend of Good Women* are featureless, enervated creatures, kept that way by the misogynistic plan of the narrator, the God of Love, and Alceste; pale Constance is assigned value by the men who trade her, and her sexuality, even as passive and mimetic as it is, is still a discomfort and confusion to the Man of Law. He denies that the mothers-in-law, with their transgressive desires, are even females of the species. The Wife of Bath, on the Other hand, actively and vociferously seeks her own sexual satisfaction. She spends the first 162 lines of her Prologue energetically defending a theology that acknowledges sexual activity, even sexual desire: our "membres," she maintains, are not only for "purgacioun / Of uryne" and for the differentiation of the sexes; they are also for "ese"—"Of engendrure," she adds, after a significant pause (115–28). Her desire for the frequent use of her "instrument" motivates this opening exegetical discourse; and in the account of her five marriages that follows, she continues to explicate her preferences and active choices. She wore out the first three old husbands "pitously a-nyght" (202), she tells us, though she makes it clear that "in bacon hadde I nevere delit" (418); she wanted to be the only source of "delit" for her adulterous fourth husband (482); and she loved her fifth the best not only because of his great legs but because "in oure bed he was so fressh and gay" (508).

The Wife's loud and happy occupation of a position that is denied by patriarchai ideology is witnessed in her full embrace of her own commodification. Lévi-Strauss attempts to cover up the implications of the commodification of women that is essential to his paradigm, as we've seen in the previous chapter; Hector in *Troilus and Criseyde* does something similar when he insists to the Trojan parliament that "We usen here no wommen for to selle" (4.182). But woman is indeed treated as a possession to be traded, "chaffare," merchandise—we think again of Criseyde as "moeble" (4.1380); of Constance, packed off as a load in a boat—and the Wife makes this explicit, assumes her position as female in the marketplace. She thus reveals the essential commodification of woman in patriarchy when she speaks the language of sexual economics.[9] Unlike Hector, the Wife clearly acknowledges that "*al* is for to selle" (414; my emphasis). She'll work the market, "make me a feyned appetit" when there's "wynnyng" to be had (416–17), withhold her sex when there's a "raunson" to be paid (409–12):

> With daunger oute we al oure chaffare;
> Greet prees at market maketh deere ware,
> And to greet cheep is holde at litel prys:
> This knoweth every womman that is wys.
>
> (521–24)

If Lévi-Strauss suggests that the law of supply and demand must regulate the masculine trade of women (scarcity of desirable women maintains the structure of exchange, as he points out in *Elementary Structures of Kinship*),[10] "wommen," the Wife contends, speaking as the excluded condition, have a "queynte fantasye" of their own: the "daungerous," withholding, scarce man generates their own desire.

Critics often argue that the Wife in her Prologue is but enacting an antifeminist stereotype of the greedy, insatiable, domineering wife—to put it in the terms of my analysis, critics argue that rather than embodying what patriarchal discourse *can't* say, she is enacting precisely what patriarchal discourse *does* say, and says endlessly (in the univocal chant of Theophrastus, Jerome, Walter Map, Andreas Capellanus, Jean de Meun, Matheolus, Gautier le Leu, Deschamps, and others such as are contained in Jankyn's book).[11] But this is another part of her process of mimicry: she not only uncovers what is hidden in the workings of patriarchal ideology but simultaneously appropriates the place of the Other that ideology openly creates; she assumes the place of the feminine (the stereotype) to which patriarchy explicitly relegates her. When the Wife rehearses to the pilgrim audience her diatribe against her three old husbands, she is repeating the very words antifeminist writers have given the out-of-control wife. Jerome, for example, quotes Theophrastus in *Adversus Jovinianum:*

> Then come curtain-lectures the live-long night: she complains that one lady goes out better dressed than she: that another is looked up to by all: "I am a poor despised nobody at the ladies' assemblies." "Why did you ogle that creature next door?" "Why were you talking to the maid?"[12]

The Wife of Bath harangues her husbands:

> Sire olde kaynard, is this thyn array?
> Why is my neighebores wyf so gay?
> She is honoured overal ther she gooth;
> I sitte at hoom; I have no thrifty clooth.
> What dostow at my neighebores hous?
> Is she so fair? Artow so amorous?
> What rowne ye with oure mayde? Benedicite!
> Sire olde lecchour, lat thy japes bel
>
> (235–42)

La Vieille, in the *Roman de la rose,* advises Bel Acueil on how a lover should play the game of love:

> He should swear that if he had wanted to allow his rose, which was in great demand, to be taken by another, he would have been weighed down with gold and jewels. But, he should go on, his pure heart was so loyal that no man would ever stretch out his hand for it except that man alone who was offering his hand at that moment.[13]

The Wife of Bath appeases her husbands just so:

> What eyleth yow to grucche thus and grone?
> Is it for ye wolde have my queynte allone?
> Wy, taak it al! Lo, have it every deel!
> Peter! I shrewe yow, but ye love it weel;
> For if I wolde selle my *bele chose,*
> I koude walke as fressh as is a rose;
> But I wol kepe it for youre owene tooth.
> (443–49)

Indeed, her words are the antifeminists' words; but she assertively, knowingly appropriates them and the position to which antifeminist writers have relegated wives ("sith a man is moore resonable / Than womman is, ye moste been suffrable" [441–42]; "Deceite, wepyng, spynnyng God hath yive / To wommen kyndely" [401–2]), and she thus rehearses this discourse with a difference. She herself remains elsewhere, with a body, a will, a desire beyond that which she is accorded by patriarchal discourse—this is "the persistence of 'matter,'" as Irigaray puts it:

> If women are such good mimics, it is because they are not simply resorbed in this function. *They also remain elsewhere:* another case of the persistence of "matter," but also of "sexual pleasure."[14]

It is the Wife of Bath as incarnation of the devalorized feminine letter in the discourse of patriarchal hermeneutics that interests me most in this consideration of the Wife and mimesis. The Wife has been dealt with by critics time and again as a more or less psychologically rounded character, expressing feminine desire and Chaucer's desire for feminine desire; but her centrality to Chaucer's poetics, it seems to me, is due less to her significance as dramatic invention than to her value as a representation of the letter, the body of the text. I read her Prologue and *Tale* as most significant in their allegorical representation of the act of reading. The Wife speaks as the literal text, insisting on the positive, significant value of the carnal letter as opposed to the spiritual gloss; moreover, in doing so she appropriates the methods of the masculine, clerkly *glossatores* themselves, thus exposing techniques that they would rather keep invisible. I want now to focus specifically on the relationship of the Wife, as literal text, to the gloss and clerkly glossators; for it is through her mimicking patriarchal hermeneutics—incarnating the excluded letter and repeating the masculine hermeneutic moves—that Chaucer suggests a revision of the paradigm of reading as a masculine activity that would acknowledge, even solicit, feminine desire. First, though, a glance at the bibliographical history of the scriptural gloss and its relationship to the biblical text is in order; glossing's totalizing function vis-à-vis the text will become apparent, and we shall be able to see the energetic proliferation of glosses themselves—although they ostensibly undertake to limit proliferation—and the self-interest of clerkly glossators, which will in fact become the Wife of Bath's theme.[15]

"Gloss" comes from the Greek *glossa* ("tongue, language"). As Francis E. Gigot notes, in early usage, Greek grammarians used the term to refer to words of Greek texts that required some exposition; later, the term came to refer to the explanation itself. Early Christian writers, commenting on Scripture, adopted the word to refer to an explanation of obscure verbal usage in the text—of foreign, dialectal, and obsolete words in particular—as opposed to an explanation of theological or doctrinal difficulties. Such glosses would be single words, written interlinearly or in the margins of the manuscript. But the word *glossa* was soon used to indicate more elaborate expositions of Scripture: from individual words to explanatory sentences to running commentaries on entire books. These longer commentaries as well would be written interlinearly and in the margins. The twelfth-century *Glossa ordinaria* ("The Gloss") sought to compile all glosses on the Bible, which themselves often consisted of layers upon layers of glosses. There were, in addition, glosses of the *Glossa*. In fact, Robert of Melun, in the mid-twelfth century (the height of glossomania) complained that the masters were reading the text only because of the gloss.[16]

But glossing activity continued, apparently unabated: notes and commentaries—*sententiae, postillae, distinctiones*—were produced vigorously. Marginal and interlinear glosses of Scripture became so elaborate, crowding the text off the page, that Sixtus V determined in 1588, on publication of his authoritative version of the Vulgate, that there would be no glosses in future copies of it—no marginal annotations of variant readings. There are words in the text of scripture as we know it now that were originally marginal or interlinear glosses—brief comments or explanations of a word—but were subsequently inserted into the text itself by scribes or owners of manuscripts. The gloss crowds out the text, the gloss becomes the text. And the gloss preserves the text from oblivion: to take a secular example, the only reason Chaucer knew a fragment of book 6 of Cicero's *Republic* is that Macrobius wrote a commentary on it, about sixteen times the length of the Ciceronian piece itself. What is supplementary, what is marginal, becomes the very condition of the primary text's existence, and itself proliferates. We might observe, too, with Graham D. Caie, that the glosses on Chaucer's own text in the Ellesmere manuscript

> are written in as large and as careful a hand as the actual text, which is placed off-centre to make room for the glosses, each of which begins with an illuminated capital in the same colours as those of the text itself. In a sense it is a misnomer to call them "marginalia" at all, and one might confidently assume that the Ellesmere scribe considered the glosses to be an important part of the work as a whole.[17]

At the same time—the twelfth century—that scriptural glossing is at its most fervent, and that Robert of Melun is complaining that the gloss is more important than the text, the word "gloss" acquires pejorative connotations. *Gloser* in French, "glosen" in English, meant "to explicate, interpret" but also "to give a false interpretation, flatter, deceive"—thus, as we say, "to gloss over." Amant, in the *Roman de la rose,* insists that Raison provide a courteous gloss for some nasty words that she uses. If she *must* talk about "testicles" ("coilles"), he maintains, she ought at least to disguise her subject with a gloss. And in the *Summoner's Tale* (following the Wife of Bath's and Friar's performances) the hypocritical and avaricious friar rejoices, "Glosynge is a glorious thyng, certeyn, / For lettre sleeth, so as we clerkes seyn" (3:1793–94). He can make the text of Holy Writ do whatever he wants via the gloss. I shall find it "in a maner glose," he states (1920), even though his meaning isn't in the letter. (And it is the very carnal fart of the enraged Thomas that puts an end to this phony spiritualizing glossing.)

This pejoration makes explicit, makes part of the very definition of the word, the self-interestedness that is always potential in the act of glossing. Glossing is a gesture of appropriation; the *glossa* undertakes to speak the text, to assert authority over it, to provide an interpretation, finally to limit or close it to the possibility of heterodox or unlimited significance. Attracted by the beauties and difficulties of the letter, the glossator opens, reveals and makes useful the text's hidden truth, recloaking the text with his own interpretation. Glossing thus registers the literal attractions of the text and the delight of understanding its spirit, but it can overwhelm the text as well. Robert of Melun complains of the aggression with which masters defended their glosses as having authority; he suggests that they were in fact ready to fight to a bloody finish for their glosses. And not only Robert charges glossators with doing violence to the literal text; Christine de Pizan's reference to an aphorism about glossing makes it clear that the view of its appropriative and totalizing nature was commonplace: in her letter to Pierre Col (about what she saw as antifeminism in the *Rose*) she remarks, "Surely, this is like the common proverb about the glosses of Orleans which destroyed the text."[18]

The Wife suggests that the appropriative nature of glossing has a particularly masculine valence. In her so-called *sermon joyeux,* the first 162 lines of her Prologue, the Wife as "noble prechour" (165) categorically opposes the text to the gloss. As I mentioned above, she has already countered the "glossing and teaching" of "lerned men" with her "joly body" in the Man of Law's Epilogue: glossing has a totalizing function much like that of masculine reading in *Troilus and Criseyde* and the *Legend,* working to turn away from the feminine body—woman and literal text. Glossing seeks to find one answer, impose one interpretation on the meaning of Christ's words to the Samaritan woman, for example:

> What that he mente therby, I kan nat seyn;
> But that I axe, why that the fifthe man
> Was noon housbonde to the Samaritan?
> How manye myghte she have in mariage?
> Yet herde I nevere tellen in myn age
> Upon this nombre diffinicioun.
> Men may devyne and glosen, up and doun . . .
>
> (20–26)

When she says "Men" in line 26, she undoubtedly means *men.* Glossing seeks to deny the functions of the body (115–24), and in particular to limit the Wife's uninhibited use of her "instrument." But the letter, she contends, authorizes her to use that "instrument / As frely as my Makere hath it sent" (149–50), even though clerks would insist that she keep her body chaste. The Wife's reliance on the letter, her heartily espousing the literal text in her justification of the fulfillment of feminine desire, is a commonplace among critics.[19] She points to a passage in Genesis when arguing against glosses on the wedding at Cana and on the Samaritan woman; she asserts that no biblical text mentions a specific number of marriages; she adduces scriptural precedents for multiple wives; appeals to the Pauline text that it is better to marry than to burn; reminds her audience that the apostle only counsels virginity and does not command it; refers to Christ's admonition that those who would live perfectly should sell all they have and give to the poor (and "that am nat I" [112]); repeats Paul's statement that the wife has power over her husband and that husbands should love their wives.

Of course, the Wife may oppose herself to them, but she is arguing here precisely like a glossator herself.[20] She poses *quaestiones,* like the twelfth- and thirteenth-century glossators. "If ther were no seed ysowe, / Virginitee, thanne wherof sholde it growe?" (71–72); "Telle me also, to what conclusion / Were membres maad of generacion?" (115–16). She works through this question logically (prompting the Friar to label her narrative "scole-matere" [1272])—the "membres of generacion" were made not only for "purgation of urine" and "to know a female from a male"; they are also for the purpose of procreation:

> Why sholde men elles in hir bookes sette
> That man shal yelde to his wyf hire dette?
> Now wherwith sholde he make his paiement,
> If he ne used his sely instrument?
>
> (129–32)

Her argumentation in these early lines of her Prologue repeats the points of
the heretical Jovinian, as has often been observed, in Jerome's *Adversus Jovinianum,* but it as well mimes Jerome's own pseudological moves in that treatise.
If the Wife of Bath's reasoning is slippery, prompting critics to castigate her,
it is because Jerome's itself is: commenting on Saint Paul's statement that it is
good for a man to be unmarried, for example, Jerome contends, "If it is good
for a man to be so, then it is bad for a man not to be so."[21] And if the Wife
amputates biblical passages to fit her scheme (forgetting, for example, the
second half of Paul's exhortation when she blithely declares: "I have the
power durynge al my lyf / Upon his propre body, and noght he. / Right thus
the Apostel tolde it unto me" [158–60]), she is but mimicking the methods
of those late glossators whom Henri de Lubac describes as "pulverizing" the
text (suppressing parts of passages, distorting and rearranging texts) to fit
their schemes.[22] In this active mimicking, the Wife reveals most powerfully
that these glossators' concerns are indeed carnal: she has made her own self-
interest explicit, and her act of appropriating their methods for openly carnal
purposes indicts their motivations as similarly carnal. She indeed affirms this
outright a little later:

> The clerk, whan he is oold, and may noght do
> Of Venus werkes worth his olde sho,
> Thanne sit he doun, and writ in his dotage
> That wommen kan nat kepe hir mariage!
>
> (707–10)

It is the bad-faith glosses written by men in order to limit and control
the feminine body that the Wife exposes, rips up, and has burned. But, curiously, it is the openly pejorated, carnal, ostentatiously masculine glossing by
the clerk Jankyn that the Wife—the body of the text—finds so appealing, so
effective, so irresistible:

> . . . in oure bed he was so fressh and gay,
> And therwithal so wel koude he me glose,
> Whan that he wolde han my *bele chose;*
> That thogh he hadde me bete on every bon,
> He koude wynne agayn my love anon.
>
> (508–12)

Flattery and blandishments cajole the Wife into bed so that Jankyn may take his pleasure of her *"bele chose"* (a foreign term in need of exposition; see also her *"quoniam"* [608]). Glossing here is unmistakably carnal, a masculine act performed on the feminine body, and it leads to pleasure for both husband and wife, both clerk and text. This glossing wipes out the Wife's immediate pain in her bones—inflicted by Jankyn, we must remember—and it does so because it satisfies the Wife's own desires even as it seeks to fulfill his. The Wife is left, of course, with bruises on her body: as she explains her love of Jankyn, she remarks,

> And yet was he to me the mooste shrewe;
> That feele I on my ribbes al by rewe,
> And evere shal unto myn endyng day.
>   (505–7)

But of all her men he is her favorite nonetheless, precisely because he—unlike Jerome's warrior—acknowledges and knows how to arouse feminine desire: "I trowe I loved hym best, for that he / Was of his love daungerous to me" (513–14).

The Wife thus describes a marriage relationship—and, allegorically, a relationship between text and gloseator—that would acknowledge the desires of both sides and would yield satisfaction to both. The conclusion of her Prologue strongly suggests that what she wants is reciprocity, despite her talk of "maistrie"; she most wants mutual recognition and satisfaction of desires. Once Jankyn apologizes to her and burns the book that has caused her so much "wo" and "pyne" (787), she becomes kind and true to him. She gains the "soveraynetee" but doesn't want to exercise it, as Donald Howard has suggested; she seeks rather to be "acorded by us selven two" (812).[23] Whether she actually has attained such complete mutuality is, despite her positive assertion of the fact, made doubtful by the language in which she expresses it: it is the language of fairy tale, rendered ironic by what has gone before (after the exposition of tricks and lies wives use, how "trewe" is "any wyf from Denmark unto Ynde"? [824]). But in the Wife's dreams, at least—in the male author's dreams that she dreams—there is full understanding between husband and wife, between clerk and text. Having married a clerk, having married him "for love" (526), she is a literal text that *wants* to disclose its hidden meaning, its truth. Her fairy-tale conclusion hints at a hermeneutic that respects the integrity and value of the literal text—Jankyn burns the book of glosses, they never have any further "debaat"—*and* that will arrive pleasurably at the spirit, the "truth" ("I was to hym . . . kynde / . . . And also trewe" [823–25]). This is a dream of a resolutely masculine reading of the feminine text—a dream of a man's reading *as* a man—that does not sacrifice the feminine in getting to the spirit but sees, in fact, that the text, stripped, reclothed, glossed, is still and ever feminine.

2

The Wife of Bath's Prologue thus renovates the patriarchal hermeneutic to accommodate the feminine, and her *Tale* continues to reveal and recover those things necessarily excluded by patriarchal discourse. She begins by immediately and forthrightly deploying the romance genre, a form relegated to women (as is clear from book 2 of *Troilus and Criseyde,* when Criseyde, reading a "romaunce," is cut off in her narration by Pandarus' allusion to Statius' "bookes twelve"), against the world of masculine authority represented by the Friar.[24] Friars gloss, as the Summoner makes clear in his tale, and the Wife uses the feminine romance against precisely such glossators—"hooly freres"—revealing, in fact, their engagement in carnal pursuits in the bushes.

Digression, dilation, delay of closure are features of this narrative form, as we've suggested in relation to Criseyde, and are in marked contrast to masculine totalizing. The Wife indeed digresses, and she does so into a classical text. Her Ovidian digression, which Lee Patterson has brilliantly analyzed, mimics such misogynistic use of the classical text as is made by the narrator of the *Legend of Good Women;* she alters the pagan text for an ostensibly antifeminist purpose: women, her fable says, can't keep secrets. But, as Patterson suggests, the Wife's use of the pagan text ends up problematizing most deeply not women's irrepressible speaking but men's listening. Midas, after all, has ass's ears; the Wife challenges male readers to resist the "immediate self-gratifications of antifeminism" in order to gain "self-knowledge."[25] The Wife manipulates the classical letter, the body, but does so to suggest something about just such a misogynistic strategy: it deprives not only the female of her significance but the male of self-understanding.

The particular narrative the Wife sets out to tell, the tale of the knight and loathly lady, makes visible and explicitly seeks to adjust the crucial structural workings of the patriarchal exchange of women. As in the Prologue, the Wife here does not seek to overthrow patriarchal power structures; the tale begins with a rape, always potential in the exchange structure that doesn't acknowledge feminine desire, and makes its central narrative problematic the correction of the rapist. The rapist, and the patriarchal power structure of possession that he enacts, must learn "what thyng is it that wommen moost desiren" (905)—must acknowledge the integrity of the feminine body and act in reference to feminine desire. That much of the energy of the first part of the narrative is devoted to enumerating the many things that women desire—"Somme seyde . . . Somme seyde . . . Somme seyde . . . Somme . . . somme . . . " (925–27)—attests to the notion that it's more important to acknowledge *that* women desire than to specify *what* it is that pleases them most. After the knight's year-long quest, the court is packed with women— "Ful many a noble wyf, and many a mayde, / And many a wydwe" (1026–27)—waiting to hear him declare, "with manly voys" (1036), what they presumably already know—waiting, that is, for the moment in which feminine desire will be acknowledged, publicly, by a man.

It is again, as in the Prologue, the Wife's allegorical working-out of the relationship between glossator and text that interests me here. As we've seen in "Adam Scriveyn," "rape" connotes not only sexual but textual violation; in *Troilus and Criseyde* and the *Legend of Philomela,* rape—the violation of the feminine—is the way misogynistic literary history is inaugurated and proceeds. In the rape and subsequent education of the rapist, the Wife of Bath works out the ideal of a hermeneutic that submits to the letter of the text and that will, as a consequence, arrive at its beautiful truth.

An act of violence is perpetrated by "a lusty bacheler" (883) on the corpus of a woman at the outset of the *Tale.* Riding out, a knight sees a "mayde" walking along, "Of which mayde anon, maugree hir heed, / By verray force, he rafte hire maydenhed" (887–88). The knight has stripped her of her protective garments and takes "hire maydenhed," the truth secreted within. He makes a whore out of her, as Macrobius would say, by exposing and soiling the pure body, a body he does not understand as anything but naked flesh. He is a brash reader, an intruder, tearing the garments, gaping at truths, violating and manhandling secrets more properly left veiled—because incomprehensible—to him.

This patently self-interested and abusive glossator's punishment is to discover "What thyng is it that wommen moost desiren" (905). How *should* he treat the body of the text? Must all glossing be violent, an unwelcome deformation of the letter? Is the alluring letter itself to be enjoyed? What is the relationship between the seductive outer garments and the wisdom underneath? Are both to be respected, are both properly sites of pleasure? The knight's quest does not, in fact, seem to promise a positive answer to questions of pleasure. For on his last day, when he approaches the dance of the four-and-twenty ladies in the forest, they vanish; and of the seductions of the letter the untutored knight, in his wantonness, is left with an ugly hag, pure wisdom with no bodily attractions to lure him toward her: "Agayn the knyght this olde wyf gan ryse" (1000), not vice versa. The old hag is the opposite of the troublesomely alluring text that torments Jerome in letter 22, to Eustochium. She is not just a text that is pure wisdom, pure spirit, with no appeal to wantonness (a *Parson's Tale,* for example); she's a literally repulsive text whose appalling letter challenges the reader to endure for the sake of its perfect spirit.

The knight is not up to the challenge of this text, even after his year-long tutelage in feminine desire. Like many men, as Patterson observes in reference to the Midas exemplum he has to be taught, it seems, yet again: on the night of their mirthless wedding, the loathly bride lectures her groom on the advantages of her lowly birth, poverty, old age, and ugliness, quoting texts of Cicero, Juvenal, Seneca, Dante (in an act, it seems, of exemplary glossing of herself). But when at last the chastened knight acknowledges her wisdom ("I put me in youre wise governance" [1231]) and her desire—and even suggests in a crucial reversal that *his* desire will conform to *hers* ("Cheseth youreself which may be moost plesance / And moost honour to yow and me also . . . / For as yow liketh, it suffiseth me" [1232–35])—she invites him to unveil her: "Cast up the curtyn, looke how that it is" (1249). The text's truth is revealed when *she* wants it to be. Here is an ideal vision of perfect reading, the ideal relation between text and glossator: the veil is respectfully, even joyfully lifted by the reader at the text's invitation, and there is full disclosure of the *nuda veritas*.

What is revealed is precisely the beautiful truth Macrobius and Richard of Bury talk about: the hidden body of woman, wise and fecund. Here is Jerome's alien woman, now arrayed for the bridal: this is, of course, the wedding night of the knight and lady.

> And whan the knyght saugh verraily al this,
> That she so fair was, and so yong therto,
> For joye he hente hire in his armes two.
> His herte bathed in a bath of blisse.
>
> (1250–53)

This is the Wife's fantasy of the perfect marriage, not unlike her fairy-tale version of her marriage to the clerk; the knight and lady live "in parfit joye" for the rest of their lives. It is a representation, further, of a specifically gendered literary act that succeeds in respecting both reader and text—both the masculine reader and the feminine read. The hag has, after all, conformed herself—her whole body—to his desire: after she lectures him on her inner goodness, after she undoes all patriarchal ideas of lineage (she argues that true "gentillesse" comes from God alone), possession (she contends that poverty is a blessed state) and feminine beauty (she maintains that her "filthe and eelde" [1215] are safeguards of chastity), she concedes, "But nathelees, syn I knowe youre delit, / I shal fulfille youre worldly appetit" (1217–18). And ever after she conforms her desires to his: the last lines of the Wife's narrative avow that "she obeyed hym in every thyng / That myghte doon hym plesance or likyng" (1255–56). The patriarchal paradigm is still in place; the trade of the captive woman, the stripping and reclothing goes on, and, as before, the Wife exploits the commodification of woman's sex that is the basis of that paradigm. She concludes her performance with a strong wish for husbands who have money and who will use it; "And olde and angry nygardes of dispence, / God sende hem soone verray pestilence!" (1263–64). But, crucially, feminine signifying value, integrity, and desire have been recognized, have been acknowledged, and the Wife celebrates "Housbondes meeke, younge, and fressh abedde" 1259) in this last passage. Her final call for wifely governance and longevity functions, I think, *within* the renovated patriarchal scheme; her final repetition of the language of mastery reveals and indicts its power of exclusion. Men's desire is still in control, as her tale shows, but feminine desire must continue to be acknowledged.

Chaucer thus responds to the imperatives raised by his representation of masculine narrators' misogynistic literary acts in *Troilus and Criseyde,* the *Legend of Good Women,* and the *Man of Law's Tale* by creating the Wife of Bath, who speaks as the excluded feminine. Her *Tale's* final vision of the joyous and mutually satisfying unveiling of the feminine is, of course, deeply gratifying to the male reader and author—one who, as we have seen, has worried about the vulnerability, even the potentially wayward afterlife of his little books (and one who, moreover, was apparently himself threatened with an accusation of rape). But Chaucer was not *only* fulfilling his masculine authorial dreams in creating the Wife. He has imagined patriarchy from the Other's point of view and has duly reckoned the costs of clerkly discourse in terms of the feminine body. The first thing we hear about the Wife is that she is permanently injured: "A good WIF was ther OF biside BATHE, / But she was somdel deef, and that was scathe" (1:445–46). The story of that injury perpetrated by a clerk motivates the narrative of the Prologue ("But now to purpos, why I tolde thee / That I was beten for a book, pardee!" [711–12]). She is deafened, and she will feel Jankyn's blows in her bones forevermore (505–7); clerks cause her emotional and physical "wo . . . and pyne" (787) for writing of women as they do.[26] That a woman would respond to patriarchal discourse in precisely these terms is dramatically affirmed by Christine de Pizan, who describes a scene that powerfully recalls the book-inspired violence of the Wife's Prologue. Christine's specific point here, one among many in her long letter to Pierre Col about the deleterious effects of the *Rose,* is that women suffer physically on account of clerkly antifeminist writing:

> Not long ago, I heard one of your familiar companions and colleagues, a man of authority, say that he knew a married man who believed in the *Roman de la Rose* as in the gospel. This was an extremely jealous man, who, whenever in the grip of passion, would go and find the book and read it to his wife; then he would become violent and strike her and say such horrible things as, "These are the kinds of tricks you pull on me. This good, wise man Master Jean de Meun knew well what women are capable of." And at every word he finds appropriate, he gives her a couple of kicks or slaps. Thus it seems clear to me that whatever other people think of this book, this poor woman pays too high a price for it.[27]

Chaucer revises and keeps the patriarchal ideology behind the image of the captive woman, but he recognizes that the achievement of respectful relationships of husband and wife, reader and text—the acknowledgement of the value of the feminine, both woman and letter—is accomplished at a dear cost and that it is still only a fantasy—the Wife's, in the fictionalized happily-ever-after of her Prologue and *Tale,* and his own fantasy, dreamed through her. In the real relations between husband and wife, clerk and text, as he makes clear, masculine glossing does not come without violence to the feminine corpus. It remains for another clerk, the pilgrim traveling on the way to Canterbury and listening to the Wife of Bath, to elaborate on the lived bodily effects of literary acts—the bodily effects on women, and the bodily effects of making literary images at all. The affinity of *this* Oxford clerk, we find unexpectedly, is with the Wife of Bath, with Griselda in his tale, with the feminine. Chaucer has not done with the Wife of Bath and "al hire secte" by any means. In her Prologue and *Tale* he represents the woman as assertively mimicking masculine discourse; the *Clerk's Tale* turns out to be a reflection on what it means for a male author to be a female impersonator.

Notes

[Ed. note: This chapter of Dinshaw's *Chaucer's Sexual Poetics* picks up from a discussion of the Man of Law's Tale in the preceding chapter. A reference (in the third paragraph) to Jerome's treatment of Deuteronomy 21 is worth glossing. As Dinshaw explains in her introduction, Jerome advocates treating classical texts as the captive woman is treated in Deuteronomy 21:10–13. When a beautiful woman is captured in battle, according to the biblical text, "Thou shalt bring her into thy house: and she shall shave her hair, and pare her nails, And shall put off the raiment, wherein she was taken: and shall remain in thy house, and mourn for her father and mother one month: and after that thou shalt go in unto her, and shalt sleep with her, and she shall be thy wife." In Jerome's analogy, the beautiful pagan text is likewise to be stripped of its seductive charms and "domesticated" (Dinshaw's word) through interpretation. See *Chaucer's Sexual Poetics,* 22–25.]

1.   The ascription of speaker to these lines is uncertain. The entire Epilogue to the *Man of Law's Tale* presents textual difficulties: it does not appear in twenty-two of the fifty-seven manuscripts of the *Canterbury Tales,* including Ellesmere, a condition that suggests to Robinson that Chaucer abandoned it in his developing plan for the *Tales.* But, as Robinson goes on to state, there is no question of its genuineness as Chaucerian. *Who* interrupts the Host at line 1178 is uncertain from the textual evidence: manuscripts ascribe the speech to the Shipman, the Squire, or the Summoner (see Robinson's summary account, in *The Works of Geoffrey Chaucer,* ed. F. N. Robinson, 2d ed. [Boston: Houghton Mifflin, 1957], pp. 696–97). I follow Robert Pratt's argument in his classic article, "The Development of the Wife of Bath" (in *Studies in Medieval Literature in Honor of Professor Albert Croll Baugh,* ed. MacEdward Leach [Philadelphia: Univ. of Pennsylvania Press, 1961], pp. 45–79), that the lines were originally written for the Wife of Bath in order to link the *Man of Law's Tale* to her tale (which was later reassigned to the Shipman after Chaucer wrote a new prologue and tale for her). Pratt, of course, follows the Bradshaw shift in putting the *Shipman's Tale* after this endlink (Fragment B[2]), but his argument about the lines' speaker doesn't necessitate this move. (For a defense of the Ellesmere order, see E. T. Donaldson, "The Ordering of the *Canterbury Tales,*" in *Medieval Literature and Folklore Studies: Essays in Honor of Francis Lee Utley,* ed. Jerome Mandel and Bruce A. Rosenberg [New Brunswick, N.J.: Rutgers Univ. Press, 1970], pp. 193–204.) The verbal echoes of the Man of Law's Epilogue in the *Shipman's Tale*—and in the later Wife of Bath's Prologue and *Tale*—are unmistakable: "joly body," for example, occurs at line 423 of the *Shipman's Tale.* Although the second and third editions of Robinson print "Seyde the Shipman" at line 1179,

both Fisher and Donaldson, in their editions, emend the text to make the Wife of Bath the speaker of these lines.

Lee Patterson, " 'For the Wyves love of Bathe': Feminine Rhetoric and Poetic Resolution in the *Roman de la Rose* and the *Canterbury Tales*," *Speculum* 58 (1983):656–95, has explicated the significance of the Wife of Bath's "joly body" in terms that prefigure my own, and makes many related points. As he puts it, "The Wife's text . . . solicits both body and mind, and it requires for its explication both an erotics and a hermeneutic" (p. 658). In observing that "the language of poetry, as enacted by the poet and received by the reader, is habitually conceived in the Middle Ages in sexual, and specifically in feminine terms" (p. 659), he suggests a structure of sexualized poetics consonant with the one I describe here, and he undertakes, as I do, to determine what the creation of the Wife means to Chaucer's masculine poetic self-definition. The Wife proposes, in Patterson's terms, a "reading at once both literal and moral" (p. 694); but while I stress the patriarchal gratifications of such a hermeneutic, Patterson proposes a more fully subversive cultural value for it.

2.   The Wife's clothing seems to have been an essential part of her character from her very beginnings as teller of the *Shipman's Tale,* as several critics, including Pratt, have observed (see n. 1 above, on the Wife of Bath as original teller of that tale). The narrator's voice, as the *Shipman's Tale* opens, insists that husbands must clothe their wives properly, "in which array we daunce jolily" (7:14). The wife in the tale needs money to pay for new clothes, so she borrows from the lascivious monk John (and pays for these "frankes" with her "flankes" [201–2]). But clothes are absorbed into the larger economic nexus of the *Shipman's Tale:* see Gerhard Joseph, "Chaucer's Coinage: Foreign Exchange and the Puns of the *Shipman's Tale*," *ChauR* 17 (1983): 341–57; and Thomas Hahn, "Money, Sexuality, Wordplay, and Context in the *Shipman's Tale*," in *Chaucer in the Eighties,* ed. Julian N. Wasserman and Robert J. Blanch (Syracuse, N.Y.: Syracuse Univ. Press, 1986), pp. 235–49. As Patterson, in "For the Wyves love of Bathe," has also suggested, although an association of the literary and the sexual is suggested in the triple pun on "taillying" at the end of the tale, it remains for the Wife of Bath, in her present Prologue and *Tale,* to develop the full hermeneutic value of her "joly body" in her fine and showy dress.

3.   It is along this continuum defined by the Hieronymian paradigm—compliant, passive, silent brides on the one end, vocal Others on the other end—that almost all the female characters of the *Canterbury Tales* can in fact be read: Alisoun of the *Miller's Tale,* May of the *Merchant's Tale,* the Prioress (a bride of Christ), and Pertelote, to name a few.

4.   For an argument supporting the claim that Chaucer intends to show respect for literal reading in his creation of the Wife as literal exegete, see Lawrence Besserman, " 'Glosynge Is a Glorious Thyng': Chaucer's Biblical Exegesis," in *Chaucer and Scriptural Tradition,* ed. David Lyle Jeffrey (Ottawa: Univ. of Ottawa Press, 1984), pp. 65–73. Besserman suggests that Chaucer's increasing respect for the letter might have derived from the contemporary, antifraternal movement as well as from late fourteenth-century English biblical translators. (On the issue of the literal, see also Douglas Wurtele, "Chaucer's *Canterbury Tales* and Nicholas of Lyre's *Postillae litteralis et moralis super totam Bibliam,*" in *Chaucer and Scriptural Tradition,* pp. 89–107.) I shall discuss Chaucer's possible response to these late fourteenth-century movements in my treatment of the *Pardoner's Tale,* in Chapter 6, agreeing with Besserman's idea but also suggesting that a good deal of anxiety about the integrity of the letter motivates that growing "respect." The argument about Chaucer's respect for literal exegesis goes counter to D. W. Robertson's famous pronouncements about the Wife in *A Preface to Chaucer* (Princeton, N.J.: Princeton Univ. Press, 1962), pp. 317–31. For more recent articulations of a basically Robertsonian position, see Graham D. Caie, "The Significance of the Early Chaucer Manuscript Glosses (with Special Reference to the *Wife of Bath's Prologue*)," *ChauR* 10 (1976): 350–60; and Sarah Disbrow, "The Wife of Bath's Old Wives' Tale," *SAC* 8 (1986): 59–71.

5.   The exact source of the *Wife of Bath's Tale* is unknown, but of the known analogues (including *The Marriage of Sir Gawain, The Wedding of Sir Gawen and Dame Ragnell,* and the *Tale of Florent* in Gower's *Confessio amantis*), none includes a rape. For a summary of possible narra-

tive sources of the rape, see the *Riverside Chaucer*, 872–73; and see, for contrast to my discussion, Bernard F. Huppé's "Rape and Woman's Sovereignty in the *Wife of Bath's Tale*" (*Modern Language Notes* 63 [1948]: 378–81), for an analysis of the rape as an "indication of the structural perfection" (p. 378) of the tale.

6. Luce Irigaray, *This Sex Which Is Not One*, trans. Catherine Porter (Ithaca, N.Y.: Cornell Univ. Press, 1985), p. 76. For an expression of the view that the Wife of Bath is "confined within the prison house of masculine language," see Patterson, p. 682; see also Hope Phyllis Weissman, "Antifeminism and Chaucer's Characterization of Women," in *Geoffrey Chaucer*, ed. George D. Economou (New York: McGraw-Hill, 1975), esp. pp. 104–10; and Susan Crane, "Alison's Incapacity and Poetic Instability in the *Wife of Bath's Tale*," *PMLA* 102 (1987): 20–28.

7. Pratt, "The Development of the Wife of Bath," p. 45.

8. Robert B. Burlin, in his *Chaucerian Fiction* ([Princeton, N.J.: Princeton Univ. Press, 1977], pp. 217–27), provides an optimistic analysis of the Wife's ability to "transcen[d] the limits of [her] own fictive universe": "When the Wife of Bath attacks Jankyn's book, which is both her enemy and the source of her being, it is as if she were usurping the role of creator, destroying the 'original' so that she might recast herself in her own image" (pp. 225, 227). But that "as if" is crucial: Chaucer is, of course, still and ever her creator, and we must ask what purpose it serves him to create a woman who *seems* to usurp the role of creator.

9. Sheila Delany uses this term in her chapter, "Sexual Economics, Chaucer's Wife of Bath, and *The Book of Margery Kempe*," in her *Writing Woman: Women Writers and Women in Literature, Medieval to Modern* (New York: Schocken, 1983), pp. 76–92. She defines it as "the psychological effects of economic necessity, specifically upon sexual mores" (p. 77) and analyzes the Wife's successful exploitation of her own commodification in terms of the profit motive and the law of supply and demand.

10. Claude Lévi-Strauss, *The Elementary Structures of Kinship*, trans. James Harle Bell, John Richard von Sturmer, and Rodney Needham, rev. ed. (Boston: Beacon, 1969), pp. 36–38; Irigaray, "Women on the Market," in *This Sex Which Is Not One*, pp. 170–71.

11. Patterson, " 'For the Wyves love of Bathe,' " provides full documentation of various antifeminist texts and Chaucer's possible use of them in creating the Wife. See, further, R. Howard Bloch's "Medieval Misogyny" (*Representations* 20 [Fall 1987]: 1–24), for a discussion of the repetitiveness and monotony of antifeminist writers, and of the ways in which antifeminist writers are themselves inescapably feminized in their ceaseless talking against women who ceaselessly talk.

12. Saint Jerome, *Adversus Jovinianum*, trans. W. H. Fremantle, in *A Select Library of Nicene and Post-Nicene Fathers of the Christian Church* (Grand Rapids, Mich.: Eerdmans, n.d.), 6:383.

> Deinde per noctes totas garrulae conquestiones: Illa ornatior procedit in publicum: haec honoratur ab omnibus, ego in conventu feminarum misella despicior. Cur aspiciebas vicinam? quid cum ancillula loquebaris? (Saint Jerome, *Adversus Jovinianum* 1. 47, in *PL* 23:276)

13. Guillaume de Lorris and Jean de Meun, *Le Roman de la rose*, trans. Charles Dahlberg, under the title *The Romance of the Rose* (Princeton, N.J.: Princeton Univ. Press, 1971), p. 227.

> . . . jurt que, s'il eüst volu
> soffrir que par autre fust prise
> sa rose, qui bien est requise,
> d'or fust chargiez et de joiaus;
> mes tant est ses fins queur loiaus

que ja nus la main n'i tendra
fors cil seus qui lors la tendra.
(*Le Roman de la rose,* vv. 13082–88 [ed. Félix Lecoy,
CFMA 98 (Paris: Honoré Champion, 1970)]).

14.   Irigaray, *This Sex Which Is Not One,* p. 76.

15.   In the following general comments about glossing, I have drawn on: the summary article by Francis E. Gigot in *The Catholic Encyclopedia* (New York: Appleton, 1909), 6: 586–88; Beryl Smalley, *The Study of the Bible in the Middle Ages,* 3d ed. (Oxford: Basil Blackwell, 1983); Henri de Lubac, *Exégèse médiévale,* 4 vols. (Paris: Aubier, 1959); C. Spicq, *Esquisse d'une histoire de l'exégèse latine au moyen âge,* Bibliothèque thomiste 26 (Paris: J. Vrin, 1944), esp. pp. 62–108, 202–88; *Cambridge History of the Bible,* ed. P. R. Ackroyd, C. F. Evans, G. W. H. Lampe, S. L. Greenslade, 3 vols. (Cambridge: Cambridge Univ. Press, 1963–70); and Hennig Brinkmann, *Mittelalterliche Hermeneutik* (Tübingen: Max Niemeyer, 1980), esp. pp. 154–163.

16.   See the *Prefatio* to his *Sententie,* in *Oeuvres de Robert de Melun,* ed. Raymond M. Martin, O.P., Spicilegium Sacrum Lovaniense (Louvain, 1947), 3:12, and Smalley's discussion of it (*The Study of the Bible,* pp. 215–30). Robert attacked not only the practice of glossing, with its removal of passages from contexts and alterations of syntax and diction (he speaks of the violence [*violentia*] done to the text [p. 17]), but also the very idea of glossing: if the gloss only repeats what the text says, it is worthless; if it changes what the text says, it is worse than worthless (pp. 13–14). As Smalley points out, Robert's critique of the authority of glosses is founded on a reverence for the inviolate word of Scripture itself. This is an impractical position for the teaching of scriptural interpretation, as Smalley says; nonetheless, it demonstrates an anxiety about the deformation and appropriation of the text by glossing (see *The Study of the Bible,* pp. 229–30)

17.   Caie, "The Significance of the Early Chaucer Manuscript Glosses," p. 350.

18.   Robert of Melun, *Prefatio,* p. 18, describes the masters as ready to fight for their glosses ("*usque ad sanguinem* pro eis, si opus esset, decertare parati" [emphasis in original]), and speaks of the violence to the literal text on p. 17; Christine de Pizan, letter 14, in *La Querelle de la Rose: Letters and Documents,* ed. and trans. Joseph L. Baird and John R. Kane (Chapel Hill: Univ. of North Carolina Dept. of Romance Languages, 1978), p. 140. "Voire, come dist le proverbe commun des gloses d'Orliens, qui destruisent le texte" (Christine de Pizan, "A Maistre Pierre Col, Secretaire du Roy Nostre Sire," in *Le Débat sur "Le Roman de la rose,"* ed. Eric Hicks [Paris: Honoré Champion, 1977], p. 144).

19.   See n. 4 above for critical discussions of the Wife's literality as an exegete.

20.   For criticism that focuses on the Wife of Bath, glossing and glossators, see Daniel S. Silvia, Jr., "Glosses to the *Canterbury Tales* from St. Jerome's *Epistola Adversus Jovinianum,*" *SP* 62 (1965): 28–39; and Graham D. Caie, "The Significance of the Early Chaucer Manuscript Glosses." Anne Kernan, in "The Archwife and the Eunuch" (*ELH* 41 [1974]: 1–25), observes in detail the Wife's relationship to exegetical commentary (which I am including under the general rubric "glossing"). The *locus classicus* for the Wife's relation to exegetes is Robertson, *Preface to Chaucer,* pp. 317–31.

21.   For comments on Jerome's pseudologicality and rhetorical excesses in *Adversus Jovinianum,* see E. Talbot Donaldson, "Designing a Camel; or, Generalizing the Middle Ages," *Tennessee Studies in Literature* 22 (1977): 1–16; Kernan, "The Archwife and the Eunuch," pp. 16–19; and Mary Carruthers, "The Wife of Bath and the Painting of Lions," *PMLA* 94 (1979): 211. Pammachius, whose initiative inspired Jerome to refute Jovinian in the first place, saw Jerome's polemic as excessive and suppressed as many copies of the treatise as he could—and this action was taken with Jerome's own approval. Douglas Wurtele, however, in "The Predicament of Chaucer's Wife of Bath: St. Jerome on Virginity" (*Florilegium* 5 [1983]: 208–36), performing a point-by-point summary and analysis of Jerome and the Wife's Prologue, finds Jerome's argument effective and the hapless Wife unable to refute it.

22.   De Lubac speaks of one of the common faults of late fourteenth-century exegesis as "la pulverization du texte" (see *Exégèse médiévale,* vol. 2, pt. 2, ch. 9, "L'Age scolastique," esp. pp. 350–53, and ch. 10, "Humanistes et spirituels," pp. 369–513).

23.   See Donald R. Howard, *The Idea of the Canterbury Tales* (Berkeley and Los Angeles: Univ. of California Press, 1976), pp. 247–55; see also H. Marshall Leicester, Jr., "Of a Fire in the Dark: Public and Private Feminism in the *Wife of Bath's Tale,*" *Women's Studies* 11 (1984): 157–78.

24.   For a sophisticated analysis of the use of the romance in the Wife's performance, see Louise O. Fradenburg, "The Wife of Bath's Passing Fancy," *SAC* 8 (1986): 31–58. Fradenburg argues that the romance, in the late fourteenth century, became the genre in which the problematics of the categories of the past and of woman intersected.

25.   Patterson's " 'The Wyves love of Bathe'" analyses the whole phenomenon of the Wife's rhetorical strategy as one of dilation, delay; his comments on her Midas digression appear on pp. 656–58.

26.   For a less sympathetic reading of the Wife's deafness, see Melvin Storm, "Alisoun's Ear," *MLQ* 42 (1981): 219–26. Storm supports the reading of Robertson: her deafness is an iconographic representation of her unregenerate Pauline oldness.

27.   Christine de Pizan, letter 14, in *La Querelle de la Rose,* trans. Baird and Kane, p. 136.

Je oÿ dire, n'a pas moult, a ·i· de ces compaingnons de l'office dont tu es et que tu bien congnois, et homme d'auctorité, que il congnoit ung home marié, lequel ajouste foy au *Ronmant de la Rose* comme a l'Euvangile; celluy est souverainnement jaloux, et quant sa passion le tient plus aigrement il va querre son livre et list devant sa fame, et puis fiert et frappe sus et dist: "Orde, telle come quelle il dist, voir que tu me fais tel tour. Ce bon sage homme maistre Jehan de Meung savoit bien que femmes savoient fere!" Et a chascun mot qu'il treuve a son propos il fiert ung coup ou deux du pié ou de la paume; si m'est advis que quiconques s'en loe, telle povre famme le compere chier. (Christine de Pizan to Pierre Col, *Le Débat sur "Le Roman de la rose,"* pp. 139–40)

The Powers of Silence:
The Case of the Clerk's Griselda

ELAINE TUTTLE HANSEN

> To take a stand would be to upset the beautiful balance of the game.
> Richard A. Lanham,
> "Chaucer's *Clerk's Tale:*
> The Poem Not the Myth"

To most Chaucerians, it is by now either commonplace or irrelevant to point out that the *Clerk's Tale,* like so many of Chaucer's poems, situates a strong female character in what one modern editor describes as "a context of masculine authoritarianism."[1] Recognizing this situation does not seem to resolve the interpreters' fundamental confusion about the Tale's meaning. This confusion, in fact, is one of the few things that a number of critics can agree upon: whatever its specific significance, this poem appears to many to be bound up with its ambiguities and contradictions, the insolubility of its many problems.[2] The force of gender conflict in the Tale is thus at once recognized and neutralized; if Chaucer takes no definitive position on the victimization of women that he so clearly depicts, then we need not raise charged and difficult questions about misogyny and great Western art, and we can instead contemplate "the beautiful balance of the game," a playful, aesthetic foreclosure of the problems of sexual politics and gendered poetics.

Here I want to recharge the question of the impenetrability of the *Clerk's Tale* with further consideration of the nature of "masculine authoritarianism" in the poem. The text offers readers a fundamentally equivocal—and hence rich and compelling—confrontation with patriarchal power, a confrontation necessitated and implicated by the literary project foregrounded in all the Chaucerian fiction I have examined thus far: the representation of a male author telling, with great verbal skill and studied, multivalent ambiguities, the story of a female character. In the first part of my discussion, focusing on

From *Chaucer and the Fictions of Gender.* © 1992 the Regents of the University of California. Reprinted by permission of the Regents of the University of California and the University of California Press.

the female character and her multiple, slippery significations, I argue that the tale of patient Griselda addresses central questions about women and power and articulates a clear paradox. Woman's insubordination is, as our lexicon suggests, a derivative of her subordination. In the second half of the chapter, focusing on the representation of the male author, I ask again what kind of men, in Chaucerian fiction, choose to tell such stories about women, and why and how such men might well prefer to play games and make jokes rather than take a stand.

"This is ynogh, Grisilde myn."
IV.365, 1051

From one point of view, the plot of Griselda's story demonstrates how a woman may rise to the highest position of hegemonic power, becoming the honored wife of a wealthy lord and a coruler of his kingdom, through her archetypally acceptable behavior: utter submissiveness and essential silence. Griselda is a complicated figure of both class mobility and the classless (or cross-class), feminized ideals of Christian thinking. She succeeds in rising from poorest peasant to ruling aristocrat—and at another level even serves, the Clerk reminds us, as an allegorical figure for the patient Christian soul— by living up to her culture's image of perfect femininity, by willfully accept- ing and even reveling in the powerlessness of her position.[3] To some modern readers, of course, Griselda may not in this way represent a positive model of female power, but rather the kind of prescriptive antifeminist propaganda for which the medieval period is well known.[4] Even from the naturalistic point of view that the Clerk sometimes at least insists on, the happy ending brings the heroine the dubious reward of permanent union with a man whom the Clerk, embellishing his sources, has characterized as a sadistic tyrant, worst of men and cruelest of husbands (although not, he suggests, unrealistic or atypical in this regard). The Clerk's peculiar handling of the Griselda story both sup- ports and complicates such responses by exploring the implications of Griselda's paradoxical position as a woman: the fact that she attains certain kinds of power by embracing powerlessness; the fact that she is strong, in other words, because she is so perfectly weak. The Tale suggests on one hand that Griselda is not really empowered by her acceptable behavior, because the feminine virtue she embodies in welcoming her subordination is by definition both punitive and self-destructive. On the other hand, the Tale reveals that the perfectly good woman *is* powerful, or at least potentially so, insofar as her suffering and submission are fundamentally insubordinate and deeply threat- ening to men and to the concepts of power and gender identity upon which patriarchal culture is premised.

The *Clerk's Tale* specifies early in the plot that even legitimate exercises of direct power only endanger a woman's well-being. Immediately after his description of Walter and Griselda's marriage, the Clerk, following his sources, points out how swiftly and remarkably the good peasant girl is transformed into the perfect noblewoman. In the space of a few stanzas (393–441), we learn that after her marriage Griselda is beloved by Walter's people and famed in many regions; people travel to Saluzzo, we are told, just to see her. Not merely a paragon of "wyfly hoomlinesse," she also serves the public interest (the "commune profit," 431) by acting in her husband's absence as a peerless adjudicator who settles all disputes with her "wise and rype wordes" (438). The passage seems in its own right to document Griselda's innate "virtue"—but the root of the word "virtue" itself, from the Latin for "male person," signals what the *Clerk's Tale* subsequently affirms: a *vir*tuous *woman,* the stuff of folk tales and saints' legends, is a contradiction, a semantic anomaly, a threat to the social order and to the stability of gender difference and hierarchy.

Walter, it appears, recognizes part of this threat right away. Griselda's public virtue, her ability to exert a power at once masculine in kind and superhuman in degree, would seem to vindicate the sovereign's willful choice of an unsuitable bride beyond his wildest dreams; people soon say, according to the Clerk, that Griselda is literally a godsend. But Walter's decision to torture and humiliate her as a wife and mother comes, according to the narrative, after she has been acclaimed as a saintly ruler, and so the narrative sequence implies on the contrary that such virtue in a woman only provokes male aggression. A woman's public powers, even if they are conferred upon her through her husband and divinely sanctioned, cannot be integrated with her proper identity as a female and a wife. Griselda's supposedly unusual and seemingly innate ability to rule wisely and well, to pass good judgments and speak in ways that men admire and respect, to assume, that is, the power and position normally assigned to the best of men, fails to empower her or enable her to escape her subordinate gendered status. Her situation may in this way remind us of a point made by modern feminist analyses of history: the occasional existence of a strong, wise, and successful female in a position of power is the exception that proves the rule; the token Virgin Mother or queen or bourgeois female entrepreneur does not alter the material position of most women or the conventional definition of the feminine. To prove her "wommanhede," Griselda must suffer and submit; the more obviously unsuitable part of her virtue—her allegedly inherent but nevertheless unnatural manliness and power—must be punished and contained.

One reason why Griselda's public virtues must be controlled, why the good woman of any social class must be defined as silent and submissive, seems patent. If a peasant woman can so easily rule as well as a noble man—or even better—then Walter's birthright and the whole feudal system on which it depends are seriously threatened. This realization is surely part of the Clerk's meaning when he remarks, near the end of the tale, that it would be "inportable," or intolerable, unbearable, if real wives behaved like Griselda. His comment seems intended to heighten the pathos and abstraction of his portrait of Griselda and to express yet again his alleged sympathy with her situation as a woman; it also suggests, however, his sympathy with Walter and his understanding that it is precisely Griselda's saintliness, her superhuman—or inhuman—goodness, her feminine ability to be just what he asks her to be, that (rightly, or at least understandably) enrages her husband. For as the tale goes on to disclose, if Walter is at first shown up, defeated, and made powerless by the position and authority he hands his wife, which she so effortlessly and successfully wields, he is again all but undone by the self-abasement that he then demands and that she, ever obedient and adaptable to her situation, so easily and successfully performs. Galled by the unbearable way in which this woman eludes his tyranny by refusing to resist and define it, he can only torture her again and again, seeking to determine her elusive identity as well as his own, to find the Other in Griselda, someone he can master in order to find himself.

The series of seemingly unmotivated trials proving Griselda's worth also emphasizes that the better Griselda is, the more she must suffer, or that the more she suffers the better she must be. While this principle is consistent with medieval Christian thought, we shall see at the close of the tale that one logical conclusion of this potentially fatal prescription for female virtue proves troubling. The end of the heroine's suffering must in a sense spell the end of her virtue, and what voice Griselda has is silenced, her story finished, when Walter finally stops torturing her. And what makes Walter stop, after the third trial, may be his eventual understanding of the paradoxical sense in which this woman continues to win, in venerable Christian fashion, by losing so fully and graciously to a tyrannical man.

The last scene of the tale becomes crucial to our understanding of the complex interaction of the subordination and insubordination of the female; Griselda almost beats Walter to the draw. She has been called back to the palace to clean it up for Walter's second wedding, and, as the nobles sit down to dinner, Walter calls the old wife over to ask how she likes his beautiful new one. But in the preceding stanza we have learned that Griselda is already busy praising the girl and her brother "So wel that no man koude hir prise amende" (1026). When Walter, who hasn't apparently noticed what she's up to, foolishly invites her to come center stage for a moment, in her rags, Griselda seizes the opportunity to protest and celebrate, at the same time, her own treatment at Walter's hands. First she wishes him well of his lovely young bride; at the same time that she once again accepts and cooperates in her own abasement here, she subtly praises herself, born again into better circumstances, and engages in the competition between women, even between mother and daughter, that her culture enforces. She goes on to warn Walter not to torment the maiden as he has tormented "mo" ("others"), as she tactfully puts it; Griselda predicts that the well-born creature could not endure what the poor one could. Her strategy recalls her earlier move when she responded to banishment with the longest, most pathetic speech in the poem

(814–89), but this time Walter knows better than to let his patient wife have the floor for more than one stanza. He is at this point said to "rewen upon hire wyfly stedfastnesse" (1050), and while the chief sense of "rewen upon" is "to feel pity or compassion for," we may also think of the more familiar sense of the verb, one which was also current in Middle English: "to regard or think of . . . with sorrow or regret, to wish that (something) had never taken place or existed."[5]

Walter must indeed regret Griselda's surpassing wifely steadfastness, because whichever way he turns, it all but defeats his lordly urge to dominate. When in the next stanza he tells Griselda, " 'This is ynogh, Grisilde myn,' " we are reminded that he said this once before, when she gave her initial promise (365), and in retrospect the repetition may underline for Walter the dangers inherent in the way Griselda from the beginning sought to exceed his demands for wifely subordination. In setting the conditions for their marriage, he asked only that she would do what he wished, and never contradict his will. She promised far more: a perilous merging of wills ("But as ye wole yourself, right so wol I" [361]), which would in fact imply her full knowledge of his will and thus destabilize the power differential and difference between them; and a surrender of her own life ("In werk ne thoght, I nyl yow disobeye, / For to be deed, though me were looth to deye,"[363–64]), which again would defeat his intention to keep her, alive, under his thumb. When, at the end of the story, he sets the limit to her excessive self-abasement, which is beginning to be coupled with the self-assertion it always entails, we cannot be sure whether he intends to call a halt to her suffering or to her emergent powers of subversive speech—powers paradoxically dependent on his continued oppression of her. When he goes on to seal Griselda's lips with kisses, her reaction is telling. She is so stunned, the Clerk says, that for a moment she cannot hear Walter's astonishing concession that she has finally proved herself in his eyes: "She herde nat what thyng he to hire seyde; / She ferde as she had stert out of a sleep" (1059–60). Griselda's temporary deafness and stupor represent, I suggest, her unwillingness to hear that the nightmare is over. She knows that any power she has lies only in continuing to excel at suffering, that she can speak only to assent to being silenced, and that the promise of a happy ending precludes her potential for martyred apotheosis, and forces her to awaken into the reality of her material, gendered powerlessness.

In the second half of this chapter I shall explore what happens after this climactic moment, in the multiple endings of the *Clerk's Tale,* as the Clerk himself confirms Griselda's powerlessness at many levels, but let me conclude this section by underscoring some implications of the reading I have just offered. Griselda has threatened to escape Walter's tyranny by willfully refusing to resist it, and it is possible to argue that he keeps testing her because given his view of selfhood and power, her behavior can only seem to him unmotivated, implausible, irritating, and even inhuman. As the Clerk says after the second trial, Walter "wondred" at his wife's patience; if he hadn't known better, he would have thought that she took some perverse or treacherous delight in seeing her children murdered (687–95), and modern readers have frequently complained that Griselda was not a good enough mother. In one way Griselda's behavior is certainly both perverse and treacherous, not because she fails to protect her children against paternal infanticide and thus to live up to ideals (and realities) of motherhood, but because she lives up all too well to certain ideals of womanhood and thus makes manifest their latent powers. Walter cannot and does not solve the mystery or negate the threat that her perfect womanly behavior poses; he merely stops trying to do so and stops giving his wife the chance to act in ways that he cannot understand or control.

Just as she remains a mystery and a threat to Walter, so too Griselda remains an unresolved problem for the Clerk and for his audiences. The *Clerk's Tale* suggests, and generations of modern interpreters confirm, that Griselda is a "humanly unintelligible" entity, as one critic puts it, comprehensible and coherent only at the allegorical level that the Clerk at once entertains and undermines.[6] In an unusual way, the inhumanity and perhaps inhumaneness of Griselda's perfect femininity confirms that the human is often posited as equivalent to the masculine in the symbolic order that reaches from the western European Middle Ages into more recent centuries. At the same time, the problem she presents—the unintelligibility of the perfectly good woman, or perhaps of any woman—is the most threatening thing about her. Griselda's embodiment of the archetypally feminine position thus not only insists on the absence and silence and powerlessness of real women in history but also marks again the limits of power for masculine authority (Walter), for the male author (the Clerk), and for the audience attempting to fix the meaning of the female character in the tale.

> Grisilde is deed, and eek hire pacience.
> IV.1177

Viewed as a poem about either a woman's subversive silence or her silenced subversion, the *Clerk's Tale* thus affirms two conclusions about the history of masculine and feminine power in Western culture. It suggests that "maleness," as Catharine MacKinnon has put it, has often been perceived as "a form of power that is both omnipotent and nonexistent, an unreal thing with very real consequences."[7] It also explains why Woman, identified as absence, is a fearsome ideal for both real women and masculine presence. Turning the focus of my reading to the Clerk now, I want to suggest that the oft-noted and characteristic ambiguity of the tale is most fruitfully read as a reflex of his position as a male storyteller, which turns out to be much the same here, where the narrator is an unbeneficed cleric writing in a specifically religious mode and explicitly translating from Latin, as when he is a secular court poet translating from the vernacular. To support and flesh out this claim, it is possible to compare the subtle Clerk of the *Canterbury Tales* with one narrator who exemplifies the coyness, insecurity, and playful evasiveness that we see in the narrators of all the earlier dream-visions and *Troilus and Criseyde:* the poet of the *Legend of Good Women.*

The *Clerk's Tale* and the *Legend of Good Women* are not, as far as I know, frequently compared, but the comparison is in fact indirectly suggested within the *Canterbury Tales,* where the Legends are invoked in the preface to the *Man of Law's Tale,* a poem that, in the most common ordering of the Tales, comes right before the *Wife of Bath's Tale,* to which the Clerk in turn is responding. The link between the *Man of Law's Tale* and the *Clerk's Tale* is reinforced by the fact that both are female saints' lives, potentially or actually bracketing the Wife's monstrous tale of feminine misrule. The Clerk may emphasize this point with his two allusions to the Man of Law's heroine, Constance: one when Walter finally admits that Griselda is "constant as a wal" (1047), and one when the Clerk says that we should all be, like Griselda, "constant in adversitee" (1146). And even if we read the tales in another order, or discount the dramatic interaction between tellers altogether, the analogies between Griselda in the *Canterbury Tales* and the female saints of the *Legend of Good Women* are obvious. All these women are represented as archetypally passive. They put the love of a man above all other responsibilities, even above life itself. As a direct consequence of this love they endure great suffering. (The heroines of the earlier poem almost all die; Griselda's survival, at least until the *Lenvoy de Chaucer* proclaims her demise, may thus indicate either a flaw in her goodness, or the story's need, like Walter's, to keep her alive in order to punish and contain her perfection.) The unremarked similarities between the men who tell this kind of story, the narrator of the *Legend* and the Clerk of Oxenford, are equally obvious and perhaps more subtly interesting, and three prominent features of their performances warrant comparison: the ostensive circumstances under which they tell their stories, the changes they make in their sources, and their closural strategies.

In both the *Legend of Good Women* and in the *Canterbury Tales,* the audience is made privy to specific circumstances or preconditions, outside and prior to the narratives of good women, that occasion each act of storytelling and hence oblige us to speculate about the dramatized motives and attitudes of both the poet/dreamer of the earlier poem and the Clerk of Oxenford, and to see each narrator's voiced personality as part of the meaning of his fiction. In the *Canterbury Tales,* not in a dream but in the framing matter of his tale, the Clerk, like the narrator of the *Legend,* is commanded to tell a story— "Telle us som murie thyng of aventures" (15)—by the Host, a figure who like Cupid in the dream assumes godlike powers of judgment and behaves like a tyrant. The Host first makes fun of the Clerk's unaggressive, even effeminate behavior: "Ye ryde as coy and stille as dooth a mayde / Were newe spoused, sittynge at the bord" (2–3). He reminds the Clerk that he agreed to submit to the Host's authority when he entered into the "pley" (10). The Clerk's professional status is also underscored by the Host's prohibitions against an overly didactic or boring tale in the "heigh style" associated with learned clerks (18). In the *Wife of Bath's Prologue* (separated from the *Clerk's Tale* only by the *Friar's* and *Summoner's Tales*), clerks in general, again like the poet/dreamer of the *Legend of Good Women,* have already been associated with and castigated for their literally antifeminism. The Clerk appears to accede more meekly to the tyrant's commands than the dreamer does, just as we would expect from the quiet, virtuous, willing learner introduced in the *General Prologue.* But even before the tale proper begins, the coy Clerk also quietly defies the Host's orders by translating, within an ostensibly disparaging framework ("Me thynketh it a thyng impertinent" [54]) almost all of Petrarch's "prohemye" to the story. This is presumably just the kind of elevated, clerkly fare that the Host hoped to forestall, and its inclusion clearly suggests that this Clerk has his own share of the impertinence he displaces onto Petrarch, that crafty impudence associated with others of his profession throughout the *Canterbury Tales.*

If we are obliged to recognize even before we begin to listen to their stories that both the Clerk and the poet/dreamer of the *Legend of Good Women* have somewhat comparable axes to grind with specific reference to a male figure of alleged sexual and literary authority, then their subsequent representations of good women confirm the wary reader's suspicions that, as in all literature, bias and resentment and special pleading color the stories. The Clerk, as we shall see, disguises himself and his motives more cleverly than the poet/dreamer of the *Legend* (or other storytellers, like the Wife of Bath and the Pardoner); he is so discreet, in fact, that at least one modern critic sees his performance as "a rarefied act of literary-critical wit," executed not in the "voiced style" of the other Canterbury pilgrims but in the manner of Petrarch himself, as "man *of letters,* a posited ideal character, created, displayed, and caught only in the act of writing."[8] This argument may disclose the Clerk's intentions quite accurately, but the alleged neutrality of the man of letters does not stand up under close inspection of the minor additions and revisions the Clerk makes to his two apparent sources, Petrarch's Latin version of Boccaccio's Griselda story and an anonymous French translation of Petrarch. In one early addition, for instance, the Clerk aims a direct blow at the Wife of Bath by supplementing the original description of Griselda with these lines: "No likerous lust was thurgh hire herte yronne. / Wel ofter of the welle than of the tonne / She drank . . ." (214–16). No such comment is found in either the Latin or French version of the story; it recalls to attentive listeners or readers the Wife's self-proclaimed drinking and sexual habits and her memorable observation that "A likerous mouth moste han a likerous tayl" (III.466). In light of the insults that the Wife hurled at clerks as a profession and at her Janekyn in particular, the Clerk's allusion cannot be accidental or innocent; and so too the subject of his tale—a patient, submissive married woman who is faithful to one husband despite his insufferable exercise of *maistrie*—must be interpreted by the audiences of the *Tales* as a central part of the interpersonal, voiced drama of the poem as a whole.

In another set of additions and revisions, the Clerk's strategy may again be profitably compared to the narrator's in the *Legend of Good Women*. As I have argued elsewhere, alterations in all of the legends consistently reshape the heroines into figures like the narrator's Cleopatra, less active, aggressive, and passionate, or like his Thisbe, less noble, more flawed, and more feminine.[9] So too, as J. Burke Severs has documented, Walter in the Chaucerian version is "more obstinately wilful, more heartlessly cruel," while Griselda's "gentleness, her meekness, her submissiveness" are more pronounced.[10] Together, these changes, like many of the alternations in the Legends, call attention to the heroine's feminine powerlessness with respect to a ruthless, self-centered, all but omnipotent man with whom she herself purports to be in love, and hence to her victimization; Griselda's suffering, no matter how we view its signification, arises specifically from the actions of a cruel, deliberate, and decidedly male oppressor, and the war between the sexes is on again. At the same time, the Clerk's version of the Griselda story, like the poet/dreamer's treatments of his good women (and his bad ones), stresses the heroine's archetypal femaleness, as Petrarch certainly does not. Note, for instance, this minor change in Walter's motivation: according to the Clerk, what he is seeking and testing in his wife is not her patience or obedience or ability to live up to her vows but her "wommanhede." Whereas in Petrarch (as in the anonymous French version) Walter is said to admire her *virtutem eximiam supra sexum supraque etatem* (a virtue beyond her sex and age),[11] the Clerk gives us Walter (here like Troilus) "Commendynge in his herte hir wommanhede, / And eek hir vertu, passynge any wight / Of so yong age" (239–41). The translation effectively alters the entire thrust of the passage; Griselda still transcends her youth, but notably she does not transcend the expected limitations of gender. Instead, she exemplifies, first and foremost, what has become an almost holy (or mock-holy) ideal in the *Clerk's Tale* as in the *Legend of Good Women*: the abstraction of certain gender-specific characteristics into the ideal state of "wommanhede." After Griselda passes her last test, Walter reiterates his motivation: " 'I have doon this deede / For no malice, ne for no crueltee, / But for t'assaye in thee thy wommanheede' " (1073–75). Again his self-justifying claim, original to the Clerk's version (and in defiance of the Clerk's subsequent injunctions), brings Griselda into line with the heroines of the Legends as type and embodiment, if not caricature, of the idealized medieval good woman.

In another set of even more obvious additions to his source materials, his own intrusive comments on the characters' behavior, the Clerk also underscores the issues of gender difference and marital conflict so central to the *Legend of Good Women* and so common in the *Canterbury Tales*. Just as Walter celebrates Griselda for her "wommanhede," the Clerk repeatedly notes that Walter's behavior is typical of a certain type of "housbonde" or "wedded" man (698, 622) who needlessly tries his "wyf" (452, 461) and her "wyfhod" (699; note that in this line "wyfhod" is mentioned before "stedefastnesse," just as in lines 239–40 "wommanhede" comes before "vertu"). In another original comment, after drawing the standard analogy between Griselda and Job in line 932, the Clerk observes:

> . . . but as in soothfastnesse,
> Though clerkes preise wommen but a lite,
> Ther kan no man in humblesse hym acquite
> As womman kan, ne kar, been half so trewe
> As wommen been, but it be falle of newe.
> (934–38)

This particular moral to the story, just one of many we will be offered, is found nowhere in Chaucer's sources, but the superiority of women to men, especially in terms of humility and fidelity, is the same highly unoriginal point that the narrator of the *Legend of Good Women* has been commanded to make. The qualifying, tonally odd turn at the end of the Clerk's comment—no man can be as humble or half as true as woman can, unless it has just happened recently—is also reminiscent of the odd jokes that the poet/dreamer often throws off at the end of his legends. Here and there such jests may indicate, like a knowing wink of the eye, the speaker's amused distance from the *querelle des femmes* and/or his actual loyalties. Moreover, the Clerk's implicit separation of himself from those other clerks who "preise wommen but a lite" is, I suggest, part of his attempt to show himself sympathetic to the cause of women, even at the expense of professional solidarity. So too in an earlier intrusion he poses a rhetorical question to the female members of his audience: "But now of wommen wolde I axen fayn / If thise assayes myghte nat suffise?" (696–97; compare the narrator of the *Legend's* "And trusteth, as in love, no man but me," 2561). The Clerk's strategy in this kind of commentary is remarkably similar to the poet/dreamer's attempts in the *Legend of Good Women* to ingratiate himself with supposed women listeners and demonstrate his unique sympathy with their gender. But despite his efforts to deny that he is the epitome of "clerkhede," to condemn needless male cruelty and to sympathize with Griselda as archvictim of patriarchal tyranny, the Clerk is finally not able or willing to distance himself from a specifically masculine attitude toward feminine virtue.

The fact that the Clerk's perspective is not morally universal, as many modern critics have assumed, not actually sympathetic to women, and not artistically neutral is dramatically confirmed at the conclusion of the tale, where what we might call the excess of endings has the same effect as the apparent incompletion of the *Legend of Good Women*.[12] Although they appear to close in such radically different ways, both endings are definitely and strategically equivocal, designed to compound readers' uncertainties about the meaning of the narratives, about the narrators' respective attitudes toward the purposes of stories and storytelling, and especially about Chaucer's attitudes toward the problematic issues of gender and marital conflict. In the case of the *Clerk's Tale,* the storyteller addresses the problem for men that he has discerned in the story of the good woman by shifting his ground, dismantling the fiction of feminine virtue by at once denying in various ways that Griselda is a woman and reaffirming that he is a man.

There are several endings to the *Clerk's Tale.* The narrative itself first concludes with a completely closed and happy ending: Walter and Griselda live "Ful many a yeer in heigh prosperitee"; their daughter is married to one of the worthiest lords in Italy; Walter brings Griselda's old father to court and takes care of him for the rest of his days; and Walter's son succeeds to the lordship of the land and makes a fortunate marriage (1128–37). At this point, the Clerk departs briefly from Petrarch to add that Walter's son, however, did not test his noble wife, and that "This world is nat so strong . . . As it hath been in olde tymes yoore" (1139–40). This comparison between the hardiness of wives then and now, between the fabular or literary and the real, implies that Griselda is not like real women, and this point will be picked up three stanzas later, where it leads directly to the Clerk's reference to the Wife of Bath and then to the envoy.

First, however, another possible ending to the story, a religious moral, is offered, prefaced by a closing call to attention, "And herkneth what this auctour seith therfoore" (1141). The subsequent moral is found in both Petrarch and the French versions; the point is not that wives should adopt Griselda's humility but that all human beings should be as "constant in adversitee" as she is: again, then, Griselda is not really a woman. Following this, a third conclusion to the tale is initiated with a second closing formula, "But o word, lordynges, herkneth er I go" (1163), and in the next two stanzas the Clerk playfully does precisely what he has just told his audience not to do. Returning to the notion that it would be hard "now-a-dayes" to find two or three live Griseldas in a town, he deallegorizes the notion of "assay" from the religious interpretation of Griselda's trials to offer this comment on material women, who fall so short of the ideal female malleability that his tale prescribes:

> For if that they were put to swiche assays,
> The gold of hem hath now so badde alayes
> With bras, that thogh the coyne be fair at ye,
> It wolde rather breste a-two than plye.
> (1166–69)

He then goes on to dedicate a blessing (in contrast to the Wife's parting curse) to the Wife of Bath and "al hire secte," who are implicitly presented as the real, living examples of that superficially fair coin that will not bend.

With a third parting call to attention—"Herkneth my song that seith in this manere" (1176)—as if he realized that our minds may well be wandering

or at least confused by this plethora of contradictory conclusions and applica-
tions of his tale, the Clerk offers what now stands as the last ending to the
text, titled in many manuscripts *Lenvoy de Chaucer.* Here, as in the preceding
two stanzas, the speaker interacts directly with the other pilgrims and links
the story we have just heard to the question of marital sovereignty. Now reading the heroine not as a paradigm for all humanity but as an historically real
character, dissociable from her ideal virtue, the speaker replicates Walter's
move, saying, in effect, "This is enough": "Grisilde is deed, and eek hire
pacience, / And bothe atones buryed in Ytaille" (1177–78). He warns husbands that they will fail if they try to test their wives. Turning to "noble
wyves," he advises them not to let any clerks tell a story about them like the
story of Griselda; and in the remaining stanzas he presents advice couched as
the most extreme version possible of the Wife's already extreme philosophy of
female dominance.

The Clerk's disclaimer two lines before the beginning of the Envoy—
"And lat us stynte of ernestful matere" (1175)—has encouraged modern
readers to see the ending as comic play that protects the seriousness of the
tale. In a frequently cited appraisal of this "concessionary comedy," for example, Charles Muscatine argues: "The Clerk admits the opposition purposely,
so willingly and extravagantly as to make safe from vulgar questioning the
finer matter that has gone before."[13] Such a reading is consistent with Freud's
view of humor as a healthy, even precious, defense mechanism wherein the
humorist takes on the psychic part of both father and child; the superego
speaks like a parent to the frightened ego, saying " 'Look here! This is all that
this seemingly dangerous world amounts to. Child's play—the very thing to
jest about.' "[14] But what, exactly, is the young male ego of the Clerk so
frightened of? And how is it the "finer matter" of Griselda's story that the
envoy makes safe?[15] As Freud further suggests, the humorist always repudiates suffering and affirms the ego's invulnerability; humor, then, would seem
far more likely to trivialize, even undercut, a heroine whose power is equivalent to her capacity to embrace suffering and who can subordinate her own
ego so completely to the cultural superego (the Law of the Father, the domination of Walter).

Given the similarity of the Clerk and the narrator of the *Legend of Good
Women,* I conclude from the nature of the jest attempted in the envoy that the
Clerk is simultaneously afraid of women and afraid of being (like) a woman.
What frightens the Clerk so much that he has to joke about it is, first, the
power of Griselda, the silenced woman, and her inhuman, celebrated capacity
to suffer. This power, within the tale, has also frightened her husband Walter,
in ways I have suggested; the envoy reveals that it is, moreover, paradoxically
reminiscent of the power attributed by the Clerk to women like the Wife of
Bath. What Griselda and the Wife seem to have in common is their capacity,
manifested in opposite ways, to escape or at least lay bare the operation of

male tyranny by exceeding, in different directions, its enunciated limits. Second, I submit, the Clerk may be frightened by his own likeness to Griselda, a parallel often drawn by readers.[16] As a youth whose manhood is openly questioned by the Host, as an unbeneficed young cleric, and as a storyteller translating a renowned author, the Clerk occupies a marginal and insecure position in the culture that wants to rule the day, the hearty manly world organized and policed both by the menacing Host of the *Canterbury Tales* and by the literary tradition embodied in the authority vested in Petrarch and the Latin source text. If Griselda exceeds the demands of her husband, so too the Clerk exceeds the demands of translation, and nowhere more than in the excess of endings to his tale. While the Clerk's sympathy with women may be suspect, then, his identification with the feminine position and hence his insight into the nature of a certain kind of psychic oppression is plausible, and it is as frightening to him as it is to a woman like the Wife.

The Clerk's strategy at the end of his tale suggests both his fears and his defense against them. By playing in the envoy at taking the shrew's part, he continues to dissociate himself—now, however, with tongue quite obviously in cheek—from the crude antifeminism of men like Walter, who seriously and mistakenly expect women to submit to masculine dominance and who underestimate the powers of their victims. At the same time, he implies that after all he has managed to transcend the merely literal response to the tale's pathos that his ostensive sympathy with Griselda might indicate and that he is in fact distanced by his superior learning and wit from the whole field of sexual warfare. Like the narrator of the *Legend of Good Women,* the Clerk finally signals that he is neither for real women nor against them; he is just playing a game, not the courtly cult of the marguerite but something not very different, a game played for and about men, and one that entails the transmission of the patriarchy's values, courtly or religious, through stories about idealized female figures. Griselda, then, is not finally unintelligible and threatening, she is just implausible; her suffering and its finer meanings can be forgotten. This is all there really is, the comic ending says, to the seemingly dangerous world of women and the war between lordly husbands and long-suffering wives—the very thing to jest about.

Freud, again like many modern Chaucerians, values humor for its "liberating" element and sees something "fine and elevating" in what he calls "the triumph of the ego": "It refuses to be hurt by the arrows of reality or to be compelled to suffer."[17] But as humor liberates the humorist, does it liberate everyone? What about people who cannot laugh off the arrows of reality, who cannot refuse to be compelled to suffer—what about people like Griselda, whose only power lies in suffering? What about those who are the targets of real arrows, the butts of jokes, like the Wife of Bath? The Clerk's humorous ending deflates rather than protects Griselda's virtue, surely, and deflects us from both the real experience and the figurative value of her suffering and endurance; in liberating and elevating himself, then, he devalues and dismisses the feminine power of silence without liberating women from the complementary myths of absence or excess. The envoy in particular not only trivializes but also preempts the voice of a woman like the Wife of Bath, exaggerating just the sort of "vulgar" response—something short of throwing his books into the fire—that she might indeed offer to a story like the Clerk's. Griselda, I have suggested, is made temporarily deaf, like the Wife, when Walter suddenly undergoes a dramatic reversal and agrees that she has proved her worth and can stop being tested; her story ends and her voice is silenced when the misogyny and fear that brings her into being finally comprehends how dangerous it is to let her suffer so visibly and well. In the same way, the Wife's position is silenced and disarmed by the Clerk's reversal when he impersonates her voice and takes up in jest precisely the kind of argument she might make.

The tale's reception, moreover, suggests that the vocal men on the pilgrimage have not been fooled into thinking that the Clerk is really on women's side in all this, or that the telling of this tale could possibly serve to liberate any wives from the domination of husbands that they are compelled to suffer outside the worlds of story and jest. In the link between the *Clerk's Tale* and the *Merchant's Tale,* we hear the Host's enthusiastic response to the story of Griselda, which he wishes his wife could hear. The Merchant, another manly man, begins the next tale in the series by comparing his own shrewish wife to Griselda. Disguised, but not completely so, as sympathetic to women, the Clerk nevertheless affirms to other men his proper maleness by offering them a comforting example of how both virtuous and vicious women alike may be silenced, and Griselda's meaning is reduced to its most minimal and least threatening level. The Host and Merchant have been accused of distorting the tale, and indeed they simply ignore the Clerk's half-hearted, clearly ambivalent and finally subverted warning that we should view Griselda not as a woman, but as a figure for the human soul.[18] But their response, biased as it may be, is invited by the Clerk's presentation.

The audience outside the poem may be more alert to the tale's subtleties, but modern critics at least have not been able to agree on its significance in a persuasive way either. And one of the problems that plagues more skillful interpreters outside the pilgrimage is the identity, not to mention the intentions, of the speaker in this poem, and especially in the envoy. Apart from the teller of the tales of *Melibee* and *Sir Thopas,* the Clerk is the character most often associated with Chaucer and his point of view, one of the few pilgrims usually thought to be treated with little irony and left in control of his own story. At the same time, the voicing of the envoy is particularly problematized by the scribal heading, *Lenvoy de Chaucer,* invoking the author's name at just the point where the joke is made. Robinson's explanatory note seems either obvious (aren't all the dramatically appropriate tales finally composed by Chaucer?) or confounding: "The song . . . is Chaucer's independent composition. But it belongs dramatically to the Clerk, and is entirely appropriate."[19] It points, however, to the importance of the fact that insofar as Chaucer speaks, it is only through the dramatic composition of other characters and other voices. Here, as in all the earlier dream-visions (and perhaps again with special relation to the *Legend of Good Women,* whose narrator also likes to make obscure little jokes about the ladies), the poet develops and plays on both the proximity and the distance between himself and the narrator of the story. To the extent that both proximity and distance remain in evidence, he creates the possibility of writing about his own limitations and biases with a penetrating self-scrutiny and an ironic self-reflexivity, and hence at the same time implying that he has in some sense escaped these limits and can be caught only in the equivocal act of writing and the liberating gesture of humor. Like Griselda, again, the figure of Chaucer transcends ostensive limits because he admits in play to perceiving and accepting them. In his marked equivocation, so central to the game, he figures himself in and as one who realizes the powers of silence and unintelligibility that he usurps from and finally denies to his female heroines.

Whereas many modern readers have posited a radical break between early and late Chaucerian fictions, one of my aims in discussing selected *Canterbury Tales* is to underscore some lines of thematic and rhetorical continuity that are especially visible to a feminist criticism interested in the problem of masculine identity and authority. The *Clerk's Tale* highlights such continuity, and we see how the evasiveness of the narrator and his position, so characteristic of all the early poems, manifests itself in an even more emphatic way in the *Tales:* through the creation of other fictive speakers altogether, with their own proper, fictive names, at different degrees of distance from the author, in the fiction of the framed collection. Here the functional moves toward the self-disguise, self-division, ambiguity, and resistance that I trace as empowering strategies in all the earlier poems proceed a logical step further toward the position of "negative capability" and aesthetic transcendence that becomes the hallmark of the humanist artist and earns Chaucer his status as Father of English poetry, even as he plays the child and perhaps identifies with children.[20] Through this further step in self-effacement, brought out so clearly in the Clerk's performance, the figure of the poet avoids precisely the predicament that the remaining male storytellers I am interested in here—the Miller, Knight, Merchant, and Franklin—to varying degrees reflect: any representation of Woman seems to entail a revelation of the male speaker's anxiety about his manliness, his status and identity. Again, this revelation goes hand in hand with a discourse that is thoroughly misogynistic, but the strategic intersection of the present, impersonated male narrator and the absent author has served to liberate Chaucer from the self-revealing, self-destructive side of the misogyny that powers the literary canon.

Notes

1. John H. Fisher, ed., *The Complete Poetry and Prose of Geoffrey Chaucer* (New York: Holt, Rinehart and Winston, 1977), p. 145. The article from which the epigraph is drawn appears in *Literature and Psychology,* 16 (1966), pp. 157–65.

2. For other readings like Richard Lanham's (cited in note 1) that locate meaning in the contradictions and tensions that the Clerk brings to his story, see Dolores Warwick Frese, "Chaucer's *Clerk's Tale:* The Monsters and the Critics Reconsidered," *Chaucer Review,* 8 (1973), pp. 133–46; Warren Ginsberg, " 'And Speketh so Pleyn': The Clerk's Tale and its Teller," *Criticism* 20 (1978), pp. 307–23; Lloyd N. Jeffrey, "Chaucer's Walter: A Study in Emotional Immaturity," *Journal of Humanistic Psychology* 3 (1963), pp. 112–19; Patrick Morrow, "The Ambivalence of Truth," *Bucknell Review* 16 (1968), pp. 74–90; J. Mitchell Morse, "The Philosophy of the Clerk of Oxenford," *Modern Language Quarterly* 19 (1958), pp. 3–20; and Robert Stepsis, "*Potentia Absoluta* and the *Clerk's Tale,*" *Chaucer Review* 10 (1975–76), pp. 129–42.

3. See Caroline Walker Bynum, *Holy Feast and Holy Fast* (Berkeley: University of California Press, 1987), for a discussion of the feminization of medieval Christian practice and theory, and especially Chapter 10, "Women's Symbols."

4. For a discussion of Chaucer's relation to the antifeminist tradition as it emerges in "images . . . which celebrate, with a precision often subtle rather than apparent, the forms a woman's goodness is to take," see Hope Phyllis Weissman, "Antifeminism and Chaucer's Characterizations of Women," in *Geoffrey Chaucer: A Collection of Original Articles,* ed. George D. Economou (New York: McGraw-Hill, 1975), pp. 93–110.

5. See Oxford English Dictionary, *rue,* v.1, sense 1.

6. Marsha Siegel, "Placing Griselda's Exemplary Value by way of the *Franklin's Tale,*" paper presented at International Congress on Medieval Studies, Kalamazoo, MI, May 1982.

7. Catharine A. MacKinnon, "Feminism, Marxism, Method, and the State: An Agenda for Theory," *Signs* 7 (1982), p. 543.

8. Anne Middleton, "The Clerk and His Tale: Some Literary Contexts," *Studies in the Age of Chaucer* 2 (1980), p. 149.

9. For a more complete discussion of this point and others in the Legends, see my "Irony and the Antifeminist Narrator in Chaucer's *Legend of Good Women,*" *Journal of English and Germanic Philology* 82 (1983), pp. 11–31, as well as the discussion in Chapter 1 of this study.

10. *The Literary Relationships of Chaucer's Clerk's Tale* (New Haven: Yale University Press, 1942), pp. 231, 233.

11. I take the Latin quotation from the convenient edition of Petrarch's *Epistolae Seniles,* Book XVII, Letter III (with a facing edition of *Le Livre Griseldis*) in *Sources and Analogues of Chaucer's Canterbury Tales,* ed. W. F. Bryan and Germaine Dempster (Chicago: University of Chicago Press, 1941), pp. 296–331. The text of Petrarch's version is translated in Robert Dudley French, *A Chaucer Handbook* (New York: F. S. Crofts, 1927), pp. 291–311.

12. For a sampling of different approaches and conclusions all based on the fundamental premise that the Clerk's answer to the Wife of Bath presents the obviously sensible, beautiful, "universal" refutation of her equally obviously monstrous and ridiculous perversion, see S. K. Heninger, Jr., "The Concept of Order in Chaucer's *Clerk's Tale,*" *Journal of English and Germanic Philology* 56 (1957); pp. 382–95; Thomas H. Jameson, "One Up for Clerks," *Arts and Sciences* (Winter 1964–65), pp. 10–13; Lynn Staley Johnson, "The Prince and His People; A Study of the Two Covenants in the *Clerk's Tale,*" *Chaucer Review* 10 (1975–76), pp. 17–29; Alfred Kellogg, "The Evolution of the *Clerk's Tale,*" in *Chaucer, Langland, Arthur: Essays in Middle English Literature* (New Brunswick, N.J.: Rutgers University Press, 1972), pp. 276–329; Morrow, "The Ambivalence of Truth"; Irving N. Rothman, "Humility and Obedience in the *Clerk's Tale,* with the Envoy Considered as an Ironic Affirmation," *Papers in Language and Literature* 9 (1973), pp. 115–27; Jerome Taylor, "Frounceys Petrak." For readings that stress the Clerk's (or Chaucer's) sympathy with women, see for example Harriet Hawkin, "The Victim's

Side: Chaucer's *Clerk's Tale* and Webster's *Duchess of Malfi,*" *Signs* 1 (1975), 339–61; Velma Richmond, "Pacience in Adversitee: Chaucer's Presentation of Marriage," *Viator* 10 (1979), pp. 323–54; and Morse, "The Philosophy of the Clerk."

13.   *Chaucer and the French Tradition* (Berkeley: University of California Press, 1957), p. 197.

14.   "Humour" (1928), in *Collected Papers,* vol. 5, ed. James Strachey (New York: Basic Books, 1959), p. 220.

15.   The term "purity" is one Muscatine insists on; see *Chaucer and the French Tradition,* p. 196.

16.   For a good analysis of the similarities between narrator and female character in this case, see Carolyn Dinshaw, *Chaucer's Sexual Poetics* (Madison: University of Wisconsin Press, 1989), pp. 135–37.

17.   "Humour," p. 217.

18.   Middleton, "The Clerk and His Tale." The Host's words, lines 1212a–g, are found in only one family of manuscripts, including the Ellesmere manuscript and Hengwrt 154. Robinson identifies them as "without doubt genuine," perhaps part of a canceled job. See also Eleanor Hammond, *Chaucer: A Bibliographical Manual* (New York: MacMillan, 1908), pp. 302–3, and Aage Brusendorff, *The Chaucer Tradition* (London: Oxford University Press, 1925), p. 76.

19.   *The Works of Geoffrey Chaucer,* note to line 1177, p. 712; John Koch argues, however, that the Envoy is spoken by the author; ("Nochmals zur Frage des Prologs in Chaucers 'Legend of Good Women,'" *Anglia* 50 [1926], p. 65); for recent comment that supports Robinson's view, see Thomas J. Farrell, "The 'Envoy de Chaucer' and the *Clerk's Tale,*" *Chaucer Review* 24 (1990), pp. 329–36.

20.   For the argument that Chaucer identifies with children and plays the childish role in the *Canterbury Tales* in particular, see Lee Patterson, " 'What Man Artow?' Authorial Self-Definition in *The Tale of Sir Thopas* and *The Tale of Melibee,*" *Studies in the Age of Chaucer* 11 (1989), pp. 117–75.

Claiming the Pardoner:
Toward a Gay Reading of
Chaucer's Pardoner's Tale

STEVEN F. KRUGER

1. THE PARDONER, 1990

At a crucial point in Allen Barnett's recent short story "Philostorgy, Now Obscure," Chaucer's Pardoner suddenly and unexpectedly appears.[1] The story's main character, Preston, returns home "[a]fter the doctor had given him his diagnosis" of AIDS (45) and begins to clean his apartment with a vengeance (45–46):

> He took blinds from the windows and soaked them in the tub. He took books from their shelves and wiped them with a damp rag. He polished brass and waxed wood and relined shelves with new paper till the apartment was astringent with the smell of powder cleanser and bleach.

Preston's housecleaning comes at the center of a story that navigates complexly back and forth between memories of the past, a present transformed by AIDS, and imaginations of the future, and the scene of cleaning functions in a complicated manner within the nexus of past, present, and future. It represents a wishful if futile attempt to deny AIDS, to cleanse the present of the tinges of disease; but it also provides Preston with an initial way, however oblique, to face his diagnosis. "[A]n addictive tonic that kept him going for three days" (46), it serves almost as a medicine that moves Preston forward into his new life. The movement forward, however, involves a confrontation with the past, and specifically a gay past whose meaning AIDS has irrevocably changed. The cleaning house entailed by Preston's diagnosis forces him to come to terms with the artifacts of his former life, and

From *Exemplaria: A Journal of Theory in Medieval and Renaissance Studies* 6 (1994): 115–39. © 1994 Pegasus Press, University of North Carolina. Reprinted by permission of Pegasus Press.

In memory of Donald R. Howard, Arturo Islas, and John J. Winkler these in turn, as if by an inexorable logic, lead him back to thoughts of disease and death. Caught up in this circular movement, Preston tries to expurgate the past, "empt[ying]" his "closets" ruthlessly (46):

> Bureau drawers gave up a T-shirt proclaiming SO MANY MEN, SO LITTLE TIME, old jock straps, unmatched socks, silk shirts and silk underwear he wouldn't be caught dead in. He had once read an article by a journalist whose neighbor had died of AIDS. The writer had described the contents of the dead man's garbage, reducing an entire life to a leather vest, chaps, and sex toys. Writing about the clothes was more invasive than wearing them would have been, he thought. And he thought about what people would find cleaning out his own apartment.

Preston's cleaning here prepares for a future, more final "cleaning out," and the confrontation of the past it involves, the gesture of "emptying closets," functions complicatedly—on the one hand, echoing the "coming out of the closet" of gay and lesbian liberation, while, on the other, discarding just those objects that, like Preston's old T-shirt, "proclaim" a gay life enabled by "coming out." Preston (and Barnett) stray dangerously close here to the homophobic moralizing equation of a certain gay "lifestyle," with its "leather vest[s], chaps, and sex toys," to disease and death, even as they, in an opposite movement, protest against "reducing an entire life" to such artifacts. The urgent question here is whether anything of a past gay life like Preston's can be salvaged now that AIDS has retrospectively rewritten that past, and rewritten it in terms disturbingly similar to those of homophobic moralizing.

At first Preston's answer seems to be no. Even though "his college notebooks slowed the process [of cleaning] down, as if there should be a reason to stave off their destruction, as if there was something in them he might have forgotten and needed learning again," these too are finally judged as "useless scribbles" (46), to be gotten rid of along with drafts of poems that are now only embarrassments (46–47):

> Better to throw it all away than to have someone find it, lay claim to it, or reduce his life to it. . . . Preston ripped the pages from their black bindings, then burned them in the sink like love letters after a divorce till there was nothing left but ash and smoke that hovered near the ceiling and made the fire alarm scream like a banshee. He needed to do the same with old friends, affect their memory of him, introduce himself anew and say, "This is me now."

But the products of his past intellectual life do give Preston pause, seeming perhaps to offer some wisdom for the present,[2] and Preston does save certain objects. What is salvaged, however, cannot remain untouched by the present; Preston's memory of it, like his old friends' "memory of him,"[3] must be made new, transformed by the experience of illness (47):

Some things he saved: letters from friends, and two papers he had written in college, one on the Pardoner from *The Canterbury Tales,* and one on Walt Whitman. "The first angry homosexual," he had written about the Pardoner, "the first camp sensibility in English literature." And then there was Whitman's vision of love between two men, almost a civic duty, and one that had flourished for a while. The latter paper he had turned in late with a note to the teacher, "I have gotten a disease in a Whitmanesque fashion, perhaps a hazard from the kind of research I have been doing lately." Something had made the glands in his legs swell up till it was impossible to walk. "Are you homosexual?" the school doctor asked, having seen the same infection in the gay neighborhood where his practice was. "Well, now that you mention it," Preston replied.

"How much space should the past be given in a one-bedroom apartment?" (46). Barnett provides an answer to this question that is finally complex, involving both the stripping away of the past and its reconstruction, the reaffirmation of connections to old friends and lovers but also the reforging of those connections in the face of radical change ("This is me now"). He especially emphasizes the need to discover and claim a particular, complicated gay history—one that includes both Whitman and the Pardoner, celebrating Whitman's "vision of love . . . that had flourished for a while" alongside the Pardoner's anger, and a "camp sensibility" that is a certain alternative to anger.[4] Such a history is complexly related to the present moment, with Whitman's joyous "vision" paradoxically bound up in the experience of disease, and the Pardoner's anger providing Preston with a model for his own angry response to the diagnosis of AIDS, a historical correlative to the "banshee" scream of the fire alarm set off as the products of a former life are converted to "ash and smoke."

Giving the Pardoner a central place in Preston's life history, Barnett points up the urgency of historical claiming at a moment in gay life when, under the pressure of AIDS, past, present, and future have all been radically transformed. While recognizing that the recent gay past with its "Whitmanesque" legacy no longer "flourishes" and can no longer be seen free of the specter of disease—and even as he strips away the artifacts of that past—Barnett's Preston salvages "Whitman's vision of love between two men." But Barnett also suggests that the openly liberatory history of Whitman and the "Whitmanesque" is not enough in the face of AIDS. Preston reaches beyond Whitman to claim the Pardoner and his anger, as though the pressures of the present echo the historical conditions that first produced "angry homosexual[s]," as though the response to AIDS needs to tap the anger and "camp sensibility" generated by centuries of homophobia. Preston looks to the violence of the past out of the violence of the present to claim a voice that might angrily challenge or campily subvert the legacies of homophobia.

2. Approaching the Pardoner

Barnett's invocation of the Pardoner does not stand alone in recent gay men's culture. Other striking gay readings of Chaucer include Pier Paolo Pasolini's *The Canterbury Tales* (1971) and Robert Glück's enigmatic short story "Chaucer" (1982), which mixes equal parts of Chaucer, Pasolini, and Hollywood Boulevard.[5] Both of these works focus attention on Chaucer's Pardoner, claiming him as a certain kind of "ancestor" and writing the *Canterbury Tales* into a history of gay subversion and resistance.[6]

Taking as their starting point the current moment in gay culture, such acts of claiming, though "historical" in that they participate in writing a certain gay history, are not necessarily "historicist." That is, they claim a certain identity with historical figures—in the case of Barnett's story, the fictional Pardoner read as "first angry homosexual" and "first camp sensibility"—but they do not as a matter of course concern themselves with a particularized understanding of the past, with what separates us from Chaucer, with the subtle or grand changes one might trace in writing a "history of sexuality." To arrive at a more fully historicized gay reading, we would need to look to recent work in the history of homosexuality like that of John Boswell and Brigitte Spreitzer[7] and to the recent elaboration of "queer theory"[8] with its (Foucauldian) awareness of the changing social construction of sexual categories. Several Chaucerians, most notably Carolyn Dinshaw, H. Marshall Leicester, and Glenn Burger, have begun to move in this direction in their readings of the Pardoner, and I hope that my discussion represents another step in elaborating this kind of reading.[9] It is important, still, not to forget the power of a reading like Barnett's—a bold claiming of the past for present ends—and to recognize that our own readings, however historicized, are always in some sense a response to the current moment.

What I want, then, to do in this essay is stage a negotiation between myself as a gay man living in 1992 to whom Barnett's invocation of Chaucer speaks powerfully and personally, and myself as a medievalist trained in a certain kind of close reading and a certain brand of historicism. I am concerned here to navigate between Chaucer's text, a historical understanding of the late-medieval construction of male homosexuality and of homophobia, and my own contemporary position, my own political stances and needs. Those needs include the need for a rediscovered or reconstructed gay history, and the ultimate question at issue for me here is what role Chaucer's Pardoner might play in the writing of such a history.

There are two main objections one might raise to Barnett's use of the Pardoner. First, can we really call the Pardoner a "homosexual," given the depiction of the character, given that the specific category "homosexual" was not available until long after the Middle Ages (1869), and given the claim of various historians that "homosexual identity" (as opposed to "homosexual behavior") first arose in Western Europe in the nineteenth (or eighteenth or seventeenth) century?[10] Second, even if we *can* argue that the Pardoner is the fourteenth-century equivalent of a gay man, do we really want what we get in claiming him?

To take the second question first: Despite the occasional sympathetic reading of Chaucer's Pardoner, Chaucerians still largely follow Kittredge in seeing the Pardoner as "an abandoned wretch," "the one lost soul among the Canterbury Pilgrims."[11] Such a view is not to be ascribed only to the critics' homophobia (though neither should we discount homophobia as an important force operating in readings of the tale);[12] Chaucer gives the critics, in the Pardoner's own words, ample ammunition for character assassination. To embrace the Pardoner, to claim the Pardoner as somehow our own, is not just to embrace a gay ancestor—if that is what he is—but also to take to ourselves a self-proclaimed hypocrite and cheat, and, worse yet, to make ourselves (as we identify with the Pardoner) the target of the strong, and violent, hatred of the tale's conclusion (the Host's verbal, but almost physical, attack on the Pardoner). The Pardoner may be intended by Chaucer to be the medieval equivalent of a gay man, but if so he is a character written out of homophobia; can we claim the Pardoner's gayness without implicating ourselves in that homophobia—without supporting the homophobic movements of the text and without making ourselves their object? Here, I think Barnett does well to focus on the Pardoner's *anger* and "camp sensibility"—those things in the character that might resist or challenge homophobia—rather than uncritically to embrace the whole character. Similarly, feminists might claim those elements of the Wife of Bath that resist patriarchy, while still recognizing that the Wife is a creation of patriarchy, and herself implicated in patriarchal ways of thinking.

But of course there is also a prior question: Can we even speak of the Pardoner as a "homosexual"? The definition of the Pardoner's sexuality has been an important issue in Chaucer criticism at least since Walter Clyde Curry argued (in 1919) that the Pardoner "carries upon his body and has stamped upon his mind and character the marks of what is known to mediaeval physiognomists as a *eunuchus ex nativitate*."[13] One strain of readings follows Curry in defining the Pardoner according to medieval medical, psychological, and spiritual categories. Thus, Robert Miller agrees with Curry's basic diagnosis, but insists on reading the Pardoner allegorically, as the *eunuchus non Dei* "sinning vigorously against the Holy Ghost."[14] Another group of readings explains the Pardoner's physical and psychic peculiarities by appealing to modern medicine and psychoanalysis: Daniel Silvia has proposed that the Pardoner suffers from Klinefelter's syndrome;[15] Beryl Rowland suggests that he is a "testicular pseudo-hermaphrodite of the feminine type";[16] and, in perhaps the most sweeping (but also most confusing) diagnosis, Eric Stockton claims that he is "a manic depressive with traces of anal eroticism, and a pervert with a tendency toward alcoholism."[17]

In recent years, much of the debate about the Pardoner's sexuality has centered particularly on the question of his homosexuality, which seems to have been first proposed in the 1940s, though the idea is, I think, also hinted at in earlier criticism.[18] Since Monica McAlpine's influential 1980 article, "The Pardoner's Homosexuality and How it Matters," the view of the Pardoner as a homosexual has been especially prominent. The evidence McAlpine brings forward strikes me as largely convincing, and other work on medieval homosexuality would support her argument that the Pardoner should be viewed "as a possible homosexual."[19] Thus, as John Boswell has shown, the "hare," to which the Pardoner is compared, is associated consistently in medieval writings with homosexual activity, particularly anal intercourse:[20]

> The hare, for example, is said to grow a new anus each year, so that he has the same number of openings as the number of years he has lived. Hence the prohibition against eating the hare represents a rejection of pederasty.[21]

> They say that the hare of the nobler sex bears the little hares in the womb. Can it be that a bizarre nature has made him a hermaphrodite? . . . Effeminate men who violate the laws of nature are thus said to imitate hares, offending against the highest majesty of nature.[22]

But while many critics have adopted a reading of the Pardoner as a homosexual, many others remain skeptical. C. David Benson argues "the weakness of th[e] entire approach" that would diagnose "the Pardoner's sexual condition," though he himself suggests that the Pardoner may best be read as an effeminate *hetero*sexual like Absolon in the *Miller's Tale*.[23] Richard Firth Green, in an article entitled "The Sexual Normality of Chaucer's Pardoner," essentially concurs, proposing for the Pardoner "a more ordinary sexual life," "ordinary in everything, perhaps, but its debilitating [and feminizing] excesses."[24] In a very different vein, Donald Howard has—I think largely out of a desire to dissociate the Pardoner's sinfulness from the attribution of homosexuality, and out of a recognition of the implicit homophobia of some other readings of the Pardoner[25]—consistently emphasized the *anomalies* of the Pardoner's sexuality, refusing to identify Chaucer's character simply as a eunuch or a homosexual or any other easily-defined type. In Howard's words,

> The Pardoner . . . is *feminoid* in a starkly physical way—his voice, his hair, his beard are involved. . . . [H]e is a mystery, an engima—sexually anomalous, hermaphroditic, menacing, contradictory.[26]

Certainly Chaucer wants to raise questions about the Pardoner's sexuality. The most explicit definition of the character's sexual identity after all presents us with alternatives rather than with one clear identification: "I trowe he were a geldyng or a mare" (I.691).[27] And if we are inclined to read the Pardoner as a homosexual, we must find some way to account for remarks made by him that seem explicitly heterosexual (and heterosexist). Interrupting the Wife of Bath, he claims, "I was aboute to wedde a wyf; allas!" (III.166); and, introducing himself to the other pilgrims before his tale, he boasts, "I wol . . . have a joly wenche in every toun" (VI.452–53).[28] Given the difficulties of the text, our imperfect understanding of medieval ideas about sexuality, our awareness (following Foucault) of how historically contingent constructions of sexuality are, and given the current consideration, in such writers as Fuss and Butler,[29] of what precisely constitutes identity, and particularly sexual identity (whether this is somehow "essential," socially constructed, discursive, performative), we should be careful not to speak too confidently about the sexual identities of the past, or to project our own notions of sexuality back onto subjects distant from (and perhaps inaccessible to) us.

I am not, in other words, concerned to "prove" the Pardoner's (indeed unprovable) homosexuality; but I am convinced that Chaucer wants us to see, as part of the Pardoner's sexual "queerness," the possibility of homosexuality. And I am convinced that reading the *Pardoner's Tale* with medieval ideas about male homosexuality in mind can generate new and exciting interpretations of the Chaucerian text.

3. MEDIEVAL HOMOPHOBIA AND THE PARDONER

Barnett's claiming of the Pardoner as "the first angry homosexual" evokes a gay history responsive to the anger of the current moment, but it neglects any specific confrontation with medieval history. A richer, if more difficult, act of claiming would situate itself in relation to both the current moment and the alterity of the Middle Ages, recognizing that the Pardoner is at least partly created out of heterosexism and homophobia, and is not just a gay ancestor to be embraced. The specific historical contexts of a text like Chaucer's, especially the particularity of late medieval sexual practices and ideas about sexuality,[30] would inform such an act of claiming. Thus, while the reading of the *Pardoner's Tale* that I wish to open here participates in a contemporary project like Barnett's concerned with writing lesbians and gay men back into a history where they too often remain absent, it also attempts to historicize the Pardoner, considering how one constellation of common medieval ideas about male homosexuality might shape an approach to Chaucer's text.

In medieval treatments of sexuality and homosexuality, linguistic and literary questions are often at issue. As Dinshaw has recently argued, acts of writing and reading are, for the Middle Ages, often depicted in a sexualized way, with the female body a common figure for the text, and with the dressing and undressing of that body common emblems of writing and of allegorical interpretation.[31] Procreative sexuality and fecundity are crucial metaphors for meaningful literature, and the most common medieval figure for allegory—"the letter covers the spirit as the chaff covers the grain"[32]—participates in this metaphoric constellation. In the formulation of Robert Holcot, "a grain sown in its covering of chaff will not as well as and quickly germinate as it would if the chaff were removed. In the same way a mystical and obscure teaching will not be so fruitful as a nude one, although it may delight the curious very much more."[33]

Given such a sexualized way of theorizing literature, it is not surprising that errors or distortions in writing or reading are often described in sexual terms, and that homosexuality is often associated with linguistic "perversion." When Hermann of Cologne, a Jew who converted to Christianity in the twelfth century, speaks of his former interpretive "blindness" (that is, his Judaism), he revealingly uses a language of perversion that, while not limited to specifically sexual senses, certainly includes them.[34] And, conversely, when homosexuality is described, it is often treated as interpretive "blindness" and linguistic abuse.[35] In the words of the most famous, and one of the most thoroughgoing, medieval attacks on "sodomy," Alain de Lille's *Plaint of Nature:*[36]

> The active sex shudders in disgrace as it sees itself degenerate into the passive sex. A man turned woman blackens the fair name of his sex. The witchcraft of Venus turns him into a hermaphrodite. He is subject and predicate: one and the same term is given a double application. Man here extends too far the laws of grammar. Becoming a barbarian in grammar, he disclaims the manhood given him by nature. . . .
>
> That man, in whose case a simple conversion in an Art causes Nature's laws to come to naught, is pushing logic too far. He hammers on an anvil which issues no seeds. The very hammer itself shudders in horror of its anvil. He imprints on no matter the stamp of a parent-stem: rather his ploughshare scores a barren strand.[37]

The barrenness of perverse sexuality, and particularly homosexual activity, is here affiliated with a linguistic barrenness, with the inability to produce the "fruyt" of meaning, and with an unproductive entrapment in the "chaff" of ungrammatical, nonsensical language. Like others (for instance, Jews and heretics)[38] who are seen as unable properly to orchestrate meaning in texts—to move from the literal "chaff" to the spiritual "fruyt"—those practicing "sodomy" are strongly associated with the body rather than the spirit, and with bodies debased particularly by their conversion of the masculine to the feminine:

> You try to be smooth and hairless below
> So that your temple there might be like that of a woman,
> So that in defiance of nature you might become a girl.
> You have declared war on nature with your filth.
> . . . .
> Your Venus is sterile and fruitless,
> And highly injurious to womankind.
> When a male mounts a male in so reprobate a fashion,
> A monstrous Venus imitates a woman.[39]

The homophobic construction I briefly sketch here—and which I hope elsewhere to elaborate more fully—is particularly suggestive for a reading of the *Pardoner's Tale*. We might in fact describe the world of that tale in the terms of the homophobic construction, that is, as a world in which the female is excluded but parodied by men, and in which the abandonment of "proper" heterosexual behavior points up abuses of language closely linked to literalness and to a deep involvement in and debasement of body.

First of all, in what has surprisingly been given little attention by the critics, the *Pardoner's Tale* is (along with the *Canon's Yeoman's Tale*) the only one of the *Canterbury Tales* that focuses solely on male characters. Though the Pardoner boasts about his own success with women and his own almost-marriage, in the story he tells—the exemplum of the three rioters—women are evoked only to be excluded. Thus, when the female appears at the center of the story, in the haunting words of the old man—

> "on the ground, which is my moodres gate,
> I knokke with my staf, bothe erly and late,
> And seye 'Leeve mooder, leet me in!' "
> VI.729–31

—it figures only as absence, only as an origin and terminus inaccessible to the characters of the tale. And while the scene of the tavern—with its

> tombesteres
> Fetys and smale, and yonge frutesteres,
> Syngeres with harpes, baudes, wafereres,
> Whiche been the verray develes officeres
> VI.477–80

—is at first a strongly feminized realm of "lecherye" (VI.481), when it comes to the actual account of the rioters, the female figures used to set the tavern scene have disappeared.

The tavern itself is thus tainted by an open display of female sexuality explicitly associated with moral depravity, and that taint cannot but adhere to the main inhabitants of the tavern, the three rioters. Still, insofar as their particular actions are described, these men move in an all-male world, encountering taverner, young boy, and old man, responding to the demise of their "felawe" (VI.672), searching for Death figured as a male "theef" (VI.675). Strikingly, the relationship among the three is depicted in terms familiar from Chaucer's representation of male homosocial relations in several of the other tales, that is, in the terms of sworn brotherhood (VI.702–4).[40] In the *Pardoner's Tale,* as in most of the other tales where this relationship of male bonding occurs, it proves to be unstable. But the instability of that relationship is, in the other tales (notably the Knight's and Shipman's), consistently tied to its competition with heterosexual attraction. Indeed, in the *Knight's Tale,* we discover the strength of the sworn bond between Palamon and Arcite only as that bond is threatened by the love each knight suddenly feels for Emily.[41] In the *Pardoner's Tale,* on the other hand, no such competition of homosocial and heterosexual loyalties exists; the object of desire that splits the brotherhood apart is not a woman, but rather the gold that is ultimately the death of all three men. The sexual is not, however, excluded from the scene of death: when two of the rioters plot the death of the third—enacting in the pairing of two against one a parody of the heterosexual triangles of tales like the Knight's and the fabliaux—they do so in language that strongly evokes the description of heterosexual activity elsewhere in the *Tales:*

> "Now," quod the firste, "thou woost wel we be tweye,
> And two of us shul strenger be than oon.
> Looke whan that he is set, that right anoon
> Arys as though thou woldest with hym pleye,
> And I shal ryve hym thurgh the sydes tweye
> Whil that thou strogelest with hym as in game,
> And with thy daggere looke thou do the same;
> And thanne shal al this gold departed be,
> My deere freend, bitwixen me and thee.
> Thanne may we bothe oure lustes all fulfille,
> And pleye at dees right at oure owene wille."
> VI.824–34

"Lustes," "wille," "game," and "pleye" are all words commonly used by Chaucer in depicting sexual "play," and the verb "struggle" is used elsewhere in the *Tales* only in sexual contexts.[42] At the heart of the Pardoner's exemplum, we find a physical penetration, a violent parody of sexual intercourse, that leads not to renewed life, or even to the rich and easy life of "pleye at dees" anticipated by the rioters, but rather to a stark and sterile death.

The turning of potentially fruitful "play" into destructive "struggle" follows inexorably in the exemplum from the rioters' consistent attachment to the physical and their consistent failure to read beyond the literal level; the depiction of the rioters thus again clearly parallels the medieval homophobic construction of male homosexuality. The rioters' brotherhood is formed out of a misunderstanding of the personification of Death, and their quest is thoroughly informed by this misunderstanding. Their ultimate error, the inability to recognize the gold treasure as itself equivalent to death, also represents a failure of allegorical reading. Firmly tied to the physical world of the tavern, of eating and drinking, of treasure and rat poison, involved in the body and its debasement even in their closest approach to spiritual discourse (as they unwittingly echo a Christian understanding of Jesus's sacrifice)—

> And many a grisly ooth thanne han they sworn,
> And Cristes blessed body they torente—
> Deeth shal be deed, if that they may hym hente!
> VI.708–10

—the rioters enact, in the destruction of their own bodies, the death associated with the purely literal.[43] The absence of the feminine from the scene of action, except as it is evoked in the rioters' violent parody of heterosexuality, emphasizes the absence of fertile, spiritual reading figured so often in the Middle Ages through the dressing and undressing of the female body.

The exemplum of the *Pardoner's Tale* thus deploys a common medieval constellation of ideas about male homosexuality: an exclusion of the female, with heterosexual behavior replaced by a homosocial parody of procreative sexuality; a failure of reading; an involvement in and debasement of body. A similar set of ideas is evoked by the larger performance of the Pardoner, in which the exemplum is framed by a diatribe against the "tavern sins" (false oaths, gambling, gluttony), and that in turn is framed by the Pardoner's self-revelation. The whole of this performance can be read, like the exemplum at its center, as a drama of reading, an exploration of allegory and allegoresis; in this drama, reading is again closely linked to sexual issues, to the body, and specifically to the feminized body of the Pardoner himself.

The "gentil Pardoner" (I.669), from his introduction in the *General Prologue,* is consistently associated with the physical, and with a particularly feminized physicality; his concern with fashion, his high voice, his long, smooth, yellow hair, his beardlessness—all lead to the conclusion that he is at least devoid of the properly masculine ("a geldyng") and perhaps fully feminine ("a mare," I.691; see I.669–91). Describing his preaching, the Pardoner himself foregrounds his physical being, focusing attention on the different bodily parts that become prominent in his public appearances:

> Thanne peyne I me to strecche forth the nekke,
> And est and west upon the peple I bekke,
> As dooth a dowve sittynge on a berne.

Myne handes and my tonge goon so yerne
That it is joye to se my bisynesse.

VI.395–99

Thanne wol I stynge hym with my tonge smerte
In prechyng.

VI.413–14

None of the other male pilgrims, and only the Wife of Bath among the women, describes him- or herself in such strongly physical terms, and as so clearly the object of the public gaze. And, as in the exemplum, physicality is here again closely tied up with questions of reading, misreading, linguistic fraud: the Pardoner's foregrounded body plays an integral role in the deception of his audiences. The strong association of the Pardoner with false relics additionally emphasizes the physical, and particularly the way in which bodies that might serve holy purposes—as might the Pardoner's own body, were he a different kind of preacher—can instead become part of an elaborate art of deception. Just as the rioters' oaths debase, by tearing apart, the holy body of Christ, the Pardoner's misuse of the institution of relics profanes the holy bodies of the saints.

But the Pardoner's larger performance raises different and more difficult questions than does the exemplum he tells. Unlike the three rioters of his story, the Pardoner shows himself aware of the linguistic and interpretive distortions in which he is involved; indeed, he celebrates these. Where the rioters are unable to escape their literalism, to move out of the realm of the physical to grasp spiritual meaning, the Pardoner is very much in control of meaning, self-consciously crafting his sermonizing as allegorical and moral. In the exemplum, a fatal misreading occurs in the rioters' insistently literal interpretation of what needs to be seen spiritually, but in the Pardoner's own use of the false relics we have an inverse problem, a situation in which what is really only material is presented as though it in fact had spiritual efficacy. The Pardoner's whole performance plays self-consciously with the relations of the material to the spiritual: presenting himself to his audiences, and finally to the Canterbury pilgrims themselves, as a spiritually efficacious force, he nonetheless also reveals to the pilgrims his status as "a ful vicious man" (VI.459).

The Pardoner, in Chaucer's portrayal, appears as especially dangerous because, while implicated in the same debasement of body and meaning as the three rioters, depicted like them in the terms of medieval homophobia, he shows himself to be much more fully in control of body and meaning than they are. And unlike the rioters, whose "immorality" of nature and of behavior mirror each other, the Pardoner, while self-confessedly "vicious," behaves in ways that may in fact have fruitful moral outcomes. In his own most succinctly self-aware formulation:

> "But though myself be gilty in that synne,
> Yet kan I maken oother folk to twynne
> From avarice and soore to repente."
> VI.429–31

As has been recognized by many critics, the Pardoner's performance consistently foregrounds the question of what happens when a moral role is played by an immoral figure (a question confronted elsewhere by medieval authors in a wide range of texts; for instance, in the Lollard and anti-Lollard debates of the late fourteenth century and in the first story of Boccaccio's *Decameron*).[44]

As presented by the Pardoner, the story of the rioters' misreadings in fact becomes a powerful allegory of what happens when people do not move beyond physical attachments, when they refuse to attend to the spiritual; as such, it should function to turn its audience away from the material world. The Pardoner deploys the medieval homophobic construction in his tale to provide a warning about the dangers of a sterile "sodomitical" relation to the world. If the central portions of the Pardoner's performance—the exemplum framed by the diatribe against the "tavern sins"—stood alone, they would unquestionably constitute, for medieval Christianity, a "moral tale" (VI.460). But the Pardoner's insistent self-presentation, the insistent foregrounding of his sinfulness, viciousness, physicality, and verbal trickery—and specifically the way he is implicated in the very homophobic construction deployed to moralizing ends in the exemplum—prevents such a comfortable reading.[45] His own debased body, placed parodically in the holy role of preacher, strongly calls attention to itself, and, as a consequence, his whole performance twists itself into paradoxes and conundrums instead of "straight" meaning. How can the straightforward Christian doctrine of the tale be recognized through the strange, feminized body and self-admittedly corrupt motives of the Pardoner? Even in the Pardoner's most orthodox preaching against gluttony and the other sins, when he speaks in the voice of St. Paul or Pope Innocent III on the sins of "throte" (VI.517) and "bely" (VI.534), how can the moral message, the spirit of the teaching, overcome the image of the corrupt teacher and his own gluttonous body?

Paradoxically, the Pardoner presents a perfect allegory of the dangers of not reading spiritually, but then, by framing this with his vivid self-confession, forces his audience away from a spiritual reading, away from submitting to the moral force of the sermon. The reader or listener is, in essence, backed into an untenable position—either to accept the Pardoner's teaching, ignoring the depravity of the teacher, or reject that teaching, turning away from what is in fact good Christian doctrine. This is the conundrum faced by the other pilgrims at the end of the tale, and the reason why, for his performance to be complete, the Pardoner must demand a direct response from them, must ask them (literally) to buy into his performance. The whole tale builds up to the point where the stark and visceral power of the exemplum—its dark and frightening "proof" of the dangers of materialism—can be baldly confronted by the Pardoner's own materialism; this point of high tension comes when the Pardoner demands a monetary "offering" from the other pilgrims. He here forces a decisive reading of his performance—either a rejection of it or a buying into it—that in fact has been made impossible by the performance itself. The tale has conspired to confound a reading that is either material or spiritual, that focuses either just on the sinful body of the Pardoner or just on the moral doctrine of his preaching. The coup de grâce in the confrontation of material and spiritual that structures the tale comes in the Pardoner's final promise of a spiritual reward in exchange for a material offering that is itself payment for spiritual guidance provided by someone openly celebrating his own material corruptions.

4. RESISTING HOMOPHOBIA

If, in the exemplum proper, Chaucer signals the dangers of literal misreading by deploying a medieval homophobic construction that associates a male exclusion and parodying of the female with excessive, debased physicality and a failure of interpretation, his deployment of a similar construction in the broader forum of the tale forces a standoff between spiritual reading and a need to respond to the Pardoner's insistent and provocative materiality—the impulse to reject even good teaching given a knowledge of the teacher's depravity. In one way, then, the tale finally reconfirms the homophobic construction that it employs: the performance of the Pardoner—this feminized man, deeply involved in body and grotesquely distorting the proper uses of language—forcefully dramatizes a fear of the loss of that meaningful signification so often affiliated, in the Middle Ages, with heterosexual fecundity. And in the final homosocial encounter of the tale, the Pardoner's challenge to the Host and the Host's angry response to the Pardoner, this fear is at least ostensibly put to rest and a heterosexual hegemony reestablished. The Host bypasses the Pardoner's linguistic constructions, refusing to respond in any direct way to what the Pardoner has said. He sidesteps the interpretive impasse to which the Pardoner's audience(s) have been brought, and launches instead an ad hominem attack couched in the terms of medieval homophobia: he associates the Pardoner with a debased physicality ("thyn olde breech" [VI.948], "with thy fundement depeint" [VI.950]), and calls attention to the proper site of his masculinity ("I wolde I hadde thy coillons in myn hond" [VI.952]) only to perform a verbal emasculation ("Lat kutte hem of" [VI.954]). In doing so, he reduces the Pardoner to speechlessness, gathering the fecund power of language to himself in a verbal act that constructs the Pardoner as outside the realm of proper masculinity even as it consolidates masculine potency for the Host himself; Harry Bailly not only promises to deprive the Pardoner of his (perhaps nonexistent) "coillons" but at the same time suggests himself as the proper bearer of their power—"Lat kutte hem of, I wol thee helpe hem carie" (VI.954). With the Pardoner thus silenced and rendered abject, the Knight can step in and smooth things over, reaffirming the social order that depends on a certain kind of communication and signification, and that has been so deeply challenged by the Pardoner's speech.

But the tale's conclusion can be read less reassuringly for the heterosexual project of signification and for the security of heterosexual self-definition over against the (homophobically constructed) medieval idea of male homosexuality, and it is such a reading that I most wish to advance here. If the Pardoner's danger lies largely in his ability to confound proper procedures of signification and interpretation, then the Host's response—especially in its rejection of any allegorical or spiritual reading of the Pardoner's performance—testifies to the Pardoner's continuing power. In his attack on the Pardoner, the Host in fact could not stand farther from Christian spirituality, and he here fully involves himself in the debased physical world presented by the Pardoner as his own:

> "Nay, nay!" quod he, "thanne have I Cristes curs!
> Lat be," quod he, "it shall nat be, so theech!
> Thou woldest make me kisse thyn olde breech,
> And swere it were a relyk of a seint,
> Though it were with thy fundement depeint!
> But, by the croys which that Seint Eleyne fond,
> I wolde I hadde thy coillons in myn hond
> In stide of relikes or of seintuarie.
> Lat kutte hem of, I wol thee helpe hem carie;
> They shul be shryned in an hogges toord!"
> This Pardoner answerde nat a word;
> So wrooth he was, no word ne wolde he seye.
> "Now," quod oure Hoost, "I wol no lenger pleye
> With thee, ne with noon other angry man."
>   VI.946–59

The angry language here strongly connects the Host to his "angry" opponent, involving itself in the physical debasement of the Pardoner's false relics and queer body even as it rejects these. The Host's language is violent, but, like the language of the rioters in the tale's exemplum, it evokes the sexual: "kisse thyn olde breech," "I wolde I hadde thy coillons in myn hand," "I wol no lenger pleye / With thee." Though reduced to silence, the Pardoner here perhaps gains a certain kind of victory. In the Host's revulsion, in what we might read as a moment of homosexual panic,[46] the Host is drawn strongly away from the spiritual and strongly into the circle of the Pardoner's body. The Knight's final act of reconciliation, while bringing the Pardoner back into the sanctioned realm of the pilgrimage, also brings the Host to "kisse" the Pardoner.[47] In any case, the complex challenges posed by the Pardoner's performance do not permit an easy reassertion of the dominant medieval paradigm of moral (allegorical) literature. The Host's response merely bypasses these challenges, and indeed represents a refusal to read spiritually; it does not put the Pardoner's paradoxical performance to rest. The dilemma of reading that the Pardoner poses for the other pilgrims is never solved; it hangs heavily over many of the tales that follow it.[48]

Chaucer thus admits in the standoff between Pardoner and Host the possibility that an angry homosexual voice might present real challenges to dominant heterosexual paradigms. Even so, of course, the Pardoner's "victory" is in part a (darker) reaffirmation of homophobia: we might hear in the conclusion of the tale the dominant voices of medieval culture lamenting what might happen if the power of language were allowed to those who could not or would not play by the rules. The Pardoner's confounding of processes of representation and interpretation, while Chaucer gives voice to it, is not something he celebrates, though certainly he recognizes (indeed creates) its power.

Still, we—gay men and lesbians, queers, anti-heterosexist critics and historians—can read the text *against* what might have been the homophobic intentions of its author, celebrating rather than condemning the Pardoner and his disruption of the heterosexual constructions of dominant medieval culture. As the classicist John J. Winkler suggests in a different context:

> [T]he larger methodological issue is whether readers should simply be trying to reproduce the author's meaning (if he had one—that is, if he had *one*) as the goal. Should we concede that much authority to the writers we read? If our critical faculties are placed only in the service of recovering and reanimating an author's meaning, then we have already committed ourselves to the premises and protocols of the past—past structures of cultural violence and their descendants in the bedrooms and mean streets and school curricula of the present. This above all we must not do. The ambiguities and contradictions within the sexual ideology of *D{aphnis} and C{hloe}*—whether they derive from the author's intention or from internal inconsistencies in the dominant cultural discourse of his age—afford us an opportunity to become resisting readers in the complex guerilla fighting of cultural studies . . . and an occasion to struggle against the tacit, conventional, and violent embrace in which we are held by the past.[49]

While Chaucer himself may present the Pardoner's "anger" and "camp sensibility" only as dangerous, only as threatening to the heterosexual model of writing and reading so central to medieval culture, we can lay claim to that threat and advance it. Most crucially, we need to show how the Pardoner's challenge to medieval heterosexist notions of signification—and Chaucer's anxiety about that challenge—lays bare the constructed nature of those notions. The very act of containing the Pardoner—the verbal violence that needs to be done to silence him—reveals the violent force needed to contain the queer; it simultaneously reveals the force, the effort needed to construct and maintain the dominance of what Harry Bailly represents. While heterosexuality elsewhere in the *Canterbury Tales,* and in medieval culture more generally, relentlessly defines itself as natural, the movement of the *Pardoner's Tale*—and especially the final movement to repress the queer—reveals the artificiality, the unnatural and violent constructedness, of heterosexual paradigms.

What do we finally get in claiming the Pardoner? In reading the *Pardoner's Tale* from a late-twentieth-century queer perspective, we at least regain for ourselves a piece of the history of homophobia, a sense of the particular medieval voicings of revulsion against persons of queer sexuality, and a sense of the kinds of issue at stake in that revulsion. Further, reading texts like the *Pardoner's Tale* as part of a process of writing queers (and women and Jews) back into the Middle Ages, we can begin to understand the ways in which a dominant medieval European culture—self-defined as Christian, heterosexual, masculinist—depended for its self-definition upon a rigorous writing-out of Judaism and Islam, of women's experience, of the sexually other. Our own historical accounts, insofar as they replicate and support the dominant view of a Middle Ages that is "naturally," effortlessly, monolithically Christian, masculinist, and heterosexual, erase the particular sites of struggle at which the female, Jewish, "heretical," queer resisted silencing even as they were brought to silence. Claiming the Pardoner, we can intervene at one such site to locate and excavate the operations of medieval homophobia, and to hear, in however muted and distorted a fashion, the queer presences against which that homophobia was anxiously erected.

Notes

Earlier versions of this paper were presented at the Graduate Center of the City University of New York and the Spring 1992 meeting of the Medieval Academy; questions and comments at each event helped shape the essay's final form. I am especially indebted to suggestions made by Sara Blair, Barbara Bowen, Sherron Knopp, Charles Molesworth, Anthony O'Brien, Judith Raiskin, Ron Scapp, and Martin Stevens, and by the anonymous readers for *Exemplaria*. [Ed. note: This note was originally endnote 1 in "Claiming the Pardoner"; all subsequent notes have been renumbered.]

1.   The story was originally published in the *New Yorker* and subsequently included, in revised form, in Barnett's collection of short stories, *The Body and Its Dangers* (New York: St. Martin's Press, 1990), 34–61. I quote from the revised version, giving page numbers parenthetically in my text.

2.   An important role is played elsewhere in the story by Preston's encounter with an old college professor, and by his memories of classes on Augustine's *Confessions;* see especially 49–51.

3.   Preston's readjustment of relations with old friends and lovers is at the center of Barnett's story.

4. Compare H. Marshall Leicester, Jr., *The Disenchanted Self: Representing the Subject in the Canterbury Tales* (Berkeley: University of California Press, 1990), 39–40:

> [T]his particular Pardoner goes out of his way to stage his abuses and make them even more blatant than those of his historically attested compeers. The same is true of his physical and sexual peculiarities. I take it that such things as his immediate echoing of the Host's "manly" oath "by Seint Ronyan" and his announced preference for jolly wenches in every town though babies starve for it . . . have in common the tactic of calling attention to the sexual oddity the *General Prologue* notes so emphatically by deliberately shamming exaggerated virility. This is a form of camp in which the hypermasculinity is as much a put-on as the mock demonism of what Patterson calls his "gross and deliberate parody of sinfulness."

5. Robert Glück, *Elements of a Coffee Service* (San Francisco: Four Seasons Foundation, 1982), 50–54. Glück's story and Pasolini's film, along with, for instance, Pasolini's *Decameron,* Melvin Dixon's *Vanishing Rooms,* and George Whitmore's *The Confessions of Danny Slocum* (the latter two rewriting, though in very different ways, Dante and his classical and Christian predecessors), participate in a claiming and revision of medieval texts by gay male writers that I hope to treat more fully elsewhere.

6. On the claiming of "ancestors" and its problematic relation to a historicist and social-constructionist understanding of sexuality, see Diana Fuss, *Essentially Speaking: Feminism, Nature and Difference* (New York: Routledge, 1989), 106:

> essentialists argue that the Foucauldian reading of sexuality as a social construct rather than a natural essence must inevitably pose a threat to a politics based on the continuity of a shared homosexual tradition. It is argued . . . that the strict social constructionist approach "denies us a history that allows us to name Plato, Michelangelo and Sappho as our ancestors" . . . and it is charged that such academic theorizing fails to speak to the lived experience and self-conceptions of most members of the gay and lesbian communities.

7. John Boswell, *Christianity, Social Tolerance, and Homosexuality: Gay People in Western Europe from the Beginning of the Christian Era to the Fourteenth Century* (Chicago: University of Chicago Press, 1980); Brigitte Spreitzer, *Die stumme Sünde: Homosexualität im Mittelalter, mit einem Textanhang,* Göppinger Arbeiten zur Germanistik, 498 (Göppingen: Kümmerle, 1988).

8. For a sampling of the kinds of questions central to "queer theory," and for an explanation of at least one rationale for the use of the term, see Teresa de Lauretis, ed., "Queer Theory: Lesbian and Gay Sexualities," *Differences: A Journal of Feminist Cultural Studies* 3.2 (Summer 1991); and see the essays collected by Diana Fuss, *Inside/Out; Lesbian Theories, Gay Theories* (New York: Routledge, 1991). Such work, and that of critics like Eve Kosofsky Sedgwick, Jonathan Dollimore, and David Halperin, consistently emphasizes an awareness of the historical situatedness of sexuality.

9. Carolyn Dinshaw, *Chaucer's Sexual Poetics* (Madison: University of Wisconsin Press, 1989), 156–84; Leicester, *Disenchanted Self,* 35–64 and 161–94; and Glenn Burger, "Kissing the Pardoner," *PMLA* 107 (1992): 1142–56. Burger's article, published after my essay was largely complete, makes especially productive use of recent critical and theoretical work concerned with re-evaluating gender, sexuality, and their interrelationships; it also responds to both Dinshaw and Leicester.

10. For a brief summary of this "social constructionist," historical view, and of the disagreement over when precisely to date the "birth" of a "homosexual identity," see Fuss, *Essentially Speaking,* 107–8. Fuss quotes the phrases "homosexual identity" and "homosexual behav-

ior" from Jeffrey Weeks, *Coming Out: Homosexual Politics in Britain from the Nineteenth Century to the Present* (London: Quartet, 1977).

11.   George Lyman Kittredge, *Chaucer and His Poetry* (Cambridge: Harvard University Press, 1915), 21 and 180. Also see 211: "The most abandoned character among the Canterbury Pilgrims is the Pardoner."

12.   Such homophobia was recognized especially clearly in Donald R. Howard's 1984 MLA talk, "The Sexuality of Chaucer's Pardoner." I am indebted to Thomas C. Moser, Jr., for providing me with a copy of Howard's corrected transcript for the talk.

13.   Walter Clyde Curry, *Chaucer and the Mediaeval Sciences,* revised ed. (New York: Barnes and Noble, 1960), 59.

14.   Robert P. Miller, "Chaucer's Pardoner, the Scriptural Eunuch, and the Pardoner's Tale," *Speculum* 30 (1955): 180–99; I quote from the reprinted article in Richard J. Schoeck and Jerome Taylor, eds., *Chaucer Criticism* (Notre Dame: University of Notre Dame Press, 1960), 1:226, 231.

15.   See Donald R. Howard, *Chaucer: His Life, His Works, His World* (New York: E. P. Dutton, 1987), 489 and 614n.

16.   Beryl Rowland, "Animal Imagery and the Pardoner's Abnormalities," *Neophilologus* 48 (1964): 58. See also Rowland's more recent treatment, "Chaucer's Idea of the Pardoner," *ChauR* 14 (1979): 140–54.

17.   Eric W. Stockton, "The Deadliest Sin in *The Pardoner's Tale,*" *Tennessee Studies in Literature* 6 (1961): 47.

18.   C. David Benson, *Chaucer's Drama of Style: Poetic Variety and Contrast in the Canterbury Tales* (Chapel Hill: The University of North Carolina Press, 1986), 159n9, attributes the first critical suggestions of the Pardoner's homosexuality to Muriel Bowden, *A Commentary on the General Prologue of the Canterbury Tales* (New York: Macmillan, 1948), 274; and Gordon H. Gerould, *Chaucerian Essays* (1952; rpt. New York: Russell & Russell, 1968), 59. Earlier hints at the Pardoner's sexual "queerness" include perhaps Kittredge's stress on the word "abandoned," with its strong sexual connotations.

19.   Monica E. McAlpine, "The Pardoner's Homosexuality and How it Matters," *PMLA* 95 (1980): 8–22, at 8.

20.   Boswell, *Christianity, Social Tolerance, and Homosexuality,* 137–38, 142, 253, 306, 317, and 356–57. Also see Edward C. Schweitzer, Jr., "Chaucer's Pardoner and the Hare," *ELN* 4 (1967): 247–50. Interestingly, in at least one exegetical treatment, the hare is also taken as standing for the Jews (Schweitzer, 250). Further, the goat, to which the pardoner is also compared, could be associated with hermaphroditism; see Rowland, "Animal Imagery," 58. Both hare and goat are more generally attached to lechery; see, for instance, D. W. Robertson, Jr., *A Preface to Chaucer: Studies in Medieval Perspectives* (Princeton: Princeton University Press, 1962), 255: "one common medieval device for illustrating lechery is to depict a man riding on a goat and either carrying or pursuing a rabbit."

21.   Clement of Alexandria, *Paedagogus* 2.10, cited in Boswell, *Christianity, Social Tolerance, and Homosexuality,* 356–57.

22.   Alexander Neckam, *De naturis rerum* 134, cited in Boswell, *Christianity, Social Tolerance, and Homosexuality,* 306.

23.   C. David Benson, "Chaucer's Pardoner: His Sexuality and Modern Critics," *Mediaevalia* 8 (1982): 337–49; the quotations are from 338, while the comparison to Absolon is on 345.

24.   Richard Firth Green, "The Sexual Normality of Chaucer's Pardoner," *Mediaevalia* 8 (1982): 351–58; the quotations are from 357. Green cites the phrase "a more ordinary sexual life" from Benson, "Chaucer's Pardoner," 345.

25.   See especially Howard's 1984 MLA talk, "The Sexuality of Chaucer's Pardoner," a response to McAlpine and Benson, as well as the comments in *Chaucer: His Life, His Works, His World,* 489 (and notes ad loc.). The following is from the transcript of the MLA talk, 5–6:

Many critics want the Pardoner to be homosexual, and some want it desperately. I think one reason is that it *defuses* the Pardoner: Chaucer meant him to be a sinister, alarming figure and meant his effect on us to be disturbing and unforgettable. But this is too much for some readers, and they want to neutralize or trivialize the figure by saying he's drunk or queer or sick, when in fact he's evil, possibly damned. Another motive is that some men want to be reassured that any two disagreeable males seen together must be queer. . . . Homophobia can produce extremes of intolerance and persecution, but in the academic world it more often produces articles. Homophobia has characterized some articles on Chaucer's Pardoner.

26. Donald R. Howard, *The Idea of the Canterbury Tales* (Berkeley: University of California Press, 1976), 344–45.

27. All citations of Chaucer are from *The Riverside Chaucer,* 3d ed., ed. Larry D. Benson et al. (Boston: Houghton Mifflin, 1987) with fragment and line numbers or, for *Troilus and Criseyde,* book and line numbers, given in my text.

28. One might indeed argue that the expression of a heterosexual drive is not inconsistent with medieval ideas about homosexuality: at least sometimes in medieval discussions, homosexual activity is seen as related to a generally increased sex drive and loss of sexual control. The homosexual poses a threat to women as well as other men. Thus, in discussing Muslim sexual abuses, Guibert of Nogent (*Gesta dei per francos*) suggests (cited in Boswell, *Christianity, Social Tolerance, and Homosexuality,* 280):

> Although it is allowed the wretches, in their opinion, to have many women, this is accounted little by them unless the value of such filth is also sullied by uncleanliness with men.

And Jacques de Vitry, in his *Oriental History,* argues that Muhammad (ibid., 281),

> the enemy of nature, popularized the vice of sodomy among his people, who sexually abuse not only both genders but even animals and have for the most part become like mindless horses or mules. . . . Sunk, dead, and buried in the filth of obscene desire, pursuing like animals the lusts of the flesh, they can resist no vices but are miserably enslaved to and ruled by carnal passions, often without even being roused by desire; they consider it meritorious to stimulate the most sordid desires.

Also see R. I. Moore, *The Formation of a Persecuting Society: Power and Deviance in Western Europe, 950–1250* (Oxford: Basil Blackwell, 1987), 91–94. Alternatively, one may read the Pardoner's claims of heterosexual interest, with Leicester, as "a form of camp in which the hypermasculinity is . . . a put-on" (*Disenchanted Self, 39*).

29. See, for instance, Fuss, *Essentially Speaking;* and Judith Butler, *Gender Trouble: Feminism and the Subversion of Identity* (London: Routledge, 1990).

30. For one of the most recent contributions in this area, see John W. Baldwin, "Five Discourses on Desire: Sexuality and Gender in Northern France around 1200," *Speculum* 66 (1991): 797–819, esp. 818–19, on homosexuality ("Only on one conclusion were the five voices unequivocal in agreement: that homosexual and bestial expressions of desire are totally reprehensible" [818]).

31. Dinshaw, *Chaucer's Sexual Poetics.*

32. From the Preface to the Canticle ascribed to St. Gregory (PL 79:471 ff.); cited in Robertson, *Preface,* 58.

33.   From Robert Holcot, *Super librum Ecclesiastici* (Venice, 1509), 3v; cited in Robertson, *Preface,* 335–36.

34.   Hermann of Cologne (Hermannus quondam Judacus), *Opusculum de conversione sua,* ed. Gerlinde Niemeyer, MGH, Quellen zur Geistesgeschichte des Mittelalters, 4 (Weimar: Hermann Böhlaus Nachfolger, 1963). See, for instance, Hermann's comment on his (unconverted) reading of certain Biblical passages: "sinistra ea qualibet interpretatione pervertebam" (chapter 9, 97) [I perverted them by some left-handed interpretation]. The textual "perversion" here is clearly and closely linked to sexual temptation, used by the Jews (and the devil acting through them) to try to prevent Hermann's conversion (see especially the immediately following sections of the text, chapter 10).

For a reading of "perversion's lost histories" especially useful for the links it draws between sexual perversion and racial difference, see Jonathan Dollimore, *Sexual Dissidence: Augustine to Wilde, Freud to Foucault* (Oxford: Clarendon Press, 1991), 103–65.

35.   See, for instance, the frequent appeal to the metaphor of "caecitas" in Peter Damian's *Liber Gomorrhianus,* PL 145:159–90. Boswell briefly discusses this text, *Christianity, Social Tolerance, and Homosexuality,* 210–12, and he translates Pope Leo IX's response to the *Liber,* 365–66.

36.   On the *De planctu Naturae,* and its (sexualized) use of the grammatical metaphor, see John Alford, "The Grammatical Metaphor: A Survey of Its Use in the Middle Ages," *Speculum* 57 (1982): 728–60; Jan Ziolkowski, *Alan of Lille's Grammar of Sex* (Cambridge: Medieval Academy, 1985); and Thomas C. Moser, Jr., "The Latin Love Lyric in English Manuscripts: 1150–1325," Ph.D. diss., Stanford University, 1987, 99–116.

37.   I cite Alan of Lille, *Plaint of Nature,* trans. James J. Sheridan (Toronto: PIMS, 1980), meter 1, 67–69. Also see Alan's prose 4 (Nature's actual complaint [136–37]):

> This great multitude of men monsters are scattered hither and thither over the whole expanse of earth and from contact with their spell, chastity itself is bewitched. Of those men who subscribe to Venus' procedures in grammar, some closely embrace those of masculine gender only, others, those of feminine gender, others, those of common, or epicene gender. Some, indeed, as though belonging to the heteroclite class, show variations in deviation by reclining with those of female gender in Winter and those of masculine gender in Summer. There are some, who in the disputations in Venus' school of logic, in their conclusions reach a law of interchangeability of subject and predicate. There are those who take the part of the subject and cannot function as predicate. There are some who function as predicates only but have no desire to have the subject term duly submit to them.

38.   Jews appear at interesting moments in the *Pardoner's Tale,* when the first of the Pardoner's false relics is described at length (VI.350–71), and when attention is focused on the figurative rending of the body of Christ through the use of oaths ("Oure blissed Lordes body they totere— / Hem thoughte that Jewes rente hym noght ynough" [VI.474–75]). In each case, a bodily corruption is associated with Judaism, and (in the first case implicitly, in the second case explicitly) tied back into the Jews' repudiation of Christ that, in medieval Christian thought, is seen as both their essential interpretive error (a massive misreading of the typology of the "Old" Testament) and the source of a distance from spiritual truth frequently figured as immersion in the literal/material and associated with the supposed degenerate quality of Jewish bodies (bleedings, male menstruation, etc.) and the supposed attacks by Jews on (holy) Christian bodies.

39.   From "Ganymede and Helen," an anonymous twelfth-century poem, translated in Boswell, *Christianity, Social Tolerance, and Homosexuality,* 381–89; I cite passages from 386–87. For similar material, see St. John Chrysostom, Commentary on Romans (*In Epistolam ad*

Romanos), Homily 4, and Peter Cantor, *De vitio sodomitico,* both translated in Boswell, 359–62 and 375–78. In medieval literary texts from a wide variety of cultures, the accusation of male homosexual behavior is closely associated with a loss of masculinity and an imputation of femininity; see, for instance, Marie de France's "Lanval," *The Lais of Marie de France,* trans. Robert Hanning and Joan Ferrante (Durham: The Labyrinth Press, 1982), 112–13, and Gíslasaga, *The Saga of Gisli,* trans. George Johnston (Toronto: University of Toronto Press, 1963), 3–4.

40.   On "male homosocial desire," see Eve Kosofsky Sedgwick, *Between Men: English Literature and Male Homosocial Desire* (New York: Columbia University Press, 1985). For a discussion of Chaucer's depiction of "sworn brotherhood" in the larger social context of late fourteenth-century England, see Paul Strohm, *Social Chaucer* (Cambridge: Harvard University Press, 1989), 96–102. Strohm discusses the *Pardoner's Tale* briefly on 97.

41.   See Palamon's speech at I.1129 ff. Only in the *Friar's Tale* of the corrupt summoner does the sworn brotherhood remain intact and only there is it, as in the *Pardoner's Tale,* unrelated to heterosexual desire. This is perhaps especially significant in that the tale is an attack on the Pardoner's travelling companion, the Summoner.

42.   "Pleye" is used to describe the (physical) filtration of Nicholas and Alison toward the beginning of the *Miller's Tale* (I.3273), as well as the sexual act itself in the *Merchant's Tale:*

> "A man may do no synne with his wyf,
> Ne hurte hymselven with his owene knyf,
> For we han leve to pleye us by the lawe."
> IV.1839–41

"Game" can connote amorous play, as in the *Monk's Tale* (VII.2288) and *Troilus and Criseyde* (II.38). "Struggle," while not so clearly sexual, appears elsewhere in Chaucer only in sexual contexts: it is used in the *Man of Law's Tale* to describe Custance's resistance to sexual assault (II.921), and, most memorably, in the denouement of the *Merchant's Tale,* as a substitute description for the sex act performed in the peer tree:

> "Was no thyng bet, to make yow to see,
> Than strugle with a man upon a tree.
> God woot, I dide it in ful good entente."
> "Strugle?" quod he, "Ye, algate in it wente!"
> IV.2373–76

These, along with the instance in the *Pardoner's Tale,* are the only occurrences of the word in Chaucer.

43.   In the vastly influential formulation of 2 Corinthians 3:6: "Littera enim occidit, Spiritus autem vivificat."

44.   The "disparity between motive and act" (Howard, *Idea,* 352) has been an important issue in recent criticism of the *Pardoner's Tale.* Alan J. Fletcher, "The Topical Hypocrisy of Chaucer's Pardoner," *ChauR* 25 (1990): 110–26, connects this issue particularly to the Wycliffite controversy contemporary with the writing of the *Pardoner's Tale* (113), as does Peggy Knapp, *Chaucer and the Social Contest* (London: Routledge, 1990), 77–84. The larger argument in both Knapp and Fletcher—that the tale should be read in the context of Lollard and anti-Lollard debate—has perhaps some connection to the question of sexuality, since, as both Boswell and Spreitzer make clear, heresy, in medieval discourse, is often associated with homosexuality. As Fletcher suggests in his brief discussion of "gelding or mare," "aberrant sexual behavior was a standard accusation in heresy charges" (120).

Robert O. Payne, "Rhetoric in Chaucer: Chaucer's Realization of Himself as Rhetor," in *Medieval Eloquence: Studies in the Theory and Practice of Medieval Rhetoric,* ed. James J. Murphy (Berkeley: University of California Press, 1978), 270–87, raises the question "can a corrupt officer perform a good service?" (274) in relation to a different tradition—the rhetorical. Martin Stevens and Kathleen Falvey, "Substance, Accident, and Transformations: A Reading of the *Pardoner's Tale*," *ChauR* 17 (1982): 142–58, take up Payne's suggestion, though they arrive at a very different conclusion—"that [for Chaucer] art and morality are inextricably linked" (156).

45.   In Lee W. Patterson's view, "Chaucerian Confession: Penitential Literature and the Pardoner," *Medievalia et Humanistica* 7 (1976): 153–73, the focusing of attention on the Pardoner's body is itself an instance of a literal-misreading (167):

> But the Pardoner egoistically misreads himself, and, like the rioters of his tale, takes letter for spirit, fleshly understanding for spiritual. . . . [H]is obsessive self-regard is directed not to his sinful acts but to his physically-maimed body. Ashamed of his literal eunuchry, he hides behind a far more shameful spiritual sterility; fearing exposure to his companions, he mocks the judgment of God; his sorrow is not *de amissione patriae celestis, et multiplici offensa Creatoris* but simply *de ipso;* and his hatred is not *vilitatis peccati* but for the vileness of his body.

46.   On the "difficult and contested definition" (19) of "homosexual panic," see Eve Kosofsky Sedgwick, *Epistemology of the Closet* (Berkeley: University of California Press, 1990), 19–21 and 182–212. Here, Sedgwick rethinks in certain ways her earlier use of the term in *Between Men.*

47.   For a fine reading of the complexities of the kiss, see Burger, "Kissing the Pardoner"; Burger also notes the ways in which the final confrontation of Host and Pardoner implicates the Host in "exactly what the Pardoner stands accused of representing" (1146).

48.   I am thinking here of the Ellesmere order, and particularly the ways in which the tales of Fragment VII take up literary questions raised by the *Pardoner's Tale.*

49.   John J. Winkler, *The Constraints of Desire: The Anthropology of Sex and Gender in Ancient Greece* (London: Routledge, 1990), 126. Also see Alan Bray, *Homosexuality in Renaissance England* (London: Gay Men's Press, 1982), 11:

> This book should be judged, firstly, by its capacity to explain the many fragments from the past bearing on homosexuality which are now coming to light, and secondly, by its ability of illuminate the world around us as history has given us it and—this above all else—to play a part in changing it.

The Authority of Fable:
Allegory and Irony in the Nun's Priest's Tale

LARRY SCANLON

1

ALLEGORY, IRONY, AND HISTORY

During the 1950's, the *Nun's Priest's Tale* abruptly became the quintessential Chaucerian text. Since then, as the tale which "fittingly serves to cap all of Chaucer's poetry,"[1] it has been the recurrent site of the central controversy in Chaucer studies: are we to read Chaucer allegorically or ironically?[2] Patristic scholars, taking literally the tale's parting injunction, "taketh the fruyt and lat the chaf be stille," have read the tale as an allegory for some doctrinal metanarrative, such as the Fall. Formalists, on the other hand, read the injunction ironically, insisting with E. Talbot Donaldson, that "the fruit of the tale is its chaff."[3] Despite the real differences in this debate, both sides share one overriding assumption—the assumption that allegory must be univocal. In the absence of any clear univocal moral at the tale's end, this conviction sends allegorists off in search of glosses from bestiaries and *specula,* at the same time that it assures ironists no coherent allegorical reading is possible.

More recently the debate seems to have reached something of a stalemate. The tale's allegorical aspirations are so clearly linked to its ironies that neither reading can convincingly account for those aspects of the text foregrounded by the other. With each succeeding contribution to the debate the general sense of the tale's complexity grows, while the possibility of giving that complexity some specific shape seems to shrink. Derek Pearsall opens his variorum edition of the tale with the warning that this state of affairs may be permanent:

> The development in recent years of more sophisticated techniques of literary analysis has been notable for the light it has thrown on this most sophisticated of Chaucer's poems, but it is likely to remain elusive. Elusiveness is indeed its character, and the life and wisdom it contains are of a kind that must necessarily defy formulation.[4]

From *Exemplaria: A Journal of Theory in Medieval and Renaissance Studies* 1 (1989): 43–68. © 1989 Pegasus Press, University of North Carolina. Reprinted by permission of Pegasus Press.

A way out of this impasse may lie with recent deconstructive accounts of allegory, which stress its affinities to the signifying play of irony, rather than its univocal reiteration of prior tradition. This newer view begins with Paul De Man's justly celebrated essay "The Rhetoric of Temporality."[5] De Man demonstrates that the structure of allegory is irreducibly double, and in this respect is entirely similar to that of irony. Both figures are signs explicitly structured by reference to a previous sign. Irony subverts an anterior sign by demystifying it. Allegory reiterates an anterior sign, but only by acknowledging the temporal distance separating the two. As an example, De Man cites Rousseau's use of the *Roman de la Rose* in *La Nouvelle Héloïse,* where the correspondences between Julie's garden and the garden of *Deduit* point up the distance between Rousseau's "moral climate" and that of medieval romance.[6] Both figures, in De Man's words, "are . . . linked in their common discovery of a truly temporal predicament."[7]

This new view is not without medieval precedent. As one version of "the implicit and rather enigmatic link between allegory and irony which moves through the history of rhetoric"[8] one may cite Isidore of Seville, who, following Quintillian, defines irony as a subclass of allegory.[9] I am not suggesting that this coincidence should be taken at face value: little is to be gained from making medieval allegory deconstructive *avant la lettre*. Indeed, even a cursory consideration exposes an important difference. For Isidore irony is a species of allegory, suggesting that what interests him in both tropes is their capacity for continuity. For De Man the opposite is true. He rescues the category of allegory for contemporary criticism precisely by making it a species of irony, by demonstrating its capacity for discontinuity. While these two views identify the same structural similarity, they thematize this similarity in entirely different ways. Negotiating this difference will clearly require a more modulated understanding of the relation between allegory and history.

Once allegory ceases to be the simple repetition of the past, then the past becomes something more than the allegorical sign's unproblematic ground. One cannot disavow the simple unity between allegory and history without disavowing unity on both sides of the dichotomy. If a linguistic form like allegory can include time, then history can include language, and the opposition between linguistic form and historical ground becomes dialectical rather than static. From this perspective a deconstructive view of language is actually close to a Marxist view of history.[10] Once history includes language, it is possible to view historical conflict as ideological as well as material. History can become the site of ideological struggle, rather than a simple succession of unified world-views (the Middle Ages believed X, the Renaissance believed Y, etc.). Allegory thus becomes implicated in the very historical process from which De Man has rightly differentiated it. The temporality of allegory becomes a specifically historical temporality.

I would be less than candid if I did not immediately concede that this is a possibility that De Man steadfastly resists. Throughout this essay he makes it clear he wants the category of temporality to be kept completely distinct from the category of history. Yet history is a category De Man can neither rehabilitate nor do without. His theoretical definition of allegory develops out of an historical argument to which its logic remains inextricably linked. This argument will be familiar, for when it comes to medieval allegory, De Man's views are entirely traditional:

> Whether it occurs in the form of an ethical conflict, as in *La Nouvelle Héloïse*, or as an allegorization of the geographical site, as in Wordsworth, the prevalence of allegory always corresponds to the unveiling of an authentically temporal destiny. This unveiling takes place in a subject that has sought refuge against the impact of time in a natural world to which, in truth, it bears no resemblance. The secularized thought of the pre-Romantic period no longer allows a transcendence of the antinomies between the created world and the act of creation by means of a positive recourse to the notion of divine will; the failure of the attempt to conceive of a language that would be symbolical as well as allegorical, the suppression, in the allegory, of the analogical and anagogical levels, is one of the ways in which this impossibility becomes manifest. . . . The relationship between the allegorical sign and its meaning (*signifié*) is not decreed by dogma; in the instances we have seen in Rousseau and in Wordsworth, this is not at all the case. We have, instead, a relationship between signs in which the reference to their respective meanings has become of secondary importance. But this relationship between signs necessarily contains a constitutive temporal element; it remains necessary, if there is to be allegory, that the allegorical sign refer to another sign that precedes it.[11]

In this passage, Christian allegory represents a univocal "transcendence" of "antinomies" which secularized allegory must renounce as mystified. The passage constantly dramatizes allegory as the movement from mystification to demystified knowledge, and the initial, mystified, moment is crucial. Allegory can unveil its "authentically temporal destiny" only after recourse to the Divine Will has been historically disallowed, and only after the subject has "sought refuge" against it in the natural world. This recognition of an authentic temporality can come about only as the complex acknowledgment of an historical loss at once personal (the subject in the natural world) and cultural (the distance between pre-Romantic thought and the Christian thought of earlier periods).

It is testimony to the sheer inertial power of the traditional view of Christian allegory that De Man reiterates it at the very point he offers a definition which would seem to undermine it. This blindness is not a momentary lapse: it causes De Man to transgress the very terms of his own argument. The very generality of his definition invalidates the historical exclusion upon which he would make the definition rest. If the structure of allegory is constituted by its registration of temporal loss, then it must always be so constituted, regardless of its historical context or ideological orientation. In his zeal to thematize the rhetorical structure of allegory, De Man commits the very error he warned against in the opening of the essay: "the association of rhetorical terms with value judgments that blur distinctions and hide the real structures." When he assumes that in Christian allegory the relation of sign to antecedent it "decreed by dogma," he is substituting value for structure.

This blindness is all the more striking when one considers how fruitful his structural description might be if applied to medieval allegory. For one thing, it would help explain why allegories as otherwise different as *De planclu Naturae, Piers Plowman,* and *Pearl* are all so centrally concerned with loss. Indeed, Christian allegory is every bit as concerned with loss as the secularized allegory of Wordsworth or Rousseau. Nor is this concern purely rhetorical. The problem of loss is written into Christian ideology as an article of faith. Just as the individual believer can never be certain he or she is saved, so the Christian allegorist can never be certain his or her allegory has faithfully recaptured the Divine Word. Like all forms of Christian figuration, Christian allegory assumes from the outset that the Divine Word it reiterates is never fully recuperable in human language. When De Man implies that in Christian allegory the relationship between sign and meaning is "decreed by dogma," he is simply wrong. There is nothing in Christian dogma that preordains the grammatical metaphors of Alain de Lille, the mourning father of the *Pearl,* or Langland's figuration of Christ and the Church as a ploughman. While Christian allegory may seem "stabler" than secularized allegory, that stability is prospective rather than retrospective: it looks forward to the end of human history and the transcendence of human language. At the moment of its production, however, a Christian allegory is as fragile and uncertain as a secularized one.

If Christian allegory and secularized allegory cannot be distinguished in structural terms, how are we to describe the difference? We must return to the category of history. We must begin by recognizing that allegorical structure itself is historically variable. What remains constant is its doubleness: sign and antecedent held together across a temporal gap. But the way that gap is thematized is subject to changes in historical context and ideological orientation. It may be thematized, as in De Man's reading of Wordsworth and Rousseau, as an irretrievable loss, a "temporal void," or it may be thematized, as in Christian allegory, as an initial loss, a fall, against which is inscribed the hope of ultimate re-unification. One thematization is not truer to the structure of the figure than the other. Though De Man clearly prefers the secularizing thematization to the Christian, this is an ideological preference, to which he certainly is entitled, but which cannot legitimately be claimed as a theoretical necessity.

If De Man's theory of allegory is to be useful beyond the writers with whom he is immediately concerned, we must discard his overly narrow thematization of its structure. His hyper-formalist, purely linguistic category of temporality must give way to a radically dialectic notion of history: the meaning of an allegory must depend on the specific historical relationship of allegorical figure to its antecedent. The same is true for irony. The ironic figure's renunciation of its antecedent does not have to be absolute. As a counter-example to the endless retreat from history De Man finds in Schlegel or Stendahl, one could cite Marx's *Communist Manifesto* or the *Eighteenth Brumaire of Louis Napoleon Bonaparte,* which ironize a specific historical situation in the hope of transforming it.[12] This possibility, irony as "the prefiguration of future recovery," is one De Man considers and rejects,[13] but he rejects it on the basis of his overly reductive view of history. If all historical action is not, as De Man assumes it must be, a lapse into mystification, then irony which aims to transform an antecedent is not necessarily less authentic than irony which aims to escape it. Like allegory, the meaning of an ironic figure depends ultimately on its historical and ideological orientation.

The question, then, for the *Nun's Priest's Tale* becomes not whether it is allegorical or ironic, but how specifically it uses allegory and irony to refigure its own past. What kind of authority does this text, composed for a court audience at the inception of a new vernacular tradition, extract from the tradition of ecclesiastical exegesis?

To answer this question one must address both the nature of the audience and the nature of the authority being appropriated. As it happens, in this case these two issues are not entirely distinct. Medieval courts were dominated by ecclesiastical discourse, not only by virtue of their recognition of the Church's spiritual authority, but also more materially by virtue of the fact that their administrative personnel were either drawn directly from the Church or at least educated by it. In both its particular procedures and in its general sense of its own authority,[14] the medieval court often drew on ideas and practices first developed within the Church. In particular, Church ideology had a strong influence on written discourse because it was the nearly exclusive purveyor of literacy.

This last circumstance has particular relevance in regard to Chaucer's audience. Though recent studies have stressed the newness of this audience, this is a point in need of some modification.[15] The social formation to which this audience belonged was indeed new: an expanded gentry which was absorbing the most prosperous of the urban bourgeoisie, even as it was acquiring greater wealth and increased political power.[16] But if the social formation was new, its ideological outlook was not. This new intermediate class was understandably conservative. Its goal was to be assimilated by the nobility, not to challenge it.

One important path toward assimilation lay with the mastery of the written word. The steadily increasing bureaucratization of noble power which marked the later Middle Ages required a steadily increasing pool of literate bureaucrats. By the end of the fourteenth century administrative and legal posts were increasingly held by university-educated laymen.[17] This mode of entrance into the ruling class came to the middle class as a double appropriation. Though its first allegiance was to the nobility which empowered it, its share in that power was refracted through the literacy it had learned from the Church. This double status may go some way towards explaining both the huge secular demand for devotional texts in later medieval England in general and Chaucer's fascination with ecclesiastical genres in particular.

The final lines of the *Nun's Priest's Tale* neatly epitomize this interest. One reason this passage has posed such difficulty is the precision with which it compresses the problem of Christian authority into six scant lines:

> But ye that holden this tale a folye,
> As of a fox, or of a cok and hen,
> Taketh the moralite, goode men.
> For Seint Paul seith that al that writen is,
> To oure doctrine it is ywrite, ywis;
> Taketh the fruyt, and lat the chaf be stille.[18]

Sincere or ironic, this much is clear: these lines portray an attempt to appropriate Christian authority. What has been less clear is the exact nature of the authority being appropriated. The lines do not offer an explicitly doctrinal moral—some unitary formula to which the tale might be reduced. On the contrary, they simply invite the reader to submit the tale to the procedures of Christian exegesis. The authority they offer is a mode of producing authority. Faced with this secular "folye" Christian exegesis has the capacity to appropriate the literal chaff of fox, cock, and hen by displacing it with the figural fruit of Christian doctrine. Christian exegesis has this capacity because, on the authority of no less a figure than Paul, there is no text Christian tradition cannot appropriate. What these lines appropriate then is precisely the Christian mode of appropriation.

The invocation of Paul demonstrates that appropriation of this sort is at the very heart of Christian exegesis. Paul's principle of inclusion is first expressed in Romans. From that point onward, inclusion through figuration was the central strategy whereby early and medieval Christianity produced and maintained the continuity of its tradition. For the bulk of Romans, Paul presents the New Law as the figural core of the Old, which displaces such literal requirements as circumcision with the nonliteral essence such requirements are meant to signify:

> For he is not a real Jew who is one outwardly, nor is true circumcision something external and physical. He is a Jew who is one inwardly and real circumcision is a matter of the heart, spiritual and not literal.[19]

Paul displaces the literally circumcised Jew with an uncircumcised non-Jew, who can still claim to be a Jew by virtue of his fidelity to a spiritual essence that exists within the Law's literal surface. This claim at once displaces Judaic law and recuperates it.

The recuperation is completed in the parenesis, which expresses the principle of inclusion in the course of exhorting his Gentile mission to be respectful of the Jews, submissive to governing authority, and at peace with one another:

> For whatever was written in former days was written for our instruction, that by steadfastness and by the encouragement of the scriptures we might have hope. May the God of steadfastness and encouragement grant you to live in such harmony with one another in accord with Christ Jesus that together you may with one voice glorify the God and Father of our Lord Jesus Christ.[20]

While one may not wish to go so far as Helmut Koester, who argues that Romans should be viewed as an "instrument of church policy" rather than a theological treatise,[21] it is clear that the immediate historical and political aims of this Epistle are not easily distinguished from its theology. Paul's problem was twofold. He had to protect his fledging Gentile mission from the external threat of Judaic tradition, while he was attempting to use that very tradition to give his mission internal coherence. His gesture of inclusion was a brilliant and extremely productive polemical maneuver. Despite his ostensible deference to the past of the Old Testament, in fact, Paul makes the Old Testament subject to the needs of his present by declaring its purpose to be "our instruction" (hemetéran didaskalían). He neutralizes previous Judaic tradition by subsuming it under the name of his own branch of Hellenistic Christianity, to which, with regard to such key social practices as circumcision and dietary law, Judaism remained unalterably opposed.

The appropriation of Judaic tradition could not be completed, however, without the figural exegesis which Paul's principle of inclusion both implied and made necessary. Figuration is what enables him to recover the instruction for his present which he finds hidden in the past. In the refiguring of the rite of circumcision in Romans, and in the more general declaration of 2 Corinthians 3:6, "the written code kills, but the Spirit gives life," Paul appropriates the Judaic past by emptying it of substance. As the letter that killeth, Judaic law is without substantial value, yet completely authoritative as the empty vessel of the Christian Spirit. By defining the practice of figural exegesis as the operation of the Living Spirit, Paul connects his present to a past more anterior than Judaism. He connects his present to God, that is, to the point of absolute origin. In effect, his program makes the present the origin of its own past.

Beyond the specific claims made for it in any particular instance, the Pauline Living Spirit is also always a figuration of "pure anteriority," to borrow De Man's phrase.[22] Even as it articulates a particular past, it always holds in reserve the possibility of further articulations more anterior and more original. As the tradition develops, movement forward can always be presented as a movement further back: changes can be presented not as fresh departures, but as the continual return to an ever purer origin. The polemical power of this notion of textual transmission should be obvious. Christianity's endless capacity to refigure the present as the past theoretically enables it to assimilate any and all historical change without acknowledging any discontinuity.

It should be stressed that this textual practice may well be the most archaic component of the Christian tradition. Not only do the Pauline letters precede the major formulations of doctrine, and all the Church's institutional structures, they also precede the Gospels and the Christology that biblical scholars tend to treat as the central concern of the early Church. The external, chronological precedence of Paul's figural program simply confirms the program's internal logic: Christianity as textual practice precedes Christianity as a dogma. Startling though this claim may seem, I mean it quite literally. Nor do I consider it to be particularly impious—though obviously it could be taken that way. Describing Christianity as a mode of reading rather than a unitary core of beliefs to which those calling themselves Christian subscribe seems a more promising way of explaining it as a historical phenomenon. It becomes a way of producing belief rather than any particular belief, which puts one in a much better position to account for the staggering variety of forms which Christian belief has historically taken.

It is certainly the case that Christian exegesis as practiced in antiquity and the Middle Ages was always thoroughly implicated in history. Like any tradition, Christian exegesis reproduces the past from the standpoint of the present, but it also privileges one part of the present—the Christian community, the Church—as wholly continuous with the past being reproduced. It is out of this necessity that Christianity's constant drive toward institutionalization is born. Christian tradition must make its reproduction of the past (its textual practice) manifest as a social force within the present. Institutionalization and the elaboration of doctrine are opposite faces of the same social process: Christian exegesis takes place within an institutional space that it must by necessity produce. Reading is the site where institutional imperative and theological tenet meet. It is therefore as much a political act as a spiritual exercise.

Chaucer's appropriation of this form of reading (this form of appropriation) must be regarded as political as well. Yet the politics have obviously shifted. His text is not ecclesiastical; nor is it in any way offered as a contribution to doctrinal debate. If Christian authority is seriously invoked here at all, it is invoked on exclusively figural terms. To understand how Chaucer can invoke on exclusively figural terms an authority that demands literal as well as figural assent, it will be necessary to extend our detour through the development of the Christian tradition a bit longer.

For Paul, Christianity defined itself primarily in relation to Judaism. As it emerged from Judaism it had to confront the classical tradition as well. Rather than being annexed wholesale like Judaism, the classical tradition is always kept at a further remove, coming to represent that part of the present discontinuous with the Christian past, the secular society within which the Church is beginning to establish its institutional space. There are two key moments in medieval Christianity's confrontation with the classical. The first is the moment of consolidation marked by Augustine. The second is the moment of expansion marked by the School of Chartres.

The growing institutional strength of the Church in the face of the deteriorating political power of the Western empire prompted Augustine to formulate a program for the diffusion of doctrine that exerted maximum textual control over a set of practitioners facing increasing political and social isolation. *De doctrina Christiana* restricts the figural exegesis of Judaic texts to the single theme of *caritas,* and completely forbids its application to classical texts. As has been often observed, the *De doctrina* is a classical rhetoric, in which Augustine strictly delineates the assimilation of classical learning to the Christian tradition.[23] Using as an analogy the Egyptian treasure stolen by the Israelites, he approves the "seizure for Christian purposes" of "liberal disciplines," certain moral precepts, and human institutions.[24] At the same time he repudiates all pagan interpretive practices, from astrology to the reading of omens. And he describes the figural exegesis of a classical text as "food not for men but for swine."[25] In short, he advocates appropriating all of classical culture which presents no challenge to Christian figural practices.

In effect, this denial of figural privilege to the classical tradition annexes it to the category of the dead letter to which Paul had consigned the immediate past of Judaism. Paul had split the past from the present by making the first a dead letter and the second a Living Spirit. Augustine brings the split right into the present itself, making the Church and its texts the sole site of the Spiritual, consigning the rest of human activity to the dead literality of the past. *De doctrina Christiana* carries forward in terms of textual practice the larger project whereby the Church was beginning to differentiate itself institutionally from non-religious social practices.

The School of Chartres represents an endpoint of sorts in this process. By the twelfth century, the Church's institutional status was well-established. The Chartrian application of figural exegesis to classical texts is part of the Church's larger turning outward at this time, as it attempted to parlay its international presence into a fuller and more manifold relation with the everyday working of secular society.[26]

Though the Chartrian project directly contravenes Augustine on the specific matter of the figurability of the classical, both the textual practice and the institutional goal are the same. With the social presence of the Church no longer in question, it becomes less necessary to deny the figurability of non-sacral texts. John of Salisbury's *Policraticus,* the first feudal "Mirror of Princes," which used classical exempla to buttress its hierocratic arguments about the superiority of the pope to the monarch, invokes Paul's principle of inclusion, and for the first time extends it to include non-Scriptural texts.[27]

In *De planctu Naturae,* after conceding that classical poets often "bewitch" their hearers with "naked falsehood," Alan of Lille insists it is still possible to treat that falsehood as an "outer shell" beneath which the "sweeter kernel of truth" is hidden.[28]

Ultimately, however, this truth remains figural,[29] and the Chartrian assimilation of the classical to the Christian must always be metaphoric, rather than literally doctrinal. The *De planctu,* for example, ends with an excommunication which is not so much a literal order of excommunication as it is a figural investment of the pagan deities of *Natura* and *Genius* with a Christian purpose. In no explicit way do these texts present themselves as contributions to doctrinal debate, nor do they ever fully define the relation between their classical figures and the Christian exegetical procedures applied to them. By leaving the relation between the Christian and the classical figural, the Chartrians protect the distinction between the secular and the ecclesiastical, even as they metaphorically proclaim the subordination of the first to the second. Articulated from within the well-established, burgeoning institutional space of the Church, Chartrian allegory carries the Pauline exegetical program to a logical conclusion: the principle of inclusion and subordination has become purely figural.

At the same time, by sanctioning a purely figural reconciliation between sacral and secular, the School of Chartres makes doctrinal authority accessible to secular writers. To the extent that the *Nun's Priest's Tale* needs a single, global moral, this is it: all writing is doctrinal. This claim occurs at the very end of the tale; it is connected, albeit tenuously, to the narrative; and it is more global than the series of practical morals which immediately precede it. In short, it is everything a reader might reasonably expect in a moral. If it has seemed incomplete or ironic to previous scholarship, that is because previous scholars have failed to recognize that the polemical power of the claim that all writing is doctrinal lies precisely in its open-endedness.

For the claim is not so much a simple proposition as it is the invocation of a practice of textual appropriation, and the meaning of an appropriation varies in accordance with the interest which motivates it. To restate the problem in slightly different terms, the claim that all writing is doctrinal never stands by itself. It is always made in order to authorize other claims. Paul makes it in order to appropriate the authority of Judaic law for social practices proscribed by it. John of Salisbury makes it in order to extend Christian exegesis to secular texts. And Chaucer makes it in order to make secular texts as authoritative as sacred ones.

It should be obvious by now that recognizing the allegorical aspirations of Chaucer's tale in no way requires one to take it as a simple affirmation of Church doctrine. What is perhaps less obvious, but no less important, is that the very same exegetical logic which enables Chaucer to be allegorical without being completely doctrinal, also enables him to be ironic without being completely subversive.

The tale's many ironic strategies—the hyperbolic descriptions of Chauntecleer and Pertelote, the continual importation of philosophical argument and epic diction, the succession of contradictory narratorial stances assumed by the Nun's Priest—complement rather than negate its allegorical appropriation. To treat the two tendencies as unalterably opposed is to assign them an historically invariant thematic value. It is to assume that allegory is always exclusively affirmative, and irony is exclusively renunciatory. By contrast, if we consider the specific position the tale takes up with relation to the exegetical tradition it appropriates, we can see its allegorical and ironic impulses not as opposed but as complementary. The final, open-ended invocation of Paul is allegorical and ironic at once. To the extent that it reiterates the doctrinal it authorizes Chaucer's text. To the extent that it subverts the doctrinal, it maintains the text's secularity. But both impulses have the same goal: to establish the adequacy of a secular text. To this end, the tale hovers between affirmation and subversion, drawing its force from both, relinquishing neither.

The secularity of the tale depends on precisely this complicated rapprochement between allegory and irony, a rapprochement to which Chaucer's choice of genre assigns an entirely traditional name: fable. Allegory and irony were both mainstays of the extremely rich tradition of medieval fable, a tradition which encompassed the corrosively ironic, anti-clerical, anti-monarchical *Roman de Renart,* and the ostentatiously allegorical moralized fables of preachers such as Odo of Cheriton. Between these extremes one finds a wealth of works such as *Ysengrimus* and the *Speculum stultorum* which combine philosophical and theological speculations with irony and satire.

These possibilities are clearly built into the genre at its most fundamental level. As Cicero defines it, a fable is neither the truth nor like the truth.[30] As an overtly false discourse, one which continually and ostentatiously declares its falsity even as it produces a coherent narrative, the table allows a maximum of discursive play to be combined with a maximum of discursive control. Its overt falsity prevents its play from ever being completely subversive; for its play is always implicitly subordinate to an external standard of truth. Even as corrosive a text as the *Roman de Renart* ultimately defers, through its generic falsity, to the external standard of Christian truth.

At the same time, fable's falsity prevents its deferral from being direct. A fable is a text without a past, a text whose indirect relation to authority means it must be written entirely in the language of the secular present. In this tale the authority of the secular is synonymous with the authority of the fictive. Chaucer uses the fictive frame of fable to insulate his text from the direct pressure of the doctrinal authority he wishes to appropriate.

2

THE AUTHORITY OF FABLE

The *Nun's Priest's Tale* is a story about the authority of utterance: who has it, where it comes from, and how it is maintained. As is appropriate in a tale which will proclaim all writing to be subsumed under a single authority, authority in this narrative has a single shape. It is patriarchal and monarchical; its position is occupied by Chauntecleer. This position will constrain utterance throughout the tale, though the continual tendency of most utterances, Pertelote's, the fox's, and even Chauntecleer's, is away from it. Chauntecleer is threatened throughout by the discourse of his subordinates, first by Pertelote's dismissal of dreams and then by the fox's flattery. Moreover, it is his own utterance that nearly does him in; crowing at the wrong time is what enables the fox to capture him. Despite this continual movement away from the authoritative position in which Chauntecleer begins, by the end the narrative has returned him to it.

It may seem a bit ludicrous to speak of Chauntecleer as patriarchal and monarchical, so I should stress that I am not describing his "character" so much as I am describing the position which that character occupies in the narrative. It is true Chauntecleer is nothing more than a talking rooster. Yet one makes sense of a beast fable in the first instance not by appealing to zoology, but by appealing to the social categories the narrative imposes on its animal characters. Chaucer makes Chauntecleer the voice of authority in the barnyard community he inhabits, and he qualifies that authority as male and royal. Thinking of a rooster as royal obviously involves ironic displacements that Chaucer exploits at every opportunity. Nevertheless, the position Chauntecleer occupies continues to structure the narrative even as the narrative demonstrates his comic inappropriateness to it. Authority as male and royal is the status quo from which the narrative begins and to which it returns.

The narrative is in two parts: the dream debate, where Chauntecleer's authority as male is threatened by the female discourse of Pertelote, and the capture, where his authority as ruler is almost destroyed by the flattery of the fox.[31] Both parts are drawn from the Renardian tradition and from one of its forerunners, Marie de France's *Fables*. In previous versions the tale is a single, continuous whole. Chaucer bifurcates it by making two changes in the previous versions. First, he shifts the role of protagonist from Renart to Chauntecleer (changing Renart's name to Russell in the process to emphasize the shift). Second, he makes Chauntecleer's dream the occasion for dramatizing two opposite modes of reading, male and female. The narrative is thus broken up into two discrete assaults on a single discursive authority embodied in Chauntecleer, with the first assault the ostensible precondition for the second.

By initially locating Chauntecleer's authority in his superiority to Pertelote, Chaucer gives the tale, as Sheila Delany has argued, a more decidedly misogynist cast than its predecessors.[32] The reason for this shift becomes clearer if we consider the differences between Chaucer's audience and the audience for the Renardian tradition from which the tale is appropriated. The Renardian tradition was also the literature of a "middle class" but one which had a much more embattled relation to the reigning social forces of Church and Crown than Chaucer's audience had. John Flinn has argued convincingly that the *Roman de Renart* was produced for the lesser provincial French nobility of the twelfth and thirteenth centuries.[33]

This subclass, continually pressured by the growing hegemony of the French and British monarchies and by the growing international hegemony of the Church, found an ironic legitimation in the incessant anti-monarchical and anti-clerical machinations of the outlaw Renart. Renart's machinations, his *engins,* are discursive ruses which consist of initially acceding to the royal authority of Noble the Lion, or the spiritual authority of a series of ecclesiastical figures, then renouncing them as soon as he is safely beyond their reach, usually in his impregnable castle Maupertuis. (In Branche I, for example, called to Noble's court to account for his crimes, he publicly repents and dons the attire of a pilgrim. Once he is safely out of the court, though not out of earshot, he tears off his clothing and reviles Noble and the Church in the most corrosive terms.)

Chauntecleer's discourse can often be as flagrantly self-interested as Renart's, but it is always under greater constraint. Renart's falsity is inventive; he is literally a plotter, a spinner of false tales, a fabulist. Chauntecleer is only an interpreter: of the heavens, of dreams, of previous textual authority. His misstatements are misreadings, not fictions invented out of whole cloth. He speaks to Chaucer's "middle class" audience, which instead of being excluded from ruling class power, is offered access to it precisely as political authority to be discursively appropriated. Chauntecleer's status as an interpreter enables him to become for this audience a figure of authority rather than an outlaw.

At the same time the social authority which Chauntecleer fictively represents already had particular social characteristics. If he is to represent this authority convincingly, even in fictional terms, he must in some way share its characteristics. It may be for this reason then that Chaucer defines Chauntecleer's interpretive power as sexual power. Sexual dominance was the *sine qua non* of noble power in the Middle Ages, for the medieval nobility was constituted primarily by primogeniture, the rule of the first-born male.[34] Defining Chauntecleer's authority in terms of his maleness gives Chaucer's audience access to noble power through its most basic and therefore broadest constituent.

Introduced against the background of the widow's "narwe cotage" and her straitened circumstances, Chauntecleer is a hyperbolic masculine splendor. His comb is redder than coral, his bill black as jet, his claws whiter than the lily, his legs azure, and his body like burnished gold. Holding seven hens "in governance," he is a fecund source of male power in a female world impoverished precisely by its lack of a man.

This male power is epitomized in his peerless crowing:

> . . . she hadde a cok, hight Chauntecleer.
> In al the land, of crowyng nas his peer.
> His voys was murier than the murie orgon
> On messe days that in the chirche gon.
> Wel sikerer was his crowing in his logge
> Than is a clokke or an abbey orlogge.
> By nature he knew ech ascencioun
> Of the equynoxial in thilke toun;
> For whan degrees fiftene weren ascended,
> Thanne crew he that it myghte not been amended.
> VII.2849–58

In the figure of Chauntecleer's crowing Chaucer has translated the dilemma of the *Nun's Priest's Tale* to its narrowest compass. On the one hand, the crowing is nothing more than the instinctive behavior of a rooster. On the other, Chaucer presents it as an act of interpretation, making it a tiny allegory for secular discourse: for discourse, that is, that derives its authority from without. Chauntecleer's reading of equinoxial ascensions translates a cosmic text into the terms of human time. If his crowing is more certain than such interpretive machines as clocks or horologes, that is because of the fidelity with which he reproduces his text. In "whan degrees fiftene weren ascended / Thanne crew he . . . ," "Thanne" follows "whan" with an immediacy that has an almost logical force: the instant Chauntecleer sees the sun rise to the proper point, he declares the beginning of day to the community.

The immediacy of his crowing reinforces the etymological sense of his name: Chauntecleer, "the clear singer," whose transparent voice contains nothing but the external reality which authorizes it. At the same time, the crowing never ceases to be crowing, that is, never ceases to be the completely inarticulate noise of an animal. But this doubleness enhances the force of the allegory rather than defeating it. Chauntecleer's crowing works as a model of secular discourse because it is both faithful to external authority and irreducibly distant from it.

The combination of these two characteristics, fidelity and referential distance, is also what enables the model to structure the rest of the narrative. Chauntecleer's position can be threatened because its authority is not inherent. He is open to temptation. Pertelote will tempt him to evade the prophetic authority of his dream, and the fox will tempt him to evade the authority of the heavens by crowing blindly. Yet he can restore himself through the same sort of evasion, flattering the fox as the fox had flattered him. Chauntecleer's authority can practice evasion because like all secular authority, it is secondary and derivative, evasive in its very essence.

This propensity is dramatized first in the dream debate, where it is increasingly linked to Chauntecleer's gender. The debate begins with a challenge to his masculinity. When he retells his frightening dream, Pertelote mocks his fear. Like D. W. Robertson's Wife of Bath, Pertelote is a carnal reader. Citing Cato, she dismisses dreams as mere symptoms of indigestion and offers Chauntecleer a laxative. He responds to this provocation with an exposition of the authority of dreams that is staggering by contrast. To Pertelote's single authority, he cites three exempla, a life of Saint Kenelm, Macrobius's commentary on the *Somnium Scipionis,* the Book of Daniel, the story of Joseph from the Book of Genesis, and the stories of Croesus and Andromache. His defense is at once authoritative and evasive: authoritative because it treats the issue of dreams correctly, and evasive because that is the wrong question. Instead of considering the implications of his dream, he is distracted by Pertelote into demonstrating his sexual superiority. When the debate concludes, and he leaves his perch to feather Pertelote twenty times, and tread her "eke as ofte," he is simply duplicating bodily the subjugation that has already taken place discursively.[35]

Moreover, despite its carnality, even this evasion begins with an act of interpretation. Chauntecleer concludes his exposition of dreams and announces his desire for love play by mistranslating a Latin authority:

> "Now let us speke of myrthe, and stynte al this.
> Madame Pertelote, so have I blis,
> Of o thyng God hath sent me large grace;
> For whan I se the beautee of youre face,
> Ye been so scarlet reed aboute youre yen,
> It maketh al my drede for to dyen;
> For al so siker as *In principio,*
> *Mulier est hominis confusio*—
> Madame, the sentence of this Latyn is,
> 'Womman is mannes joye and al his blis.' . . ."
>
> VII.3157–66

Mulier est hominis confusio is the beginning of a sardonic definition of woman so widely circulated in the Middle Ages that Susan Kavanaugh, in her notes to the tale, calls it "almost proverbial."[36] As given in the *Speculum historiale* of Vincent of Beauvais, the complete definition runs as follows:

> What is woman? The confusion of man. An insatiable beast. A continual trouble. An unceasing battle. The wreck of the continent man. A human slave.[37]

Chaucer's deployment of the definition makes its irony double-edged. On the one hand, it serves as an ironic summation of the entire first half of the tale: what has been presented is the confusion of a male by a female. Yet for that very reason the ultimate target of the definition is not Chauntecleer but Pertelote. To the extent that Chauntecleer's invocation and mistranslation of the definition undercut his pretension to authority, they also illustrate the definition's essential truth. Chauntecleer is a figure of ridicule at this point not because he has not resisted Pertelote, but because he has not resisted her enough. He chooses to luxuriate in the superiority of his position rather than confront the threat posed to that position which his dream foretells.

It should be noted as well that Chaucer presents this evasion in very precise terms as a breakdown between sacral and secular authority. When Chauntecleer claims that the proposition *"Mulier est hominis confusio"* is "also siker as *In principio,"* he is presenting it as a second *Verbum;* that is, he is presenting it as a truth as certain and originary as "In principio erat Verbum" or "In principio creavit Deus caelum et terram." Yet *"Mulier est hominis confusio"* can never have the stability of the Divine Word because it expresses not stability but confusion. The confusion extends even to the manner in which the Divine Word is here invoked. The fact that the abbreviated phrase *In principio* can stand for either the opening of John or the opening of Genesis or both at once is a sign of its vulgarization. The repetition of these sentences had for Chaucer's audience become such a regular part of everyday routine that their sacral authority had become overlaid by the sheer fact of their continual reiteration.

From this perspective, Chauntecleer's mistranslation is simply a more extreme case of the inevitable loss that marks the passage from sacred to secular. The secular translation of the sacred will always be a mistranslation: while Chauntecleer's mistranslation may expose the contradiction of his position, it does not invalidate his authority. Since secularization never fully commands the authority it claims, the simple fact of Chauntecleer's pretention is not less significant than its failures. Chaucer clearly expects his audience to find Chauntecleer's exuberance appealing even as he undercuts it. The conclusion of the dream debate is a triumph of what one critic has inelegantly but accurately called Chauntecleer's "cockiness."[38] If his dream threatens to displace him from his authoritative position, the energy which he devotes to subjugating Pertelote reinforces his position even though it fails to meet the threat. Perhaps it is for this reason that Chaucer twice calls him royal in the last ten lines of this half of the tale:

> Real he was, he was namoore aferd.
> He fethered Pertelote twenty tyme,,
> And trad hire eke as ofte, er it was prime.
>
> . . . .
>
> Thus roial, as a prince is in his halle,
> Leve I this Chauntecleer in his pasture,
> And after wol I telle his aventure.
> VII.3176–79; 3184–86

The note of triumph in these lines is hyperbolic and ironic in the extreme; it is triumphal nonetheless.

Moreover, the hyperbole looks ahead to the actual moment of crisis, which is staged more straightforwardly as the crisis of a prince. Flattery was for the Middle Ages a predominantly political problem: making the fox a flatterer casts Chauntecleer in the role of a prince or great lord, about to be trapped in the discursive exchange of his own court. *Renart le contrefait,* Chaucer's most immediate extant source for the tale, opens with a scene at the court of Noble the Lion in which Renart plays the flatterer.[39] Behind this Renardian topos lies the didactic tradition of the Mirror of Princes and other political writings, a point the Nun's Priest emphasizes by pausing to warn "ye lordes" that "many a fals flatour / Is in youre courtes. . . ." John of Salisbury's *Policraticus,* which marks the beginning of this tradition in the high Middle Ages,[40] presents flattery (*adulatoria*) as one of the chief means by which courtiers manipulate the power of their superiors, and the foremost agency of the *concupiscentia* which destroys the public welfare. John makes flattery the cause of Rome's decline, claiming that its end (*finis*) is the destruction of liberty and the promotion of tyranny.[41] Such theoretical discussions frequently found practical issue in accusations of bad counsel, one of the commonest, and probably one of the safest, ways to complain about a medieval king. This line of attack was used consistently against Richard II almost from the moment he began to rule on his own in 1380 to his deposition in 1399. The most serious threat before 1399 came in exactly this form in the Merciless Parliament of 1389. The thirty-nine charges offered by the Lords Appellant, though actually directed against Richard's concentration of royal power within his household, were framed entirely as an attempt to protect him from the encroachment of his personal advisors.[42] In both theory and practice, the concept of flattery often served the same function it does in this tale: to stake out a zone of completely degraded, completely false discourse against which more authoritative political discourse could be defined. As the flatterer, the fox is able to displace Chauntecleer by convincing him that political authority could be self-contained and inherent. He ingratiates himself by praising the inherent beauty of Chauntecleer's voice and by likening it to "my lorde youre fader." When he asks, "konne ye youre fader countrefete?," he is tempting Chauntecleer to claim a place in the artificially inflated patrilineage he has just constructed.

Though both characters will continue to communicate in the degraded language of flattery throughout this scene they do so under severe discursive constraint. The fox must flatter Chauntecleer by appealing to his lineage: he cannot imagine a new form of power; he can only manipulate the proper form. Similarly, the only difference between the authorized and unauthorized versions of Chauntecleer's crowing is a negative one: in the unauthorized version he closes his eyes. Moreover, the authority Chauntecleer abdicates remains ironically present throughout the scene in the form of the resultant anarchy.

In a social world where authority has a single shape, the displacement of Chauntecleer can have no other result but anarchy. The pursuit that follows his capture draws every member of his community, including the bees who swarm from their hive, away from their accustomed places. Chaucer compares the mob first to fiends in hell and then to the English Rising of 1381:

> So hydous was the noyse—a, benedicitce!—
> Certes, he Jakke Straw and his meynee
> Ne made never shoutes half so shrille
> Whan that they wolden any Flemyng kille
> As thilke day was maad upon the fox.
>
> VII.3393–97

The reference to Jack Straw, a leader in the Rising, is one of a very few topical allusions in the *Canterbury Tales*. It is usually dismissed as a curiosity, but viewed in relation to Chauntecleer's ruse immediately following, it acquires a somewhat larger significance:

> This cok, that lay upon the foxes bak,
> In al his drede unto the fox he spak,
> And seyde, "Sire, if that I were as ye,
> Yet sholde I seyn, as wys God helpe me,
> 'Turneth agayn, ye proude cherles alle!
> A verray pestilence upon yow falle!
> Now I am come unto the wodes syde;
> Maugree youre heed, the cok shal heere abyde.' "
>
> VII.3405–12

When Chauntecleer suggests that the fox address this anarchic mob as proud churls and command them to turn back, he tempts the fox to speak with the authority of a prince. The turning point in the Rising occurred when Richard, then twelve years old, went to negotiate with the rebels massed at Smithfield and convinced them to disperse. Most of the chronicles, irrespective of their general view of Richard, portray his role in the Rising as that of the sole authoritative voice, decisively pacifying an anarchic mob through the sheer assertion of his privileged position in public discourse. The fullest example of this view is Walsingham's. After Wat Tyler is mortally wounded during negotiations and a riot seems imminent,

The king with marvellous presence of mind and courage for so young a man, spurred his horse towards the commons and rode around them, saying "What are you doing? Surely you do not wish to fire on your own king? Do not attack me and do not regret the death of that traitor and ruffian. For I will be your king, your captain and your leader. Follow me into that field where you can have all things you would like to ask for."

The mob follows him to a nearby open field, "before they had fully decided whether they ought to kill the king or be quiet and return home," and there they are easily surrounded by an armed band hastily summoned by the mayor of London.[43]

In effect, Chauntecleer invites the fox to make the same gesture as Richard—to restore order through the power of his voice. True to his character as Flatterer, the fox cannot resist the prospect of completing his appropriation of Chauntecleer's authority. The attempt to complete the appropriation immediately exposes its momentary and illusory character. As soon as the fox opens his mouth to speak Chauntecleer escapes, and the power Russell had apparently appropriated disappears.

It is a final irony that Chauntecleer must resort to flattery in order to escape the Flatterer. Like the other ironies in this tale, however, this one also serves the status quo which structures the narrative. While the fox's flattery simply misconstrues the authority Chauntecleer represents and has no other aim than anarchy, the purpose of Chauntecleer's flattery is restorative. It forces the fox to face the impossibility of any form of authority other than the one he would destroy and ultimately returns Chauntecleer's world to the position of stability from which the narrative began. Chauntecleer's descent into the language of flattery is justified by the authority he represents.

Chauntecleer's descent is also Chaucer's: this final act of flattery—this final, ungrounded linguistic figuration—is necessary to secure the coherence of Chaucer's narrative. It is only fitting that a narrative that aspires to achieve the stability of Christian authority through the detour of fable should turn on an instance of linguistic evasion. Like Chauntecleer's, Chaucer's discourse is authoritative in its very evasions, its competence enabled by an antecedent structure it steadfastly resists.

Chaucer never relinquishes the shifting, contradictory space between the allegorical and the ironic, for the contradictions that constrain his authority are the very conditions which make it possible. In order to maintain its secularity, this authority must always remain implicit; it must advance its claims ironically. Against the explicit, overtly systematic discourse of Christian doctrine, it must mobilize the less direct, but no less powerful resources of fabular narrative. Chaucerian authority is critical yet profoundly conservative, ironically self-conscious yet deferential to the status quo. It is precisely his critical examination of previous authority which enables him to appropriate it. If modern scholarship has too often failed to recognize either the range of his formal self-consciousness, or the depth of his social conservatism, then that is because it is the great blindness of the modern humanist tradition to equate critical self-consciousness with its own ideological predispositions. The strong counter-instance Chaucer provides does not so much present a fully formed alternative to humanist assumptions, as suggest the urgent need for their reappraisal. Acknowledging authority is not always an act of deference, and renouncing the past is not always an act of liberation.[44]

Notes

[Ed. note: Much of this essay appears, in different form, in Scanlon's *Narrative, Authority, and Power: The Medieval Exemplum and the Chaucerian Tradition* (Cambridge: Cambridge University Press, 1994).]

    1.   Charles Muscatine, *Chaucer and the French Tradition* (Berkeley: University of California Press, 1957), 238.

    2.   Cf. Stephen Knight, *Geoffrey Chaucer* (Oxford: Oxford University Press, 1986), 1. I list here only the most important contributions to this debate. For a comprehensive critical history of the tale, see Derek Pearsall, ed., *The Nun's Priest's Tale,* vol. II, pt. 9 of *A Variorum Edition of the Works of Geoffrey Chaucer* (Norman: University of Oklahoma Press, 1984), 30–81. From the patristic perspective: Mortimer Donovan, "The *moralite* of the Nun's Priest's Sermon," *JEGP* 52 (1953): 493–508; Charles Dahlberg, "Chaucer's Cock and Fox," *JEGP* 53 (1954): 277–90; D.W. Robertson, Jr., *A Preface to Chaucer* (Princeton: Princeton University Press, 1959), 251–52; Bernard F. Huppé, *A Reading of the Canterbury Tales,* rev. ed. (Albany: SUNY Press, 1967), 174–84; Bernard S. Levy and George R. Adams, "Chauntecleer's Paradise Lost and Regained," *MS* 29 (1967): 178–92. Donovan and Dahlberg lay out the general lines of the argument, and marshall an impressive array of evidence from theological sources. Donovan identifies the cock with the preacher and the fox with the devil, while Dahlberg introduces additional evidence that associates the fox with the friars. Robertson produces iconographic support for the argument and Huppé and Levy and Adams broaden its focus, seeing the tale as an allegorical reworking of the Fall. Judson Boyce Allen, "The Ironic Fruyt: Chauntecleer as Figura," *SP* 66 (1969): 25–35, also derives his evidence from theological sources but argues Chaucer's use of them was ironic, that Chauntecleer fails to live up to his exegetical models. The formalist reading begins with Muscatine, *Chaucer and the French Tradition*. Muscatine concludes his account this way: "Unlike fable, the *Nun's Priest's Tale* does not so much make true and solemn assertions about life as it tests truths and tries out solemnities" (242). Recapitulating this line of argument in various ways have been E. Talbot Donaldson, ed., *Chaucer's Poetry* (New York: Ronald Press, 1958), 940–44; Stephen Manning, "The Nun's Priest's Morality and the Medieval Attitude toward Fables," *JEGP* 59 (1960): 403–16; Stanley Fish, "The Nun's Priest's Tale and Its Analogues," *CLAJ* 5 (1962): 223–38; Jill Mann, "The *Speculum Stultorum* and the Nun's Priest's Tale," *ChaurR* 9 (1975): 262–82; A. Paul Shallers, "The 'Nun's Priest's Tale': An Ironic Exemplum," *ELH* 42 (1975): 319–37; Alfred David, *The Strumpet Muse: Art and Morals in Chaucer's Poetry* (Bloomington: Indiana University Press, 1976), 223–31; Donald R. Howard, *The Idea of the Canterbury Tales* (Berkeley: University of California Press, 1976), 280–307; Robert B. Burlin, *Chaucerian Fiction* (Princeton: Princeton University Press, 1977), 229–37.

    3.   E. Talbot Donaldson, *Speaking of Chaucer* (New York: Norton, 1970), 150.

    4.   Pearsall, *Variorum,* 3.

    5.   Paul De Man, "The Rhetoric of Temporality" in *Blindness and Insight: Essays in the Rhetoric of Contemporary Criticism* (Minneapolis: University of Minnesota Press, 1983), 187–228. The possibility of applying this essay to Chaucer was initially suggested to me by my former colleague at Reed College, Robert Knapp. For a different application, see his "Penance, Irony, and Chaucer's Retraction," *Assays* 2 (1983): 45–67.

    6.   De Man, "Rhetoric," 203.

7. De Man, "Rhetoric," 222.

8. De Man, "Rhetoric," 208.

9. Isidore of Seville, *Etymologiae,* cited in John MacQueen, *Allegory* (London: Methuen, 1970), 49. I am grateful to Clare Carroll of Wesleyan University for having brought this fact to my attention.

10. This is an historical fact as well as a theoretical convergence. The Marxism of Louis Althusser developed within the same Parisian milieu as Jacques Derrida's deconstruction, often contesting the same fundamental concepts. The affinities are signalled by the similarity in categories. De Man's blindness and insight are anticipated by Althusser's blindness and oversight (Althusser and Etienne Balibar, *Reading Capital,* trans. Ben Brewster [London: Verso, 1979], 18–22). Pierre Macherey, one of Althusser's leading disciples, outlined a theory of literature based on the notion of absence in *A Theory of Literary Production* (trans. Geoffrey Wall [London: Routledge, Kegan Paul, 1978]), which originally appeared in 1966, a year before Derrida's *Of Grammatology.* For Macherey and Althusser, textuality is an absence, but a determinate absence, which always presents a reader with material to work on. The text is the "raw material" from which the labor of reading produces meaning (though like any other raw material the text is already the product of previous labor). This theory of reading is as totalizing as deconstruction, but its insistence on the material character of each new reading allows it to retain the materiality of history, which the residual idealism of deconstruction always deflects. I am heavily indebted to this theory for both my adaptation of De Man and my subsequent reading of the *Nun's Priest's Tale.*

11. De Man, "Rhetoric," 206–07.

12. Cf. Hayden White, *Metahistory: The Historical Imagination in Nineteenth-Century Europe* (Baltimore: The Johns Hopkins University Press, 1973), 317–30.

13. De Man, "Rhetoric," 219.

14. For the dependence of secular notions of political authority on ecclesiastical tradition, see M. J. Wilks, *The Problem of Sovereignty in the Later Middle Ages* (Cambridge: Cambridge University Press, 1963).

15. Paul Strohm, "Chaucer's Audience," *Literature and History* 5 (1977): 26–41; and Anne Middleton, "Chaucer's New Men," in *Literature and Society: Papers from the English Institute (1978),* ed. Edward Said (Baltimore: The Johns Hopkins University Press, 1980), 15–56.

16. Janet Coleman, *Medieval Readers and Writers 1350–1400* (New York: Columbia University Press, 1981), 13–57. For the absorption of the bourgeoisie into the bottom ranks of the nobility, see K. P. McFarlane, *The Nobility of Later Medieval England* (Oxford: Oxford University Press, 1963), 142–67.

17. Coleman, *Medieval Readers,* 31–32.

18. Geoffrey Chaucer, *The Riverside Chaucer,* 3rd ed., ed. Larry D. Benson, *et al.* (Boston: Houghton-Mifflin, 1987), 261 (VII.3438–43). All subsequent citations are from this edition and will hereafter be given in the text.

19. *Nestle-Aland Greek-English New Testament,* 26th rev. ed., the 2nd ed. of the R.S.V. and the text of the Novum Testamentum Graece in the tradition of Eberhard Nestle and Erwin Nestle, ed. Kurt Aland, *et al.* (Stuttgart: Deutsche Bibelgesellschaft, 1979), Romans 2:28–29.

20. *Nestle-Aland,* Romans 15:4–6.

21. Helmut Koester, *History and Literature of Early Christianity,* vol. 2 of *Introduction to the New Testament* (Philadelphia: Fortress Press, 1982), 5. For a different view, see Norman Perrin, *The New Testament, An Introduction: Proclamation and Paranesis, Myth and History* (New York: Harcourt Brace Jovanovich, 1974), 106–14.

22. De Man, "Rhetoric," 207.

23. James J. Murphy, *Rhetoric in the Middle Ages: A History of Rhetorical Theory from Saint Augustine to the Renaissance* (Berkeley: University of California Press, 1974), 48–49.

24. Augustine, *De doctrina Christiana* 2.40.60, ed. William M. Green (Vienna: Hoeld-Pichler-Tempsky, 1963), CSEL 80:75.

25.   Augustine, *De doctrina* 3.7.11.

26.   M. D. Chenu, *Nature, Man, and Society in the Twelfth Century,* ed. and trans. Jerome Taylor and Lester K. Little (Chicago: University of Chicago Press, 1968), 297–308.

27.   John of Salisbury, *Policraticus* 3.8, ed. C.C.J. Webb, 2 vols. (Oxford: Clarendon Press, 1909), 1:194. For John's use of exempla, see Peter Van Moos, "The Use of *Exempla* in the *Policraticus* of John of Salisbury," in *The World of John of Salisbury,* ed. Michael Wilks (Oxford: Basil Blackwell, 1984), 207–61. For his advocacy of the hierocratic view that secular rulers were politically subordinate to the Church, see Beryl Smalley, *The Becket Conflict and the Schools: A Study of Intellectuals in Politics* (Totowa, NJ: Rowman and Littlefield, 1973), 87–108.

28.   Alain de Lille, *De planctu Naturae,* Prose 4, trans. James J. Sheridan (Toronto: Pontifical Institute of Medieval Studies, 1980), 140.

29.   Winthrop Wetherbee, *Platonism and Poetry in the Twelfth Century* (Princeton: Princeton University Press, 1972), 210.

30.   Cicero, *De inventione* 1.19; cited in Murphy, *Rhetoric,* 13.

31.   In what follows, I rely heavily on Robert A. Pratt, "Three Old French Sources of the Nonnes Preestes Tale," *Speculum* 47 (1972): 422–44, 646–68. What I have called the "capture" Pratt calls the "fable."

32.   Sheila Delany, *"Mulier est hominis confusio':* Chaucer's Anti-popular *Nun's Priest's Tale,"* *Mosaic* 17 (1984): 1–8.

33.   J. F. Flinn, "Littérature bourgeoise et *Le Roman de Renart,"* in *Aspects of the Medieval Animal Epic,* Proceedings of the International Conference, Louvain, May 15–17, 1972, ed. E. Rombauts and A. Welkenhuysen (The Hague: Martinus Nijhoff, 1975), 11–23.

34.   For a brief discussion, see Marc Bloch, *Feudal Society,* 2 vols., trans. L. A. Manyon (Chicago: University of Chicago Press, 1961), 1:199–210.

35.   Ian Bishop, *"The Nun's Priest's Tale* and the Liberal Arts," *Review of English Studies,* 30 (1979): 266.

36.   Kavanaugh, *Riverside Chaucer,* 939.

37.   *Speculum historiale* 11.71; cited in Carleton Brown, "Mulier est Hominis Confusio," *MLN* 35 (1920): 479–82.

38.   Shallers, " 'The Nun's Priest's Tale,' " 332.

39.   *Le Roman de Renart,* ed. Gaston Raynaud and Henri Lemaître (1914; reprint, Geneva: Slatkine Reprints, 1975), 5–9, lines 415–788.

40.   Wilhelm Berges, *Die Fürstenspiegel des hohen und spälen Mittelalters* (Leipzig: K. W. Hiersemann, 1938), 3–8.

41.   John of Salisbury, *Policraticus* 3.4–10 (1:177–205), 8.17 (2:162).

42.   Anthony Tuck, *Richard II and the English Nobility* (London: Edward Arnold, 1973), 122–23.

43.   Thomas Walsingham, *Historia Anglicana* 1:456–67, excerpted and trans. in *The Peasants' Revolt of 1381,* ed. R. B. Dobson (London: Macmillan, 1970), 178–79.

44.   A somewhat shorter version of this essay was presented to the Center of the Humanities at Wesleyan University during my stay there in the academic year 1987–88. Comments offered by the other Fellows, Nancy Armstrong, Hazel Carby, Emmet Flood, Fred Pfeil, Kachig Tölöyan, and Director of the Center, Richard Vann, were extremely helpful in formulating this current version. I also received helpful suggestions from Sheila Delany and Aline Fairweather.

Chaucer's Criseyde:
Woman in Society, Woman in Love

DAVID AERS

Retornyng in hire soule ay up and down
The wordes of this sodeyn Diomede,
His grete estat, and perel of the town,
And that she was allone and hadde nede
Of frendes help; and thus bygan to brede
The cause whi, the sothe for to telle,
That she took fully purpos for to dwelle.
                Troilus and Criseyde, V, ll. 1023–9

Anyone attempting to contribute to the understanding of Chaucer's achievement and meaning in creating the figure of Criseyde will be aware that, in
reaction to much previous criticism, influential commentators in recent
decades eschewed interpretations which might seem to treat medieval writing
as though it held any affinities with the kind of "naturalism" medievalists
associate with nineteenth-century novels.[1] So in his important study of
Chaucer it is not surprising that R. O. Payne praised modern critics who had
evolved approaches to "the patterns of characterization which remove it from
the realistic and motivational-psychological categories in which earlier criticism had sought to define it." He himself wished to demonstrate that there is
no ground in the poem for any "naturalistic reconstruction of 'personalities,'"
nothing approaching "individual psychologies." In common with others, such
as D. W. Robertson, Payne's treatment of *Troilus and Criseyde* assumed that all
late medieval poetry was governed by the same unambiguous "ultimate
moral principles," while the past was viewed as a straightforward "series of
illustrations of intellectual abstractions." The function of characters in art was
to convey already known "typical significances" through fixed symbols quite
isolated from the contingencies of "actual existence." Criseyde, for example,
"is a way of saying something about the lovely vanity of human wishes."[2]
Thus, the multifarious and dynamic forms of human existence were transformed into a set of unproblematic abstractions and judgments as medieval

Reprinted from *Chaucer, Langland, and the Creative Imagination* by David Aers, ed. (1980) by permission of the publisher, Routledge: New York and London.

art allegedly eliminated individuals in the service of clearly presented and static universals. However, as the previous chapters [of Aer's book—ed.] have suggested, such approaches blind us to central currents in both Langland's and Chaucer's poetry, and I now wish to show how, in creating the figure of Criseyde, Chaucer developed a social psychology which comprised a profound contribution to the understanding of interactions between individual and society. His astonishing achievement in making Criseyde included an exploration of the ways in which individual action, consciousness and sexuality, the most intimate areas of being, are fundamentally related to the specific social and ideological structures within which an individual becomes an identifiable human being. Far from either simply transporting his readers "away from contemporary reality to a distant and romantic Troy,"[3] or exemplifying unproblematic ethical and metaphysical universals, this exploration paid particular attention to the position of women in courtly society, ideology and literary traditions. Choosing Boccaccio's tale, placed in Troy, may have made it easier for him to engage in detailed and imaginatively sympathetic explorations of love, sexuality and female consciousness without constantly addressing himself to the dominant attitudes and judgments of conventional Christianity, but it did not entail a flight from the world of his own audience.[4] Quite the contrary, his treatment of Criseyde shows concern with women *in* the social group for which he wrote—the expectations they cherished, the manipulative pressures they had to accept and use, the contradictory self-images and realities with which they were presented. He also, as he would do later in the *Canterbury Tales,* showed great interest in women's complex mixture of opposition, accommodation and positive complicity in a situation where they were a subordinate group, at all social levels.

In much romance writing and courtly literature there is an attempt to remove love from the compromises, confusions and institutionalized miseries of the contemporary world. Instead of constructing utopian images and fictions which were made to encounter the present world in a critical and earnest examination of it, romances could be used to offer far more simple and comforting escape. The formula of an outstanding knight committing his existence to the devoted service of a woman fulfilled a psychological and perhaps growing need to create a more satisfying alternative to the real organization of Eros and marriage in medieval society. Customary practices and ideology (secular as well as ecclesiastic) demanded the subordination of women to men and to land, aristocratic marriages being primarily land transactions and family alliances. This is the context in which courtly literature evolved images and conventions in which the normal relations between women and men were inverted, the knight serving the woman, paying homage and devotion to her. The role of female patronesses in shaping such literature is no coincidence, and Eileen Power's suggestion that it served a psychological function for upper-class women not dissimilar to that served by modern romantic stories and magazines for working-class women may be plausible, for the image of women as goddesses worshipped by aristocratic males sorted very ill with their actual position.[5] It seems to me that Chaucer was fascinated by these contradictions and was not prepared to leave them peacefully coexisting. In *Troilus* he actually used the romance genre and conventions of courtly literature to explore the tensions between the place women occupied in society and the various self-images presented to them. He set out to imagine his way into the psychic cost for men and women in the situation he perceived so sharply, returning to society in his own art.

At the very opening of the poem Chaucer shows that he wants his audiences to take Criseyde's social situation seriously. He emphasizes her sense of isolation in Troy at this point in her life, her danger as the daughter of a traitor in a long war, and her immediate need for a male protector.

Chaucer reports the general view that not only Criseyde's father, but all his kin "Ben worthi for to brennen," so her fear is most understandable:

> For of hire lif she was ful sore in drede,
> As she that nyste what was best to rede;
> For bothe a widewe was she and allone
> Of any frend to whom she dorste hir mone.
> (*Troilus and Criseyde,* I, ll. 90–1, 95–8)

Before critics venture any remarks about Criseyde's "weakness" or "slydynge of corage" they need to project their imaginations into this situation, following Chaucer. Her fear is justified and has specific grounds, her weakness is a genuine aspect of a social reality in which women are a subordinate group, and her feelings of isolation are a subjective registering of both the particular crisis she faces and a more general vulnerability and precariousness in the position of woman.[6] In these circumstances her chief asset, her leverage on the powerful, is her sexuality. She understands this well enough, so that although she is "Wel neigh out of hir wit for sorwe and fere" (I, 1. 108), she still approaches Hector, one of the most powerful men in the city:

> On knees she fil biforn Ector adown
> With pitous vois, and tendrely wepynge,
> His mercy bad, hirselven excusynge.
> (*T & C,* I, ll. 110–12)

This scene offers an interesting contrast to images of the male prostrate before the female, and it is significant that it precedes the enactment of these images by Troilus and the arch-manipulator Pandarus (III, ll. 183–4, 953, 1079–80). Yet even before he has introduced Troilus, Chaucer invites such contrasts by introducing her frightened act of homage with a very conventional description of her "aungelik" beauty and her appearance as "an hevenyssh perfit creature" (I, ll. 100–5). To survive in this culture the woman needs to make use of her sexuality and whatever courtly sexual conventions, fictions or male fantasies may serve her.[7]

She does so, and we should not miss the way Chaucer has opened his poem by placing the courtly forms of sexual relations and language in a setting which stresses the "aungelik" female's subordinate position and her urgent need for male protection. It is Hector, responding to her beauty and helpless sorrow, responding to her as a woman, who guarantees her safety and "hir estaat" (I, ll. 113–31). The esteem in which she is held by Hector and the royal family is very important to her, and during her first discussion with Pandarus in Book II she asks directly after Hector, the potentate whose goodwill and existence appears necessary for her own well-being and relative security within the community. Similarly, when later it seems that there is a threat to her property, the importance of the royal family as her patrons who can protect her is made clear (II, ll. 1414–91, 1611–36). And being reliant on this group Criseyde is influenced by their opinions, whether about Troilus, when her mixed feelings are soothed by hearing these powerful people praise him (II, ll. 1583–94), or when she considers Troilus' proposal that they elope, a scene we shall examine later.

The first interview between Pandarus and Criseyde confirms Chaucer's interest in the processes of interaction between individual consciousness and various social pressures, manipulations and values, often bewilderingly conflicting (II, ll. 87–597). Criseyde's natural impulses and fears, her joys and her anxieties, are carefully situated in the context established in the first book. It is May, and Pandarus asks her to cast aside her self-possession and dance. At once Criseyde turns to one possible social role (in Chaucer's society) to protect herself from risks that could be involved in her uncle's invitation:

> "I? God forbede! "quod she," be ye mad?
> Is that a widewes lif, so God yow save?
> By God, ye maken me ryght soore adrad!
> Ye ben so wylde, it semeth as ye rave.
> It sate me wel bet ay in a cave
> To bidde and rede on holy seyntes lyves;
> Lat maydens gon to daunce, and yonge wyves."
> (*T & C*, II, ll. 113–19)

Criseyde may be playing with her uncle, but the game involves genuine and, as we saw, well-founded fears. Here she confronts them by using her widowhood, a state which allowed contemplative withdrawal from the threatening life of the world and the repression of natural instincts, with all the risks these carried. Of course, Criseyde does not claim this is what she wants, as her uncle knows, only that it would be a legitimate and decorous defence, one she has not yet been driven to. As we shall see, she can assess the potential of widowhood and its acknowledged values in yet another way.

In the ensuing gossipy conversation the war is the overtly central topic, another source of fear (II, 1. 124) being used by Pandarus to bring Troilus into mind, until Criseyde consults Pandarus about her "estat" and "governaunce" (II, ll. 212–20). This focusses on his relationship to her as uncle, elder male relative and guide to subordinate female, and the gamesome quality in the exchanges should not conceal the authority relations here, for as the narrator notes, nieces should obey uncles (II, ll. 232–52, 295–8; III, 1. 581). Pandarus uses his position in these roles to push Troilus' interest at her. Chaucer's handling of Criseyde's situation here is, as throughout this work, extraordinarily delicate. Its vulnerability has been stressed and Pandarus' circumlocutions both deliberately play on her fears and excite her (II, ll. 267–315). When he has done this, he introduces the core of his matter:

> Now, nece myn, the kynges deere sone,
>
> . . . .
>
> The noble Troilus, so loveth the,
> That, but ye helpe, it wol his bane be.
> (*T & C,* II, ll. 316–20)

Pandarus emphasizes the social status of the lover, the king's son—the personal name only follows three lines after the identification of rank and power. He uses this as a bait, but also as a threat, for what would become of Criseyde if she should be held responsible for his sickness or death (II, ll. 320–50)? In a similar manner, Pandarus adds to the pressure by stating that if she does not acknowledge Troilus then he, her uncle, will cut his own throat (II, ll. 323–9). This added threat has a double force, for Criseyde is not only subordinate to him but fond of his company. She plays for time and seeks clarification, using the social roles Pandarus has elected for the moment—" 'Now em,' quod she, 'what wolde ye devise? / What is your reed I sholde don of this?' " Her uncle's reply is unequivocal and recommends total fulfilment of Troilus' sexual desires (II. ll. 386–406). Criseyde tries to forestall this demand by appealing to his identity as her quasi-father (ll. 408–28). This tactic fails completely, for Pandarus renews his previous threats and gets up to leave. Her response is then carefully traced in the next three stanzas, emphasizing how she "wel neigh starf for feere, / So as she was the ferfulleste wight" (II, ll. 449–69). Her fear has again been given a thoroughly sufficient social basis and there is no reason to treat it as a peculiar flaw. Thinking of her uncle's threats and their social repercussions, she thinks about her own social survival, the dangers for her if Pandarus and Troilus are in earnest, and her uncle's personal survival. Her comment (to herself) that, "It nedeth me ful sleighly for to pleie," suggests how aware she is that her uncle manipulates her and uses the courtly forms of game as they suit him. She must try and out-play him and shifts to the area where, as we mentioned, convention allowed women a seemingly dominant role—"love." This allows her to assert that she cannot love anyone against her own will, and she takes a certain initiative in the role of powerful beauty able to bring even a king's son to woe (II. ll. 462–504). But the rules of the game were neither designed nor controlled by women, and Pandarus may well smile, for he sees her move as the concession essential to Troilus' gratification. By the time this interview between uncle and niece concludes, Chaucer has taken us far into one of the central problems he was exploring— the contradictions between aristocratic love conventions, in which woman was an exalted and powerful figure, and the reality in which she was a subordinate being to be manipulated and made serviceable to men.

We begin to see the ways in which the realities of the situation actually pervade these conventions in a subtle confirmation of the existing order and power relations. Furthermore he has shown us that he explores the problem concretely, as it was lived out in Criseyde's own consciousness and actions.

When Pandarus, sure of his success, leaves Criseyde, she withdraws "into her closet" to examine her own feelings. But "as she sat allone" and thought that to give or withhold love was something in which she was free, Troilus rides past her house in military triumph, almost presented as an event stimulated by Criseyde's meditations (II, ll. 599–647). The diversity and fluidity of her movements of consciousness are marvellously evoked by Chaucer as he expanded and changed Boccaccio's work here.[8] She responds to Troilus' presence, "And leet it so softe in hire herte synke," part passive, part agent, a delicately realized "process" which the narrator notes a few lines later when he comments that "she gan enclyne / To like hym" but gradually his own being "Made love withinne hire herte for to myne." She tries to analyse his qualities and "his estat," but while she does not try to repress her sexual feelings, we are reminded that she is "allone" and fully understand her need to take into account her social circumstances and the psychological risks of loving (ll. 649 ff.). Her mind moves to the implications of any involvement with Troilus for her own social existence:

> Al were it nat to doone,
> To graunte hym love, ye, for his worthynesse,
> It were honour, with pley and with gladnesse,
> In honestee with swich a lord to deele,
> For myn estat, and also for his heele.
> Ek wel woot I my kynges sone is he;
> And sith he hath to see me swich delit,
> If I wolde outreliche his sighte flee,
> Peraunter he myghte have me in dispit,
> Thorugh whicch I myghte stonde in worse plit.
> (*T & C*, II, ll. 703–12)

The opening two lines of this quotation imply grounds for not giving Troilus her love but at the moment they are vague and convey some confusion, easily sliding over into positive grounds for involvement, within legitimizing social conventions ("honour," "honestee") themselves equivocal as to precise content. Having followed Chaucer's stress on her estate and its uncertain position, we appreciate with sympathy this blend of self-preservation and care of another, characteristically realized by a poet with a fine care for the complexity of motivation. Indeed, the complications increase within the quoted passage as Criseyde recalls that her "estat" might not only be protected by "my kynges sone" but could be threatened from two distinct directions. If she rejects him he could certainly undermine her position even further and she would be in a far "worse plit" than at present, protected as she is by Hector. Her assessment is thoroughly realistic, as the court-poet well knew, and it again displays the real power relations underlying the forms and conventions of courtly and literary love. The second direction from which she envisages a threat is stated some lines later, and although very different is equally realistic in terms of Chaucer's own world: the threat of marriage. A widow in medieval society, a basic model for this fictional Trojan aristocracy, had a privileged position in relation to married women as long as she had adequate means of subsistence. As soon as she married the legal and economic rights she had as a widow were removed and her husband took total control of her and her lands. These are the factors Criseyde bears in mind when she thinks of the re-marriage:

> I am myn owene womman, wel at ese,
> I thank it God, as after myn estat,
> Right yong, and stonde unteyd in lusty leese,
> Withouten jalousie or swich debat:
> Shal noon housbonde seyn to me "chek mat!"
> (*T & C*, II, ll. 750–4)

Doubtless this confident statement includes some idealization of her present state and its anxieties, an independence which is clearly dependent on Hector and other males. But it does bring out the unpleasant problems of having the male protector in the form of a husband who would destroy whatever measure of precarious independence she had.[9] Throughout the entire period before she commits herself to Troilus in bed, threatened as she is, she constantly expresses fears about losing the relative independence she has and becoming totally dominated, fears Troilus tries not to arouse as she becomes directly involved with him.

Finally she is aware that the relevant problems go beyond the issue of marriage and male domination to embrace the way any full and serious love for another person necessarily involves risking oneself, jeopardizing a self-possession often won with great pain and difficulty. The whole process of genuine commitment to another opens out the self and is experienced as both joy and taxing constraint. She puts these risks well:

> Allas! syn I am free,
> Sholde I now love, and put in jupartie
> My sikernesse, and thrallen libertee?
> Allas! how dorst I thenken that folie?
> May I naught wel in other folk aspie
> Hire dredfull joye, hire constreinte, and hire peyne?
> Ther loveth noon, that she nath why to pleyne.
>
> (*T & C*, II, ll. 771–7)

This fear is quite distinct in theory from the more material group previously discussed, but in practice it overlaps, and Chaucer once more discloses the inextricable connections between objective social factors and the individual psyche.[10]

Chaucer's preoccupation with the issues under discussion is manifest in the dream about the eagle which Criseyde has after the delicate and many-layered scene in the garden. She dreams,

> How that an egle fethered whit as bon,
> Under hire brest his longe clawes sette,
> And out hire herte he rente, and that anon,
> And dide his herte into hire brest to gon,
> Of which she nought agroos, ne nothyng smerte;
> And forth he fleigh, with herte left for herte.
>
> (*T & C*, II, ll. 926–31)

This dream exhibits the violence and perils of loving concealed behind the traditional and cosy conceit of an exchange of hearts. Chaucer shows that although the dreamer feels no pain she perceives herself as passive in the face of an aggressive and dominating male. Her feelings are described in negatives ("she *nought* agroos, *ne nothyng* smerte"), and there is a striking absence of any tenderness, mutuality or pleasure. There is also an absence of security, for although the eagle inserts his heart, he actually flies on. True enough, this is a dream focussing Criseyde's fears rather more than her hopes, but the point here is that these fears are well grounded in the realities with which women had to cope, and the consequences these had for intimate areas of experience. It is in such terms, if any, that Chaucer creates the "typical" and "universal," a universal which does not dissolve the individual consciousness or particular social circumstances, a universal only apprehensible in and through individuals.

As the third book progresses, Troilus' behaviour gradually melts away Criseyde's fears as she comes to rely on him as one who, although her male social superior, is a loving protector willing to leave her identity and status free from domination by him (III, ll. 463–83). She remains subordinate to male initiatives and commands, but we also see that she may perhaps be using this submission while conforming. For example, she dutifully *obeys* her uncle, "as hir ought" when he tells her to stay the night in his house (III, ll. 575–81); but Chaucer reminds us that we cannot have complete knowledge of a consciousness such as Criseyde's, even though he is the poet creating her for us, and he implies that she may be doing so for her own advantage (the possibility of seeing Troilus) without having to accept responsibility as initiator or decision-maker. Yet he only implies it by encouraging us to guess at "What that she thoughte" when Pandarus denied that Troilus was in the house, even while he himself claims he does not know ("Nought list myn auctour fully to declare"). This interchange embodies the way that in noticing the possible uses of her subordination and imposed passivity, the poem does not allow us to go to the extreme of claiming that the woman is really the controlling manipulator, as some readers have asserted.[11] Even at this point, in a Book which contains one of the most powerful celebrations of fulfilled human love, of what Blake called "the lineaments of gratified desire" and what Chaucer called "the grete worthynesse" in love, we see that her final coming together with Troilus still needs the offices and presence of her uncle. This is especially noteworthy for it is a very different matter in Boccaccio's text, where his Criseida organizes the consummation, sends Pandarus to bring Troilo to her and needs no third party on the night.[12] Far from this version, Chaucer shows the effects of the pressures and the overall situation he has realized so fully, and we see Criseyde's real confusions, social anxieties, distress at Troilus' alleged jealousy, her sexual desires, all interacting to bring her to her "wittes ende" and place her in Pandarus' hands, "I am here al in youre governaunce."[13]

However, once the uncle completes his offices by throwing the fainting Troilus into her bed ("O nece, pes, or we be lost!"—still playing on her fears as much as her erotic desires (III, ll. 1065–118)) Criseyde takes the sexual initiative, kissing and reassuring Troilus.[14] Once she has done so she delicately and trustingly hands over the initiative to him, in a transaction Chaucer describes with marvellous tact and insight (III, ll. 1177–83). Troilus, "with blisse of that surprised," responds joyfully and the poet creates an atmosphere of mutual discovery and shared stimulation as a new serenity encompasses them which contrasts most strikingly with the manipulative but socially inescapable love-games played out previously.

Yet, even in this admirable transition, there are still images to remind us that the subordinate position of women leaves its imprint on this mutually satisfying and intimate relationship. The timorous "mouses herte" Troilus, anxiously swooning at Criseyde's bedside (III, ll. 736, 1092), is transformed into a predatory bird not so dissimilar from the one in her own violent dream:

> What myghte or may the sely larke seye,
> Whan that the sperhauk hath it in his foot?
> (*T & C*, III, ll. 1191–2)

The power relations are again overt, the predatory nature of the sparrow-hawk undisguised. Well may the narrator muse about what the lark might say from this position. Chaucer leaves the lark and turns to the newly confident Troilus. Far from thanking Criseyde for bringing him to erotic life and so generously giving him the sexual initiative, he unreflexively starts thanking the seven planetary gods (1. 1203), and then addresses Criseyde in a conventional but revealing image. This also presents their relationship in terms of male hunter and female vanquished prey (ll. 1205–11), mirroring the sparrow-hawk/lark image. The effects of male domination and egotistic predatoriness, legitimized in social practice and ideology, are reflected even in the most personal acts where there is genuine love.

While this needs pointing out, it would be very wrong to leave the passage by emphasizing these aspects of what is a characteristically multi-faceted piece of writing. Despite the social and ideological forces Chaucer has evoked with such imaginative depth, and despite his refusal to make them just vanish away, he does certainly create a most powerful example of the way in which fulfilled Eros enables individuals to transcend social pressures, repressions and fears. Mutual love, involving the total person, is achieved, and in this mutuality we celebrate not only the triumph over adverse forces but the momentary and joyful abandonment of anxious selfhood as together they "Felten in love the grete worthynesse." The conflicts of power and the distortions of energy are transcended in an oasis of "hevene blisse," the "perfit joie" of a generous love which informs body, mind and affections (II, ll. 1219–414).

The final point I wish to make about the third book concerns the aubade (ll. 1429–70). Here the coming of morning symbolizes not some inquisitorial sun of righteousness against which the evil worldlings are in rebellion being damned by Chaucer, but the re-intrusion of day-to-day society into their lives, the society in which practices and ideas concerning women have the deforming and elaborately contradictory effects we have followed,a society fighting a war initiated by male aggression and the rape of a woman. It is a society which subordinates human relations and Eros to power structures and militaristic glory, with disastrous results—"many a lovere hastow slayn, and wilt" (1. 1459). Nevertheless, although the lovers curse the day and promise an eternity of the kind of love they have just experienced, they do not yet question their own resumption of aristocratic life, accepting that "it mot nedes be" (1. 1520), however antagonistic it is to their own love. They accept the society's downgrading of the magnificent human achievement that their love is, accept the claims of the society's values and the war. It will not always be thus for Troilus, nor should it be so for Chaucer's readers.

The Prologue to Book IV opens with the narrator castigating the abstraction "Fortune" for causing the misery we are about to witness. This way of talking about events was traditional enough, and in fact here Chaucer is virtually translating the final stanza of part three in Boccaccio's *Filostrato*. Yet it is actually far less relevant to what Chaucer's own poem reveals than many readers, and perhaps even the author himself, have been prepared to admit. His work, as we have seen, portrays individual consciousness and the relationship between Criseyde and Troilus in a mode which incorporates relevant social and ideological dimensions, as different to Boccaccio's poem as to most medieval romances. It makes us unwilling to accept claims that "Fortune" cast him out of Criseyde's grace, for Chaucer has concentrated so intensely on human processes that such statements come as evasory, pseudo-explanations, the irrelevant vestiges of a tradition which needed them to provide some sense of understanding about troubling, obscure and seemingly inexplicable events and changes. Book IV confirms this impression, for it carefully describes the prime importance of social organization and cultural values in determining what happens to Criseyde and the consequences of this in her relationship with Troilus. It too makes addresses to Fortune (and even more metaphysical speculations about destiny) seem an unnecessarily vague and mystifying discourse in which to grasp the events of the last two books, a discourse which can only conceal human practices revealed in the poetic processes Chaucer created.

Immediately the fourth book brings the crucial social contexts to our attention (ll. 29–231). First, Chaucer reminds readers that Troy had immersed itself in a long war (ll. 29–56), and we might be expected to remember that its origins lay not in "Fortune" but in specific acts of male social aggression and greed leading to the present state of continuous legalized violence. Chaucer reports a day-long battle in which men fight with all kinds of weapon, "And with hire axes out the braynes quelle" (IV, ll. 43–6). The Trojans suffer severe losses and seek a truce and negotiations with the Greeks for exchange of prisoners. At this point the sudden intervention of Calkas underlines a key element in the social structure: woman is seen as a passive object to be disposed of by a patriarchal ruling group. Calkas decides that he wants his daughter to join him, now blaming his cruelty in leaving her in a place he felt sure was soon to be destroyed. However strange such paternal care may now seem from the father who abandoned his daughter to face hostility and possible persecution when he left the city, no one questions his right to claim her, nor her right to be consulted (ll. 64–147). Although her alienation from her treacherous father is as complete as her wish to remain in her home (ll. 659–871, 1128–69), neither Calkas, Greeks nor Trojans consider that a mere woman is a being with needs, desires and choices to be honoured, even though she is close to court circles. Troilus sees this quite clearly, and he reminds Criseyde that her father will be able to marry her off as he sees fit, persuading her verbally or by using violence as he wishes.[15]

Chaucer highlights these issues for us as ones we should continue to take very seriously, and he moves us from Calkas and the Greek assembly to the Trojan "parlement" (IV, ll. 141–217). The purpose of the parliament is to discuss the exchange of prisoners (1. 146), the Greek delegation's request for Criseyde and Toas in exchange for Antenor. The assumptions here are extremely revealing. Because Criseyde is a woman and a daughter without a husband (whose authority would replace the father's), she has no different status from that of a prisoner. We now see from yet another perspective how Hector's promise to protect the fair woman, the "aungelik" creature of courtly convention, contradicted many major elements in existing social organization. Hector does have the integrity to remember his promise and speak out at the parliament:

> "Syres, she nys no prisonere," he seyde;
> . . . .
> "We usen here no wommen for to selle."
> (*T & C*, IV, ll. 179–82)

This gets to the nub of the matter. Criseyde is not officially a prisoner, and once this is acknowledged then it becomes clear that the proposal under consideration is simply to sell her, to handle her as a commodity in a social market organized by and for male possessing groups. Parliament's decision to sell her is realistic enough and also acts as a symbol for the position of women in relation to men (fathers, husbands, rulers) in Chaucer's world as much as the fictional one of his poem. The Trojan Antenor is "Daun Antenor . . . so wys and ek so bold baroun . . . ek oon the grettest of this town," whereas Criseyde is reduced to having no identity other than, "This womman" (ll. 188–92). The fact that after the immediate threats to her survival (following Calkas' treachery) had been weathered Criseyde became "both of younge and olde / Ful wel biloved" (I, 1. 130–1), that she "nevere dide hem scathe" (IV, 1. 207), that Hector is correct in asserting she is not officially a prisoner, and that she desperately wishes to remain, all this is irrelevant before her social status as "womman." Parliament naming and classifying her like this signifies the exact power structure being invoked as once more the realities beneath and within the various courtly forms of love and respect for women are made plain at a key juncture in the poem. Hector is soon silent.

As the transaction takes place we are thus shown quite clearly that the ensuing disintegration of the love between Troilus and Criseyde, and the psychic disintegration they each suffer, is precisely grounded in the social structure and conventional male attitudes to women. Criseyde can be sold because she is a female without a personal male owner in Troy (husband) and belongs to a male ruling group now prepared to cash her suddenly increased value. Chaucer added Hector's intervention to the narrative he found in Boccaccio, and in doing so he drew further attention to the centrality of male attitudes and public practices to the tragic destruction of a great human achievement.[16] But he was also to focus on the complex processes by which the dominant culture is made psychologically active in even those it does not benefit.

The long discussion between the lovers, once they have gone to bed after the parliament's decision, actually exemplifies such processes, despite their great love and commitment to each other.[17] Just as Criseyde took the sexual initiative on their first night together in Book III, so she does now in offering comfort and reassurance that they will be re-united (ll. 1261 ff.). It seems like a brave attempt to make the best of a bad situation without capitulating to it, an initiative taken in the face of and against tremendous pressures. But as we scrutinize this passage more closely we find that her admirable attempt at initiating action turns into the complex submission of a victim to the dominating groups that control her world. Chaucer's own insight and art is especially subtle as he shows how her seemingly confident claims of being an initiating agent are gradually undermined within her own discourse by womanly accommodation and compliance to a specifically *social* fate. A fundamental social conservatism, the product of her whole life, traps her into total accommodation with an alien reality in which she is sacrificed to the self-interest of a male ruling group.

The overt claims of her role as agent are illustrated in sentences like the following:

> Now, that I shal wel bryngen it aboute,
> To come ayeyn, soone after that I go,
> Thereof am I no manere thyng in doute.
> (*T & C,* IV, ll. 1275–7)

This bodes well for Troilus. But having said that the urgency of the occasion means she will have to cram "an heep of weyes" by which she will effect this "in wordes fewe" she expends the next twelve stanzas without specifying one way in which *she* will ensure the desired outcome, let alone a heap (ll. 1279–365). What does happen is significant, for she is not only completely vague: when she does envisage some ways by which she could be with Troilus again the agents in these cases act quite independently of her:

> Men trete of pees; and it supposid is
> That men the queene Eleyne shal restore,
> And Grekis us restoren that is mys.
> (*T & C,* IV, ll. 1346–8)

From being agent in a process she initiates ("I shal wel bryngen it aboute") she has now become syntactically absolutely deleted, invisibly waiting upon events under the control of "men" and rumours about what "men purposen" (l. 1350). This shift characterizes these twelve stanzas. She may then sense that her promising opening has not been maintained and she says, "Have here another wey, if it so be / That al this tyng ne may yow nat suffise" (ll. 1366–7). This involves persuading her father to send her back to Troy to collect, and intercede for, his property (ll. 1368–414). Again the original initiatory role is dissolved as she substitutes accepted male authorities for herself in effecting her deliverance from misery. Her socialization as woman has been so successful that she has internalized the values and norms of her male governors, leaving her unable to imagine any coherent opposition to their utterly selfish and cruel decrees—"My goyng graunted is by parlement / So ferforth that it may nat be withstonde / For al this world" (ll. 1297–9). It is important to notice how in this she is quite unlike the male aristocrat Troilus, for despite his own deep vested interest in the *status quo,* his training and life has encouraged a far more active and independent role in the social world. He proposes that they defy the parliament's ruling and elope. He sees that their only way of surviving as fulfilled and happy lovers is to break out of this society, so inimical to their relationship (ll. 1501–26). Nor is this an irresponsible flight of fancy, for he is a well-proven knight who has also taken thought of their need for material subsistence and survival (ll. 1513–26). It is Criseyde who refuses to pursue this rebellious course (though she later regrets it, V, ll. 736–65), and the terms in which she does so again emphasize the manner in which the repressed and subordinate learn to internalize the values and assumptions of the repressing and dominant groups—to their own detriment and destruction.[18] It is not mere idiosyncratic timidity that guides Criseyde, but official (male) ideology about women and values. She says:

> But that ye speke, awey thus for to go
> And leten alle youre frendes, God forbede,
> For any womman, that ye sholden so!
> (*T & C,* IV, ll. 1555–7)

Here she, a woman, downgrades the full heterosexual love of a man for a woman in relation to inter-male friendship and the cohesion of the male aristocracy, and she downgrades women. Next she places a male-instigated war above their love (ll. 1558–9) and uncritically accepts crude militaristic notions of "honour" (ll. 1561, 1575) rather than the claims of so fully humanizing a love as we saw celebrated in Book III. She moves on to consider what "the peple ek al aboute / Wolde of its seye?" (ll. 1569–70). This is a fine representation of the uncritical nature of her ideology, for these are the very same "peple" we listened to in the parliament, in a scene already discussed (IV, ll. 183 ff.). They showed a total contempt for Criseyde's identity as a mere woman, and no hesitation in selling her for their own (supposed) immediate advantage. Yet their obnoxious but conventional attitudes and behaviour are the norms their victim appeals to in a crisis where her own aristocratic lover advocates flight and rebellion. The power of training, habitual subordination and convention could not be more powerfully demonstrated. So profoundly has she internalized anti-feminist norms, and the downgrading of Eros, that she defends a dominant ideology in which war, male self-interest and the defence of the male ruling group are more important than human love and her own survival and happiness.[19] Chaucer rounds off this brilliant exploration by having her appeal to stoical "reason" and "patience" to confirm her resignation in the face of a social fate against which cogent human action was, as Troilus asserted, possible (IV, ll. 1583–9). There is not space to develop this observation here and it will have to suffice simply to note that this use of stoical and Boethian stances pervades Book IV. That is, the Book shows the narrator, Troilus, and Criseyde using Boethius to rationalize and sanctify resignation in the face of a social order willing to trade human beings and wage long and totally destructive war. As so often in the history of thought and religion we see metaphysics being used to construct defences of contemporary social organization. But the movements of the poetry subvert such strategies, as they disclose human agency, ideology and history at the core of metaphysical projections, however attractive and fascinating these projections were to Chaucer.[20]

By the opening of Book V Troilus and Criseyde have accommodated themselves to the crippling social reality against which Troilus suggested they rebel. Chaucer shows them fully controlled as Criseyde is "muwet, milde, and mansuete" (V, 1. 194) and Troilus completely involved in subduing his feelings and behaving in a supposedly manly fashion in public. To me it seems that criticism of the poem has again paid insufficient attention to Chaucer's continuing evolution of a rich social psychology in which the final disintegration of the mutual love is placed in a social situation imaginatively and aesthetically realized with precision and depth.

Chaucer stresses how Criseyde's weak and subordinate position, her social heritage as a woman (not as a morally weak or oddly timid individual), is made many times worse in the Greek camp (V, ll. 687–765). She is a prisoner of the enemy army, much more isolated than in Troy, even at the beginning of Book I, and completely lacking in that most vital of stays—warm human support. Whereas Troilus at least has Pandarus to talk with and is in his own customary milieu, a powerful figure with friends and public identity, Criseyde is frighteningly alone, "With wommen fewe, among the Grekis stronge. . . . There was no wight to whom she dorste hire pleyne . . . she was allone and hadde nede / Of frendes help."[21] The poet's emphasis is unmistakable, and the word "dorste" is well chosen. When her father-ruler refuses to let her return she is frightened of attempting a clandestine escape. Her soliloquy about these fears is very moving and once more shows Chaucer imagining his way into individual consciousness and history, in a manner quite untypical of medieval characterology represented by Lydgate, Gower or saints' legends. Away from any idealizing literary conventions, Criseyde voices her real and justifiable social and sexual fears, fear of the Greek state, fear of rape.[22] Her movement away from commitment to Troilus must always be discussed in these contexts which Chaucer has created so understandingly. His approach is the absolute antithesis to the abstract inquisitorial moralism favoured by certain groups in many ages and countries.

Her total situation, with all its pressures working on an individual trained by her society to *accommodate* to an antagonistic reality rather than rebel (as Troilus recommended) now expands to include a new aristocratic lover, Diomede (V, ll. 771 ff.). In her painful isolation she is cruelly exposed to Diomede, for whom she is a (doubtlessly goddess-like) fish to be netted (ll. 775–7). So when we come to the now famous phrase describing aspects of her being as "slydynge of corage" (1. 825), we have been given ample grounds for grasping this in the full light Chaucer has cast on the crippling social reality and ideology which constitute her circumstances. He has created a profound vision of a social individual whose bad faith was almost impossible to avoid, encouraged and prepared for by the habits and practices of the very society which would, of course, condemn such a betrayal with righteous moral indignation. (The contradiction Chaucer grasps so clearly has had a long life in western society and ethics.) The poet himself should be quoted as he realizes this theme in Criseyde's shift away from Troilus:

> Retornyng in hire soule ay up and down
> The wordes of this sodeyn Diomede,
> His grete estat, and perel of the town,
> And that she was allone and hadde nede
> Of frendes help; and thus bygan to brede
> The cause whi, the sothe for to telle,
> That she took fully purpos for to dwelle.
> (*T & C,* V. ll. 1023–9)

This explicitly encourages the reader to acknowledge the central role of social organization and individual situation in breeding the fundamental grounds of moral and spiritual failure. It is a statement which draws our attention to the poem's social psychology and rejects the simpler paths of abstract moral accusation and judgment favoured by the Parson in *The Canterbury Tales,* and those many conventional moralists like him. Furthermore, it is worth noticing how syntax is made to enhance our imaginative participation in the movements of Criseyde's consciousness, contributing to our understanding of the nature of what we would tend to describe as human choice basic to moral action. The first line in the passage just quoted begins with the word "Retornyng," a present participle which helps convey the circular processes within the lonely woman's mind, a continuous present that seems to dissolve any possibility of an initiating, controlling act of self-determination. The next three-and-a-half lines mime the fragmented and undirected way imposed circumstances are mediated in her receptive consciousness, beautifully showing us how she experiences events in this stage of her overwhelming isolation and unhappiness. Chaucer then leaves the original present participle ("Retornyng") in a strikingly incomplete from for he does not give it the subject noun or pronoun (Criseyde, or she) we expect. Instead he begins a new sentence, "and thus bygan. . . ." This also enacts the elimination of anything we could readily define as volitional powers at this stage of her life, as Chaucer decides not to let her feature as the direct initiating subject in a sentence involving agent, verb (describing the process), effected participants and results.

In the new sentence he strengthens this impression by presenting her "purpos for to dwelle" in a way which again suggests that mental events now seem to happen *to* her, or *in* her, rather than to be the outcome of her mental activity: "and thus bygan to brede / The cause whi"—by· choosing the infinitive "to brede" the poet once more removes any specific agent from the process in question (*who* is breeding . . .), if anything implying that the fragmented events breed her purpose. We are left to realize that in cases such as this one can hardly say that the person made a decision with certain specifiable motives, for we are shown, in the minutest particulars of the poet's art, how the interactions between her desolate circumstances and her subjugated consciousness breed a daily state in which a great escape, a decisively rebellious act of will, was quite unimaginable.[23]

Chaucer also reveals wonderful comprehension and sympathy in his depiction of Criseyde's real misery at betraying Troilus, during the very processes out of which that betrayal emerges, allied to a simultaneous and pathetic, but authentic wish to move from the extremely unsatisfying life in which she is now immersed to one more structured by freely chosen fidelity:

> Ther made nevere woman moore wo
> Than she, whan that she falsed Troilus.
> . . . .
> But syn I se ther is no bettre way,
> And that to late is now for me to rewe,
> To Diomede algate I wol be trewe.
>   (*T & C,* V, ll. 1052–3,
>   1069–71; see 1051–85)

This desperate fantasy is poignant, for the fine relationship that we have just followed is not the kind that is easily replaced, and the new man, with his "hook and lyne" is using her for his present gratification in a context where the word "trewe" could have little meaning. The sadness here, the power and universal relevance of this psychological realization should never be lost by attempting to collapse Chaucer's art into the conventional norms of medieval characterization and abstract moralism.

Criseyde's final appearance in the poem shows her using her genuine fears and miserable resignation in a letter designed to manipulate the sympathies of the lover she has now betrayed, perhaps even to keep him hanging on to her a little longer (V, ll. 1590–631, especially ll. 1618–20, 1627). In Troilus' response, free of all the earlier egotistical histrionics, Chaucer manifests the quality of love and commitment that this relationship has developed in his own being:

> Thorugh which I se that clene out of youre mynde
> Ye han me cast; and I ne kan nor may
> For al this world, withinne myn herte fynde
> To unloven yow a quarter of a day!
> In corsed tyme I born was, weilaway,
> That yow, that doon me al this wo endure,
> Yet love I best of any creature!
> (*T & C,* V, ll. 1695–701)

Troilus still cannot see the primary role of his own culture and social organization in creating the present tragedy, and so he perceives Criseyde's actions in a very different perspective from the one open to Chaucer's readers. But this only increases the intensity of his admirable commitment to Criseyde. This evokes the real possibilities and achievements of human relationships, even as it makes us grieve over the intolerable pressures to which they may be subjected and their frequent, painful failures. It is Pandarus who represents this society's deepest conventional wisdom in the tragedy it has prepared. Having treated Criseyde as an amiable creature whose sole object in life should be the gratification of his male friend, he now turns on her in blind outrage:[24]

> What sholde I seyen? I hate, ywys, Cryseyde;
> And, God woot, I wol hate hire evermore!
> ⋅
> And fro this world almyghty God I preye
> Delivere hire soon! I kan namore seye.
> (*T & C,* V, ll. 1732–3, 1742–3)

Chaucer's own work should have delivered us not only from any such reaction, quite lacking in reflexive imagination and psychological insight, but also from all abstract moralization which comfortably ignores social realities and cultural controls. In doing so, one of its central achievements was the poetic evocation of a social psychology which grasped complex interactions between individual consciousness, action, conflicting ideologies and social organization.

At the end of the poem Criseyde is left in the Greek camp, Chaucer's study of this stage of her development left as he sets about closing his work. The relationship between the supreme achievements we have been following and the lines following the death of Troilus is primarily one of contrast in poetic modes and styles of thought, as Elizabeth Salter and others have maintained. The very last function they can serve is to provide an authoritative and relevant lesson in how to read *Troilus and Criseyde* and extract its meaning.[25] For these lines (ll. 1807–55) are marked by a simple and unreflexive assertiveness which is the antithesis of the modes created in the treatment of Criseyde and the antithesis of the complex moral thought integral to these modes. This trait is exemplified in the conventional observations the "goost" of Troilus allegedly makes (ll. 1807–25). From the eighth sphere he begins to "despise" our world as "al vanite" compared with heavenly felicity and "dampned al oure werk that foloweth so / The blynde lust, the which that may nat laste." The language is so generalized that within its terms one could not discriminate between Troilus and Diomede, between Criseyde and, say, Damyan in the *Merchant's Tale*—"al" would be despicable "vanite," all damned as "blynde" such static generalizations are substituted for the subtle realizations of human processes we have followed through the work. There is no attempt to create any poetic specificity for the abstraction "felicite" leaving it instead as a generalization which could be filled with Boethian, epicurean or other contents. Even the instruction to set "al oure herte on heven" fails to become more than a conventionally pietistic gesture, since it does not begin to notice the problematic nature of this recommendation for the incarnate beings inevitably engaged in social practices which make the question asked in *The Canterbury Tales* a serious religious one: "How shal the world be served?" (*General Prologue*, 1. 187). No more than *Piers Plowman* does Chaucer's work encourage glib answers.

Similar comments are called for by the language and moral postures of the incantatory stanzas about the rather vague end of Troilus, pagan religions, "thise wrecched worldles appetites" and the homiletic address to the youth of today, instructing them to return from "worldly vanite" to love of Christ (ll. 1828–55).[26] Even some of the same phrases used by the "goost" of Troilus reappear and when the speaker typically insists that we should think "al nys but a faire / This world, that passeth soone as floures faire," he fails to notice some very relevant aspects of the image. If life is a medieval "faire" then we are the producers, the buyers and sellers in a community without which there would be neither individuality nor human spirituality, for we are not ghosts but incarnate beings whose choices and actions are necessarily and as profoundly affected by the "faire" as were Criseyde's.[27] Speakers who exclude this awareness from their own discourse exclude a reflexivity which proved essential to Chaucer's imagination. It is natural for a Christian to invoke Christ as the supreme model of faithful love:

> For he nyl falsen no wight, dar I seye,
> That wol his herte al holly on hym leye.
> And syn his best to love is, and most meke,
> What nedeth feynede loves for to seke?
> (*T & C*, V, ll. 1845–8).

Far from suggesting that we humans need and should engage with feigned and imperfect earthly versions of divine love, as some have supposed, it puts

forward the incoherent idea that people who want stable, mutual and committed relationships deliberately seek "feynede loves," asking why they do so.
Yet the poem has just created an example of human and thoroughly sexual
love that is not "feyned" but so great and powerful that even when Criesyde
proves unable to withstand the pressures she is subjected to, after the Trojan
parliament trades her to the Greeks, Troilus' love for her never changes,
becoming a memorable image of commitment and fidelity attainable in heterosexual (and non-Christian relationships). The invocation just quoted is also
inadequate in religious terms. The question about why people seek "feynede
loves" when a true and faithful love that is totally satisfying awaits them,
could stimulate real and troubling religious questions—ones concerning the
corruption of the will, the individual's ability to commit himself "al holly" to
God, predestination, grace.[28] Of course, *Troilus and Criseyde* is not *Piers Plowman,* and this was not the place to pursue such questions, but my point is that
the mode fails to present them as problematic questions, proving as superfi-
cial in its religious orientation as in its psychological, moral and literary directions. It is Chaucer's own poetic processes which teach us to see the inadequacies in style of thought and language in the closing lines, however well they
may fit conventional didactic and moralistic formulations. It is not a language
for serious moral, religious or psychological inquiry, not the mode in which
Chaucer undertook his creative exploration of Criseyde.

In my own view there are two plausible accounts of why Chaucer composed the closing lines in the manner I have outlined. The first has been
splendidly explained by Monica McAlpine:[29] the statements of the "goost"
of Troilus are partial and limited, a further example of his personal development and vision. To emphasize the lack of definitive authority here the poet
refuses to speculate about God's judgment of Troilus and does not give him
any clear location in the after-life to which he refers (1. 1827). The other
stanzas are also treated as the utterance of a speaker other than the poet—
the narrator. Chaucer uses this figure to exhibit the conventional wishes for
clear-cut closures and simple and fixed judgments on the poem's characters
and the issues they raise. He himself undermined these aspirations (while
acknowledging their importance in his culture), and carefully established the
limitations and the inevitable partiality of human knowledge and fictions.
He wished to suggest that all attempts at total and impersonal judgment
will, like the narrator's in the face of *Troilus and Criseyde,* prove hopelessly
inadequate to the complex processes being judged. As the final stanza of the
poem reminds us, there is a divine perspective on human life which is inaccessible to us and demands that our own approach be self-reflexive and
open-ended.

The second plausible account has been fruitfully discussed by Elizabeth
Salter and Alfred David:[30] Chaucer, the Christian poet, was deeply disturbed
by the implications of his own work and felt the need to retreat into a more

affirmative position with regard to conventional forms of moral judgment and didactic discourses concerning human and sexual love, even though his own poetic processes quite superseded such forms. In this account the closing lines represent understandable and powerfully felt divisions within the writer's own imagination and intellect.

The first account comes close to the comments on Chaucer's reflexive and critical treatment of the *Parson's Tale,* in the last chapter, the second to those made on the pressures and fears which divided Chaucer from his own creative achievements in his "retractions." I believe that both accounts of the conclusion to *Troilus and Criseyde* can be convincingly maintained through analysis of the text and attention to the writer's cultural and ideological situation. If a reader decides between them this will probably be based on his overall version of narrative voices in the poem and his views about the development of Chaucer's vision at the time he completed *Troilus and Criseyde.* What I wish to stress here is that his poetic exploration of the complex and fluid interactions between individual and circumstances, his grasp of the real contexts and processes of human choice, makes it impossible for an attentive reader to go on repeating conventional formulae about unambiguous vices and virtues propagated in the mass of contemporary homiletic work. This was inevitably disturbing to traditional and seemingly uncomplicated certainties as it works to subvert all absolutes and static finalities. Leszek Kolakowski's essay on the antagonism between what he calls "the priest and the jester" seems relevant:[31]

> The priest is the guardian of the absolute; he sustains the cult of the final and the obvious as acknowledged by and contained in tradition. The jester is he who moves in good society without belonging to it, and treats it with impertinence; he who doubts all that appears self-evident . . . to unveil the nonobvious behind the obvious, the nonfinal behind the final.

Chaucer (unlike many of his exegetes) was, in the sense Kolakowski expounds, a jester rather than a priest or inquisitor. Nevertheless, as Kolakowski adds, "there are more priests than jesters at a king's court, just as there are more police-men than artists in his realm," and the poet must have realized the unsettling implications of his own profoundly social psychology and imaginative ethical thought, the disturbing implications of being a jester in a culture where priests and intellectual policemen played a major role. But as for Criseyde, woman in society and woman in love, Chaucer was neither of her party without knowing it, nor one of the conventional moralists' party against her. Instead this jester at a king's court developed a complex, profoundly dialectical grasp of the interactions between individual and society which is subversive of all priestly absolutes, and which is as meaningful today as it was in his own culture.

216 ◆ DAVID AERS

Notes

[Ed. note: This essay is a chapter in Aers's book *Chaucer, Langland, and the Creative Imagination*, and occasionally refers in passing to arguments made in other chapters. Those interested in following Aers's thinking on *Troilus and Criseyde* will also want to read "Masculine Identity in the Courtly Community: The Self Loving in *Troilus and Criseyde*," chap. 3 in *Community, Gender, and Individual Identity: English Writing 1360–1430* (London: Routledge, 1988).]

1. An earlier version of this chapter was written and submitted to *Ch Rev* in summer 1977, published vol. 13, winter, 1979. It is deeply indebted to the generous help of Yvonne McGregor, and I am also very grateful to the commentaries on the earlier version of this chapter offered by Elizabeth Salter and Derek Pearsall. I have also been influenced by an essay I greatly admire, Elizabeth Salter's "*Troilus and Criseyde*: a reconsideration," in *Patterns of Love and Courtesy,* ed. J. Lawlor, Arnold, London, 1966, pp. 86–106.

2. R. O. Payne, *The Key of Remembrance,* Yale University Press, 1963, pp. 81, 181–3, 221, 222, 226, 223. He particularly praises A. Mizener, "Character and action in the case of Criseyde," *PMLA,* 54 1939, pp. 65–79; similarly R. M. Jordan, *Chaucer and the Shape of Creation,* Harvard University Press, 1967, pp. 99–100; for D. W. Robertson see *Preface to Chaucer,* Princeton University Press, 1963 and "Chaucerian tragedy," *ELH,* 19, 1952, pp. 1–37. For like-minded comments to the ones offered here, M. E. McAlpine, *The Genre of Troilus and Criseyde,* Cornell University Press, 1978, pp. 193 n. 11, 208–13, 230–3. (This interesting book was published after my own essay had been submitted to *Ch Rev* but I have now added reference to her arguments where relevant, especially to chapter 6, "The Boethian tragedy of Criseyde.")

3. See K. Young, "Chaucer's *Troilus and Criseyde* as romance," *PMLA,* 53, 1938, pp. 38–63.

4. He shifted Boccaccio's setting to a courtly one, and concentrated on developing the subtle ambivalences of feeling which emerge as Criseyde encounters and absorbs social and ideological pressures in determinate circumstances whose relevance Chaucer articulates in a way quite unknown to Boccaccio. Italian text in *Opere minori in volgare,* Rizzoli, Milan, 1970, English translation R. K. Gordon, *The Story of Troilus,* Dutton, New York, 1964, pp. 25–127. On the different treatment of desire and sensuality in the two poets, and on the role of circumstance in Chaucer's treatment of Criseyde, see two essays by R. P. ap Roberts, "Love in the *Filostrato*," *Ch Rev,* 7, 1972, pp. 1–26, and "Criseyde's infidelity," *Speculum,* 44, 1969, pp. 383–402. On political dimensions, J. P. McCall, "The Trojan scene in Chaucer's *Troilus*," *ELH,* 29, 1962, pp. 263–75.

5. I take up the issues of medieval marriage, religious dimensions and utopian elements in Chaucer's own imagination in chapter 6. For conventional romances referred to here, E. Power, *Medieval Women,* Cambridge University Press, 1975, pp. 16–28; A. David, *The Strumpet Muse: Art and Morals in Chaucer's Poetry,* Indiana University Press, 1976, pp. 17, 55–6; P. Gradon, *Form and Style in Early English Literature,* Methuen, London, 1971, p. 220; M. A. Gist, *Love and War in the Medieval Romances,* University of Pennsylvania Press, Philadelphia, 1947. For the positive role of dream and reverie in opposition to social norms, see the outstanding essay by J. Frappier, "Sur un procès fait à l'amour courtois." *Romania,* 93, 1972, pp. 145–93.

6. See Monica McAlpine's excellent comments on the way Criseyde "suffers under all the disabilities of being a woman, the king's subject, Calkas' daughter, and her husband's widow," *Genre of Troilus and Criseyde,* pp. 191–2, 199–200.

7. Yvonne McGregor points out to me that in choosing not to channel her request through her uncle (transformed by Chaucer into an older man), apparently the only male relative left to her in Troy, Criseyde could be showing a measure of strong-willed independence.

Her later comments on marriage (II, ll. 750–6) confirm the plausibility of this suggestion; but it is also true that she will get a better deal by prostrating her own body before that of the most powerful male in Troy.

8.   Contrast *Filostrato,* II, st. 68–72 with Chaucer's expansion, *T & C,* II, ll. 596–749.

9.   See Power, *Medieval Women,* p. 38; F. R. H. Du Boulay, *Age of Ambition,* Nelson, London, 1970, p. 95; and Christine de Pisan's views as recounted by C. C. Willard, "A fifteenth century view of women's role in medieval society: Christine de Pisan's *Livre des trois vertus,*" pp. 90–120 in *The Role of Women in the Middle Ages,* ed. R. T. Morewedge, Hodder & Stoughton, London, 1975, here pp. 105–6 on the privileges *and* added vulnerability of widows. H. A. Kelly's thesis on the clandestine marriage of Troilus and Criseyde is strangely forgetful of these issues and the force of II, ll. 750 ff., an oversight which gravely distorts his approach to the poem—*Love and Marriage in the Age of Chaucer,* Cornell University Press, 1975, pp. 217–42.

10.   See too the resistance to making "hirselven bonde / In love" (II, ll. 1197–225) and in III, ll. 169–72 she still reminds him of this in a brilliantly equivocal passage. On the "risks of intimacy," see also McAlpine, *Genre of Troilus and Criseyde,* pp. 199–200.

11.   For example, P. Elbow, *Oppositions in Chaucer,* Wesleyan State University Press, pp. 55–8.

12.   See *Filostrato,* III, st. ll. 21 ff.; for the need of Pandarus in Chaucer's poem, eg. III, ll. 274–7, 785–98, 855–980 *passim* and his reappearance at Criseyde's bed, ll. 1555–82.

13.   See III, ll. 939–45 and the use of broken syntax to enact the confused movements of Criseyde's consciousness at III, ll. 918 ff.

14.   See III, ll. 1116–34: Boccassio's Criseida is little else but 'sexual initiative' in *Filostrato,* III, and Chaucer's subtle explorations of movements of consciousness and sexual desire are quite foreign to the Italian text.

15.   IV, ll. 1471–5: here again Chaucer mediates medieval patriarchal realities (see chapter 6 n. 1 and discussion at opening of that chapter: I am grateful for conversations about the role of Calkas with Yvonne McGregor). For an interesting example of Chaucer's critical stance towards patriarchal powers see the *Physician's Tale,* where a "fadres pity" is exposed in all its cruel and self-righteous egotism (although the physician himself cannot see this)—see especially ll. 218–26.

16.   On these issues see too McCall, *The Trojan Scene,* and McAlpine, *Genre of Troilus and Criseyde,* pp. 198–9, 201.

17.   IV, ll. 1242 ff.; the poet makes Criseyde's commitment clear: IV, ll. 699–700, 708–14, 731–945, 1128–69. It is noticeable that whereas Troilus thinks only of himself and consoles himself with metaphysics, Criseyde actually thinks about her own grief *and* about how her lover will fare—IV, ll. 794–5, 890–903, 942. Here I think Monica McAlpine (*Genre of Troilus and Criseyde,* p. 166) wrong to deny Troilus' "self-absorption" at this stage.

18.   Here I disagree with Monica McAlpine's reading of this episode: she constantly insists that what is at issue is a "rape" of Criseyde analogous to the rape of Helen, and she simply admires Criseyde *and* Troilus for not carrying it out (*Genre of Troilus and Criseyde,* pp. 160–2, 188–90). But what is discussed in the interview is voluntary and mutual secession from a society bent on destroying the greatest human achievement we are shown, and itself to boot! The major aspects I am discussing are quite ignored by J. Bayley's bizarre diagnosis that Criseyde's "trouble" is her "absence of passion" (*The Characters of Love,* (1960), Chatto & Windus, London, 1968, p. 107). The dialectic Chaucer develops here is a universal one in our civilization, though medievalists have been largely closed to it: cf. D. Aers, "Blake and the dialectics of sex," *ELH,* 44, 1977, pp. 500–14.

19.   These considerations are, once more, quite alien to his source, here being followed fairly closely by Chaucer (*Filostrato,* IV). It is characteristic that Boccaccio should climax the arguments of his Criseida by having her claim that things are not so bad really since their love can give pleasure only because they have to act furtively and see each other rarely, whereas if they were together often their love and desire would soon vanish (IV., st. 153). Nothing could

be further removed from Chaucer's Criseyde or his overall approach and he does not translate this passage.

20.   On this both Elizabeth Salter ("Troilus and Criseyde") and David, *Strumpet Muse,* chapter 2, have pertinent comments.

21.   See V, ll. 688, 728, 1026–7. Monica McAlpine's *Genre of Troilus and Criseyde* provides similar emphasis in some excellent comments on pp. 200–4.

22.   Here see V, ll. 701–6, 712–14, On the real threat of rape to medieval women and awareness of this in literature, see Gist, *Love and War,* pp. 75 ff., and the emphasis on real "insecurity" even in peace and supposed "hospitality" (pp. 82–3); in war, the situation was even worse, for women were part of the spoils of war (pp. 83 ff.); similarly McAlpine, *Genre of Troilus and Criseyde,* p. 204.

23.   I am grateful for Derek Pearsall's suggestion that I expand the commentary offered in my earlier version of this chapter to take the syntax into closer account.

24.   One could also recall the first advice offered Troilus, that if Criseyde had to leave Troy he should simply take another woman, since "newe love out chaceth ofte the olde," and all "is but casuel plesaunce" anyway. This is a good example of exploitative norms in much traditional male sexuality, combined with characteristic double standards of morality, although the narrator (Chaucer?) steps in to say that "douteles" Pandarus did not really mean it, only saying it to "help his freend" (V, ll. 400–31). Still, he *did* say it, at length too, and in what sense could something one believed was false and evil be said to "help"?

25.   Salter, *Troilus and Criseyde,* pp. 103–6, and for reference to some of the many studies on the 'Epilogue' see McAlpine, *Genre of Troilus and Criseyde,* pp. 177 n. 17, and 237 n. 19.

26.   See Salter, *Troilus and Criseyde,* p. 106.

27.   This theme has been discussed in relation to both the poetry of Langland and Chaucer in the previous four chapters.

28.   See reference to P. Brown's explication of Augustine's psychological analysis of these issues, chapter 2, n. 31.

29.   McAlpine, *Genre of Troilus and Criseyde,* pp. 177–81, 235–46.

30.   See Salter, *Troilus and Criseyde,* pp. 103–6.

31.   L. Kolakowski, *Marxism and Beyond,* Pall Mall Press, London, 1969, especially "The Priest and the Jester," pp. 29–57.

Complicity and Responsibility in Pandarus' Bed and Chaucer's Art

Evan Carton

Jankyn, parish clerk and fifth husband to the Wife of Bath, proudly possessed an anthology of classical and religious writings that traced the wickedness of wives throughout history. Night and day he would rehearse the stories in this book, ostensibly to edify Alisoun but mainly to establish external authority for his restriction of her freedom. Jankyn's use of his text exemplifies the attitude that, in C. S. Lewis' view, was fundamental to the development of the medieval world picture. At the outset of *The Discarded Image,* Lewis emphasizes "the overwhelmingly bookish or clerkly character of medieval culture." He continues:

> When we speak of the Middle Ages as the ages [sic] of authority we are usually thinking about the authority of the Church. But they were the age not only of her authority, but of authorities. If their culture is regarded as a response to environment, then the elements in that environment to which it responded most vigorously were manuscripts. Every writer, if he possibly can, bases himself on an earlier writer, follows an *auctour:* preferably a Latin one.[1]

In a single sentence several pages later Lewis sums up the most important implication of this faith in the authority of the written word: "They [poets, as well as common men] would have felt that the responsibility for their cosmological, or for their historical or religious, beliefs rested on others" (p. 17).

A tradition of reverence for, and reliance upon, the ancient wisdom contained in books, combined with their rarity and costliness, rendered almost any book authoritative to the point of inviolability. So, when the Wife of Bath finally can stand no more of her husband's recitations of the wisdom of his "auctours," her retaliation strikes at some deep-seated cultural values:

> And whan I saugh he wolde nevere fyne
> To reden on this cursed book al nyght,
> Al sodeynly thre leves have I plyght

Reprinted by permission of the Modern Language Association of America from *PMLA* 94 (1979): 47–61. © 1979 the Modern Language Association of America.

> Out of his book, right as he radde, and eke
> I with my fest so took hym on the cheke
> That in oure fyr he fil backward adoun.
> (III. 788–93)[2]

By ripping out the three pages, Alisoun symbolically denies the book's authority (even if she confirms its estimation of a woman's temperament) and rejects the role of acquiescent auditor. The concomitant assault on Jankyn disallows any claim he might make to the passivity or innocence of his position as a reader and judges him responsible for the words he speaks. Finally, she forces him to respond directly to her, rather than to a type of wicked womanhood. His direct response is a blow to his wife's head that permanently deafens her in one ear. But, in the remorseful aftermath, he burns his book, grants her authority over her life, and ceases to restrict her experience of the world.

The Wife's famous claim for the significance of worldly experience is implicit in the conceptual frame of the *Canterbury Tales;* the pilgrimage to Canterbury is, allegorically, the voyage of life. Near the end of the General Prologue, the narrator promises shortly to "telle of our viage / And al the remenaunt of oure pilgrimage" (I. 723–24). But we hear nothing about the pilgrimage except the stories that are told and the responses that they elicit. This intercourse, this community of speaking and hearing, *is* the pilgrimage, is experience in the world.[3] Chaucer's claim for experience, and for its rootedness in the common activity of exchanging stories, challenges both the authority of authorities and the responsibility-exempt status of those who obey them; it also attributes more importance to human communication in general, and to Chaucer's own literary creation in particular, than was customarily allowed.

The pilgrimage frame enables Chaucer to demonstrate his claim without having to state it outright and to present his self-authorized work while deferring, until the end, the issue of his personal responsibility for it. By having his characters tell the stories, Chaucer constructs the pretense, and plays on the convention, of external authority for his words; then, adopting the role of diligent hearer-recorder, he insists on the words:

> For this ye knowen al so wel as I,
> Whoso shal telle a tale after a man,
> He moot reherce as ny as evere he kan
> Everich a word, if it be in his charge,
> Al speke he never so rudeliche and large,
> Or ellis he moot telle his tale untrewe,
> Or feyne thyng, or fynde wordes newe.
> (I.730–36)

Through such role playing, Chaucer disguises—and facilitates by disguising—his underlying commitment to his creative freedom. The precedents he marshals in support of literal recital wryly convey this commitment and suggest its weight:

> Crist spak hymself ful brode in hooly writ,
> And wel ye woot no vileynye is it.
> Eek Plato seith, whoso that kan hym rede,
> The wordes moote be cosyn to the dede.
>
> (I.739–42)

Christ's "auctour" was the Father, with whom he was one; Chaucer's ostensible "auctours" include an anachronistic knight, an epicurean monk, and a drunken miller. Here, this contextual distinction is collapsed, as is the Platonic kinship between word and deed. In the *Canterbury Tales* the word is the deed, and, as we shall see, the same is true, with a vengeance, of the *Troilus*.

No deed performed by language, however, is finished when the word is spoken. That the speaker must accept responsibility for what he says is dramatized by the ineffectual posturings and disclaimers of the Miller and the Pardoner and darkly reaffirmed by the Manciple's Tale. But the hearer completes the act of communication and shares its burden. The Reeve's self-accusing "Stynt thy clappe!" (I.3144) helps shape the Miller's Tale and provides an ulterior meaning; the Host's violent response at the end of the Pardoner's Tale implicates himself and the other laughing pilgrims in the Pardoner's cynical judgments. Like the Pardoner, Chaucer does not allow his audience to remain coolly unimplicated. The reader of the *Canterbury Tales* must choose how—or even, Chaucer suggests, whether—to read each tale and then must live with his decision:

> And therfore, whoso list it nat yheere,
> Turne over the leef and chese another tale;
> For he shal fynde ynowe, grete and smale,
> Of storial thyng that toucheth gentillesse,
> And eek moralitee and hoolynesse.
> Blameth nat me if that ye chese amys.
>
> (I.3176–81)

We will find gentility, morality, and holiness, although Chaucer does not pair these attributes with specific tales. We are free to create our own reading experience, but not entirely free. The last line of the Miller's Prologue, spoken by Chaucer, is admonitory: "And eek men shal nat maken ernest of game." In his poems and in his interaction with his audience, Chaucer is deeply concerned with the relationship of teller to listener, with the conditions and consequences of what William Faulkner called "some happy marriage of speaking and hearing." For him, as for Faulkner, the relationship is frequently tempestuous, but it is always a marriage.

I

The narrator of *Troilus and Criseyde* assumes the role of a reader. He is also a mediator; he makes available to us, his English-reading audience, the text of his fictional Latin chronicler, Lollius. He further characterizes himself as "the sorwful instrument, / That helpeth loveres" (I.10–11) and parodies the pope's title when he begins the third stanza, "For I that God of Loves servauntz serve" (I.15). Finally, he is a Christian. Morton W. Bloomfield, in his influential essay "Distance and Predestination in *Troilus and Criseyde*," contends that the narrator's position amounts to that of an interested and sympathetic but consistently aloof historian, an expositor who can no more violate his data than God can violate his own divine rationality.[4] This view finds its major support in the narrator's frequent disclaimers of responsibility for the events he narrates. "Bound by his self-imposed task of historian, he both implies and says directly that he cannot do other than report his tale," writes Bloomfield (II, 197). The narrator's aloofness, combined with the Christian message of the notorious palinode in which Troilus laughs from the heights of the eighth sphere and we are told that Christ is the only lover who will betray no one, leads Bloomfield to conclude:

> It seems to me that, if we regard the framework of the poem—the role that Chaucer sets himself as a commentator—as a meaningful part of the poem and if we consider the various references to fate and destiny in the text, we can only come to the conclusion that the Chaucerian sense of distance is the artistic correlative to the concept of predestination. *Troilus and Criseyde* is a medieval tragedy of predestination because the reader is continually forced by the commentator to look upon the story from the point of view of its end and from a distance. The crux of the problem of predestination is knowledge. So long as the future is not known to the participants in action, they can act as if they were free. But once a position of distance from the action is taken, then all can be seen as inevitable. And it is just this position which Chaucer the commentator takes and forces upon us from the very beginning. (II, 204)

Bloomfield's account of narration, reading, and significance in the *Troilus* is not only inadequate to the complexity of the reader's and the narrator's experience but, as I hope to demonstrate, absolutely incorrect. True distance never is achieved by the narrator or by the reader, although both know the outcome of the love affair from the poem's first line: "The double sorwe of Troilus to tellen" (I.1). It is, in fact, precisely the illusion of the possibility of such distance that the *Troilus* constantly explodes—for the narrator, for Pandarus, for Criseyde, and for us. To write, read, or act in *Troilus and Criseyde* is to be a partner in the polygamy of speaking and hearing that at once makes up the poem and constitutes its main subject. Each partner performs both as speaker and as hearer, as author and as reader. Each, except perhaps Troilus, seeks to construe or manipulate language and linguistic relationships to attain maximum control over events and over others, with minimum responsibility for the consequence; and each discovers that personal control is always incomplete and that responsibility is always shared. This is what it means to be a partner, a reader, a lover, a member of a community.

The narrator's disclaimers of control and responsibility, like Pandarus' equivalent self-extrications, are the increasingly desperate evasions of a character who recognizes his deep complicity in a series of events that features seduction and culminates in betrayal.[5] I am suggesting not only that the narrator implicates himself in his plot but that self-implication is unavoidable; he can no more tell the story "from the point of view of its end and from a distance" than Criseyde can live it, or we can read it, that way. It would make no sense to say that we and the narrator are predestined to be caught up in the desires and recriminations that frame the union of Troilus and Criseyde. Bloomfield rightly insists that predestination, as a force in the poem, depends on the alignment of reader and narrator with God. If such an alignment, despite our foreknowledge, does not occur—if instead, as I believe, narrator and reader participate in the plot as fully and in the same way as do the other characters—it signifies that, even when we know or suspect the future, we cannot but act as if we were free, because from a human standpoint—the only one available to us and the only one from which Chaucer presumed to write—we are. Our freedom consists in the ability to shape, interpret, and respond to the world; it is, in short, the freedom of involvement, which fails to comprehend only transcendent, unimplicated noninvolvement. Chaucer did not misconstrue his Boethius. He recognized that God's detached and all-encompassing view of the world depends not on his knowing more than we do but on his knowing differently. God, we might say, does not have to read; indeed, he cannot read. And, "to look upon [*Troilus and Criseyde*] from the point of view of its end and from a distance," to try to imitate God's view, is precisely not to read it—not, at least, in the active and responsible sense of reading that I think the poem demands and that its characters are constantly modeling.

II

A man who makes texts available to readers (or listeners) and readers to texts, a "sorwful instrument, / That helpeth loveres," a priest of love, a dealer in words—these descriptions apply to both the narrator and the pander of

Troilus and Criseyde. In order to appreciate the reader of Lollius, with his jittery concern that we shall mistake his intentions and his pledge to treat lovers "As though I were hire owne brother dere" (I.51), we must understand the role of his closest counterpart—the man who insists that he, too, is but a sympathetic reader and reporter of others' desires, the man whose own pure intentions the narrator staunchly defends through scene after compromising scene, the man who often addresses Troilus as his "brother dere" and declares himself ready to procure for him either of their sisters. Pandarus is undeniably central to the plot of *Troilus and Criseyde,* but many critics have denied, or failed to recognize, that he is also central to its meaning, that his activity is, in fact, paradigmatic for all participants in the narrative.

Pandarus enters Troilus' chamber unexpectedly, hears his friend groaning, and asks the cause of his sorrow. Troilus at first refuses to tell him, but, when Pandarus accuses him of cruel distrust, Troilus relents and, like any amorous neophyte, makes his plaint in charmingly wooden verse:

> "Love, ayeins the which whoso defendeth
> Hymselven most, hym alderlest avaylleth,
> With disespeyr so sorwfulli me offendeth,
> That streight unto the deth myn herte sailleth."
> (I.603–06)

Pandarus responds that Troilus has been a fool; perhaps, he suggests, "thou myghte after swich oon longe / That myn avys anoon may helpen us" (I.619–20). Before he even knows the identity of Troilus' lady, Pandarus has translated private and passive love-longing into a communal venture. This participatory impulse is reflected in the plural first-person pronoun that he habitually employs when he has no immediate stake in dissociating himself from one or both of the lovers.

Troilus' doubt that he can be helped by a man whose failure in love is well known elicits Pandarus' first metaphor involving a sharp implement or weapon; metaphors of cutting and piercing thereafter recur in his speech and in the narrator's. The statement "A wheston is no kerving instrument, / But yet it maketh sharppe kervyng tolis" (I.631–32) indicates, if we grant its sexual suggestiveness, that Pandarus has interpreted the aim of love-longing for Troilus, or for anyone, and has graphically imagined his own role in its achievement. Neither Troilus' aim nor Pandarus' role, however, has yet been constituted. Despite Pandarus' arguments that to share one's sorrow is to halve it and that consultation is the first step toward resolution, despite his pledge to support his friend's suit, even if its object be Troilus' sister-in-law Helen, and despite his rather odd and unsolicited assurance that Troilus need not fear him to be a deceiver, Troilus refuses to name his lady. Shocked rejection greets Pandarus' first offer to serve as go-between, and several subsequent temptations fail before Pandarus hits upon an argument commensurate with Troilus' courtliness, or naïveté: Love is its own reward, and, should a knight serve a lady for twenty years without receiving so much as a kiss for his trouble, the very opportunity for devotion is to be considered a thousand times the requital he deserves.

Troilus breaks down and asks his friend to tell him what to do, but Pandarus never provides overt direction that does not appear to be authorized by one of the lovers. In every instance, he manipulates until he is in a controlling position, but he will not exercise control until he has received at least tacit agreement that he speaks the desires of the lovers and acts out their intentions. Here, he answers, "If the like, / The beste is that thow telle me al thi wo" (I.829–30). Troilus must follow his own inclination, but, if allowed, Pandarus will furnish speedy relief. "Were it for my suster, al thy sorwe, / By my wil she sholde al be thyn to-morwe," Pandarus vows (I.860–61).

Pandarus hears the confession with glee, discourses on Criseyde's beauty, virtue, and availability, and plays the priest when he makes Troilus beg forgiveness from the god of love for his years of heresy. When Troilus persists in dreading Criseyde's anger or the possibility that she will refuse to hear of his love from her uncle, Pandarus loses his patience. "Whi, Lord, I hate of the thi nyce fare!" (I.1025). Troilus finally agrees to let Pandarus represent him, but with one qualification: Pandarus must not imagine that he desires anything that will involve harm or villainy; he would rather die than have Criseyde think that. In response to this plea, Pandarus laughs and utters a puzzling exclamation: "And I thi borugh?" (I.1038).[6] Troilus no doubt reads this as a rhetorical question: "Aren't I, Criseyde's uncle, your guarantee against impropriety?" It is more consistent with Pandarus' emerging attitude toward love, and with his prefatory laugh, to read it as a piece of ironic self-recognition: "And I, Pandarus, the guarantor of your love's chastity!" Pandarus, on several subsequent occasions, accuses himself of being a pimp to give himself an opportunity to refute the accusation. This is complex and insistent self-awareness; it may be deferred or disguised but never eradicated. As Book I concludes, Pandarus plots his strategy. His meditations are represented by lines that liken him to a builder, lines that Chaucer borrowed from Geoffrey of Vinsauf's *Poetria Nova,* in which they describe the writing of a poem.

Awakening on the fourth of May to the strains of the swallow Procne lamenting her husband's incestuous rape of her sister, Pandarus sets out toward his niece's palace; the narrator entreats Janus, the double-faced "god of entree" (I.77), to guide the go-between. Criseyde and her maids have been reading about Oedipus in a romance of Thebes. Pandarus suggests that she put away her book and her widow's veil and come dance with him; "Lat us don to May som observaunce," he urges (II.112). Criseyde reacts, in John Speirs' words, with "the exaggerated holiness and pretense of outraged decorum."[7]

"I? God forbede!" quod she, "be ye mad?
Is that a widewes lif, so God yow save?

> By God, ye maken me ryghte soore adrad!
> Ye ben so wylde it semeth as ye rave.
> It sate me wel bet ay in a cave
> To bidde and rede on holy seyntes lyves;
> Lat maydens gon to daunce, and yonge wyves."
>
> (II.113–19)

Criseyde is warning her uncle not to assume too much. In this grandiloquent refusal, however, she engages herself—as an equal partner who will not always allow Pandarus to lead—in the verbal dance that makes up most of Book II.

Undaunted by her rebuke, Pandarus observes that he could tell her a thing to make her play. Tell me, uncle dear, she rejoins. The siege, perhaps, is over? Five times better than that, he replies. Criseyde does not know what he means. "And I youre borugh, ne nevere shal, for me, / This thyng be told to yow," he says (II.134–35). Pandarus, it is interesting to note, guarantees not that the thing will never be told by him but that it will not be told for his sake. Criseyde casts down her eyes; never has she wanted more to know something "sith the tyme that she was born" (II.143), but she assures Pandarus she shall not press him against his will. They lapse into pleasantries and then converse admiringly about Troy's greatest warriors, Hector and Troilus, until Pandarus rises to leave. Criseyde bids him stay; she needs to consult with him. She speaks, we are told in the most general terms, of "hire estat and of hire governaunce" (II.219). When she finishes this unrecorded speech, Pandarus again declares his intention to leave but first offers her another chance to dance with him. "Shall I nat witen what ye meene of this?" (II.226), she responds this time. Pandarus plays on courtly convention: he had better hold his tongue than say a truth against her will. Finally, Criseyde authorizes him to speak familiarly and to say what he likes. "Gladly," he replies, and kisses her.

She again casts down her eyes. He coughs a little before asserting that, since the intended result is the measure of any story, he will be direct. Then he stares at Criseyde until she becomes uncomfortable and asks him whether he has never seen her before. "Yis, yys," quod he, "and bet wole er I go!" (II.278). His intentions are good, Pandarus continues; if she doubts this he will never see her again. "For Goddes love," says Criseyde, "whither it be wel or be amys, / Say on" (II.313–14). Pandarus obliges: Troilus is dying for love of her. If she lets him die, he—Pandarus—will "with this knyf my throte kerve" (II.325).[8] Troilus desires nothing "but youre frendly cheere" (II.332), and this is no trick:

> "For me were levere thow and I and he
> Were hanged, than I sholde ben his baude,
> As heigh as men myghte on us alle ysee!
> I am thyn em; the shame were to me,

> As wel as the, if that I sholde assente,
> Thorugh myn abet that he thyn honour shente."
> (II.352–57)

In case she suspects he is a pimp, he denies it. If he were, though, and if he procured her for Troilus, all three of them would be guilty. He reiterates: she need only give Troilus better welcome than she has done heretofore. This is "plainly oure entente, / God help me so, I nevere other mente!" (II.363–64). The shift from "oure entente" to "I nevere other mente" is telling; Pandarus foresees the result of his labor and is building the case for acquittal into the crime. But, like the Pardoner, he makes little effort to hide his disingenuousness. To do that would be to absolve the listener from responsibility. He proceeds, instead, to suggest that Criseyde take precaution against gossip by cloaking her relationship with Troilus in the mantle of friendship. No one will wonder at Troilus' visits to her palace, Pandarus contends, and he supports this opinion with perhaps the most shocking and cynical analogy in the poem: Who will judge, when they see a man enter a temple, that he goes to eat the idols (II.373–74)?

"I shal felen what he meneth, ywis" (II.387) is Criseyde's cool first thought. He means for her to seize the day, Pandarus says, and Criseyde begins to weep and to accuse her uncle of moral and rhetorical treachery. By God, Pandarus swears, he will not see her for the rest of the week; in fact, he will go off to die. He starts up and leans or stretches toward the door—"and on his wey he raughte" (II.447) seems to suggest a studied deliberateness— until Criseyde catches his garment. The narrator here offers an explanation of Criseyde's motives (we shall shortly consider his own involvement in these negotiations). But, because his attitude toward her is always ambivalent, he complicates more than he clarifies. Criseyde, he tells us, is the most fearful person imaginable; in addition, she recognizes "the sorwful ernest of the knyght, / And in his preier ek saugh noon unryght" (II.452–53). Her recent outburst seemed to indicate that she saw little "ernest" and much "unryght," but the narrator ignores such discrepancies and proceeds to quote her next thought:

> "And if this man sle here hymself, allas!
> In my presence, it wol be no solas.
> What men wolde of hit deme I kan nat seye,
> It nedeth me ful sleighly for to pleie."
> (II.459–62)

Although she has just stopped him from leaving, Criseyde now seems to be concerned that "this man" might kill himself in her presence, an act that others could misinterpret in any number of ways. She agrees to give Troilus her pity, but only to save her uncle's life. Both Pandarus and Troilus may die, however, before she will sacrifice her honor. "Honor" is an ambiguous term in

the poem. After the consummation, Criseyde and Pandarus use it to refer to
their public image; before, Criseyde seems to equate it with her chastity. At
all times, "honor" is a particularly public word, and Criseyde's public stance,
as she outlines it in her letter to Troilus later in Book II, is always that she will
please him as a sister would (II.1224).

Pandarus accepts her terms. Like her, he has only engaged himself in this
business to save an innocent life, and he swears "that myn entente is cleene, /
Take heede therof, for I non yvel mene" (II.580–81). This assertion of clean
intent, like the preceding one, is immediately followed by lines that are
meant to falsify it:

> "And ryght good thrift, I prey to God, have ye,
> That han swich oon ykaught withouten net!
> And, be ye wis as ye be fair to see,
> Wel in the ryng than is the ruby set.
> Ther were nevere two so wel ymet,
> Whan ye ben his al hool, as he is youre:
> Ther myghty God yet graunte us see that houre!"
> (II.582–88)

Thomas W. Ross has noted the iconography of coition in the figure of the
ruby set in the ring, a significance that may be reinforced by the succeeding
line—"Ther were nevere two so wel ymet"—and by the available play on
"hool" in the next.[9] Criseyde also seems to recognize the innuendo and signals
her recognition with a laugh and a playful scolding:

> "Nay, therof spak I nought, ha, ha!" quod she;
> "As helpe me God, ye shenden every deel!"
> "O, mercy, dere nece," anon quod he,
> "What so I spak, I mente naught but wel,
> By Mars, the god that helmed is of steel!
> Now beth naught wroth, my blood, my nece dere."
> "Now wel," quod she, "foryeven be it here!"
> (II.589–95)

Here, brilliantly, Chaucer breaks off the scene. The colloquy may end without
another word because both Pandarus and Criseyde have tacitly acknowledged
their complete understanding of each other and of the game they already
have begun to play. The rules allow both of them to author and to disclaim
authority, to read and even to misread, but not to avoid involvement. They
have committed themselves not to some fixed set of facts but to the shared
process of creating those facts. It is the moment of purest complicity.

In the last several pages, I have been helping to shape the process that
will bring Criseyde to bed. I have established the facts out of what is said,
unsaid, and half-said, I have developed my position, and I have convinced

myself that my "auctour" is at least partly responsible for all this. I have participated exactly as the characters do, as the narrator does, and as all parties to the dynamics of communication must.

III

The narrator's emotional involvement in the story begins to emerge in his opening hymn and pledge of devotion to lovers. His repeated denials of personal experience in love suggest a vicarious interest akin to Pandarus'. He does not try to parlay this inexperience into evidence of his detachment and blamelessness until the proem to Book II (II.12–14), and he does not issue his more urgent disclaimers of responsibility until much later, but his language seems evasive and betrays ambivalence from the outset. His peculiar relationship to his text is most apparent when he speaks of Criseyde. He sometimes transgresses the boundaries of a recorder's role by offering his own opinion, as he does, for example, in commenting that, "As to my doom" (I.100), Criseyde was the fairest creature in Troy. At other times, he seeks to regain his distance or to produce the impression of distance by abruptly asserting his inability to give us a particular detail. A characteristic instance of this increasingly frequent and invariably subversive move occurs in the midst of the description of Troilus' lovesickness:

> But how it was, certeyn, kan I nat seye,
> If that his lady understood nat this,
> Or feynede hire she nyste, oon of the tweye.
> (I.492–94)

We have had no reason to suspect Criseyde of feigning ignorance of Troilus' love, and never would have suspected her; now we must take responsibility for rejecting a notion that, at least momentarily, we have been guilty of entertaining. Throughout the poem, the narrator specifies things that he cannot or will not say and leaves us to decide whether or not they have been said and, if so, by whom. Our decisions, whatever they are, become part of the poem and give us a stake in it and a share of the responsibility.

Apart from the indications I have mentioned—the devotion to lovers, the strategically placed bits of noninformation, the prayer to Janus, the peculiar treatment of Criseyde—the narrator's involvement is not so evident in the early scenes as it becomes later. His intrusions are more direct and more frequent as he is caught up first in the seduction and then in the implications of the betrayal. The problem of his involvement turns, as it does for each man in the poem, on his relation to Criseyde. As a servant of courtly love, the narrator has an interest in representing her as a proper courtly lover. But, if

Criseyde is innocent of bald sexual desire and unaware of Pandarus' thinly disguised intent, the narrator participates in, and publicizes, a violation of her trust and her honor. The apportionment of blame for her betrayal presents the same problem in a slightly different form. If she is a victim of circumstances, who shaped and championed those circumstances? Criseyde's characterization both generates and is generated by this problem; she emerges as a puzzling mixture of lusty complicity and maidenly resistance. E. T. Donaldson, with habitual suavity, pronounces the effect of this mixture to be "curiously endearing."[10] It is, in fact, downright provocative. Narrator and reader not only participate but, like Pandarus, participate eagerly in the seduction of Criseyde and rejoice that the indefiniteness of her complicity allows her to be, in some measure, seduced. Such prurient interest is a secret that the narrator must try to guard; so, when Criseyde sees Troilus riding handsomely by and whispers, "Who yaf me drynke?" (II.651), the narrator jumps to refute the hypothetical and unlikely accusation that her love is too sudden. "I sey naught," he assures us, "that she so sodeynly / Yaf hym hire love" (II.673–74). He proceeds to equivocate with much verbiage, but the question remains: Exactly whom is he defending?

When Pandarus reports the success of his errand, Troilus burns to know the next step. How long, he asks, until Criseyde again receives his representative. Even now, when his affection has been at least provisionally accepted, Troilus never considers initiating anything. His first impulse is always self-containment. He loves hopelessly and hermetically until Pandarus defines love as a passion that seeks palpable fulfillment; Troilus seems to accept this definition, but he never shows a clear sense of what such fulfillment entails. "O mercy, God, what thing is this?" (III.1124), he exclaims when he wakes from his swoon during the assignation scene to find himself undressed and in bed with Criseyde. Only after receiving many kisses and caresses does he begin to understand what is expected of him. The most crucial manifestation of Troilus' self-containment, however, is his speech. Communication in *Troilus and Criseyde* is constitutive. Words do not merely express preestablished facts and feelings or affirm a preauthorized reality; rather, the activity of speaking and hearing constitutes reality and constitutes the identities of the speakers and hearers. It is only Troilus who neither creates nor is created by this activity. His speech is confessional, never strategic; it is self-absorbed, not self-conscious. He is as fundamentally constant in an unstable world as he will be in the eternity of the eighth sphere. For this reason, Troilus does not engage us as the other characters do. He may be an object of our admiration, pity, or scorn, but he remains an object. What complicates our relation to Troilus is the ironic awareness we share with Pandarus and the narrator that, despite our more active involvement, we serve as the instrument to his unmediated fulfillment and only derive our fulfillment from his success. I shall now proceed more quickly toward this fulfillment and its consequences.

The next step, Pandarus suggests, is a letter. He will not write it for Troilus, but he gives detailed instructions. When Troilus balks, Pandarus characteristically makes a point of declining to exert pressure: "and if that thow nylt noon, / Lat be, and sory mote he ben his lyve, / Ayeins thi lust that helpeth the to thryve" (II.1055–57). Troilus writes the letter, and the narrator's indirect account of it—twenty-one lines of parataxis that produce the impression of breathless and empty-headed redundancy—is almost undisguisedly scornful. (Boccaccio quotes Troilus' letter, and it is a model of courtly elegance.) Pandarus returns to Criseyde and, after some preliminary banter, shows her the letter. She refuses to take it at first, but his final argument is convincing:

> "Refuse it naught," quod he, and hente hire faste,
> And in hire bosom the lettre down he thraste,
> And seyde hire, "Now cast it awey anon,
> That folk may seen and gauren on us tweye."
> (II.1154–57)

Criseyde smiles and asks Pandarus to write her response. He will be happy to write, if she will dictate. She laughs at this, and they go in to dine. When Troilus, as arranged, rides under the window, the narrator intrudes with startling vehemence. His metaphor, which Pandarus repeats in Book III (III.1104–05), recalls others that Pandarus has used:

> To God hope I, she hath now kaught a thorn,
> She shal nat pulle it out this nexte wyke.
> God sende mo swich thornes on to pike!
> (II.1272–74)

Book II concludes with the planning and execution of Pandarus' plot to bring about a meeting between the lovers or, as Pandarus puts it, to drive the deer to Troilus' bow (II.1535). The narrator cuts short the details of Criseyde's reception at Deiphebus' house and proposes to pass swiftly to her interview with the ostensibly bedridden Troilus. "For for o fyn is al that evere I telle," he says (II.1596), echoing Pandarus' ambiguous assertions of single-minded purpose.

When Criseyde enters his chamber, Troilus at first forgets his lines. Finally, he stammers out a plea for mercy. Pandarus weeps "as he to water wolde" (III.115), and Criseyde asks to be told again "the fyn of his entente. / Yet wiste I nevere wel what that he mente" (III.125–26). Troilus means nothing but worship and chivalry, and Criseyde, after stipulating that her honor will not be sacrificed and that not even a king's son shall have sovereignty over her in love, accepts and kisses him. Pandarus sinks to his knees and thanks the gods who have wrought this miracle. He tells the lovers that he shall arrange a meeting at his house to facilitate further conversation:

> "And lat se which of yow shal bere the belle
> To speke of love aright!"—therwith he lough—
> "For ther have ye a leiser for to telle."
>
> (III.198–200)

The joke in these lines strikes at the heart of Pandarus', the narrator's, and our involvement in the events of the poem. It also begins to explain Pandarus' fondness for sexual puns and innuendo and his amused intolerance of others' denials of sexual intent. Pandarus here offers his house not really for conversation but for coition, and he laughs at how neatly he can make the one serve as a private euphemism for the other. Later, the narrator reenacts the substitution of verbal for sexual intercourse when he restates Pandarus' desire to bring the lovers to his house, "Whereas at leiser all this heighe matere, / Touchyng here love, were at the fulle upbounde" (III.516–17). And, early in the assignation, Pandarus asks Criseyde to let Troilus sit "upon youre beddes syde al ther withinne, / That ech of yow the bet may other heere" (III.976–77). When language is functioning as an instrument intimate and powerful enough to make love with, one can easily and appropriately refer to speech and mean sex.

Pandarus, as we have seen, recognizes early the nature of his role in the affair, but he explicitly confesses to pandering only when he and Troilus are left alone after his promise to arrange a meeting. The confession is wrapped in a denial of responsibility; Pandarus has intended only "That al shal ben right as thiselven liste" (III.259). Still, he admits, if it were known that he had manipulated his niece "To doon thi lust and holly to ben thyn" (III.276), the world would consider it the worst treachery ever committed. He asks that Troilus hold his tongue and "that thow us nevere wreye" (III.284)—meaning, by "us," himself and Criseyde—and launches into a forty-two-line harangue on the evil consequences of loose speech. The worst culprits are men who boast about the conquest of women:

> "Swich manere folk—what shal I clepe hem?
>   what?—
> That hem avaunte of wommen, and by name,
> That nevere yet bihyghte hem this ne that,
> Ne knewe hem more than myn olde hat!
> No wonder is, so God me sende hele,
> Though wommen dreden with us men to dele."
>
> (III.317–22)

Pandarus has turned an apparent confession into a conferral of responsibility upon Troilus and finally into a condemnation of men who prattle about women, and by name, from whom they never received favors or whom they never even knew. Pandarus has no label for such a man, but we may recognize that, from one perspective, he has perfectly described the narrator.

The narrator's active involvement is increasing. He will skip over the correspondence between Troilus and Criseyde and get to the point—the meeting. The preparations, he tells us, have gone smoothly and the event is imminent:

> Now al is wel, for al the world is blynd
> In this matere, bothe fremed and tame,
> This tymbur is al redy up to frame;
> Us lakketh nought but that we witen wolde
> A certeyn houre, in which she comen sholde.
> (III.528–32)

The architectural metaphor recurs significantly at the threshold of fulfillment. *We* lack nothing but to know the hour when she will come; as Pandarus implicates Troilus and Criseyde by his use of the plural first-person pronoun, the narrator here implicates himself and us. There remains little to do, he notes, as Pandarus goes on a storm-threatening day to invite Criseyde to dinner. "Ye han wel herd the fyn of his entente" (III.553), says the narrator. Of course, we have never heard it directly, but we well know it. Criseyde asks if Troilus will be present. Pandarus swears not and quickly adds that, even if he were, no one would know it. The narrator breaks in to state that his "auctour" does not say whether Criseyde believed her uncle or not. In either event, she accepts the invitation with a sentence chosen to deflect responsibility toward Pandarus: "Em, syn I must on yow triste, / Loke al be wel, and do now as yow liste" (III.587–88). The "houre, in which she comen sholde," is now established.

The expected storm materializes at the end of the meal, and Pandarus deposits his weather-bound niece in a private bedroom. He then goes to the closet in which Troilus is hiding and repeats that "it shal be right as thow wolt desire" (II.709). Troilus begins to pray nervously to every god he can think of; Pandarus calls him a "wrecched mouses herte" (III.736) and passes through a trapdoor into Criseyde's room. Startled, Criseyde begins to call her attendants, but her uncle stops her. "God forbede it sholde falle / . . . that ye swich folye wroughte! / They myghte demen thyng they nevere er thoughte" (III.761–63). Pandarus' intimation is clear: what the attendants have never thought before but might now imagine is incest. He, evidently, has imagined it; and by this time—given his vows to procure sisters, his vicarious delight in the anticipation of Troilus' success, and the many signs of his "physical and verbal intimacy" with Criseyde, which Beryl Rowland justly terms "lover-like" (p. 9)—we are not shocked. We may even imagine, shortly, that it comes to pass.

Criseyde suggests that she send a token to Troilus (who supposedly has heard a rumor of her faithlessness) or that their meeting be postponed until morning. Pandarus deems these measures inadequate, assures her that "harm

may ther be non, ne synne; / I wol myself be with yow al this nyght"
(III.913–14), and offers to fetch Troilus "whan yow liste" (III.917). Criseyde
declares herself in a quandary but accedes, characteristically, by saying "doth
herof as yow list" (III.939). Soon, Pandarus promises, "We shul ben alle
merye" (III.952). After establishing Troilus at Criseyde's bedside, he retreats
to the fireplace "and fond his contenaunce, / As for to looke upon an old
romaunce" (III.979–80). It cannot and need not be determined whether he
looks upon a literary romance or regards the one being enacted before him as
if it were a book; in either event, he models our activity. "With a full good
entente" (III.1188), the narrator tells us, Pandarus installs Troilus in bed,
once the lover has been stripped and revived from an initial faint, and advises
him, "Swouneth nought now" (III.1190). The narrator's blithe defense of
Pandarus' intent, on the verge of his scheme's consummation, is anything but
innocent and the statement we might have expected instead—that Pandarus
leaves the room—is conspicuously absent.

Troilus now, with belated assertiveness, tells Criseyde she can do nothing
but yield. She would hardly be here, Criseyde responds, had she not yielded
already. The narrator begs every woman to take heed and act in the same way
if the opportunity arises. When Criseyde recognized Troilus' truth and clean
intent, he continues, she "Made hym swich feste, it joye was to seene"
(III.1228). The lovers wrap themselves around each other like honeysuckle
vines around tree trunks; and, at last, "Criseyde, whan hire drede stente, /
Opned hire herte, and tolde hymn hire entente" (III.1238–39).

Throughout this long scene, the reader is kept aware of his own presence
and participation. Pandarus and the narrator remind us that we are looking
but do not tell us what we see. The delights are unspeakable, but we are
free—indeed, we are bound—to imagine them.[11] The narrator's repeated
declarations of his inarticulateness are often accompanied by an appeal to us
for help:

> Of hire delit, or joies oon the leeste
> Were impossible to my wit to seye;
> But juggeth ye that han ben at the feste
> Of swich gladnesse, if that hem liste pleye!
> (III.1310–13)

The feast we have attended is the feast that, a hundred lines before, "it joye
was to seene." Troilus, Criseyde, Pandarus, the narrator, and the reader have
all partaken of this feast—despite Troilus' passivity, despite Criseyde's displays of weakness and "simulated misunderstanding" (Speirs' phrase, p. 93),
despite Pandarus' skillful pretensions to pure service, despite the narrator's
and our claims merely to have taken the words of others. All have performed
as partners in a cozy ménage à cinq, founded upon the shared activity of
speaking and hearing. In a last attempt to transfer responsibility from himself

to the reader, the narrator offers us this advice: if he has added any word to Lollius' account, "Doth therwithal right as youreselven leste" (III.1330). Pandarus and Criseyde have spoken the same phrase many times. Its disguised purpose is always self-extrication, and it is always, therefore, an admission of involvement and responsibility. At the same time, the course it urges on the hearer or reader is inevitable:

> For myne wordes, heere and every part,
> I speke hem alle under correccioun
> Of yow that felyng han in loves art,
> And putte it al in youre discrecioun
> To encresse or maken dymynucioun
> Of my langage, and that I yow biseche.
>   (III.1331–36)

Nothing more or less could happen to any word generated by the poem's insular community—we "that felyng han in loves art"—because language, being communal, never entirely allows its speakers to control it or its hearers to disclaim it.

After exchanging vows with his lover, Troilus returns to his palace at dawn and, the narrator adds somewhat deflatingly, drops into bed "To slepe longe, as he was wont to doone" (III.1536). For the rest of us, however, there is one more scene in Criseyde's bedroom, a scene that is wholly Chaucer's invention:

> Pandare, o-morwe which that comen was
> Unto his nece and gan hire faire grete,
> Seyde, "Al this nyght so reyned it, allas,
> That al my drede is that ye, nece swete,
> Han litel laiser had to slepe and mete.
> Al nyght," quod he, "hath reyn so do me wake,
> That som of us, I trowe, hire hedes ake."
>
> And ner he com and seyde, "How stant it now
> This mury morwe? Nece, how kan ye fare?"
> Criseyde answerde, "Nevere the bet for yow,
> Fox that ye ben! God yeve youre herte kare!
> God help me so, ye caused al this fare,
> Trowe I," quod she, "for al youre wordes white.
> O, whoso seeth yow, knoweth yow ful lite."
>
> With that she gan hire face for to wrye
> With the shete, and wax for shame al reed;
> And Pandarus gan under for to prie,
> And seyde, "Nece, if that I shal be ded,
> Have here a swerd and smyteth of myn hed!"

With that his arm al sodeynly he thriste
Under hire nekke, and at the laste hire kyste.

I passe al that which chargeth nought to seye.
What! God foryaf his deth, and she al so
Foryaf, and with here uncle gan to pleye,
For other cause was ther noon than so.
But of this thyng right to the effect to go,
Whan tyme was, hoom to here hous she wente,
And Pandarus hath fully his entente.

(III.1555–82)

Criticism has widely ignored or failed to appreciate the suggestiveness of this
scene because its tone and the nature of its suggestion deeply threaten traditional interpretations of the poem. Donaldson's passing remark that it is a
"delightful scene . . . [which] is not without a hint of prurience" (p. 972)
comprised, for some time, the riskiest and most sustained analysis of it. In the
last few years, at least three articles have argued that Pandarus goes to bed
with his niece, but each essay trivializes the point as soon as it is advanced,
because the author does not have an overall reading to account for it. Thus,
Beryl Rowland uses the scene to support her psychological analysis of Pandarus as a protomodern bisexual pimp who is doomed to suffer the fate of
Tantalus (pp. 3–15); Peter Christmas sees the scene as the crowning instance
of Chaucer's "*chiaroscuro* presentation of characters";[12] and Haldeen Braddy
asserts that Criseyde's casual episode with her uncle hardly undermines the
impact of her betrayal because, "within the given military setting, her actions
of consorting with the enemy and of becoming Diomede's mistress constitute
the greater crime."[13]

It seems to me that the first and perhaps most crucial observation to be
made about this postnuptial encounter is that it is, if nothing else, the con-
summate instance of evasive language. Here, more inexorably than anywhere
else in the poem, the reader is responsible for the meaning he produces; and
that, I believe, is the meaning of the scene. No amount of receptivity to its
sexual suggestiveness will *give* us the incest, but any amount should make us
reexamine interpretations of the poem that can only survive by flatly rejecting such a possibility. Pandarus' greeting to Criseyde—with its feigned innocence of what both know took place during the night, its pointed concern
that she has had "little laiser for to slepe and mete," and its casual reference to
his own wakefulness—is bawdy and self-titillating, if not downright lecher-
ous. Criseyde's spunky and colloquial response—given her willing, if not
aggressive, acceptance of Troilus, given her playful intimacy with Pandarus
throughout, and given the absurdity of her continuing to act the surprised
innocent at this late date—admires and invites more than it accuses. She
hides beneath the sheet. Pandarus pries underneath and offers her a sword,
clearly not intending that she literally should slay him; instead, he thrusts an

arm under her neck and "at the laste" kisses her. The narrator intrudes—his timing could not appear more incriminating—to say that he will skip what need not be said. He only announces that she forgave him (we remember the circumstances of her earlier act of forgiveness, which ended their first interview) as Christ forgave his executioners (this shocking comparison neatly insinuates the magnitude of her forgiveness as it defensively pretends to explain it away) and that at the end of their play (the word sometimes connotes sex and sometimes does not) Criseyde went home and "Pandarus hath fully his entente." To take Criseyde himself is the logical extreme and the ultimate gratification of Pandarus' constant "entente," and, as I have shown, narrator and reader are aligned with Pandarus. Chaucer, in writing this scene, makes available to all three the possibility of such gratification, and there he stops. We must reach out to seize our prize; if the possibility is to be realized, we must realize it in our reading. But, in the instant we do, we (like Pandarus) strip ourselves of our last defense, the vicariousness of our involvement, and come face to face with the thoroughness of our complicity in all that has occurred. Speaking and hearing are united.

IV

Early in Book III, Pandarus seems to anticipate the fate that lies in store for his name. If it were known that he had become "swich a meene / As maken wommen unto men to comen, . . . all the world upon it wolde crie" (III.254–55, 277). In Book v, Criseyde predicts her own historical identity:

> "Allas! of me, unto the worldes ende,
> Shal neyther ben ywriten nor ysonge
> No good word, for thise bokes wol me shende.
> O, rolled shal I ben on many a tonge!"
> (V.1058–61)

Pandarus and Criseyde are finally attractive characters, I think, because their self-awareness is rooted in their implicit recognition that history is always being shaped by individuals in the present, that it is not a fixed and impersonal set of facts and rules. This recognition distinguishes them from Troilus, whose muddled disquisition on predestination is the measure of his unique separateness from the network of personal agency that generates most of the poem's action. Troilus' argument is that of the prisoner Boethius before he is corrected by Lady Philosophy; it is an argument that, as J. L. Shanley aptly remarks, "started from its conclusion";[14] its force, moreover, is dissipated by everything that has preceded it and by his and Criseyde's consideration of the various alternatives to separation in the latter half of Book IV.

The equivalent of predestination, for the narrator, is the text of his "auctour," and he begins to invoke it often as the poem advances toward Criseyde's exchange and betrayal. The feeling he displays, however, when he passes on to Lollius the responsibility for this turn of events, is not relief but discomfort. The narrator is trapped; his emotional interest and eager complicity in the development and consummation of the love plot are irreconcilable with the stance of detached and foreknowing historian that, for self-protection, he must now assume. He equivocates desperately and only succeeds in uprooting the support he leans on:

> For how Criseyde Troilus forsook,
> Or at the leeste, how that she was unkynde,
> Moot hennesforth ben matere of my book,
> As writen folk thorugh which it is in mynde.
> Allas! that they sholde evere cause fynde
> To speke hire harm, and if they on hire lye,
> Iwis, hemself sholde han the vilanye.
>
> (IV.15–21)

Each of the three stanzas that render the betrayal stipulates that its information is directly transcribed from the story's source. The narrator, however, feels compelled to challenge the authority on which he has insisted; in the last line of the second of these stanzas, he proclaims, "Men seyn—I not—that she yaf hym hire herte" (V.1050). The succeeding lines, typically, enact his return to the authorized position:

> But trewely, the storie telleth us,
> Ther made nevere woman moore wo
> Than she, whan that she falsed Troilus.
>
> (V.1051–53)

As the narrator grapples with the implications of his involvement in a story that has turned sinister, his ambivalence toward Criseyde becomes more pronounced. Pandarus can go through the motions of self-extrication by offering to get Troilus other women who will make him forget the "casuel pleasaunce" (IV.419) that Criseyde has provided or, when her betrayal is certain, by making a show of his hatred for her and assuring Troilus that, from beginning to end, "I dide al that the leste" (V.1736). Neither condemnation nor vindication of Criseyde, however, can absolve the narrator from responsibility for his part in the affair, so he careens violently between the two. As F. D. Covella suggests, "if the defense becomes more insistent, the insinuations become less subtle."[15] The narrator states that Criseyde sat through the first stage of Diomede's suit "As she that was with sorwe oppressed so / That, in effect, she naught his tales herde" (V.177–78), but he qualifies this already qualified assertion by admitting in the next line that she did make out "her and ther . . . a word or two" (V.179). He bitterly punctuates one of Criseyde's soliloquies in which she vows to return soon:

> But God it wot, er fully monthes two,
> She was ful fer fro that entencioun!
> For bothe Troilus and Troie town
> Shal knotteles thorughout hire herte slide.
> (V.766–69)

A few lines later, he interrupts Diomede's courtship to insert formal portraits of Diomede, Criseyde, and Troilus. Here he introduces the information that Criseyde was of average stature, liked to let her hair fall down her back, and was flawed only by eyebrows that joined together. When Diomede approaches Criseyde on the tenth day, she answers his questions but, the narrator comments unemphatically, "as of his entente, / It semed nat she wiste what he mente" (V.867–68). Criseyde's role concludes with a patently dishonest letter that Chaucer invents for her to send to Troilus. After promising to return at some unspecified future date, Criseyde apologizes for her letter's brevity but reminds Troilus that "Th'entente is al, and nat the lettres space" (V.1630). The line echoes similar sentiments expressed by Pandarus and the narrator; its hollowness in this final context serves as an apt judgment upon all proclaimed intentions in *Troilus and Criseyde*. The narrator asks that his lady readers "be nat wroth with me" (V.1775) for Criseyde's treachery. He has told his tale, he claims, mainly to warn them against those who "with hire grete wit and subtilte / Bytraise yow!" (V.1782–83). "Beth war of men" (V.1785), he concludes; it is not so odd a moral from a character who knows that most of the partners in his community of deception have been male.

V

When Pandarus half-admits that he is a pander, Troilus defends him by insisting that his friend's motives are noble: "compaignie" and "felawship" (III.396, 403). We recognize these as terms that Chaucer often uses to describe the Canterbury pilgrims and the purpose of their storytelling venture. Whatever the violations perpetrated by Pandarus and by the pilgrims upon the ideals of "compaignie" and "felawship," the terms are fitting in both circumstances. Pandarus, through his and others' language, creates a community that overcomes spatial, temporal, moral, and intellectual differences among the individuals it comprises. The language of the pilgrims, too, breaks down numerous distinctions among them; it establishes and explores their common ground, often over their own objections. The insidious resistance of all strict categories and complacent certainties is the perpetual task of

Chaucer's language. And it is a beautifully easy task, one that is sure of achievement whenever language is turned loose among a group of diverse and interested individuals. Thus, the Miller takes possession of motifs and phrases from the Knight's Tale and reconstructs them into a totally different but closely related fiction that exposes puns and possibilities in the Knight's language that he never intended but could not exclude; the Wife of Bath puts forth terms and issues that are taken up and reworked from several perspectives in the Clerk's, Merchant's, Squire's, and Franklin's tales; the Nun's Priest's Tale plays on the rhetorical and intellectual pretensions of nearly all medieval literature.

The great moral danger for religious pilgrims was that they would be distracted by the persons they met and the adventures they had along the way. By Chaucer's time, the Church discouraged pilgrimages because the participants could not seem to avoid secular temptations; some, like the Wife of Bath, had no other reason for going. Chaucer's fictional pilgrimage never reaches Canterbury and never was meant to reach it; instead, it explores the communal way, the unstable and impure world that we create through the stories we tell one another. The goal—Canterbury, salvation—is that which we can only gesture at, and the *Canterbury Tales* dutifully concludes with such a gesture. The Manciple's Tale grimly advocates keeping one's mouth shut; the lesson of the crow is that no storyteller, whether he speaks truth or falseness, can escape implication in his story. The Parson's sermon follows, sweeping away the pretense of a company of storytelling pilgrims. As Donald R. Howard points out, the Parson gives us not a tale but a book that instructs us to look to our own souls and that we approach with no sense of being part of a community (*Idea,* pp. 376–81). When the Parson has finished, Chaucer issues his retraction. Fellowship has given way to solitude, language to silence.

It would be impossible, I believe, to read the *Canterbury Tales* from the perspective of Chaucer's retraction, even though the tales mark the way to that perspective. In the *Troilus,* the evolution of sexual and linguistic relationships marks the way to the palinode's repudiation of all things earthly. But, here too, it is the *way* that interests Chaucer and that involves us as readers. The conclusion of an article on the *Troilus* by Robert Jordan, who more or less follows Bloomfield, makes my point:

> The distinctions between past and present, life and death, fortune and misfortune dissolve in the eternal simultaneity of divine vision. Within this perspective, the affairs of humanity—including loving and writing of lovers—can be contemplated only with cool, assured laughter.[16]

"The eternal simultaneity of divine vision" is the ultimate authority because it constitutes a perspective above and beyond the flux of human relationships and language. For this reason, it is a perspective that no writer or reader, no speaker or hearer, ever attains. The problem for the Christian storyteller is to avoid being paralyzed by this knowledge, to make himself give free and serious play to the only "matere" he has—his experience of language and the world. The otherworldly goal remains, but the storyteller willingly suspends his belief in its absoluteness; like the narrator of the *Troilus,* he immerses himself in the life of his story despite his awareness that the ardor of his involvement will make repudiation difficult when the time comes. Chaucer's greatness lies in his determined openness to the experience of the way; and the end of the *Troilus,* like the end of the *Canterbury Tales,* should be seen as his acknowledgment of responsibility for this openness. Troilus, whom death has finished grooming for the eighth sphere, ascends and damns "al oure werk that followeth so / The blynde lust, the which that may nat laste" (V.1823–24). Through Troilus, Chaucer can gesture toward the absolute, but he, like the other implicated participants in the story, remains below to participate again in the complicity of worldly language and affairs. If this means that, for now, Troilus gets the last laugh, I—as one unrepentant accomplice— am prepared to let him have it.

Notes

[Ed. note: This article receives, in the *Riverside Chaucer,* the distinction of being attacked without being named. The editor of *Troilus and Criseyde,* Stephen A. Barney, writes in his explanatory note to III.1555–82: "The now widespread view that Pandarus here seduces or rapes Criseyde, or that Chaucer hints at such an action, is baseless and absurd. The statement, for example, published in 1979, that 'criticism has widely ignored or failed to appreciate the suggestiveness of this scene' is incorrect; all too much has been written about its 'suggestiveness.' " Readers of Carton's essay will of course want to judge the validity of Barney's critique, and may also perhaps want to ask how a response like Barney's fits into Carton's interpretive scheme. Carton himself says of this article, in a personal communication, "Over the years, responses to this essay have brought me pleasure and amusement, without—given the circumstances of its composition—the usual mixture of professional anxiety." Carton is himself not a medievalist; his fields of specialization are American literature and critical theory, and this article, his first publication, was originally written for a graduate seminar.]

1. Lewis, *The Discarded Image* (Cambridge: Cambridge Univ. Press, 1964), p. 5.
2. Quotations of Chaucer's works herein are from *The Works of Geoffrey Chaucer,* ed. F. N. Robinson, 2nd ed. (Boston: Houghton, 1957). Line numbers are noted within parentheses in the text.
3. The best extended treatment of the *Canterbury Tales* as "a book about the world" is Donald R. Howard's *The Idea of the Canterbury Tales* (Berkeley: Univ. of California Press, 1976).
4. Bloomfield, *PMLA,* 72 (1957), 14–26; rpt. in *Chaucer Criticism,* ed. Richard J. Schoeck and Jerome Taylor, II (Notre Dame: Univ. of Notre Dame Press, 1961), 196–210.
5. Dorothy Bethurum argues that the narrator's "reiteration that he is only an outsider and the power and truth of his picture are completely contradictory and produce the ambivalence that is so strikingly characteristic of the poem" ("Chaucer's Point of View as Narrator in the Love Poems," *PMLA,* 74 [1959], 511–20; rpt. in *Chaucer Criticism,* II, 211–31). I agree with this general statement. What I hope to do here is to specify the nature and the

implications of the ambivalence that Bethurum notes and to suggest that the narrator's denials of involvement are belied, not by anything as abstract and undemonstrable as "the power and truth of his picture," but by the entire conception and operation of communication in the poem. Donald R. Howard in "Chaucer the Man" (*PMLA*, 80 [1965], 337–43) offers, in passing on to other concerns, several observations about the *Troilus* narrator. He notes that the narrator is "a reader" and that he is "therefore like ourselves." Howard also calls Pandarus "a kind of mirror image of this narrator." Finally, E. Talbot Donaldson, in his *Speaking of Chaucer* (New York: Norton, 1970, 1972), pp. 65–83, deftly points up some of the oddities and ambiguities of Criseyde's characterization and attributes them to the narrator's "wildly emotional attitude" (p. 68) and inability to see his heroine "from any consistently detached, objective point of view" (p. 67). Again, I am attempting to address—more squarely, I believe, than has been done—the issue of what it means, to the poem and to us, for observations like these to be correct.

6. Troilus, it may be noted, never laughs until he looks down from the eighth sphere, but Pandarus and Criseyde laugh often, and their laughter invariably functions in one of two ways: either it ironically punctuates a disavowal of sexual inference or it signifies recognition of a sexual pun or conspiratorial suggestion.

7. Speirs, *"Troilus and Criseyde," Scrutiny*, 11 (1942), 93.

8. Beryl Rowland in "Pandarus and the Fate of Tantalus" (*Orbis Litterarum*, 24 [1969], 10) notes occasions—in the Merchant's, Wife's, and Parson's Tales—when Chaucer plays on the phallic suggestiveness of the knife. In Criseyde's bedroom, on the morning after the consummation of her affair with Troilus, Pandarus offers her a sword and asks her to behead him. The context strongly supports the case for a sexual meaning.

9. Ross, *"Troilus and Criseyde*, II.582–87: A Note," *Chaucer Review*, 5 (1970), 137–39.

10. Donaldson, *Chaucer's Poetry* (New York: Ronald, 1958), p. 968.

11. Donald R. Howard also makes this point in his suggestive essay "Literature and Sexuality: Book Three of the *Troilus*" (*Massachusetts Review*, 8 [1967], 446–48).

12. Christmas, *"Troilus and Criseyde:* The Problems of Love and Necessity," *Chaucer Review*, 9 (1975), 290.

13. Braddy, "Chaucer's Playful Pandarus," *Southern Folklore Quarterly*, 34 (1970), 80.

14. Shanley, "The *Troilus* and Christian Love," *ELH*, 6 (1939), 277; rpt. in *Chaucer Criticism*, II, 142.

15. Covella, "Audience as Determinant of Meaning in the Troilus," *Chaucer Review*, 2 (1968), 239.

16. Jordan, "The Narrator in Chaucer's *Troilus*," *ELH*, 25 (1958), 257.

Dante and the Poetics of *Troilus and Criseyde*

Winthrop Wetherbee

This essay[1] aims to define the dynamics of the relationship established in *Troilus and Criseyde* between Chaucer and those writers whom he called "poets," the classical epic poets and the Dante of the *Commedia*.[2] Chaucer was deeply engaged with classical poetry in the *Troilus,* and his engagement was largely mediated by Dante, whose great theme was love, but who saw himself as extending the tradition of Latin epic, to the point of claiming a place for himself among the *bella scola* of the disciples of Homer.

For Dante this assimilation is simultaneously an appropriation of the stylistic resources of his chosen poets, and he makes us aware of the presumption and the risk that such an appropriation involves. There are moments in the *Inferno* when one may sense that the rhetorical weapons he deploys are beyond his power to fully control, that he stands condemned by the very force with which he condemns the sins of others. The other side of this profound involvement is a high degree of intuitive sympathy with what is most congenial in ancient poetry, and it is this that makes possible the astutely selective, "redemptive" readings, allowing him to place Lucan's Cato at the threshold of Purgatory, or discover in Ovidian metamorphosis a repertory of metaphors for spiritual transformation.

Chaucer offers nothing like Dante's direct imitation of the ancient poets, but in encasing his narrative in a dense framework of allusion to ancient poetry, he is doing something closely analogous. Like Dante, he allows the ancient poets' view of history and human destiny—a vision at once severely limited and painfully aware of its limitations—to inform his own. The effect is in one sense to circumscribe his narrator's spiritual awareness by confirming him in his obsessive involvement with the sorrows of love in their seemingly tragic aspect. But the *poetae* also significantly enlarge Chaucer's perspective on his story, compelling him to see beyond the romantic tragedy of Troilus to the larger tragedy of epic history. In the process, he moves, as I intend to show, from what can be called an "infernal" to a "purgatorial" relation to his poem and its tradition—from a position comparable to that of the Dante who weeps for Paolo and Francesca to that of the Dante

This essay was written specifically for this volume and is published here for the first time by permission of the author.

who discovers a new, potentially transcendent significance in the dark world of the *Thebaid* of Statius.

The differences between Chaucer's discovery and Dante's are *again* very great. Dante's engagement with the *poetae* is an important theme of the *Commedia* from the outset,[3] whereas Chaucer's sense of his indebtedness emerges belatedly and as if by accident. We can see its first stirrings as Chaucer's narrator, approaching the end of the *Troilus,* introduces an elaborate series of concluding gestures, suggesting various morals for his love story, offering his "litel bok" to the world, and defining for it a humble, "subject" relation to the works of the great poets of the classical past:

> But litel book, no makyng thow n'envie,
> But subgit be to alle poesye;
> And kis the steppes where as thow seest pace
> Virgile, Ovide, Omer, Lucan, and Stace.[4]

He goes on to voice his anxiety about the survival and reception of his poem, in the absence of any normative standard of written or spoken English. Then, quite unexpectedly, he recalls a "purpose" still unaccomplished, and the poem abruptly begins again:

> The wrath, as I bigan yow for to seye,
> Of Troilus the Grekis boughten deere,
> For thousandes his hondes maden deye,
> As he that was withouten any peere,
> Save Ector, in his tyme, as I kan heere,
> But—weilawey, save only Goddes wille,
> Dispitously hym slough the fierse Achille.
> (5.1800–1806)

There is nothing more bewildering in this complex poem than the elaborate movement of the next few stanzas. As the narrator seeks by various means to impose formal closure on his story, Troilus, unfulfilled and desperate to avenge his loss of love, is allowed to break down a series of rhetorical barriers, reemerging first as the epic hero and then, as if in reward of his final display of heroism, ascending the spheres to attain for the first time an incipiently spiritual perspective on his life and his world. It would seem that the possibility of a fuller and more coherent rendering of Troilus's experience has here been momentarily revealed to us, one that would conform to the formal and moral demands of poetry in its nobler classical aspect, and we are bound to ask just what relationship is being suggested between this new heroic and sapiential dimension and the experience of Troilus the lover as it has been presented up to this point.

We may be tempted to take Troilus's epic renewal as a declaration that the spirit that had sensed a transcendent meaning in the love of Criseyde could also find expression in heroic and authentically spiritual forms. I suggest that Chaucer is deliberately disclaiming any serious epic intention in these stanzas by underlining the arbitrariness of the rhetorical gestures they involve. Chaucer's evocation of Troilus's "wrath" clearly recalls the opening of the *Iliad*, but its placement at the end of the poem rather than the beginning is faintly absurd. The revelation that it is an afterthought ("as I bigan yow for to seye") is clearly so, and so is the displacement of the hero's name to an unemphatic position in the next line, a bathos comparable to the "yif I kan" that intrudes on the opening line of the *Aeneid* as rendered in the *House of Fame* (143 ff.).

The stanza ends, appropriately enough, with Achilles, who emerges to reclaim his Homeric role and bring Troilus's heroic moment to an abrupt close. The effect of the stanza as a whole is to remind us that Troilus's "wrath" is a medieval embellishment of Dares Phrygius,[5] as alien to Chaucer's carefully fashioned classical world as Pandarus himself. For the classical Troilus Chaucer knew is Virgil's, the "miserable boy" whom Aeneas weeps to behold amid the panorama of the Trojan War, in the temple of Juno in Dido's Carthage. The panorama shows the Trojan people thronging the Palladion, where the story of Chaucer's Troilus begins, juxtaposing this scene with a picture of how that story ends:

> parte alia fugiens amissis Troilus armis,
> infelix puer atque impar congressus Achilli,
> fertur equis curruque haeret resupinus inani,
> lora tenens tamen; huic ceruix comaeque trahuntur
> per terram, et uersa puluis inscribitur hasta.
>
> (*Aeneid* 1.474–78)

[In another place Troilus, in flight, his arms abandoned, a miserable boy and no match for Achilles, is dragged supine by his horses and empty chariot, still holding the reins. His neck and hair are dragged over the ground, and his inverted spear writes in the dust.]

This is not the wrathful slayer of thousands, the "Ector the secounde" to whom Chaucer's poem so often refers. But Chaucer must have had this hapless Troilus very much in mind as he adapted a narrative that is in effect the story of the *infelix puer* that his spear, writing aimlessly in the dust of the battlefield, cannot tell. For Virgil's Troilus is no less congruent than Dares' vaunted warrior with the Troilus Chaucer's poem has actually shown us. We are assured that this figure is noble and brave, "fulfilled of heigh prowesse," but the Troilus we mainly see is a confused adolescent, fearful of public opinion, and incapable of decisive action, someone Pandarus and Criseyde manipulate at will. From the moment of his submission to love, moreover, the impulses of the warrior are subordinated to those of the lover,[6] and it is by no means clear why this "sely" figure should be so abruptly transformed into an epic figure of quasi-transcendent significance.[7]

Historically, too, the significance of the death of Troilus is equivocal. From the outset Chaucer's hero is plainly a figure for Troy itself: the structure of the poem's opening couplet and its assonantal linkage of "Troilus" and "Troye" suspend him in a closed space, emotional and physical, as Troy and its fate will circumscribe his existence.[8] He is neither Hector, whose death at the hands of Achilles is plainly identified as the pivotal event in the fall of Troy (5.1541–54), nor Aeneas, whose divinely engineered escape from Achilles' wrath will ensure the foundation of Rome. Instead Troilus resembles those beautiful, doomed figures, Camilla, Nisus, Euryalus, sacrificial victims whom Dante's Virgil, their creator, recalls with deep irony as having "died for" Italy (*Inferno* 1.106–8), emblems of what must be destroyed to make way for the new.

Chaucer goes beyond Boccaccio in pointing up the historically marginal status of a Trojan story that both writers narrate with only an occasional sidelong glance at the great process of translation and foundation in which the Trojan War is the pivotal event. If Troilus is representative of Troy, it is insofar as his life and death are defined by, his nobility and bravery in thrall to, the besetting Trojan infatuation with "joye," Virgil's *falsa gaudia,* which the shade of Deiphobus repents in recalling the city's last night (*Aen.* 6.513–14). Beautifully and powerfully told, the tale of Troilus that Chaucer takes from Boccaccio is more than any earlier *roman d'antiquité* a love story, with its own beginning and end; history is confined to a series of sporadic reminders, most of them cryptically or allusively conveyed, and even the story of Troilus himself is reduced in the end to the occasion for a confrontation between the poem's narrator and the literary tradition with which he has been half-consciously engaged. Then, in a series of elaborate rhetorical gestures, the story of Troilus is apparently rejected altogether.

Why Chaucer should have introduced the stanzas that report Troilus's death and posthumous fortunes is a question to which I am not prepared to offer a complete answer. But there are, as I have argued, enough grounds for seeing them as inappropriate to Troilus's role, both in the poem and in epic history, to suggest that these stanzas are in one aspect, at least, only another in the series of abortive attempts at closure that punctuate the final stanzas of the poem. They may express a lingering desire to "value" Troilus, but they provide no certain knowledge.[9] This in turn should remind us that Chaucer has expressly delimited the theme of his poem at several points. The opening lines announce Troilus's adventures "in loving," and say nothing of "wrath" or "arms"; the "Troian gestes" with which all the characters are involved are explicitly excluded (1.143); and the poem's long conclusion can be said to begin with the poet's reminder that his concern has been, not the arms of Troilus, but his love (5.1765–69).

Whatever importance we assign to Troilus's story in determining the meaning of the "Book of Troilus" as a whole, then, must depend first of all on our recognizing that it is primarily and finally a story of love. But we must then ask why the *Troilus,* unlike the *Filostrato,* should be so fraught with allusion to classical epic poetry, and why the complex transformation the narrator undergoes in the final stanzas of book 5—where he moves from an intense involvement with the story of Troilus to the transcendent perspective affirmed in the prayer that concludes the poem—should center on his discovery of his indebtedness to Homer, Virgil, and Statius. What relation is being suggested between their poetry and that of a narrator who is at pains to focus his poem on what may serve the servants of the god of love? Here as at so many points in the *Troilus,* the crucial element is the presence of Dante.

Critics have tended to underplay the role of direct engagement with the classical past in both the *Troilus* and the *Commedia,* emphasizing instead the well-attested medieval hermeneutical practices that neutralized the "seductive authority" of pagan texts and opened them to new meaning by more or less "violent" acts of interpretative appropriation.[10] But it is only by considering moments in which we can see Dante or Chaucer responding to the seductive and unredeemed qualities of this poetry—abandoning themselves to its inherent power and experiencing the alien and potentially hostile character of its spiritual universe as fully as possible—that we can appreciate the complexity of their sense of how literary tradition is formed and the depth of their awareness of the continuity that linked them to the ancient poets. I would like to look closely at two such moments, passages that show the medieval poets submitting themselves to the influence of their pagan forebears at its most intense.

The Dante who accepts Virgil's invitation to descend to the lower world, home of the "antichi spiriti dolenti" (*Inf.* 1.116), knows that for Virgil this had been largely a world of tragic unfulfillment, its moral and spiritual order uncertain and circumscribed by darkness. He is aware also that in appropriating Virgil's poetic style, as he claims to have done in *Inferno* 2, he is deploying a resource as ominously ambiguous in its power as the Golden Bough itself. The moment that illustrates this most plainly is also one of Dante's most sustained and detailed echoings of Virgil, though the borrowing is perhaps so obvious as to have seemed perfunctory and has received relatively little notice. The passage climaxes the Pilgrim's first encounter with the souls of the damned, in a series of similes that describe how these souls hurl themselves from the shore of Acheron at the command of Charon, who will ferry them to the realm of the damned. I would like to examine one of these similes:

> Come d'autunno si levan le foglie
> l'una appresso de l'altra, fin che 'l ramo
> vede a la terra tutte le sue spoglie,
> similmente il mal seme d'Adamo
> gittansi di quel lito . . .
> (*Inf.* 3.112–16)

[As the leaves fall in autumn, one after another, until the bough sees all its spoils upon the ground, so the evil seed of Adam fling themselves from that shore . . .]

We have been told explicitly that the catalyst of the process here described is the cruel words, the "parole crude" of "Caron demonio" (100–102, 109). Virgil had applied the adjective *cruda* to the strange, demonic vitality of Charon himself in his old age (*Aen.* 6.304); Dante's use of the Italian cognate imputes a darker version of the same energy to Charon's speech and points up the importance of language in the episode as a whole. Throughout we must see the Pilgrim responding not only to what he sees and hears but also to the remembered words in which Virgil had described the same scene:

> huc omnis turba ad ripas effusa ruebat,
>
> . . . .
>
> quam multa in siluis autumni frigore primo
> lapsa cadunt folia . . .
>
> (Aen. 6.305, 309–10)

[Here the whole throng [of souls] rushed forward to the bank . . . : as many as the leaves which fall in the forest at the first chill of autumn . . .]

If we compare Dante's lines with their Virgilian original, we can see that the Pilgrim, too, like the damned souls responding to the words of Charon, has been caught up as if by a demonic force. The focus of Dante's simile is not the fallen leaves, but the bough that "sees" them on the earth. The leaves, moreover, fall one by one, "ech after other," as Chaucer will later translate Dante's phrase (*Troilus* 4.226). The unnatural details draw us away from the beauty of the imagery and point to the new role this images has assumed. The bough is the Pilgrim; the leaves falling in sequence mirror the word-by-word sequentiality of his imaginative and verbal response to the controlling influence of Virgil's poetry, as audible here, beneath the surface of Dante's Italian rendering, as at any point in the *Commedia*.

The simile thus expresses Dante's sense of the challenge implicit in imitating his great poetic forebear. So deeply has he felt Virgil's power that he has momentarily assimilated also the deep sadness that lies behind it. Thus the imagery represents not only the self-destruction of the damned souls, but the self-diminishing effect of Dante's identification with them. The leaves are his own words, the means whereby, under Virgil's programmatic influence, he emulates the self-abandonment of the "evil seed of Adam" in an ejaculation of vicarious desire for participation in the scene he beholds. The peril of thus succumbing to Virgil's "parole crude" is clear in the shock the Pilgrim undergoes when confronted with the contrast between this imaginative suicide and the promise of salvation implicit in Charon's reaction to his presence in hell (90–93, 127–36). Disoriented by his self-indulgent response to the pathos of the Virgilian moment, he had lost all sense of his true mission. What he has learned remains inarticulate, to be assimilated gradually by the altered self that will emerge from an experience which, in a moment of profound dividedness, has drawn him to the brink of psychological chaos.[11]

Chaucer's awareness of the power of the dislocating and potentially demoralizing power of classical poetry emerges plainly in the invocation to the Fury Tisiphone that concludes the opening stanza of the *Troilus:*

> Thesiphone, thow help me for t'endite
> Thise woful vers, that wepen as I write.
>
> (1.6–7)

The effect of this shocking and puzzling invocation is further complicated by its allusion to the Roman poet Statius, whose major work, the *Thebaid,* is a horrifying account of the war between the two sons of Oedipus, Eteocles and Polynices, over the lordship of Thebes. Calling out to the "cruel furie" from the "darkness" of his loveless isolation, Chaucer's narrator bears a strange resemblance to the blinded Oedipus who appears at the opening of the *Thebaid,* and, in the "eternal night" of his self-inflicted damnation, summons this same "cruel goddess" from the underworld to inflict a fatal madness on his sons and thereby sets in motion the plot of Statius's poem.[12]

The narrator's banal justification for appealing to Tisiphone—her "dreariness" is appropriate to his own sad mood and story—suggests an innocence of intention in sharp contrast to the deliberate impiety of Statius's embittered Oedipus, to whom Tisiphone is a kind of patron. But Chaucer's Fury is true to her epic role insofar as she reinforces in her human agent a radically subjective and limited outlook on the coming action. Though the narrator is linked to his protagonists by a vicarious identification with their love rather than by hatred, his attachment has a desperate intensity such that at times the fulfillment of his own emotional need through their union will become all-important to him, rendering any larger, more enlightened perspective on their situation inaccessible.

The narrator's rueful reflections on the "unlikeliness" that somehow disables him as a lover are more than a comic touch. Like Pandarus, whose emotional involvement with the lovers can never be trusted, he has invested all hope of happiness in their love. At the moment of consummation he can imagine trading his soul for an instant of such bliss as he imagines them to know. Like Statius's Oedipus, though for different reasons, he is motivated in large part by deprivation, and one function of the invocation of Tisiphone is to warn us that the need underlying his vicarious identification with Troilus is contaminated by frustration and envy. Like the narrator, the goddess weeps as she torments her victims, and like Tisiphone the narrator is inescapably a collaborator in the infliction of the pain he describes.[13] Statius, too, though he takes elaborate pains to assert his authorial distance from the horrors with which his poem must deal, also gives way to moments of deep pessimism and caustic bitterness that deepen the poem's prevailing atmosphere of despair and make plain the extent to which the spiritually enervating burden of Theban history has diminished his power to affirm the meaning of love, piety, and heroic virtue. For both poets Tisiphone marks an obsessive involvement with the tragic action from which the narrators of both poems will ultimately free themselves, but which poses a recurrent threat to their morale and sense of purpose during the course of their narratives.

In both the *Troilus* and Dante's *Commedia* the influence of this "infernal" vision, dominated by the sense of individual tragedy and historical fatalism, coexists with an idealizing poetics of love. In Dante's personal myth, the "good courage" that sustains his pilgrimage through the afterlife descends to him, mediated by the "noble speech" that he puts into the mouth of Virgil, from Beatrice, the "Donna di virtù" who is the focal point of his spiritual aspirations (*Inf.* 2.52–138). Chaucer's narrator is vaguer and more cryptic in expressing his idealism, but there will be moments when the love he seeks to affirm appears to him with something like the heavenly aspect it has for Dante, leading him to celebrate its power in inspired outbursts that echo the visionary flights of the *Commedia,* and the poetry of the *dolce stil novo* in which Dante's idealizing of Beatrice is grounded.[14]

In both poems the affirmation of human love is shown to be a psychologically complex, and at times an ominously ambiguous, undertaking. The story adumbrated in the opening stanzas of the *Troilus*—the story, ultimately, of Troilus's double sorrow for love of a Criseyde who "forsook hym er she deyde" (1.56)—conforms in its prevailing emphases to the representation of human love in canto 5 of Dante's *Inferno,* the canto of Dido, Francesca, and all the "donne antiche e' cavalieri" whose love proved stronger than reason.[15] Though the private darkness from which Chaucer's narrator speaks to us is not that of Dante's underworld, we know, inescapably, from the outset, that the love of Troilus is doomed,[16] and we are made to feel the narrator's difficulty in coming to terms with this knowledge. Like the Dante who responds to the plight of Paolo and Francesca by imagining the sweet thoughts and sighs that drew them to the "doloroso passo," Chaucer's narrator defines his role in terms of his vocation to give expression to the woes of lovers (*Tr.* 1.10–11, 15). He is not, of course, so clearly implicated in the scene he presents as the Pilgrim, whose *pietà* for Francesca is a connoisseur's unreflecting response to the sheer pathos of her tale, and whose deathlike swoon at the end of canto 5 is a telling comment on the "sweet style" that evokes such vicarious feeling. Chaucer's narrator, indeed, shows himself capable of a certain detachment and is ready to respond to the misery he foresees with something closer to true charity than Dante's self-regarding pity (*Tr.* 1.48–51). But this tentative awareness cannot sustain itself in the face of his need to affirm the quasi-religious status of love, a need which, if not as intense as Dante's identification with Francesca, will cause him to ignore his own surer instincts until the complex realization of the poem's final stanzas.

For both poets, love's power is underscored by powerful reminders of classical antecedents. Dante's encounter with Francesca reenacts Augustine's description of the effect on his younger self of Virgil's account of the suicide of Dido.[17] It is also pervaded, like Augustine's reading, and to a much greater extent, by the guilty compassion with which Aeneas addresses Dido's shade in the underworld of *Aeneid* 6, seeking to reaffirm a bond that he himself had broken, and one wholly at odds with his larger mission.[18] In thus creating a tension between his narrator's dominating concern with love and the allusively conveyed awareness of a larger context of tragic history that sets that love in a diminishing perspective, Chaucer is again following Dante, defining for himself a complex relation not only to classical poetry but also to courtly romance. The Pilgrim's experience in the circle of the lustful, where the mere name of Dido evokes a world of suppressed meaning, shows how these elements could be isolated and enhanced in a sensibility conditioned by *courtoisie*. And as the beauty of Francesca's narrative, with its echoes of *stilnovo* lyric and its unconscious tribute to the insidious power of romance, ennobles desire and disguises the destructive power of which Dido is the emblem, so the *roman d'antiquité*—the tradition to which Chaucer owes the story of Troilus—had assimilated the history of Troy and Thebes by muting the emphasis of Virgil and Statius on the pain and irresolution of human experience, and stressing the redemptive power of love. Chaucer exploits the license provided by the *roman d'antiquité,* allowing his narrator to pursue his love story in willful blindness to the darker questions it raises, while at the same time his self-reflecting classical allusions—like Dante's evocations of the guilty *pietà* of Aeneas—suggest the ambiguous nature of his enterprise.

For Dante, of course, every engagement with human love is fundamentally conditioned by his love of Beatrice, which evolves over the course of his pilgrimage into a full appreciation of her role as a vessel of truth. The love Chaucer's narrator seeks to affirm remains hostage to human frailty and human history, and the narrator is finally compelled to recognize it as inferior, the "feynede" emulation of a transcendent love. What the narrator retains from his earlier engagement with Troilus and his world is critically important to his subsequent realizations, but his transformation clearly diverges fundamentally from the model of Dante's own role as the Christian love-poet par excellence. At the same time it brings the narrator very close to the model provided by the one ancient *poeta* to whom Dante himself assigns a Christian significance, the Statius of the *Purgatorio,* who is still identifiably the author of the *Thebaid*—with its despairing images of a spiritually bankrupt paganism—but who surfaces in Purgatory, reborn as a Christian penitent.

Dante makes plain that Statius's new spiritual enlightenment is the fulfillment of insights tentatively expressed in his own *Thebaid.* His account of his first exposure to Christianity evokes the description, in the final book of the *Thebaid,* of the altar of the goddess Clementia, where a new spirituality seems to have emerged. The cult of Clementia is itself a new dispensation, and one that Statius compares to the gods' bestowal of the gifts of law, religion, and agriculture, "laws, and a new man, and sacred rites, and seeds descending into the empty earth" (*Thebaid* 12.501–2), language that he recalls in Purgatory to describe the early preachers who had made the world "pregnant" with the seeds of true belief (*Purgatorio* 22.76–78). The Lemnian princess Hypsipyle—whose story forms a long digression at the center of the *Thebaid,* a minor epic of female heroism and loss wholly at odds with the prevailing emphasis of the poem as a whole—is one of a number of figures whose incipient spirituality, fearful and uncertain in the savage atmosphere of the Theban world, is allusively recalled and granted an imaginative fulfillment in the experience of Dante's Statius.[19]

The most striking instance of this retrospective validation of Statius's religious intuition involves the Theban prince Menoeceus, whose ritual suicide, prompted by the declaration of Tiresias that this act alone can save the city, is presented by Statius more as the means to spiritual fulfillment of a new and higher kind than as an act of patriotism (*Theb.* 10.604–20). Statius's account of how the goddess Virtus prepares Menoeceus for his immortalizing self-sacrifice becomes the basis for the description, in the discourse of Dante's Statius on the origin and destiny of the human soul, of how the powers of the natural organism are transformed and reoriented when informed by divine *vertù* (*Purg.* 25.70–72). Dante's delegation of Statius to trace the development of human life from the origin of the natural embryo to its consummation in the soul is an important symbolic gesture in itself, pointing clearly to the presence of an embryonic spirituality in the *Thebaid* itself.

In creating his Christian Statius, Dante thus subjects the *Thebaid* to a rigorously selective reading, one that omits nearly all trace of the narrative proper and grants certain seemingly random moments in the poem a kind of intuitive, almost visionary authority. From the perspective of the *Purgatorio,* Statius's Theban history is devoid of inherent value, significant only as the vehicle of these intuitions, even as earthly existence, in his account of human life, is reduced to a mere interval in the soul's pursuit of its destiny. It is by an essentially similar shift of perspective that the heroic and even the "Dantean" dimensions of the experience of Chaucer's Troilus are finally revealed as devoid of meaning, save insofar as their articulation has been a necessary catalyst for the narrator's progress, through poetry, to that spiritual perspective from which Troilus and his world, like Statian Thebes, will suddenly become all but invisible. Chaucer goes beyond Dante to show us the actual stages of the narrator's rejection of his story, punctuated by the invective that reduces the hero's love and bravery to worldly folly and subject his pagan beliefs to a virtual exorcism. These elaborate gestures create a distance between the narrator and his story comparable to that which separates the redeemed Statius of the *Purgatorio* from the world of the *Inferno,* where motifs drawn from the *Thebaid* are made to set off the enormity of a number of major sins.[20]

The invoking of Tisiphone in the opening stanza of the *Troilus* establishes the bond between Chaucer's narrator and the Statius of the *Thebaid,* and the same stanza clearly evokes Dante's Statius as well. The "double sorwe" of Chaucer's opening line echoes the *Purgatorio,* where Dante's Virgil, reflecting on his encounter with Statius, sums up the plot of the *Thebaid* as "the cruel arms of Jocasta's twofold sorrow"[21] and notes the incongruity of Statius's grim narrative with his newly revealed Christian vocation. The allusion, the first of a host of often cryptic reminiscences of Statius's Theban narrative, implicates not only Troilus and the historical action in which he is inextricably involved, but the narrator himself, whose intense engagement with his characters and their love will cause him repeatedly to lose sight of the history that looms inevitably over the action and will reduce him to a collaborator in the pattern of "disordered memory and fatal repetition"—the hapless rehearsal of "a past both forgotten and obsessively remembered"—that make the Theban legend Chaucer's chosen model of the fatally repetitive character of secular history.[22]

Like Dante's Statius, Chaucer's narrator will finally manage to escape from his involvement with the action of his "tragedy," but the experience of both figures is a long trajectory that begins in darkness. In the opening lines of the *Thebaid* Statius speaks, like his own Oedipus, from the shadows of a spiritually embittered world, seemingly cursed to relive its violent history indefinitely, whereas Chaucer's narrator acknowledges the dark depths of his obsession with the woes of lovers from whose experience he is irredeemably alienated, both by his "unliklynesse" for love and by the futility of compassion in the face of the certainty of their doomed history. And for both Chaucer and Statius, the spiritual evolution that will finally become their central concern is inseparable from their activity as poets. The Statius who dates his baptism by reference to his progress in composing the *Thebaid* (*Purg.* 22.88–89), and marks the stages of his spiritual growth in terms of a growing understanding of Virgil, provides a unique standard of comparison for the progress of Chaucer's narrator, who comes at last, in a passage that strongly evokes both the Statius cantos of *Purgatorio* and the conclusion of Statius's own *Thebaid,* to a sense of the spiritual meaning of his poem.

Chaucer's representation of this evolving understanding of poetic experience is marked by what Dante himself calls "resurgence" (*Purg.* 1.7). Chaucer's equivalent for Dante's reinvigorating escape from infernal despair is the renewal of a poetry that had seemed to have expended all its desiring energy in celebrating the poem's all-too-human lovers, and the renewal is at the same time a demarcation, for it involves a clear recognition of all that separates the mortal joys of Troilus and Criseyde from the ongoing spiritual life accessible to the poet and his audience. At the same time, like the *Purgatorio,* but more explicitly, the conclusion of the *Troilus* shows Chaucer coming to terms with the ongoing poetic tradition that joins the living and the dead, Christian and pagan alike,[23] and a reverent recognition of what he owes the great classical poets, from Homer to Statius himself. The process of breaking away from Troilus's earthbound desire and entering the realm of charity is inseparable from a recognition that the vehicle through which he has attained his new insight into love has been "the forme of olde clerkes speche / In poetrie" (5.1854–55). His final vision is largely dependent on the sympathetic, even reverent assimilation of the flawed but profoundly humane vision of these poets; and by the end the poem's central concern has become his discovery of what it means to be, first, a poet, and, second, a Christian poet.

The experience the narrator undergoes in the final stanzas of book 5 can be said to begin with the ending of the love story, which I take to occur once and for all in the following passage:

> And if I hadde ytaken for to write
> The armes of this ilke worthi man,
> Than wolde Ich of his batailles endite;
> But for that I to writen first bigan
> Of his love, I have seyd as I kan . . .
> (5.1765–69)

The last line, surely as weak and halting a line as Chaucer ever wrote, tells its own story. The long slow decline of the love affair has finally ended, and this line is the exhausted last gasp of the narrator's inspiration to tell that story, a moment that corresponds very broadly to the swoon of Dante's Pilgrim, exhausted by his self-indulgent weeping for Francesca and Paolo.

The energy that moves the poem forward beyond this point is Troilus's desire to compensate his loss on the battlefield, and what happens to the narrator in the next few stanzas happens unawares as he labors to cancel the poem's new lease on life and impose formal closure. Throughout he seems at sea regarding his own intention in the *Troilus*, yet there is no moment in the poem at which he is closer to Dante and the ancient poets, and he now somehow arrives at a new appreciation of the role and capacities of poetry.

> Go, litel bok, go, litel myn tragedye,
> Ther God thi makere yet, ere that he dye,
> So sende myght to make in som comedye!
> (5.1786–88)

The opposition of tragedy to comedy here has been explained as balancing the *Troilus,* now almost complete, against the as-yet-unwritten *Canterbury Tales;* but in the context of the conclusion as a whole, the lines may be seen as referring to the precarious generic status of the *Troilus* itself at this crucial stage in its unfolding, when the significance of its twofold debt to both the tragic vision of the classical poets and the spiritual perspective of Dante's *Commedia* is still uncertain. As the narrator reflects further on the possible destiny of his "litel bok," his sense of working as a "maker"[24] gives way to a recognition of his more significant role as a participant in a larger continuum of poetic experience and poetic tradition:

> But, litel book, no makyng thow n'envie,
> But subgit be to alle poesye;
> And kis the steppes where as thow seest pace
> Virgile, Ovide, Omer, Lucan, and Stace.
>
> (5.1789–92)

After the insistent repitition of "makere," "make," "makyng" in lines 1787–89, "poesye" is introduced into the poem in line 1790. Now for the first time the chimerical Lollius and the tyrannizing book of "myn auctor" are replaced by the names of real poets. In bidding his book revere these poets, Chaucer recalls both Statius, who had bidden his *Thebaid* follow reverently in the foot-steps of Virgil (*Theb.* 12.816–17), and Dante's Statius, who seeks to embrace the feet of Virgil when the two poet-shades meet on the steps of Purgatory (*Purg.* 21.130–32). In thus affirming his affinity with Statius and his own more tentative claim to a place in the poetic canon, the narrator passes from the service of the god of love and the rhetoric of sentiment to a concern with universal values, and with poetic tradition as the repository of these values. As one "subject" to ancient poetry he does not claim the name of poet for himself, but his new, increasingly conscious role is very far from the hapless state in which, blinded by desire, he had first abandoned himself to Tisiphone.

In the context of this new departure, Chaucer's use of the term *poesye* to characterize the living tradition he has discovered is highly suggestive. Unlike "poetrie" (used of "olde clerkes speche" a few stanzas later), "poesye" occurs only here in Chaucer's work, and it is framed in a way that indicates a special significance. The stanza in which it appears is unique in the *Troilus* in that it sustains a single rhyme through five lines, and the sequence of "tragedye," "comedye," and "poesye" stands out with the effect of Dantean *terza rima*. Followed as it is, first by the self-dedicatory gesture of the stanza's final couplet, then by a sudden renewal of narrative energy, the passage bears a certain resemblance to the passage that includes Dante's only use of the equivalent term, *poesì,* at the opening of the *Purgatorio:*

> Ma qui la morta poesì resurga,
> O sante Muse, poi che vostro sono . . .
>
> (*Purg.* 1.7–8)

[But here let dead poesy rise up again, O holy Muses, since I am yours . . .]

For both poets, this unique use of "poesye"/"poesì" occurs as part of the expression of a new sense of commitment to their vocation as poets; and for both, its appearance marks the recovery of vital contact with the classical tradition. But it must be acknowledged that this renewal is easier to locate in the *Purgatorio* than in the *Troilus.* Lucan, Ovid, and Statius, as well as Virgil, will play significant roles in the experience of the Pilgrim as he ascends the mountain of Purgatory, and now their roles will be clearly integrated into the economy of his spiritual evolution; his one further concession to the treacherous appeal of the Virgilian *lacrimae rerum* will occur in the lines in which he responds to the disappearance of Virgil himself (*Purg.* 30.49–54).

Chaucer's sense of renewal is harder to define in either literary or spiritual terms, and in its initial stages what may impress us most is his narrator's seeming diffidence in accepting its implications. The literalism of bidding his poem "kis the steppes" where the *poetae* have walked suggests a lingering sense of his own slightly comic ineptitude in comparison with the great masters. In the next stanza he accepts at last his own responsibility for the language of his poem, but this assertion of autonomy is balanced by anxiety as to whether his words will survive the process of transmission—thoughts very far from the concluding reflections of Ovid, or even Statius, on the enduring power of their art, let alone Dante's intense pride in his refinement of the mother tongue.

Nonetheless, when the narrator discovers simultaneously the depth of his indebtedness to "poesye" and the ultimate independence of his own poem, he holds the key to final liberation from his obsession with the story of Troilus. And it is by comparing his experience to that which Dante dramatizes in the later stages of the *Purgatorio* that we can best reconcile the importance of what he is undergoing with his evident uncertainty. In both cases it is a peculiarly "poetic" experience, communicable only through poetry—and almost entirely through one poet's insights into the work of another.

The symbol of this experience is Dante's Statius, and its nature is indicated by the purely intuitive character of the knowledge that has guided his transformation from pagan poet to purified Christian soul. The catalyst for his conversion was the language of Virgil, which, through partial misreading and half-conscious translation, came to seem to him "consonant" with the words of Christian preachers (*Purg.* 22.37–42, 67–81). In Purgatory, too, Statius's knowledge remains wholly intuitive. He candidly confesses his inability to explain the unchanging climate of upper Purgatory, or why the mountain trembles at the release of each purified soul from its purgation, and his bafflement is in keeping with his own experience: the process of purgation is imperceptible even by those who undergo it, and its only confirmation is the sudden "surprising" of the soul by its newly liberated will (*Purg.* 21.61–63).

It is important to recognize the claim being made for poetry in Dante's resurrection of Statius. Dante's Statius claims that his poetic and religious lives had diverged during the period when, as he tells us, his crypto-Christianity was concealed by an outward paganism (*Purg.* 22.88–91), but his poetry remains the sole documentary basis for Dante's account of his career, and reminds us that we too must rely mainly on intuition in seeking to gauge the spiritual significance of a poetic text. The kind of reading needed to bring Statius into line with the spiritual biography Dante assigns him is close to the kind of reading Dante credits Statius with having applied to the poetry of Virgil (*Purg.* 22.64–73) and depends on assigning a privileged meaning to elements in the text that may have had a very different value for the poet himself. Inventing for Statius's own poetry a spiritual-historical context that can be made to illumine the authentically spiritual elements latent in it is Dante's way of affirming the continuity that links the classical and Christian worlds, the texts of the *poetae* and the poetry of Dante himself.

It is a continuity that can only be understood intuitively, an interaction of imaginative and spiritual experience as impervious to analysis as the image of sunlight transformed to wine that climaxes Statius's discourse on the soul (*Purg.* 25.76–78). And it is clear that what a poetic invention like the apotheosis of Menoeceus comes to represent in the spiritual career of Statius as reimagined by Dante is what this same act of reimagining represents for Dante himself, a growth to maturity through poetry, which will be illustrated in the *Purgatorio* by his encounters with Bonagiunta and other vernacular poets. By a series of engagements in which poetic and spiritual experience are indistinguishable, Menoeceus's encounter with *Virtus* in the *Thebaid* leads directly to the moment when Dante will discover himself able to explain the inspiration of his own poetry as a response to the inbreathing of love:

> "I'mi son un che, quando
> Amor mi spira, noto, e a quel modo
> ch'e' ditta dentro vo significando."
> (*Purg.* 24.52–54)

[I am one who, when Love inspires me, take note, and according to the form of what is spoken inwardly I go on to express it.]

For this passage and the process it describes closely anticipate the moment when Dante's Statius, in lines that recall the apotheosis of Menoeceus in the *Thebaid,* describes the infusion of the human soul:

> lo motor primo a lui si volge lieto
> sovra tant'arte di natura, e spira
> spirito novo, di vertù repleto . . .
> (*Purg.* 25.70–72)

[The First Mover turns to [the fully formed fetus], rejoicing at Nature's artistry, and breathes into it a new spirit, replete with virtue . . .]

We can no more see or analyze the process that brings about Dante's self-discovery than we can detect the moment of the animation of the human embryo. In both cases, in Dante's terms, we are *surprised*—as we are surprised by the apotheosis of Menoeceus; as we are surprised by the appearance of Statius in Purgatory, and his retrospective unveiling of a history that had been latent but invisible in his poetry; as the soul is surprised by the sudden liberation of the purified will. And it is as a surprise of the same order that

Chaucer's narrator will realize the power to resolve his poem in a new way, such that its completion leads to the discovery of new spiritual meaning.

In simplest terms, the narrator of the final dozen stanzas of the *Troilus* bears the same relation to the narrator of the poem up to this point that Dante's Statius bears to the Statius of the *Thebaid*. But Chaucer goes further than Dante in emphasizing his narrator's subservience to tradition and his inability to understand what is happening to him. As the narrator bids farewell to his "litel bok," he is clearly unaware that he is soon to gain a new perspective on his story and break free once and for all from his acquiescence in its tragic message. If the processes through which Statius embraces Christianity and Dante achieves poetic self-awareness are left obscure, their equivalent in the case of Chaucer's narrator seems to be a subliminal instinct that carries the poet forward almost in spite of himself.

The narrator's futile attempt to conclude the story reflects the persistence of his idolatrous and desperate attachment to it. He seeks to cut it off at the point when it threatens to outgrow his sentimental notion of tragedy and challenge him with moral and spiritual questions he feels unable to resolve. So Dante had foundered in *pietà* when confronted with Francesca and Paolo, and so Statius had turned away from the disastrous implications of his narrative to end the *Thebaid* by joining in the general lament over the dead. In their several ways all three poets show themselves irresolute in facing the implications of their themes, and it is only the shaping power of "poesye" that renders these themes in a form sufficiently definitive that maturer vision can discern their full significance. We sense, as the Pilgrim of *Inferno* 5 cannot, the importance of his lurking awareness that Paolo and Francesca come to him from the company "where Dido is," the deep level at which he responds to Virgil's account of Dido's fatal passion by inventing a story of fatal passion that inevitably refers us to Dido as its archetype. We can see ahead, as the historical Statius could not, to the completion of his insight into the death of Menoeceus in his account of the birth of the soul in *Purgatorio* 25, where Dante, reading Statius from his own Christian vantage point, revises the *Thebaid* in a way that brings out a potential significance of Statius's poetic rendering of spiritual experience. In both situations what we observe is the work of a "poesye" that, by giving stable and enduring form to human experience, makes possible the creation of new poetry that develops the intuitions of the old and ensures the essential conformity of the new to what is universal in the old. The "truth" of poetry is its fidelity to its own tradition and its capacity to reveal new meaning in the light of evolving historical and spiritual perspectives on that tradition. And Chaucer, in reducing his narrator to a virtually unconscious collaborator in the discovery of his true poetic vocation, is demonstrating by this comic means just how far it is possible to proceed in the direction of enlightenment under the influence of the great poets. In the absence of any conscious application of craft or knowledge on the narrator's part, it is "poesye"—the normative influence of poetic tradition—that guides his hand, enabling him to complete his artistic task and express fully what is of enduring value in the story he has told.

The first confirmation of the narrator's new sense of vocation appears in the four stanzas that describe Troilus's death and posthumous vision, and as I have suggested, it is important to recognize how little meaning these events possess in themselves. Taken as the completion of the story of Troilus himself, they may be seen as an attempt to vindicate the abortive spiritual impulse that has issued at last in Troilus's desperate resolve to seek his own death on the battlefield (5.1716–19), but his final display of heroism is devoid of historical significance, and the religious status of his posthumous vision, although it may seem an appropriate tribute to the Dantean spiritual capacities with which Chaucer has endowed him, is at best equivocal. Rich with echoes of the *Somnium Scipionis* and the *Paradiso,* it nonetheless suspends the hero in a spiritual void, and there is no category of religious experience to which we can confidently refer these stanzas. Troilus ascends to the eighth sphere only to set forth again with Mercury, to a place of which the poem tells us nothing.

The inherent unmeaning of Troilus's ascent is further suggested in that Chaucer's report of it is borrowed, virtually intact, from the account of the death of Arcite in Boccaccio's *Teseida.* Not only does the very portability of so seemingly solemn a passage imply a certain arbitrariness in its deployment, but the significance of Arcite's life and death in moral and historical terms is as equivocal as in the case of Troilus. Like the *Troilus,* the *Teseida* tells a historically marginal story with no ancient authority. Arcite, like Troilus, is a historical footnote; his life occupies a small space in the murky interval of world history that separates the fall of the house of Oedipus from the outbreak of the Trojan War. The events that lead to his death amount to a final spasm of Theban violence, and though his reconciliation with Palamon can perhaps be taken *in bono* as an emblem of the neutralizing of "Thebanism" by the moral spirit of a newly ascendent Athens, the *Teseida* offers little clear evidence for such a reading.

Thwarted in love and war, both Arcite and Troilus are finally as tragic as we choose to make them, but we must recognize that their bravery and high-mindedness, unlike the *pietas* of a Hector or Menoeceus, are an exercise in courtly-chivalric convention. The real importance of Troilus's end is in its significance for the narrator himself. Whether or not we choose to see the heavenly journey as a fitting final articulation of Troilus's spiritual capacities, it clearly marks the narrator's first conscious exercise in his newfound role as a participant in the tradition of the great poets. Like the apotheosis of Menoeceus, viewed in the light of Dante's retrospective account of Statius's career, Troilus's ascent is ultimately most meaningful insofar as it adumbrates the narrator's transcendence of the world of his poem.

In the final six stanzas of the *Troilus,* the voice we hear is that of a poet who has been finally liberated from his long darkness and distanced himself from his narrative to the point at which it can assume the status proper to a work of art, an embodiment of aesthetic and human qualities that may be appreciated for themselves and for their exemplary value, with no danger that they will be confused with the spiritual values that are now the poet's primary concern. The first three of these stanzas balance the ultimately abortive love of Troilus against the feelings of the young lovers in Chaucer's audience, whose love is not circumscribed by the horizons of paganism and can be matured and refined in the light of inner vision to the point at which it becomes an all-consuming love of God. The three stanzas, and the three types or stages of love to which they refer, form a sequence like that of Inferno, Purgatory, and Paradise, and it is perhaps in this evolving pattern that we may find the essential meaning of the poet's emancipation from the world-view imposed by his pagan story. He has sent forth his book and commended its fortunes to God, only to have his little tragedy return to him, incorporated now into a larger divine comedy, so that its tragic aspect has suddenly come to seem little more than a distant memory.

But this transformation and distancing are not absolute, and we are reminded in various ways that they have been achieved at great emotional cost. Troilus among the spheres views the distant world not only harshly ("this wrecched world") but tenderly ("This litel spot of erthe that with the se / Embraced is"), and the poet, too, vacillates between harsh moralism and a need to preserve a sympathetic bond with the story he has told. Thus the stanza that begins with the heavy repetition of "Swich fyn!" ends in a couplet that traces the arc of Troilus's experience, with no hint of condemnation:

> And thus bigan his lovyng of Criseyde,
> As I have told, and in this wise he deyde.
> (5.1833–34)

These lines have the moral gravity of the preceding exorcism, without the violence. They focus on the sad fact of Troilus's loss in a way that lends urgency to the following stanza, in which the poet reminds his young hearers that they, at least, have an alternative to "feynede loves." The very force of the exorcism that precedes them purges the narrator's tone of any trace of senti-mentality, and so makes possible their combination of objectivity and com-passion. So too in the *Thebaid,* as Statius condemns the dead sons of Oedipus to the punishments of hell, he thinks simultaneously of the sad condition of humankind (*Theb.* 11.574–76), and immediately mitigates even his judgment on the princes themselves by depicting the mourning of the bereaved father, Oedipus, who comes at last to a rediscovery of piety and the bonds of nature (*Theb.* 11.605–9). The fulfillment of the curse of Tisiphone, the completion of the story told under her inspiration, releases in both poets the capacity for a larger, more humane perspective.

But we are made to linger over Troilus's experience by more than com-passion. The narrator's attitude is hardly distinguishable from Troilus's own as they ascend the spheres, and Troilus speaks for both of them in his sensitive response to his vision of the universe. Only then, and as if prompted by Troilus himself, does the narrator emerge, suddenly and decisively, as a Christian poet, and even at this moment of transcendence, the barrier so firmly imposed between the narrator's new condition and his old attachment to Troilus and his world is oddly permeable. The force of the poet's appeal to his young readers is largely due to the sadness and finality of the couplet that is his last word on Troilus's love, and there is a significant continuity between the moral content of the lines that appeal to the higher feelings of "yonge, fresshe folke" and that of Troilus's posthumous vision in the preceding stanzas. Looking down on the world, Troilus had dismissed

> . . . al oure werk that foloweth so
> The blynde lust, the which that may nat laste,
> And sholden al oure herte on heven caste . . .
> (5.1823–25)

Though these are ostensibly Troilus's own final reflections, we should note the marked shift of emphasis in the third line and the syntactic disjunction ("And sholden . . .") that sets it apart from the tightly structured phrases that precede it. In fact *we cannot say who speaks this line* that seems at first only the completion of Troilus's realization but also expresses the narrator's lingering, futile desire to draw Troilus toward the affirmation that would be the spiritual complement to the *contemptus mundi* he has already come to feel. So heard, the line might also herald a resurgence of the narrator's own Christian instincts, as artless and apparently unconscious as the charity he expresses at the end of the opening proem.

It is thus hard to locate the point at which the narrator's insight into Troilus's experience becomes distinguishable from Troilus's own. It is as if the religious lesson the narrator goes on to offer were being vouchsafed to him by Troilus, and the continuity of their experience is set off by a continuity of language: the injunction to "caste" our hearts on heaven is echoed in the narrator's beautiful appeal to his young hearers to "cast up" their inner vision to God. The point so simply made is profound: the love that "upgroweth" in Chaucer's young Christian lovers has grown also in Troilus. What separates his "blynde lust" from their power to attain the vision of God and Christ is a body of knowledge that the poet now recalls with paternal simplicity:

> And of youre herte up casteth the visage
> To thilke God that after his ymage
> You made, and thynketh al nys but a faire,
> This world . . .
> (5.1838–41)

The unobtrusive artistry with which the highly Latinate syntax here sets off the meanings conveyed by "herte," "visage," and "ymage" is an emblem of the long poetic schooling that has issued in the narrator's recovery of what he now offers as simple truth: we see truly with the eyes of the spirit; we are made in the image of God; the beauty we behold outwardly will pass away. The absence of such certainties, so fundamental as to be taken for granted and all but forgotten by the "yonge, fresshe" Christian reader, is what caused Troilus to fall short, to worship an ephemeral incarnation of the divine presence he had sensed so strongly at the heart of his experience of love.

The final three stanzas of the poem again follow an ascendant pattern, moving from a rejection of paganism, and the submission of Chaucer's own text for the scrutiny of learned friends, to a final prayer. The emphasis has shifted from the poem to the poet, but in the first of these stanzas he balances a vigorous rejection of pagans and their gods with a couplet that states plainly his debt to the world he is rejecting, as his final reference to Troilus and his love had balanced the strident moralizing of the "Swich fyn!" stanza:

> Lo here, the forme of olde clerkis speche
> In poetrie . . .
>
> (5.1854–55)

The narrator has finally separated himself from his story and set it in a larger, transforming perspective, but the form around which his spiritual intuitions have taken shape is that of a poem in the classical tradition. His relation to that poem is, as I have said, a version of the relationship of Dante's redeemed Statius to the Statius of the *Thebaid*, the poet of Oedipus and Tisiphone. Like Statius's account of Menoeceus viewed from the perspective of Dante, the experience embodied in Chaucer's Troilus can now be seen to bear a broadly typological relation to Chaucer's own experience in creating *Troilus and Criseyde*, an experience that has culminated in the rediscovery of religious truth.

In the *Troilus* our sharing of the narrator's exposure to the spiritual uncertainties of the world of the ancient poets is not controlled by the rigid terms of the *Inferno*. We are made vividly aware of its potential dangers, but the deeper effect of Chaucer's engagement with ancient poetry is to enlarge our sense of human community, even as we withdraw to the religious distance of the poem's final stanzas. We do not need to speculate on the salvation of the righteous heathen to find value in an experience of poetry that withholds the final orientation of a religious perspective until we have been made to see in the condition of Troilus, and the Ovidian victims and Statian heroes with whom he is compared, the lineaments of the love that "upgroweth" in the hearts of Chaucer's hearers. The motive for such a use of the poets is continuous with that which will lead Chaucer to create the violent secular world of the *Canterbury Tales* and seek out the spiritual element in the lives of its most worldly and tormented inhabitants.

Even the prayer that concludes the *Troilus* conveys something of this sense of human community. Its seriousness is beyond question, and it constitutes the first and sole moment at which we hear the poet speak with no reference to the poem itself or to his activity as poet. Yet even here there are signs that Troilus is within his purview. It is based on the song of the souls in Dante's Paradise who await the perfecting sacrament of reunion with their earthly bodies:

> Quell'uno e due e tre che sempre vive
> e regna sempre in tre e 'n due e 'n uno,
> non circunscritto, e tutto circunscrive . . .
> *(Paradise* 14.28–30)

> Thow oon, and two, and thre, eterne on lyve,
> That regnest ay in thre, and two, and oon,
> Uncircumscript, and al maist circumscrive . . .
> *(Tr.* 5.1863–65)

The translation is virtually word-perfect, beautiful English that is at the same time a complete rendering of the Italian. Chaucer and Dante here speak with one voice. But Chaucer's allusion is at least partly prompted by Boccaccio, who echoes Dante's prayer, in the second part of the *Filostrato,* when Pandaro assures Criseida that "since he who circumscribed the universe made the first man," no being has ever possessed a soul finer than that of Troiolo, the extent of whose love for her it would be impossible to define (*Filostrato* 2.41.4–8). The contrast between God's emphatic delimiting of the cosmos and the alleged illimitability of Troiolo's love is one of Boccacio's many half-mocking evocations of the idealizing of love in earlier medieval poetry, and the irony of the passage, if not the mockery, anticipates a number of moments at which Chaucer will comment obliquely on the deluded idealism of Troilus. But Chaucer—in this as in so many respects an older, wiser version of the author of the *Filostrato*—has rendered the sorrow of Troilus's abortive vision in greater depth. If we hear his concluding prayer as recalling simultaneously the fatally circumscribed spirituality of Troilus and the glory of the bodily regeneration promised to the souls in Dante's Paradise, his allusive use of Dante's lines may be heard as a plea for the reintegration of human life, for the redemption of imagination and the resolution of the psychological schism that has allowed Troilus to invoke love in the language of Dante's Saint Bernard yet allowed him also to believe that Paradise is the love of Criseyde.

But of course the allusion is first and last to Dante, and it may be seen both as acknowledging Chaucer's indebtedness and as marking the point at which the two poets part company. Dante allows his disembodied souls a lingering concern with the spiritual well-being of others who had been dear to them in the world, but his emphasis in the prayer as a whole is on the supernatural radiance that the resurrected body will exhibit. Poetry, too, is for Dante only a means. In the *Paradiso* he has already distanced himself immeasurably from the world that poetry can claim to engage.

Chaucer never turns so decisively away. His concern is more with aspiration than with transcendence—he is, we might say, most at home in Purgatory—and to the end of his career he affirms the importance for him of poetry as a mode of vision, albeit a flawed and ambiguous one. In the "F" Prologue to the *Legend of Good Women* we can see him pondering the implications of his vocation, in terms which show him still concerned over the conflicting impulses that inform his poetry. On the one hand he is the poet of love, subject to the feminine power that he symbolizes in the daisy:

> My word, my werk is knyt so in youre bond
> That, as an harpe obeieth to the hond
> And maketh it soune after his fyngerynge,
> Ryght so mowe ye oute of myn herte bringe
> Swich vois, ryght as yow lyst, to laughe or pleyne.
> Be ye my gide and lady sovereyne!
> *(Legend* F 89–94)

These lines express the aspiration of *fin amor,* a submissiveness that recalls Troilus at his most Dantean, and a self-consecration virtually as pure and complete as that of the Psalmist. A few lines later we see the poet, quickened by the "fire" of his devotion to the daisy, preparing to go forth at dawn,

> For to ben at the resurreccion
> Of this flour, whan that yt shulde unclose
> Agayn the sonne, that roos as red as rose,
> That in the brest was of the beste, that day,
> That Agenores doghtre ladde away.
> *(Legend* F 110–14)

Here the phonic echoes ("roos," "rose"; "brest," "beste") punctuate a chain of associations that leads from the rising of the sun to the abduction of Agenor's daughter and inescapably implies a further linkage between the fire of "glad devotion" in the poet's breast and the desire that provoked the ancient act of rape. The poet of the "F" Prologue presents himself as a servant of love, capable of active desire and thus at a clear remove from the futile isolation in which we encounter the narrator of the proem to the *Troilus*. Yet his imaginative world is in a sense only the primal version of that of the *Troilus* narrator. It is a world where the poet's devotion cannot exist independent of his role as "subjit" to the *poetae;* his flights of *courtoisie* participate in the same energy that led Jove to ravish Europa, and thereby inaugurate the long terrible history of Thebes. It is a world where imagination is always exposed to the threat of tragic realization, where love can never exist free of the constraints of history, where Troilus is always desiring, and the war goes on.

Notes

1. The essay is a reworking of the final chapter of my book *Chaucer and the Poets: An Essay on* Troilus and Criseyde (Ithaca, N.Y.: Cornell University Press, 1984), and incorporates portions of earlier chapters, largely rewritten. The present version is much the better for careful readings by Tom Stillinger and Richard Neuse.

2. Chaucer uses the terms *poet* and *poetry* sparingly, almost always in reference to classical literature. The only exceptions, apart from general references in the *House of Fame,* are citations of Dante by the Monk and the Wife of Bath, and the Clerk's famous praise of Petrarch, whom he would see as a Latin writer. Dante, then, is the one vernacular writer Chaucer calls a poet. See J. S. P. Tatlock, "The Epilogue of Chaucer's 'Troilus,' " *Modern Philology* 18 (1920–21): 630–32; Anne Middleton, "Chaucer's 'New Men' and the Good of Literature in the *Canterbury Tales,*" in *Literature and Society,* ed. Edward W. Said (Baltimore: Johns Hopkins University Press, 1980), 24–39, 53–54 n. 15; Glending Olson, "Making and Poetry in the Age of Chaucer," *Comparative Literature* 31 (1979): 272–90.

3. See my "*Poeta che mi guidi:* Dante, Lucan, and Virgil," in *Canons,* ed. Robert von Hallberg (Chicago: University of Chicago Press, 1984), 131–48.

4. *Troilus and Criseyde* 5.1789–92. Here and throughout I cite the text of Stephen Barney, *The Riverside Chaucer,* 3d ed., ed. Larry D. Benson (Boston: Houghton Mifflin, 1987).

5. On the ancient and medieval background of Chaucer's Troilus, see N. R. Havely, *Chaucer's Boccaccio* (Cambridge, England: D. S. Brewer, 1980), 164–86.

6. It is love that provokes Troilus's feats of arms at 1.1072–75, 3.1772–78, and 5.1751–64 (with which cp. 5.1716–22). In 5.1564–68, Troilus's grief at the death of Hector turns imperceptibly into the sorrow of love.

7. Even John M. Steadman, arguing for an affirmative reading of Troilus's ascent, notes that his life has not been of the sort traditionally assigned a heavenly reward; *Disembodied Laughter: Troilus and the Apotheosis Tradition* (Berkeley: University of California Press, 1972), 137–42.

8. Contrast the opening of the *Aeneid,* which locates Aeneas as the man who left Troy for Italy. For Dante's Virgil, too, the *Aeneid* tells of the just son of Anchises "che venne di Troia" (*Inferno* 1.74). I cite the *Commedia* in the edition of Charles Singleton (Princeton: Princeton University Press, 1970–75). Translations are my own.

On the opening couplet, see Thomas Stillinger, *The Song of Troilus: Lyric Authority in the Medieval Book,* (Philadelphia: University of Pennsylvania Press, 1992), 159.

9. See Barry Windeatt, *Oxford Guides to Chaucer:* Troilus and Criseyde (Oxford: Oxford University Press, 1992), 307: "That the hero's soul ascends 'ful blisfully' and that he has the satisfaction of hearing the harmony of the music of the spheres . . . seem to be signals that the flight is some endorsement of value in the hero, even though his more permanent abode remains uncertain."

10. The language is that of Giuseppe Mazzotta, *Dante, Poet of the Desert* (Princeton: Princeton University Press, 1979), 191.

11. On such moments in the *Aeneid,* see Sanford Budick, "The Prospect of Tradition: Elements of Futurity in a Topos of Homer and Virgil," *New Literary History* 22 (1991): 23–37.

12. *Thebaid* 1.56–87. A. C. Spearing finds this parallel "extravagantly remote" ("*Troilus and Criseyde:* The Illusion of Allusion," *Exemplaria* 2 (1990): 268). What is extravagant is the choice of Tisiphone as in effect the Muse of the *Troilus*. The *Thebaid* provides the one invocation

of Tisiphone that Chaucer could have known, and the parallel, though I am likely enough to have missed some of its implications, is too striking to be simply dismissed.

13. Leonard Michael Koff, "Ending a Poem before Beginning It, or The 'Cas' of Troilus," in *Chaucer's* Troilus and Criseyde: *"Subjit to Alle Poesye,"* ed. R. A. Shoaf (Binghamton, N.Y.: Medieval and Renaissance Texts and Studies, 1992), 167, notes Tisiphone's "disturbingly helpless role." I am intrigued by his suggestion that she weeps out of compassion for her victims, but I am also perplexed. Unlike some infernal powers, the Furies have no human past, but are simply a primal daimonic force. Tisiphone's sorrow is an unfulfilled desire to inflict pain and is surely to be contrasted with the sorrow of the narrator, who will feel the stirrings of an authentic charity for his lovers, and even with the pain of Statius's Oedipus, who will weep in spite of himself over his dead sons (*Thebaid* 11.605–33).

14. For a somewhat overstated view of this aspect of the poem, see my *Chaucer and the Poets,* 46–49, 80–84, 176–78.

15. On *Troilus* and *Inferno* 5, see the rich discussion of Karla Taylor, *Chaucer Reads the Divine Comedy* (Palo Alto, Calif.: Stanford University Press, 1989), 50–77.

16. On the importance of this knowledge, see Koff, "Ending a Poem."

17. See Mazzotta, *Dante, Poet of the Desert,* 165–70.

18. See my *"Poeta che mi guidi,"* 137–39.

19. See my essay "Dante and the *Thebaid* of Statius," in *Lectura Dantis Newberryana,* vol. 1, ed. Paolo Cherchi and Antonio C. Mastrobuono (Evanston, Ill.: Northwestern University Press, 1988), 71–92.

20. See the references to Capaneus (*Inf.* 14.49–72; cp. *Theb.* 10.827–939) and the fatal duel of the sons of Oedipus (*Inf.* 26.52–54; cp. *Theb.* 12.419–32). Recalling the fate of Ugolino and his children, Dante calls Pisa "novella Tebe" (33.89), and Ugolino, gnawing at the neck of Archbishop Ruggieri, imitates Tydeus's cannibalizing of Melanippus (*Inf.* 32.127–32; *Theb.* 8.739–62).

21. See *Purg.* 22.55–56: ". . . le crude arme / de la doppia trestizia di Giocasta." "Doppia trestizia" is commonly taken as a reference to Jocasta's twin sons, whose fatal struggle is the subject of Statius's poem, but there are obviously many ways in which Jocasta could be said to know a "double sorrow," and I suspect that both Dante and Chaucer use the phrase to suggest the complex perspective in which Theban and Trojan history must be viewed.

22. See Lee Patterson, *Chaucer and the Subject of History* (Madison: University of Wisconsin Press, 1991), 75, 130–36; and David Anderson, "Theban History in Chaucer's *Troilus,"* *Studies in the Age of Chaucer* 4 (1982): 109–33.

23. Neglect of this continuity flaws John V. Fleming's *Classical Imitation and Interpretation in Chaucer's* Troilus (Princeton: Princeton University Press, 1990), the fullest study of the poem's classical aspect. A good corrective is Richard Neuse, *"Troilus and Criseyde:* Another Dantean Reading," in Shoaf, *Chaucer's* Troilus and Criseyde, 199–210.

24. The term may mean simply "craftsman," one who practices an art, or may denote specifically one who writes love verse to the specifications of a courtly audience. See Olson, "Making and Poetry."

Index

♦

The Volume Editor

Thomas C. Stillinger is associate professor of English at the University of
Utah. He holds degrees from Yale University (B.A.), Goddard College
(M.F.A.), and Cornell University (M.A. and Ph.D.). He is the author of *The
Song of Troilus: Lyric Authority in the Medieval Book* (Philadelphia: University of
Pennsylvania Press, 1992).

The General Editor

Zack Bowen is professor of English at the University of Miami. He holds degrees from the University of Pennsylvania (B.A.), Temple University (M.A.), and the State University of New York at Buffalo (Ph.D.). In addition to being general editor of this G. K. Hall series, he is editor of the James Joyce series for the University of Florida Press and the *James Joyce Literary Supplement*. He is the author and editor of numerous books on modern British, Irish, and American literature. He has also published more than 100 monographs, essays, scholarly reviews, and recordings related to literature. He is past president of the James Joyce Society (1977–86), former chair of the Modern Language Association Lowell Prize Committee, and currently president of the International James Joyce Foundation.